American Bible Union

The New Testament of Our Lord and Saviour Jesus Christ

The common English Version. Second Revision

American Bible Union

The New Testament of Our Lord and Saviour Jesus Christ
The common English Version. Second Revision

ISBN/EAN: 9783337313890

Printed in Europe, USA, Canada, Australia, Japan

Cover: Foto ©Lupo / pixelio.de

More available books at **www.hansebooks.com**

THE

NEW TESTAMENT

OF OUR

LORD AND SAVIOR JESUS CHRIST.

THE COMMON ENGLISH VERSION, CORRECTED BY THE FINAL COMMITTEE OF THE
AMERICAN BIBLE UNION.

Second Revision.

NEW YORK:
AMERICAN BIBLE UNION.
LONDON:
TRÜBNER & CO., 60 PATERNOSTER ROW.
1869.

20th thousand.] [*Pica 8vo Edition*

NOTE.

This Revised Testament has been prepared under the auspices of the American Bible Union, by the most competent scholars of the day. No expense has been spared to obtain the oldest translations of the Bible, copies of the ancient manuscripts, and other facilities to make the revision as perfect as possible.

The paragraph form has been adopted in preference to the division by verse, which is a modern mode of division, never used in the ancient scriptures. But, for convenience of reference, the numbers of the verses are retained.

All quotations from the Old Testament are distinctly indicated, and the poetic form is restored to those which appear as poetry in the original.

The revisers have been guided in their labors by the following rules prescribed by the Union:

RULES FOR THE REVISION OF THE ENGLISH NEW TESTAMENT.

The received Greek text, critically edited, with known errors corrected, must be followed.

The common English version must be the basis of revision, and only such alterations must be made as the exact meaning of the text and the existing state of the language may require.

The exact meaning of the inspired text, as that text expressed it to those who understood the original Scriptures at the time they were first written, must be given in corresponding words and phrases, so far as they can be found in the English language, with the least possible obscurity or indefiniteness.

☞ The *numbering* of the *chapter* is omitted, where it would break the connection; as in John viii., 1 Cor. xi., xiii., xiv., Philipp. iv., Col. iv., 1 Peter iii.

Entered according to Act of Congress, in the year 1865, by THE AMERICAN BIBLE UNION, in the Clerk's Office of the District Court of the United States for the Southern District of New York.

LANGE, HILLMAN & LANGE,
Steam Book and Job Printers,
207 Pearl Street, near Maiden Lane, N. Y.

THE
NEW TESTAMENT.

THE GOSPEL ACCORDING TO MATTHEW.

1. Book of the generation of Jesus Christ, son of David, son of Abraham. ² Abraham begot Isaac; and Isaac begot Jacob; and Jacob begot Judah and his brothers; ³ and Judah begot Pharez and Zarah, of Tamar; and Pharez begot Hezron; and Hezron begot Ram; ⁴ and Ram begot Amminadab; and Amminadab begot Nahshon; and Nahshon begot Salmon; ⁵ and Salmon begot Boaz, of Rahab; and Boaz begot Obed, of Ruth; and Obed begot Jesse; ⁶ and Jesse begot David the king; and David begot Solomon, of the wife of Uriah; ⁷ and Solomon begot Rehoboam; and Rehoboam begot Abijah; and Abijah begot Asa; ⁸ and Asa begot Jehoshaphat; and Jehoshaphat begot Joram; and Joram begot Uzziah; ⁹ and Uzziah begot Jotham; and Jotham begot Ahaz; and Ahaz begot Hezekiah; ¹⁰ and Hezekiah begot Manasseh; and Manasseh begot Amon; and Amon begot Josiah; ¹¹ and Josiah begot Jeconiah and his brothers, at the time of the removal to Babylon. ¹² And after the removal to Babylon, Jeconiah begot Salathiel; and Salathiel begot Zerubbabel; ¹³ and Zerubbabel begot Abiud; and Abiud begot Eliakim; and Eliakim begot Azor; ¹⁴ and Azor begot Zadock; and Zadock begot Achim; and Achim begot Eliud; ¹⁵ and Eliud begot Eleazar; and Eleazar begot Matthan;

and Matthan begot Jacob; ¹⁶ and Jacob begot Joseph the husband of Mary, of whom was born Jesus, who is called Christ.

¹⁷ All the generations, therefore, from Abraham unto David are fourteen generations; and from David unto the removal to Babylon, fourteen generations; and from the removal to Babylon unto the Christ, fourteen generations.

¹⁸ Now the birth of Jesus Christ was after this manner. His mother Mary having been betrothed to Joseph, before they came together she was found with child by the Holy Spirit. ¹⁹ And Joseph her husband, being just, and not willing to expose her openly, desired to put her away privately. ²⁰ But while he thought on these things, behold, an angel of the Lord appeared to him in a dream, saying: Joseph, son of David, fear not to take to thee Mary thy wife; for that which is begotten in her is of the Holy Spirit. ²¹ And she shall bring forth a son, and thou shalt call his name Jesus; for he shall save his people from their sins.

²² And all this has come to pass, that it might be fulfilled which was spoken by the Lord through the prophet, saying:

²³ Behold, the virgin shall be with child,
And shall bring forth a son.
And they shall call his name Immanuel;

which is interpreted, God with us.

²⁴ And Joseph, awaking from sleep, did as the angel of the Lord bade him, and took to him his wife; ²⁵ and he knew her not till she brought forth a son; and he called his name Jesus.

II. And Jesus having been born in Bethlehem of Judaea, in the days of Herod the king, behold, there came wise men from the east to Jerusalem, ² saying: Where is he that is born King of the Jews? For we saw his star in the east, and came to do him homage. ³ And the king, Herod, hearing it, was troubled, and all Jerusalem with him. ⁴ And having

---

V. 19. *In some ancient copies;* to make her an example.
V. 23. *Or, which interpreted* is
V. 25. *In some ancient copies:* her first-born son

CHAPTER II.

assembled all the chief priests and scribes of the people, he inquired of them where the Christ should be born. ⁵ And they said to him: In Bethlehem of Judæa; for thus it is written by the prophet:

⁶ And thou Bethlehem, land of Judah,
Art by no means least among the princes of Judah;
For out of thee shall come forth a Governor,
Who shall rule my people Israel.

⁷ Then Herod, having secretly called the wise men, inquired of them exactly the time of the appearing of the star. ⁸ And he sent them to Bethlehem, and said: Go and inquire strictly concerning the child; and when ye have found him, bring me word again, that I also may come and do him homage. ⁹ And they, having heard the king, departed; and lo, the star, which they saw in the east, went before them, till it came and stood over where the child was. ¹⁰ And seeing the star, they rejoiced with exceeding great joy. ¹¹ And coming into the house, they saw the child with Mary his mother, and fell down, and did homage to him; and opening their treasures, they presented to him gifts, gold and frankincense and myrrh. ¹² And being warned by God in a dream, not to return to Herod, they departed into their own country by another way.

¹³ And when they had departed, behold, an angel of the Lord appears to Joseph in a dream, saying: Arise, and take the child and his mother, and flee into Egypt, and be there until I bring thee word; for Herod is about to seek the child to destroy him. ¹⁴ And he arose and took the child and his mother by night and departed into Egypt, ¹⁵ and was there until the death of Herod; that it might be fulfilled which was spoken by the Lord through the prophet, saying: Out of Egypt I called my son.

¹⁶ Then Herod, seeing that he was mocked by the wise men, was exceedingly enraged; and he sent forth, and slew all the male children that were in Bethlehem, and in all its borders, from two years old and under, according to the time which he had exactly learned from the wise men. ¹⁷ Then was fulfilled that which was spoken through Jeremiah the prophet, saying:

> ¹⁸ A voice was heard in Ramah,
> Weeping, and great mourning;
> Rachel weeping for her children,
> And would not be comforted, because they are not.

¹⁹ But when Herod was dead, behold, an angel of the Lord appears in a dream to Joseph in Egypt, ²⁰ saying: Arise, and take the child and his mother, and go into the land of Israel; for they are dead who sought the child's life. ²¹ And he arose, and took the child and his mother, and came into the land of Israel. ²² But hearing that Archelaüs reigned in Judæa instead of Herod his father, he was afraid to go thither; and being warned by God in a dream, he retired into the region of Galilee. ²³ And he came and dwelt in a city called Nazareth; that it might be fulfilled which was spoken through the prophets: He shall be called a N a z a r e n e.

III.

In those days comes John the Immerser, preaching in the wilderness of Judæa, ² and saying: Repent, for the kingdom of heaven is at hand. ³ For this is he that was spoken of through the prophet Isaiah, saying:

> The voice of one crying in the wilderness,
> Prepare the way of the Lord,
> Make straight his paths.

⁴ And he, John, had his raiment of camel's hair, and a leathern girdle about his loins; and his food was locusts and wild honey.

⁵ Then went out to him Jerusalem, and all Judæa, and all the region about the Jordan; ⁶ and they were immersed by him in the Jordan, confessing their sins. ⁷ But seeing many of the Pharisees and Sadducees coming to his immersion, he said to them: Brood of vipers, who warned you to flee from the coming wrath? ⁸ Bring forth therefore fruit worthy of repentance; ⁹ and think not to say within yourselves, We have Abraham for our father; for I say to you, that God is able of these stones to raise up children to Abraham. ¹⁰ And already the axe is

---

V. 18. *In some ancient copies:* lamentation and weeping

CHAPTER IV.

laid to the root of the trees; therefore every tree that brings not forth good fruit is cut down, and cast into the fire. ¹¹ I indeed immerse you in water unto repentance; but he that comes after me is mightier than I, whose sandals I am not worthy to bear; he will immerse you in the Holy Spirit and fire; ¹² whose fan is in his hand, and he will thoroughly cleanse his threshing-floor, and will gather his wheat into the garner; but the chaff he will burn up with fire unquenchable.

¹³ Then Jesus comes from Galilee to the Jordan, to John, to be immersed by him. ¹⁴ But John sought to hinder him, saying: I have need to be immersed by thee, and dost thou come to me? ¹⁵ And Jesus answering said to him: Suffer it now; for thus it becomes us to fulfill all righteousness. Then he suffered him. ¹⁶ And having been immersed, Jesus went up immediately from the water; and lo, the heavens were opened to him, and he saw the Spirit of God descending, as a dove, and coming upon him. ¹⁷ And lo, a voice out of heaven, saying: This is my beloved Son, in whom I am well pleased.

IV. Then Jesus was led up by the Spirit into the wilderness, to be tempted by the Devil. ² And having fasted forty days and forty nights, he afterwards hungered. ³ And coming to him, the tempter said: If thou art the Son of God, command that these stones become loaves of bread. ⁴ But he answering said: It is written, Man shall not live on bread alone, but on every word that proceeds out of the mouth of God.

⁵ Then the Devil takes him into the holy city, and sets him on the pinnacle of the temple, ⁶ and says to him: If thou art the Son of God, cast thyself down; for it is written:

He will give his angels command concerning thee;
And on their hands they will bear thee up,
Lest haply thou dash thy foot against a stone.

⁷ Jesus said to him: Again it is written, Thou shalt not tempt the Lord thy God.

⁸ Again the Devil takes him into an exceedingly high mountain, and shows him all the kingdoms of the world, and the

MATTHEW.

glory of them; ⁹ and says to him: All these things I will give thee, if thou wilt fall down and worship me. ¹⁰ Then Jesus says to him: Get thee hence, Satan; for it is written: T h o u s h a l t   w o r s h i p   t h e   L o r d   t h y   G o d,   a n d   h i m o n l y   s h a l t   t h o u   s e r v e. ¹¹ Then the Devil leaves him; and behold, angels came and ministered to him.

¹² And hearing that John was delivered up, he retired into Galilee. ¹³ And leaving Nazareth, he came and dwelt in Capernaum, which is by the sea, in the borders of Zebulun and Naphtali; ¹⁴ that it might be fulfilled which was spoken through Isaiah the prophet, saying:

¹⁵ The land of Zebulun, and the land of Naphtali,
　By the way of the sea, beyond the Jordan,
　Galilee of the Gentiles,
¹⁶ The people that sat in darkness, saw great light,
　And to those sitting in the region and shadow of death
　　light sprang up.

¹⁷ From that time Jesus began to preach, and to say: Repent, for the kingdom of heaven is at hand. ¹⁸ And walking by the sea of Galilee, he saw two brothers, Simon called Peter, and Andrew his brother, casting a net into the sea; for they were fishermen. ¹⁹ And he says to them: Come after me, and I will make you fishers of men. ²⁰ And they, immediately leaving the nets, followed him. ²¹ And going on from thence, he saw other two brothers, James the son of Zebedee, and John his brother, in the ship with Zebedee their father, mending their nets; and he called them. ²² And they, immediately leaving the ship and their father, followed him.

²³ And Jesus went about all Galilee, teaching in their synagogues, and preaching the good news of the kingdom, and healing every sickness and every infirmity among the people. ²⁴ And his fame went forth into all Syria; and they brought to him all that were sick, taken with divers diseases and torments, and possessed with demons, and lunatic, and palsied; and he healed them. ²⁵ And great multitudes followed him from Galilee, and Decapolis, and Jerusalem, and Judæa, and from beyond the Jordan.

CHAPTER V.

V. AND seeing the multitudes, he went up into the mountain; and he having sat down, his disciples came to him. ² And he opened his mouth, and taught them, saying:
³ Happy the poor in spirit; for theirs is the kingdom of heaven.
⁴ Happy they that mourn; for they shall be comforted.
⁵ Happy the meek; for they shall inherit the earth.
⁶ Happy they that hunger and thirst after righteousness; for they shall be filled.
⁷ Happy the merciful; for they shall obtain mercy.
⁸ Happy the pure in heart; for they shall see God.
⁹ Happy the peacemakers; for they shall be called sons of God.
¹⁰ Happy they who are persecuted for righteousness' sake; for theirs is the kingdom of heaven.
¹¹ Happy are ye, when they shall revile and persecute you, and shall say all evil against you falsely, for my sake. ¹² Rejoice, and exult; because great is your reward in heaven, for so they persecuted the prophets that were before you.
¹³ Ye are the salt of the earth; but if the salt become tasteless, wherewith shall it be salted? It is thenceforth good for nothing, but to be cast out, and to be trodden under foot by men.
¹⁴ Ye are the light of the world. A city that is set on a hill can not be hid. ¹⁵ Nor do they light a lamp and put it under the bushel, but on the lamp-stand; and it shines to all that are in the house. ¹⁶ Thus let your light shine before men, that they may see your good works, and glorify your Father who is in heaven.
¹⁷ Think not that I came to destroy the law, or the prophets; I came not to destroy, but to fulfill. ¹⁸ For verily I say to you, till heaven and earth pass, one jot or one tittle shall not pass from the law, till all be fulfilled. ¹⁹ Whoever therefore shall

V. 5. *Or*, the land
V. 11. *Some ancient copies omit:* falsely.

break one of these least commandments, and shall teach men so, shall be called the least in the kingdom of heaven; but whoever shall do and teach them, he shall be called great in the kingdom of heaven.

²⁰ For I say to you, that except your righteousness shall exceed that of the scribes and Pharisees, ye shall not enter into the kingdom of heaven.

²¹ Ye heard that it was said to those of old: T h o u s h a l t n o t k i l l; a n d w h o e v e r s h a l l k i l l s h a l l b e i n d a n g e r o f t h e j u d g m e n t. ²² But I say to you, that every one who is angry with his brother, without cause, shall be in danger of the judgment; and whoever shall say to his brother, Raca! shall be in danger of the council; and whoever shall say, Thou fool! shall be in danger of hell-fire. ²³ Therefore if thou bringest thy gift to the altar, and there rememberest that thy brother has aught against thee; ²⁴ leave there thy gift before the altar, and go, first be reconciled to thy brother and then come and offer thy gift.

²⁵ Agree with thine adversary quickly, while thou art in the way with him; lest haply the adversary deliver thee to the judge, and the judge deliver thee to the officer, and thou be cast into prison. ²⁶ Verily I say to thee, thou shalt not come out thence, till thou hast paid the uttermost farthing.

²⁷ Ye heard that it was said: T h o u s h a l t n o t c o m m i t a d u l t e r y. ²⁸ But I say to you, that every one who looks on a woman, to lust after her, has already committed adultery with her in his heart. ²⁹ And if thy right eye causes thee to offend, pluck it out and cast it from thee; for it is profitable for thee that one of thy members perish, and not thy whole body be cast into hell. ³⁰ And if thy right hand causes thee to offend, cut it off and cast it from thee; for it is profitable for thee that one of thy members perish, and not thy whole body be cast into hell.

V. 21. *Or, by those*
V. 22. without cause, *is omitted in many ancient copies.*
Ib. Raca, *a term of angry reproach.*

CHAPTER V.

[31] And it was said: Whoever shall put away his wife, let him give her a writing of divorcement. [32] But I say to you, that whoever shall put away his wife, save for the cause of fornication, makes her commit adultery; and whoever shall marry her when put away, commits adultery.

[33] Again ye heard, that it was said to those of old: Thou shalt not swear falsely, but shalt perform to the Lord thine oaths. [34] But I say to you, swear not at all; neither by heaven, for it is God's throne; [35] nor by the earth, for it is his footstool; nor by Jerusalem, for it is the city of the great King. [36] Nor shalt thou swear by thy head; because thou canst not make one hair white or black. [37] But let your word be, Yea, yea, Nay, nay; for that which is more than these comes of evil.

[38] Ye heard that it was said: An eye for an eye, and a tooth for a tooth. [39] But I say to you, that ye resist not evil; but whoever shall smite thee on thy right cheek, turn to him the other also. [40] And if any man will sue thee at the law, and take thy coat, let him have thy cloak also. [41] And whoever shall compel thee to go one mile, go with him two. [42] Give to him that asks of thee, and from him that would borrow of thee turn not away.

[43] Ye heard that it was said: Thou shalt love thy neighbor, and shalt hate thine enemy. [44] But I say to you, love your enemies, and pray for those who persecute you; [45] that ye may be sons of your Father who is in heaven; for he causes his sun to rise on the evil and the good, and sends rain on the just and the unjust. [46] For if ye love those who love you, what reward have ye? Do not also the publicans the same? [47] And if ye salute your brethren only, what do ye that excels? Do not also the heathen thus? [48] Be ye therefore perfect, even as your Father who is in heaven is perfect.

V. 33. *Or*, by those of old

VI. Take heed that ye do not your righteousness before men, to be seen by them; otherwise ye have no reward with your Father who is in heaven. ² Therefore when thou doest alms, do not sound a trumpet before thee, as the hypocrites do in the synagogues and in the streets, that they may have glory of men. Verily I say to you, they have in full their reward. ³ But when thou doest alms, let not thy left hand know what thy right hand does; ⁴ that thine alms may be in secret; and thy Father who sees in secret will himself reward thee.

⁵ And when ye pray, ye shall not be as the hypocrites; for they love to pray standing in the synagogues and in the corners of the streets, that they may be seen by men. Verily I say to you, they have in full their reward. ⁶ But thou, when thou prayest, enter into thy closet, and having shut thy door, pray to thy Father who is in secret; and thy Father who sees in secret will reward thee.

⁷ But when ye pray, use not vain repetitions, as the heathen do; for they think that they shall be heard for their much speaking. ⁸ Be not ye therefore like to them; for your Father knows what things ye have need of, before ye ask him. ⁹ Do ye, therefore, pray after this manner:

Our Father who art in heaven, hallowed be thy name.
¹⁰ Thy kingdom come; thy will be done, as in heaven, so also on the earth.
¹¹ Give us this day our daily bread.
¹² And forgive us our debts, as also we forgave our debtors.
¹³ And bring us not into temptation, but deliver us from evil.

¹⁴ For if ye forgive men their trespasses, your heavenly Father will also forgive you; ¹⁵ but if ye forgive not men their trespasses, neither will your Father forgive your trespasses.

¹⁶ And when ye fast, be not as the hypocrites, of a sad coun-

---

V. 11. *Or,* our needful bread
V. 13. *The words omitted are wanting in all the ancient copies.*

CHAPTER VI.

tenance; for they disfigure their faces, that they may appear to men to fast. Verily I say to you, they have in full their reward. ¹⁷ But thou, when thou fastest, anoint thy head, and wash thy face; ¹⁸ that thou appear not to men to fast, but to thy Father who is in secret; and thy Father who sees in secret will reward thee.

¹⁹ Lay not up for yourselves treasures on the earth, where moth and rust consume, and where thieves break through and steal. ²⁰ But lay up for yourselves treasures in heaven, where neither moth nor rust consumes, and where thieves do not break through nor steal. ²¹ For where your treasure is, there will your heart be also.

²² The lamp of the body is the eye. If therefore thine eye be single, thy whole body will be light; ²³ but if thine eye be evil, thy whole body will be dark. If therefore the light that is in thee is darkness, how great the darkness! ²⁴ No man can serve two masters; for either he will hate the one, and love the other, or he will hold to one and despise the other. Ye cannot serve God and Mammon.

²⁵ For this cause I say to you, take not thought for your life, what ye shall eat, or what ye shall drink; nor for your body, what ye shall put on. Is not the life more than food, and the body than raiment? ²⁶ Behold the birds of the air, that they sow not, nor reap, nor gather into barns; and your heavenly Father feeds them. Are ye not much better than they? ²⁷ And which of you by taking thought can add one cubit to his stature? ²⁸ And why take ye thought for raiment? Consider the lilies of the field, how they grow. They toil not, nor spin; ²⁹ and I say to you, that even Solomon in all his glory was not arrayed like one of these. ³⁰ And if God so clothes the grass of the field, which to-day is, and to-morrow is cast into the oven, will he not much more you, ye of little faith? ³¹ Take not thought therefore, saying, What shall we eat? or, What shall we drink? or, Wherewith shall we be clothed? ³² For after all these do the Gentiles seek. For your heavenly

---

V. 27. *Or,* to his age

Father knows that ye have need of all these. ³³ But seek first the kingdom of God, and his righteousness; and all these shall be added to you. ³⁴ Take not thought, therefore, for the morrow; for the morrow will take thought for itself. Sufficient for the day is the evil thereof.

VII. Judge not, that ye be not judged. ² For with what judgment ye judge, ye shall be judged; and with what measure ye mete, it shall be measured to you. ³ And why beholdest thou the mote that is in thy brother's eye, but perceivest not the beam that is in thine own eye? ⁴ Or how wilt thou say to thy brother: Let me cast out the mote from thine eye; and behold, the beam is in thine own eye? ⁵ Hypocrite! first cast out the beam out of thine own eye; and then thou wilt see clearly to cast out the mote out of thy brother's eye.

⁶ Give not that which is holy to the dogs, nor cast your pearls before the swine; lest they trample them with their feet, and turn and rend you.

⁷ Ask, and it shall be given you; seek, and ye shall find; knock, and it shall be opened to you. ⁸ For every one that asks receives; and he that seeks finds; and to him that knocks it shall be opened. ⁹ Or what man is there of you, of whom if his son ask bread, will he give him a stone? ¹⁰ And if he ask a fish, will he give him a serpent? ¹¹ If ye then, being evil, know how to give good gifts to your children, how much more will your Father who is in heaven give good things to those who ask him? ¹² Therefore all things whatever ye would that men should do to you, so also do ye to them; for this is the law and the prophets.

¹³ Enter in through the strait gate; because wide is the gate, and broad the way, that leads to destruction, and many are they who go in thereat. ¹⁴ Because strait is the gate, and narrow the way, that leads to life, and few are they who find it.

¹⁵ Beware of false prophets, who come to you in sheeps' clothing, but inwardly are ravening wolves.

V. 14. *In some ancient copies:* How strait

CHAPTER VIII.

¹⁶ Ye shall know them from their fruits. Do men gather grapes from thorns, or figs from thistles? ¹⁷ So every good tree brings forth good fruit; but the corrupt tree brings forth evil fruit. ¹⁸ A good tree can not bring forth evil fruit, nor a corrupt tree bring forth good fruit. ¹⁹ Every tree that brings not forth good fruit is cut down, and cast into the fire. ²⁰ So then, from their fruits ye shall know them.

²¹ Not every one that says to me, Lord, Lord, shall enter into the kingdom of heaven; but he that does the will of my Father who is in heaven. ²² Many will say to me in that day: Lord, Lord, did we not prophesy in thy name, and in thy name cast out demons, and in thy name do many miracles? ²³ And then will I profess to them, I never knew you; depart from me, ye who work iniquity.

²⁴ Every one, therefore, who hears these sayings of mine, and does them, I will liken him to a wise man, who built his house on the rock. ²⁵ And the rain descended, and the streams came, and the winds blew, and fell upon that house; and it did not fall, for it had been founded on the rock. ²⁶ And every one who hears these sayings of mine, and does them not, shall be likened to a foolish man, who built his house on the sand. ²⁷ And the rain descended, and the streams came, and the winds blew, and beat upon that house, and it fell; and great was the fall of it.

²⁸ And it came to pass, when Jesus ended these sayings, that the multitudes were astonished at his teaching. ²⁹ For he taught them as having authority, and not as the scribes.

VIII. WHEN he had come down from the mountain, great multitudes followed him. ² And, behold, there came a leper and bowed down to him, saying: Lord, if thou wilt, thou canst cleanse me. ³ And stretching forth his hand, he touched him, saying: I will; be thou cleansed. And immediately his leprosy was cleansed. ⁴ And Jesus says to him: See thou tell no one; but go, show thyself to the priest,

---

V. 24. *In some ancient copies:* my sayings

and offer the gift that Moses commanded, for a testimony to them.

⁵ And as he entered into Capernaum, there came to him a centurion, beseeching him, ⁶ and saying: Lord, my servant lies at home palsied, grievously tormented. ⁷ And Jesus says to him: I will come and heal him. ⁸ The centurion answered and said: Lord, I am not worthy that thou shouldst come under my roof; but only say in a word, and my servant will be healed. ⁹ For I am a man under authority, having soldiers under me, and I say to this one, Go, and he goes; and to another, Come, and he comes; and to my servant, Do this, and he does it. ¹⁰ And Jesus hearing it marveled, and said to those who followed: Verily I say to you, I found not so great faith, even in Israel. ¹¹ And I say to you, that many will come from the east and west, and will recline at table, with Abraham, and Isaac, and Jacob, in the kingdom of heaven; ¹² but the sons of the kingdom will be cast out into the outer darkness. There will be the weeping, and the gnashing of teeth! ¹³ And Jesus said to the centurion: Go thy way; and as thou didst believe, be it done to thee. And his servant was healed in that hour.

¹⁴ And Jesus, coming into the house of Peter, saw his mother-in-law lying, and sick with fever. ¹⁵ And he touched her hand, and the fever left her; and she arose, and ministered to him. ¹⁶ When evening was come, they brought to him many that were possessed with demons; and he cast out the spirits with a word, and healed all that were sick; ¹⁷ that it might be fulfilled which was spoken through Isaiah the prophet, saying: Himself took our infirmities, and bore our sicknesses.

¹⁸ And Jesus, seeing great multitudes about him, commanded to depart to the other side. ¹⁹ And a certain scribe came, and said to him: Teacher, I will follow thee whithersoever thou goest. ²⁰ And Jesus says to him: The foxes have holes and the birds of the air nests; but the Son of man has not where he may lay his head. ²¹ And another of his disciples said to him: Lord, suffer me first to go and bury my father. ²² But Jesus said to him: Follow me, and let the dead bury their own dead.

CHAPTER IX.

²³ And when he had entered into the ship, his disciples followed him. ²⁴ And, behold, there arose a great tempest in the sea, so that the ship was covered by the waves; but he was sleeping. ²⁵ And the disciples came and awoke him, saying: Lord, save us; we perish. ²⁶ And he says to them: Why are ye fearful, ye of little faith? Then rising, he rebuked the winds and the sea; and there was a great calm. ²⁷ And the men marveled, saying: What manner of man is this, that even the winds and the sea obey him!

²⁸ And when he had come to the other side, into the country of the Gadarenes, there met him two possessed with demons, coming out of the tombs, exceedingly fierce, so that no one was able to pass by that way. ²⁹ And, behold, they cried out, saying: What have we to do with thee, Son of God? Camest thou hither to torment us before the time? ³⁰ And there was afar off from them a herd of many swine feeding. And the demons besought him, saying: ³¹ If thou cast us out, send us away into the herd of swine. ³² And he said to them, Go. And they, coming out, went away into the swine; and, behold, the whole herd rushed down the steep into the sea, and perished in the waters. ³³ And the herdsmen fled, and went away into the city, and told every thing, and what had befallen the possessed with demons. ³⁴ And, behold, all the city came out to meet Jesus; and seeing him, they besought that he would depart from their borders.

IX. And entering into the ship he passed over, and came to his own city. ² And, behold, they brought to him one that was palsied, lying on a bed. And Jesus, seeing their faith, said to the palsied man: Child, be of good cheer; thy sins are forgiven. ³ And, behold, certain of the scribes said within themselves: This man blasphemes. ⁴ And Jesus knowing their thoughts said: Wherefore think ye evil in your hearts? ⁵ For which is easier, to say: Thy sins are forgiven; or to say: Arise, and walk? ⁶ But that ye may know that the

---

V. 28. *In some ancient copies:* Gergesenes

Son of man has power on earth to forgive sins, (then says he to the palsied man) Arise, take up thy bed, and go to thy house. ⁷ And rising up he departed to his house. ⁸ And seeing it the multitudes feared, and glorified God, who gave such power to men.

⁹ And Jesus, passing on from thence, saw a man named Matthew, sitting at the place of receiving custom ; and he says to him : Follow me. And he rose up and followed him. ¹⁰ And it came to pass that, as he reclined at table in the house, behold, many publicans and sinners came and reclined at table with Jesus and his disciples. ¹¹ And the Pharisees, seeing it, said to his disciples : Why does your teacher eat with the publicans and the sinners ? ¹² And Jesus hearing it, said : They who are well need not a physician, but they who are sick. ¹³ But go, and learn what this means : I desire mercy and not sacrifice ; for I came not to call righteous men, but sinners.

¹⁴ Then come to him the disciples of John, saying : Why do we and the Pharisees fast often, but thy disciples fast not ? ¹⁵ And Jesus said to them : Can the sons of the bridechamber mourn, so long as the bridegroom is with them ? But days will come when the bridegroom will be taken from them, and then they will fast. ¹⁶ And no one puts a piece of unfulled cloth on an old garment ; for that which fills it up takes from the garment, and a worse rent is made. ¹⁷ Nor do they put new wine into old skins ; else the skins burst, and the wine runs out, and the skins are destroyed. But they put new wine into new skins, and both are preserved together.

¹⁸ While he was speaking these things to them, behold, there came a ruler, and bowed down to him, saying : My daughter just now died ; but come and lay thy hand upon her, and she will live. ¹⁹ And Jesus arose and was following him, he and his disciples. ²⁰ And behold, a woman, having a flow of blood twelve years, came behind, and touched the fringe of his garment. ²¹ For she said within herself : If I only touch his gar-

---

V. 15. *Or,* Can the bride-men mourn

CHAPTER IX.

ment, I shall be made whole. [22] And Jesus, turning and seeing her, said: Daughter, be of good cheer; thy faith has made thee whole. [23] And the woman was made whole from that hour. And Jesus, coming into the house of the ruler, and seeing the minstrels and the crowd making a noise, [24] said: Give place; for the maiden is not dead, but is sleeping. And they laughed him to scorn. [25] But when the crowd was put forth, he went in, and took hold of her hand, and the maiden arose. [26] And this report went abroad into all that land.

[27] And as Jesus passed on from thence, two blind men followed him, crying, and saying: Have mercy on us, Son of David. [28] And when he had come into the house, the blind men came to him. And Jesus says to them: Believe ye that I am able to do this? They say to him: Yea, Lord. [29] Then he touched their eyes, saying: According to your faith be it done to you. [30] And their eyes were opened. And Jesus sternly charged them, saying: Take heed, let no one know it. [31] But they, going out, spread abroad his fame in all that country.

[32] And as they were going out, behold, they brought to him a man dumb, possessed with a demon. [33] And the demon being cast out, the dumb spoke. And the multitudes marveled, saying: It was never so seen in Israel. [34] But the Pharisees said: He casts out the demons through the prince of the demons.

[35] And Jesus went about all the cities and villages, teaching in their synagogues, and preaching the good news of the kingdom, and healing every sickness and every infirmity. [36] And seeing the multitudes, he was moved with compassion for them, because they were harassed, and scattered, as sheep having no shepherd. [37] Then he says to his disciples: The harvest indeed is great, but the laborers are few. [38] Pray therefore the Lord of the harvest, that he will send forth laborers into his harvest.

V. 36. *Or*, and cast off

MATTHEW.

X. And calling to him his twelve disciples, he gave them authority over unclean spirits, so as to cast them out, and to heal every sickness and every infirmity. ² And the names of the twelve apostles are these; first Simon, who is called Peter, and Andrew his brother; James the son of Zebedee, and John his brother; ³ Philip, and Bartholomew; Thomas, and Matthew the publican; James the son of Alpheus, and Lebbeus surnamed Thaddeus; ⁴ Simon the Cananite, and Judas Iscariot, who also betrayed him.

⁵ These twelve Jesus sent forth, and charged them, saying: Go not into the way to the Gentiles, and into a city of Samaritans enter not. ⁶ But go rather to the lost sheep of the house of Israel. ⁷ And as ye go, preach, saying: The kingdom of heaven is at hand. ⁸ Heal the sick, raise the dead, cleanse lepers, cast out demons. Freely ye received, freely give. ⁹ Provide not gold, nor silver, nor brass in your girdles; ¹⁰ nor bag for the journey, nor two coats, nor sandals, nor staff; for the laborer is worthy of his living. ¹¹ And into whatever city or village ye shall enter, inquire who in it is worthy; and there abide till ye go thence. ¹² But when ye come into the house, salute it. ¹³ And if the house be worthy, let your peace come upon it; but if it be not worthy, let your peace return to you. ¹⁴ And whoever shall not receive you, nor hear your words, when ye go out of that house or city, shake off the dust of your feet. ¹⁵ Verily I say to you, it shall be more tolerable for the land of Sodom and Gomorrah in the day of judgment, than for that city.

¹⁶ Behold, I send you forth as sheep in the midst of wolves; be therefore wise as serpents, and simple as doves. ¹⁷ But beware of men; for they will deliver you up to councils, and will scourge you in their synagogues; ¹⁸ and before governors also and kings will ye be brought for my sake, for a testimony to them and to the Gentiles.

V. 4. Cananite, (*as some suppose*) = Zelotes.
V. 8. *Some ancient copies omit:* raise the dead

CHAPTER X.

¹⁹ But when they deliver you up, take not thought how or what ye shall speak; for it shall be given you in that hour what ye shall speak. ²⁰ For it is not ye that speak, but the Spirit of your Father that speaks in you.

²¹ And the brother will deliver up the brother to death, and the father the child; and children will rise up against parents, and cause them to be put to death. ²² And ye will be hated by all, for my name's sake; but he that has endured to the end, the same shall be saved.

²³ But when they persecute you in this city, flee into the other; for verily I say to you, ye shall not have gone over the cities of Israel, till the Son of man come.

²⁴ A disciple is not above the teacher, nor a servant above his lord. ²⁵ It is enough for the disciple that he be as his teacher, and the servant as his lord. If they called the master of the house Beelzebul, how much more those of his household!

²⁶ Fear them not therefore; for there is nothing covered that shall not be revealed, and hid that shall not be known. ²⁷ What I say to you in the darkness, that speak ye in the light; and what ye hear in the ear, that proclaim upon the house-tops. ²⁸ And be not afraid of those who kill the body, but are not able to kill the soul; but rather fear him who is able to destroy both soul and body in hell.

²⁹ Are not two sparrows sold for a penny? And one of them shall not fall on the ground without your Father. ²⁰ But the very hairs of your head are all numbered. ³¹ Fear not therefore; ye are of more value than many sparrows.

³² Every one, therefore, who shall acknowledge me before men, him will I also acknowledge before my Father who is in heaven. ³³ But whoever shall deny me before men, him will I also deny before my Father who is in heaven.

³⁴ Think not that I came to send peace on the earth; I came not to send peace, but a sword. ³⁵ For I came to set a man at variance with his father, and a daughter with her mother, and a bride with her mother-in-law; ³⁶ and a man's foes will be they of his household.

³⁷ He that loves father or mother more than me, is not worthy

MATTHEW.

of me; and he that loves son or daughter more than me, is not worthy of me. ³⁸ And he that does not take his cross and follow after me, is not worthy of me. ³⁹ He that finds his life shall lose it; and he that loses his life for my sake shall find it.

⁴⁰ He that receives you receives me; and he that receives me receives him who sent me. ⁴¹ He that receives a prophet in the name of a prophet shall receive a prophet's reward; and he that receives a righteous man in the name of a righteous man shall receive a righteous man's reward. ⁴² And whoever shall give to drink a cup of cold water only to one of these little ones, in the name of a disciple, verily I say to you, he shall not lose his reward.

XI. And it came to pass, when Jesus made an end of commanding his twelve disciples, that he departed thence to teach and to preach in their cities.

² And John, having heard in the prison the works of the Christ, sent by his disciples, ³ and said to him: Art thou he that comes, or look we for another?

⁴ And Jesus answering said to them: Go and report to John what ye hear and see. ⁵ The blind receive sight and the lame walk, lepers are cleansed and the deaf hear, the dead are raised, and to the poor good tidings are published. ⁶ And happy is he, whoever shall not be offended at me.

⁷ And as these were departing, Jesus began to say to the multitudes concerning John: What went ye out into the wilderness to behold? A reed shaken by the wind?

⁸ But what went ye out to see? A man clothed in soft raiment? Behold, they who wear soft clothing are in king's houses.

⁹ But what went ye out to see? A prophet? Yea, I say to you, and more than a prophet. ¹⁰ For this is he of whom it is written:

    Behold, I send forth my messenger before thy face,
    Who shall prepare thy way before thee.

V. 9. *In some ancient copies:* But why went ye out? To see a prophet?

CHAPTER XI.

[11] Verily I say to you, among those born of women, there has not risen a greater than John the Immerser. But he who is least in the kingdom of heaven is greater than he. [12] And from the days of John the Immerser until now, the kingdom of heaven suffers violence, and the violent seize upon it. [13] For all the prophets and the law prophesied until John. [14] And if ye are willing to receive it, he is the Elijah that should come. [15] He that has ears to hear, let him hear.

[16] But to what shall I liken this generation? It is like to children sitting in the markets, who call to their fellows, [17] and say: We piped to you, and ye danced not; we sang the lament, and ye did not beat the breast. [18] For John came neither eating nor drinking, and they say: He has a demon. [19] The Son of man came eating and drinking, and they say: Behold a glutton and a wine-drinker, a friend of publicans and sinners. But wisdom was justified on the part of her children.

[20] Then began he to upbraid the cities wherein most of his miracles were done, because they repented not. [21] Woe to thee, Chorazin! Woe to thee, Bethsaida! For if the miracles, that were done in you, had been done in Tyre and Sidon, they would have repented long ago in sackcloth and ashes. [22] But I say to you, it will be more tolerable for Tyre and Sidon in the day of judgment, than for you.

[23] And thou, Capernaum, that wast exalted to heaven, shalt go down to the underworld. For if the miracles, that were done in thee, had been done in Sodom, it would have remained until this day. [24] But I say to you, that it will be more tolerable for the land of Sodom in the day of judgment, than for thee.

[25] At that time Jesus answered and said: I thank thee, O Father, Lord of heaven and earth, that thou didst hide these things from the wise and discerning, and reveal them to babes; [26] yea, O Father, that so it seemed good in thy sight! [27] All things were delivered to me by my Father; and no one

---

V. 23. *In the oldest copies:* shalt thou be exalted to heaven? Thou shalt
V. 23. Underworld: *the abode of the dead, represented (figuratively, as in the Old Testament) as underneath, in contrast with heaven above. See Philipp.* ii., 10; *Rev.* v., 3, 13; *Luke* xvi., 23.

knows the Son but the Father; nor does any one know the Father but the Son, and he to whom the Son is pleased to reveal him.

²⁸ Come unto me all ye that labor and are heavy-laden, and I will give you rest. ²⁹ Take my yoke upon you, and learn from me; for I am meek and lowly in heart; and ye shall find rest for your souls. ³⁰ For my yoke is easy, and my burden light.

XII. At that time Jesus went on the sabbath through the grain-fields; and his disciples were hungry, and began to pluck ears of grain, and to eat. ² And the Pharisees seeing it said to him: Behold, thy disciples are doing that which it is not lawful to do on the sabbath. ³ And he said to them: Have ye not read what David did, when he hungered, himself and those with him; ⁴ how he entered into the house of God, and ate the show-bread, which it was not lawful for him to eat, nor for those with him, but for the priests alone? ⁵ Or have ye not read in the law, that on the sabbath the priests in the temple profane the sabbath, and are blameless? ⁶ But I say to you, that a greater than the temple is here. ⁷ But if ye had known what this means, I d e s i r e m e r c y a n d n o t s a c r i f i c e, ye would not have condemned the blameless. ⁸ For the Son of man is Lord of the sabbath.

⁹ And departing from thence, he went into their synagogue. ¹⁰ And behold, there was a man, having his hand withered. And they asked him, saying: Is it lawful to heal on the sabbath? that they might accuse him. ¹¹ And he said to them: What man will there be of you, that shall have one sheep, and if this fall into a pit on the sabbath, will not lay hold of it, and raise it up? ¹² How much better then is a man than a sheep! So that it is lawful to do well on the sabbath. ¹³ Then he says to the man: Stretch forth thy hand. And he stretched it forth; and it was restored whole, as the other.

¹⁴ And the Pharisees went out, and took counsel against him, how they might destroy him. ¹⁵ But Jesus, knowing it, withdrew from thence; and great multitudes followed him, and he

CHAPTER XII.

healed them all. ⁱ⁶ And he charged them that they should not make him known; ¹⁷ that it might be fulfilled which was spoken through Isaiah the prophet, saying :
¹⁸ Behold my servant, whom I chose,
My beloved, in whom my soul is well pleased.
I will put my spirit upon him,
And he will declare judgment to the Gentiles.
¹⁹ He will not strive, nor cry ;
Nor will any one hear his voice in the streets.
²⁰ A bruised reed he will not break,
And smoking flax he will not quench,
Till he send forth judgment unto victory.
²¹ And in his name will Gentiles hope.

²² Then was brought to him one possessed with a demon, blind, and dumb; and he healed him, so that the blind and dumb both spoke and saw. ²³ And all the multitudes were amazed, and said : Is this the Son of David ? ²⁴ But the Pharisees hearing it said : This man does not cast out the demons, except through Beelzebul, prince of the demons. ²⁵ And Jesus, knowing their thoughts, said to them : Every kingdom divided against itself is brought to desolation ; and any city or house divided against itself shall not stand. ²⁶ And if Satan cast out Satan, he is divided against himself; how then shall his kingdom stand ? ²⁷ And if I through Beelzebul cast out the demons, through whom do your sons cast them out ? Therefore they shall be your judges. ²⁸ But if I through the Spirit of God cast out the demons, then is the kingdom of God come near to you. ²⁹ Or how can any one enter into a strong man's house, and seize upon his goods, except he first bind the strong man ? And then he will plunder his house.

³⁰ He that is not with me is against me ; and he that gathers not with me scatters abroad.

³¹ Therefore I say to you, every sin and blasphemy will be forgiven to men; but the blasphemy against the Spirit will not be forgiven. ³² And whoever speaks a word against the

---

V. 22. *The oldest copies omit*, blind, and both.

MATTHEW.

Son of man, it will be forgiven him; but whoever speaks against the Holy Spirit, it will not be forgiven him, neither in this world, nor in that which is to come. ³³ Either make the tree good and its fruit good, or make the tree corrupt and its fruit corrupt; for from the fruit the tree is known. ³⁴ Brood of vipers! How can ye, being evil, speak good things? For out of the abundance of the heart the mouth speaks. ³⁵ The good man out of the good treasure sends forth good things; and the evil man out of the evil treasure sends forth evil things. ³⁶ But I say to you, that every idle word that men shall speak, they shall give account thereof in the day of judgment. ³⁷ For from thy words thou shalt be justified, and from thy words thou shalt be condemned.

³⁸ Then certain of the scribes and of the Pharisees answered him saying: Teacher, we desire to see a sign from thee. ³⁹ But he answering said to them: An evil and adulterous generation seeks after a sign; and no sign shall be given to it, but the sign of Jonah the prophet. ⁴⁰ For as Jonah was three days and three nights in the belly of the fish, so shall the Son of man be three days and three nights in the heart of the earth. ⁴¹ Men of Nineveh will rise in the judgment with this generation, and will condemn it; because they repented at the preaching of Jonah, and behold, a greater than Jonah is here. ⁴² A queen of the south will rise up in the judgment with this generation, and will condemn it; for she came from the utmost parts of the earth to hear the wisdom of Solomon, and behold, a greater than Solomon is here.

⁴³ But when the unclean spirit is gone out from the man, he goes through dry places seeking rest, and finds it not. ⁴⁴ Then he says, I will return into my house from whence I came out; and coming he finds it empty, swept, and set in order. ⁴⁵ Then he goes, and takes with him seven other spirits more wicked than himself, and they enter in and dwell there; and the last state of that man becomes worse than the first. So shall it be also with this wicked generation.

⁴⁶ While he was yet speaking to the multitudes, behold, his

CHAPTER XIII.

mother and his brothers were standing without, seeking to speak to him. ⁴⁷ And one said to him : Behold, thy mother and thy brothers are standing without, seeking to speak to thee. ⁴⁸ But he answering said to him that told him : Who is my mother, and who are my brothers ? ⁴⁹ And stretching forth his hand toward his disciples, he said : Behold my mother and my brothers ! ⁵⁰ For whoever shall do the will of my Father who is in heaven, he is my brother, and sister, and mother.

XIII. And on that day Jesus went out of the house, and sat by the sea-side. ² And great multitudes were gathered together to him, so that he went into the ship and sat down ; and all the multitude stood on the beach. ³ And he spoke many things to them in parables, saying :

⁴ Behold, the sower went forth to sow. And as he sowed, some fell by the way-side, and the birds came and devoured them. ⁵ And others fell on the rocky places, where they had not much earth ; and forthwith they sprang up, because they had not depth of earth. ⁶ And when the sun was up, they were scorched ; and because they had not root, they withered away. ⁷ And others fell upon the thorns ; and the thorns came up, and choked them. ⁸ And others fell on the good ground, and yielded fruit, some a hundredfold, some sixty, some thirty. ⁹ He that has ears to hear, let him hear.

¹⁰ And the disciples came and said to him : Why dost thou speak to them in parables ? ¹¹ And he answering said to them : To you it is given to know the mysteries of the kingdom of heaven ; but to them it is not given. ¹² For whoever has, to him shall be given, and he shall have abundance ; but whoever has not, even what he has shall be taken from him. ¹³ Therefore I speak to them in parables ; because seeing they see not, and hearing they hear not, nor understand. ¹⁴ And in them is fulfilled the prophecy of Isaiah, which says :

With the hearing ye will hear, and will not understand ;

V. 9. *In some ancient copies:* He that has ears, let him hear.
V. 11. *Or,* Because to you it is given

And seeing ye will see, and will not perceive.
¹⁵ For the heart of this people is become gross,
And their ears are dull of hearing,
And their eyes they have closed ;
Lest haply they see with their eyes,
And hear with their ears,
And understand with their heart,
And turn, and I shall heal them.

¹⁶ But happy are your eyes, because they see; and your ears, because they hear. ¹⁷ For verily I say to you, that many prophets and righteous men desired to see what ye are beholding, and did not see, and to hear what ye are hearing, and did not hear.

¹⁸ Hear therefore the parable of the sower. ¹⁹ When any one hears the word of the kingdom, and understands not, then comes the evil one and snatches away what was sown in his heart. This is that which was sown by the way-side.

²⁰ And that sown on the rocky places, this is he that hears the word, and immediately with joy receives it ; ²¹ and has not root in himself, but is only for a time ; and when tribulation or persecution arises because of the word, immediately he is offended.

²² And that sown among the thorns, this is he that hears the word, and the care of this world and the deceitfulness of riches choke the word, and it becomes unfruitful. ²³ And that sown on the good ground, this is he that hears the word and understands; who bears fruit, and produces, some a hundredfold, some sixty, some thirty.

²⁴ Another parable he put forth to them, saying : The kingdom of heaven is likened to a man that sowed good seed in his field. ²⁵ But while men slept, his enemy came and sowed darnel among the wheat, and went away. ²⁶ And when the blade sprang up and produced fruit, then appeared the darnel also. ²⁷ And the servants of the householder came and said to him : Sir, didst thou not sow good seed in thy field? From whence then has it darnel? ²⁸ He said to them : An enemy did this. The servants said to him : Wilt thou then that we go

CHAPTER XIII.

and gather them up? ²⁹ He said: Nay, lest while ye gather up the darnel, ye root up the wheat with them. ³⁰ Let both grow together until the harvest. And in time of harvest I will say to the reapers: Gather up first the darnel, and bind them in bundles to burn them; but gather the wheat into my barn.

³¹ Another parable he put forth to them, saying: The kingdom of heaven is like to a grain of mustard, which a man took and sowed in his field. ³² Which is the least indeed of all seeds; but when it is grown, it is greater than the herbs, and becomes a tree, so that the birds of the air come and lodge in its branches.

³³ Another parable he spoke to them: The kingdom of heaven is like to leaven, which a woman took and hid in three measures of meal, till the whole was leavened.

³⁴ All these things Jesus spoke to the multitudes in parables; and without a parable he spoke nothing to them; ³⁵ that it might be fulfilled which was spoken through the prophet, saying:

I will open my mouth in parables;
I will utter things hidden from the foundation of the world.

³⁶ Then having sent away the multitudes, he went into the house. And his disciples came to him, saying: Explain to us the parable of the darnel of the field. ³⁷ And answering he said to them:

He that sows the good seed is the Son of man. ³⁸ The field is the world. The good seed, these are the sons of the kingdom; but the darnel are the sons of the evil one, ³⁹ and the enemy that sowed them is the Devil. The harvest is the end of the world; and the reapers are angels. ⁴⁰ As therefore the darnel are gathered up and are burned with fire, so shall it be in the end of the world. ⁴¹ The Son of man will send forth his angels, and they will gather out of his kingdom all the causes of offense, and those who do iniquity, ⁴² and will cast them into the furnace of fire; there will be the wailing, and the gnashing

---

V. 36. *Or,* Then leaving the multitudes

of teeth! ⁴³ Then will the righteous shine forth as the sun in the kingdom of their Father. He that has ears to hear, let him hear.

⁴⁴ Again, the kingdom of heaven is like to a treasure hidden in the field, which a man found and concealed; and for joy thereof, he goes and sells all that he has, and buys that field.

⁴⁵ Again, the kingdom of heaven is like to a merchant seeking goodly pearls; ⁴⁶ and having found one pearl of great price, he went and sold all that he had, and bought it.

⁴⁷ Again, the kingdom of heaven is like to a net, cast into the sea, and gathering together of every kind. ⁴⁸ Which, when it was filled, they drew up upon the beach, and sat down and gathered the good into vessels, but cast the bad away. ⁴⁹ So will it be in the end of the world. The angels will go forth, and will separate the wicked from among the just, ⁵⁰ and will cast them into the furnace of fire; there will be the wailing, and the gnashing of teeth!

⁵¹ Did ye understand all these things? They say to him, Yea, Lord. ⁵² And he said to them: Therefore every scribe, instructed in the kingdom of heaven, is like to a householder, who brings forth out of his treasure new and old.

⁵³ And it came to pass, when Jesus finished these parables, that he departed thence. ⁵⁴ And coming into his own country, he taught them in their synagogue; so that they were astonished, and said: Whence has this man this wisdom, and the miracles? Is not this the carpenter's son? ⁵⁵ Is not his mother called Mary, and his brothers, James, and Joseph, and Simon, and Judas? ⁵⁶ And his sisters, are they not all with us? Whence then has this man all these things? ⁵⁷ And they were offended at him. But Jesus said to them: A prophet is not without honor, save in his own country, and in his own house. ⁵⁸ And he did not many miracles there, because of their unbelief.

V. 43. *In some ancient copies:* He that has ears, let him hear.
V. 44. *Or, and because of his joy,*
V. 55. *In some ancient copies:* Joses

CHAPTER XIV.

XIV. At that time Herod the tetrarch heard the fame of Jesus. ² And he said to his servants : This is John the Immerser ; he is risen from the dead, and therefore do these powers work in him.

³ For Herod laid hold of John, and bound him and put him in prison, for the sake of Herodias, the wife of Philip, his brother. ⁴ For John said to him : It is not lawful for thee to have her. ⁵ And though desiring to put him to death, he feared the multitude, because they held him as a prophet. ⁶ But when Herod's birthday was kept, the daughter of Herodias danced before them, and pleased Herod. ⁷ Whereupon he promised with an oath, to give her whatever she should ask. ⁸ And she, being urged on by her mother, says : Give me here, on a platter, the head of John the Immerser. ⁹ And the king was sorry ; but for the sake of the oath, and of those who reclined at table with him, he commanded it to be given. ¹⁰ And he sent, and beheaded John in the prison. ¹¹ And his head was brought on a platter, and was given to the damsel, and she brought it to her mother. ¹² And his disciples came and took up the body, and buried it ; and they went and reported it to Jesus.

¹³ And when Jesus heard it, he withdrew from thence by ship, into a desert place apart. And the multitudes hearing of it, followed him on foot from the cities. ¹⁴ And going forth he saw a great multitude, and had compassion on them, and he healed their sick.

¹⁵ And when it was evening, his disciples came to him, saying : The place is desert, and the time is already passed away ; dismiss the multitudes, that they may go away into the villages, and buy themselves victuals. ¹⁶ But Jesus said to them : They need not go away ; give ye them to eat. ¹⁷ And they say to him : We have here but five loaves, and two fishes. ¹⁸ He said : Bring them hither to me. ¹⁹ And he commanded that the multitudes should lie down on the grass, and took the five

---

V. 2. *Or*, the powers

MATTHEW.

loaves and the two fishes, and looking up to heaven he blessed, and broke, and gave the loaves to the disciples, and the disciples to the multitudes. ²⁰ And they all ate, and were filled; and they took up of the fragments that remained twelve baskets full. ²¹ And they who ate were about five thousand men, besides women and children.

²² And straightway he constrained his disciples to enter into the ship, and to go before him to the other side, while he dismissed the multitudes.

²³ And having dismissed the multitudes, he went up into the mountain apart to pray; and when evening was come, he was there alone. ²⁴ But the ship was already in the midst of the sea, vexed by the waves; for the wind was contrary. ²⁵ And in the fourth watch of the night he went to them, walking on the sea. ²⁶ And the disciples, seeing him walking on the sea, were troubled, saying: It is a spectre. And they cried out for fear. ²⁷ But straightway Jesus spoke to them, saying: Be of good cheer; it is I, be not afraid. ²⁸ And Peter answering him said: Lord, if it is thou, bid me come to thee on the water. ²⁹ And he said: Come. And coming down from the ship, Peter walked on the water, to go to Jesus. ³⁰ But seeing the wind boisterous, he was afraid; and beginning to sink, he cried out, saying: Lord, save me. ³¹ And immediately Jesus, stretching forth his hand, took hold of him, and said to him: Thou of little faith, wherefore didst thou doubt?

³² And when they had entered into the ship, the wind ceased. ³³ And those in the ship came and worshiped him, saying: Of a truth, thou art the Son of God.

³⁴ And passing over, they came into the land of Gennesaret. ³⁵ And the men of that place, knowing him, sent out into all that country round, and brought to him all that were diseased; ³⁶ and besought him that they might only touch the fringe of his garment; and as many as touched were made whole.

V. 33. *Or*, and bowed down to him

CHAPTER XV.

XV. ¹ THEN there came to Jesus the scribes and Pharisees from Jerusalem, saying: ² Why do thy disciples transgress the tradition of the elders? For they wash not their hands when they eat bread. ³ And he answering said to them: Why do ye also transgress the commandment of God, for the sake of your tradition? ⁴ For God commanded, saying: Honor thy father and mother; and he that curses father or mother, let him surely die. ⁵ But ye say: Whoever says to his father or his mother, It is a gift, whatever thou mightest be profited with from me, ⁶ shall not honor his father or his mother ; and ye made the word of God of no effect, for the sake of your tradition.

⁷ Hypocrites ! Well did Isaiah prophesy of you, saying :
⁸ This people honor me with their lips,
But their heart is far from me.
⁹ But in vain they worship me,
Teaching as doctrines commandments of men.

¹⁰ And calling to him the multitude, he said to them: Hear, and understand. ¹¹ Not that which enters into the mouth defiles the man ; but that which comes out of the mouth, this defiles the man.

¹² Then came to him his disciples, and said to him : Knowest thou that the Pharisees, when they heard the saying, were offended? ¹³ And he answering said : Every plant, which my heavenly Father planted not, shall be rooted up. ¹⁴ Let them alone ; they are blind leaders of the blind ; and if the blind lead the blind, both will fall into the ditch.

¹⁵ And Peter answering said to him : Explain to us this parable. ¹⁶ And he said : Are ye also even yet without understanding? ¹⁷ Do ye not yet understand, that whatever enters into the mouth goes into the belly, and is cast out into the drain? ¹⁸ But the things that proceed out of the mouth come forth out of the heart ; and they defile the man. ¹⁹ For out of

---

V. 4. *In the oldest copies:* For God said :
V. 6. *In some ancient copies:* the commandment of God

the heart proceed evil thoughts, murders, adulteries, fornications, thefts, false-witnessings, blasphemies. ²⁰ These are the things that defile the man; but to eat with unwashen hands defiles not the man.

²¹ And Jesus, going forth from thence, withdrew into the region of Tyre and Sidon. ²² And behold, a woman of Canaan, coming out from those borders, cried to him, saying: Have mercy on me, O Lord, Son of David; my daughter is grievously possessed with a demon. ²³ But he answered her not a word. And his disciples came and besought him, saying: Dismiss her; because she cries after us. ²⁴ But he answering said: I was not sent except to the lost sheep of the house of Israel. ²⁵ But she came and bowed down to him, saying: Lord, help me. ²⁶ But he answering said: It is not good to take the children's bread, and cast it to the dogs. ²⁷ And she said: Yea, Lord; for the dogs also eat of the crumbs that fall from their masters' table. ²⁸ Then Jesus answering said to her: O woman, great is thy faith; be it done to thee as thou wilt. And her daughter was healed from that hour.

²⁹ And departing from thence, Jesus came near to the sea of Galilee; and going up into the mountain, he sat down there. ³⁰ And great multitudes came to him, having with them lame, blind, dumb, maimed, and many others, and laid them down at his feet, and he healed them; ³¹ so that the multitudes wondered, when they saw the dumb speaking, the maimed whole, the lame walking, and the blind seeing; and they glorified the God of Israel.

³² And Jesus, having called to him his disciples, said: I have compassion on the multitude, because they continue with me now three days, and have nothing to eat; and I will not dismiss them fasting, lest they faint in the way. ³³ And his disciples say to him: Whence should we have so many loaves in the wilderness, as to fill so great a multitude? ³⁴ And Jesus says to them: How many loaves have ye? And they said: Seven, and a few little fishes. ³⁵ And he commanded the multitudes to lie down on the ground. ³⁶ And he took the seven loaves and the fishes, and gave thanks, and broke, and

CHAPTER XVI.

gave to his disciples, and the disciples to the multitude. ⁵⁷ And they all ate, and were filled. And they took up of the fragments that remained seven baskets full. ⁵⁸ And they who ate were four thousand men, besides women and children. ⁵⁹ And dismissing the multitudes, he entered into the ship, and came into the borders of Magdala.

XVI. And the Pharisees and Sadducees came to him, and tempting desired him to show them a sign from heaven. ² And he answering said to them : When it is evening, ye say : Fair weather! for the sky is red. ³ And in the morning : A storm to-day! for the sky is red and lowering. Ye know how to discern the face of the sky, but can ye not the signs of the times ?

⁴ An evil and adulterous generation seeks after a sign ; and no sign shall be given to it, but the sign of Jonah. And he left them, and departed.

⁵ And coming to the other side, his disciples forgot to take bread. ⁶ And Jesus said to them : Take heed, and beware of the leaven of the Pharisees and Sadducees. ⁷ And they reasoned among themselves, saying : Because we took no bread ! ⁸ And Jesus knowing it said : Ye of little faith, why reason ye among yourselves, because ye took no bread ? ⁹ Do ye not yet understand, nor remember the five loaves of the five thousand, and how many baskets ye took up ? ¹⁰ Nor the seven loaves of the four thousand, and how many baskets ye took up ? ¹¹ How is it that ye do not understand, that I spoke not to you of bread ? But, beware of the leaven of the Pharisees and Sadducees ! ¹² Then they understood, that he did not bid them beware of the leaven of bread, but of the teaching of the Pharisees and Sadducees.

¹³ And having come into the region of Cæsarea Philippi, Jesus asked his disciples, saying : Who do men say that the Son of man is ? ¹⁴ And they said : Some, John the Immerser ; and others, Elijah ; and others, Jeremiah, or one of the prophets.

V 13. *In many ancient copies :* that I the Son of man am

¹⁵ He says to them : But who do ye say that I am? ¹⁶ And Simon Peter answering said : Thou art the Christ, the Son of the living God. ¹⁷ And Jesus answering said to him : Happy art thou, Simon Bar-jonah; for flesh and blood did not reveal it to thee, but my Father who is in heaven. ¹⁸ And I also say to thee, that thou art Peter, and upon this rock I will build my church; and the gates of the underworld shall not prevail against it. ¹⁹ And I will give to thee the keys of the kingdom of heaven; and whatever thou shalt bind on earth shall be bound in heaven; and whatever thou shalt loose on earth shall be loosed in heaven.

²⁰ Then he charged his disciples, that they should tell no one that he is the Christ.

²¹ From that time Jesus began to show to his disciples, that he must go to Jerusalem, and suffer many things from the elders and chief priests and scribes, and be put to death, and rise on the third day.

²² And Peter taking him aside began to rebuke him, saying : Be it far from thee, Lord; this shall not be to thee. ²³ But he turned and said to Peter : Get thee behind me, Satan; thou art an offense to me; for thou thinkest not the things of God, but those of men.

²⁴ Then Jesus said to his disciples : If any one will come after me, let him deny himself, and take up his cross, and follow me. ²⁵ For whoever will save his life shall lose it; and whoever may lose his life for my sake, shall find it. ²⁶ For what is a man profited, if he shall gain the whole world, and forfeit his soul? Or what shall a man give as an exchange for his soul? ²⁷ For the Son of man will come in the glory of his Father, with his angels; and then he will reward each one according to his works.

²⁸ Verily I say to you, there are some of those standing here, who shall not taste death, till they see the Son of man coming in his kingdom.

V. 17. Bar-jonah : *that is*, Son of Jonah.
V. 18. Peter : *that is*, rock.
Ib. *Or*, my congregation
V. 23. *Or*, adversary
V. 26. *Or*, as a ransom

CHAPTER XVII.

XVII. And after six days Jesus takes with him Peter, and James, and John his brother, and brings them up into a high mountain apart. ² And he was transfigured before them; and his face shone as the sun, and his garments became white as the light. ³ And behold, there appeared to them Moses and Elijah, talking with him. ⁴ And Peter answering said to Jesus: Lord, it is good for us to be here. If thou wilt, let us make here three tents; one for thee, and one for Moses, and one for Elijah. ⁵ While he was yet speaking, behold, a bright cloud overshadowed them. And behold, a voice out of the cloud, saying: This is my beloved Son, in whom I am well pleased; hear ye him. ⁶ And the disciples, hearing it, fell on their face, and were exceedingly afraid. ⁷ And Jesus coming to them touched them, and said: Arise, and be not afraid. ⁸ And lifting up their eyes, they saw no one save Jesus only.

⁹ And as they came down out of the mountain, Jesus charged them, saying: Tell no one the vision, until the Son of man is risen from the dead.

¹⁰ And his disciples asked him, saying: Why then say the scribes that Elijah must first come? ¹¹ And he answering said: Elijah indeed comes, and will restore all things. ¹² But I say to you, that Elijah is already come, and they knew him not, but did with him whatever they would. So also is the Son of man about to suffer by them.

¹³ Then the disciples understood that he spoke to them of John the Immerser.

¹⁴ And when they were come to the multitude, there came to him a man, kneeling down to him, and saying: ¹⁵ Lord, have mercy on my son; for he is lunatic, and is sorely afflicted; for ofttimes he falls into the fire, and oft into the water. ¹⁶ And I brought him to thy disciples, and they could not cure him. ¹⁷ And Jesus answering said: O faithless and perverse generation, how long shall I be with you? How long shall I bear with you? Bring him hither to me. ¹⁸ And Jesus rebuked him; and the demon went out from him, and the child was cured from that hour.

¹⁹ Then the disciples, coming to Jesus apart, said: Why could not we cast him out? ²⁰ And he said to them: Because of your want of faith. For verily I say to you, if ye have faith as a grain of mustard, ye shall say to this mountain, remove hence to yonder place, and it shall remove; and nothing shall be impossible to you. ²¹ But this kind goes not forth, except by prayer and fasting.

²² And while they abode in Galilee, Jesus said to them: The Son of man is about to be delivered into the hands of men; ²³ and they will put him to death, and he will rise on the third day. And they were exceedingly sorrowful.

²⁴ And they having come to Capernaum, those who received the half-shekel came to Peter, and said: Does not your teacher pay the half-shekel? ²⁵ He says, Yes. And when he came into the house, Jesus anticipated him, saying: What thinkest thou, Simon? Of whom do the kings of the earth take customs, or tribute? Of their sons, or of strangers? ²⁶ He says to him: Of strangers. Jesus said to him: Then are the sons free. ²⁷ But that we may not offend them, go to the sea and cast a hook, and take the fish that first comes up; and opening its mouth thou wilt find a shekel; that take, and give to them for me and thee.

XVIII. At that time came the disciples to Jesus, saying: Who then is greatest in the kingdom of heaven?

² And Jesus, calling a little child to him, placed it in the midst of them, ³ and said: Verily I say to you, if ye do not turn and become as the little children, ye shall not enter into the kingdom of heaven. ⁴ Whoever therefore shall humble himself as this little child, he is the greatest in the kingdom of heaven. ⁵ And whoever shall receive one such little child, in my name, receives me. ⁶ But whoever shall cause one of these little ones that believe on me to offend, it were better for him that an upper millstone were hanged about his neck, and he were plunged in the depth of the sea.

V. 24. Half-shekel; see *Exodus* xxx., 13, 15.

CHAPTER XVIII.

⁷ Woe to the world, for causes of offense! For it must needs be that causes of offense come; but woe to that man, through whom the cause of offense comes! ⁸ But if thy hand or thy foot causes thee to offend, cut it off, and cast it from thee. It is better for thee to enter into life lame or maimed, than having two hands or two feet to be cast into the everlasting fire. ⁹ And if thine eye causes thee to offend, pluck it out and cast it from thee. It is better for thee to enter into life with one eye, than having two eyes to be cast into hell-fire.

¹⁰ Take heed that ye despise not one of these little ones; for I say to you, that their angels in heaven always behold the face of my Father who is in heaven. ¹¹ For the Son of man came to save that which was lost.

¹² What think ye? If a man has a hundred sheep, and one of them is gone astray, does he not leave the ninety and nine upon the mountains, and go and seek that which is gone astray? ¹³ And if it be that he find it, verily I say to you, he rejoices over it more than over the ninety and nine that went not astray. ¹⁴ So it is not the will of your Father who is in heaven, that one of these little ones perish.

¹⁵ But if thy brother shall sin against thee, go show him his fault between thee and him alone. If he shall hear thee, thou hast gained thy brother. ¹⁶ But if he hear not, take with thee one or two more, that in the mouth of two or three witnesses every word may be established. ¹⁷ And if he shall neglect to hear them, tell it to the church; and if he neglect to hear the church also, let him be to thee as a heathen and a publican. ¹⁸ Verily I say to you: Whatever ye shall bind on earth shall be bound in heaven; and whatever ye shall loose on earth shall be loosed in heaven.

¹⁹ Again I say to you, that if two of you shall agree on earth, concerning any thing that they shall ask, it shall be done for them by my Father who is in heaven. ²⁰ For where two or three are gathered together in my name, there am I in the midst of them.

²¹ Then Peter came to him, and said: Lord, how often shall my brother sin against me, and I forgive him? Until seven

times? ²² Jesus says to him: I say not to thee, until seven times, but until seventy times seven.

²³ Therefore is the kingdom of heaven likened to a certain king, who desired to make a reckoning with his servants. ²⁴ And when he had begun to reckon, there was brought to him one, who owed ten thousand talents. ²⁵ But as he was not able to pay, his lord commanded him to be sold, and his wife, and children, and all that he had, and payment to be made. ²⁶ The servant therefore, falling, prostrated himself before him, saying: Have patience with me, and I will pay thee all. ²⁷ And the lord of that servant, moved with compassion, released him, and forgave him the debt. ²⁸ But that servant went out, and found one of his fellow-servants, who owed him a hundred denáries; and laying hold of him he took him by the throat, saying: Pay me that thou owest. ²⁹ Therefore his fellow-servant fell down and besought him, saying: Have patience with me, and I will pay thee. ³⁰ And he would not; but went and cast him into prison, till he should pay the debt. ³¹ And his fellow-servants, seeing what was done, were very sorry, and came and disclosed to their lord all that was done. ³² Then having called him, his lord says to him: Thou wicked servant; I forgave thee all that debt, because thou besoughtest me. ³³ Shouldest not thou also have had pity on thy fellow-servant, as I too had pity on thee? ³⁴ And his lord was angry, and delivered him to the tormentors, till he should pay all that was due to him. ³⁵ So also will my heavenly Father do to you, if ye from your hearts forgive not every one his brother.

XIX. And it came to pass, when Jesus finished these sayings, that he departed from Galilee, and came into the borders of Judæa beyond the Jordan. ² And great multitudes followed him, and he healed them there.

³ And the Pharisees came to him, tempting him and saying: Is it lawful for a man to put away his wife for every cause?

V. 24. Talent (*Syrian*), about *fifteen hundred denáries*.
V. 28. Denáry, *seven and a half pence sterling, or fifteen cents*.

CHAPTER XIX.

⁴ And he answering said to them: Have ye not read, that he who made them from the beginning made them male and female, ⁵ and said: For this cause shall a man leave father and mother, and shall cleave to his wife, and the two shall be one flesh. ⁶ So that they are no longer two, but one flesh. What therefore God joined together, let not man put asunder.

⁷ They say to him: Why then did Moses command to give a writing of divorcement, and to put her away? ⁸ He says to them: Moses, for your hardness of heart, suffered you to put away your wives; but from the beginning it was not so. ⁹ And I say to you, that whoever shall put away his wife, except for fornication, and shall marry another, commits adultery; and whoever marries her when put away, commits adultery.

¹⁰ His disciples say to him: If the case of the man with the woman is so, it is not good to marry. ¹¹ But he said to them: Not all can receive this saying, but they to whom it is given. ¹² For there are eunuchs, who were so born from the mother's womb; and there are eunuchs, who were made eunuchs by men; and there are eunuchs, who made themselves eunuchs for the sake of the kingdom of heaven. He that is able to receive it, let him receive it.

¹³ Then were brought to him little children, that he might put his hands on them and pray; and the disciples rebuked them. ¹⁴ But Jesus said: Suffer the little children, and forbid them not to come to me; for to such belongs the kingdom of heaven. ¹⁵ And he laid his hands on them, and departed thence.

¹⁶ And, behold, one came to him and said: Teacher, what good shall I do, that I may have eternal life? ¹⁷ And he said to him: Why dost thou ask me concerning good? One is the Good. But if thou desirest to enter into life, keep the commandments. ¹⁸ He says to him, Which? Jesus said: Thou

---

V. 4. *In some ancient copies:* who created them

shalt not kill; Thou shalt not commit adultery; Thou shalt not steal; Thou shalt not bear false witness; [19] Honor thy father and thy mother; and, Thou shalt love thy neighbor as thyself. [20] The young man says to him: All these I kept; what do I yet lack? [21] Jesus said to him: If thou desirest to be perfect, go, sell what thou hast, and give to the poor, and thou shalt have treasure in heaven; and come, follow me. [22] But when the young man heard this saying, he went away sorrowful; for he had great possessions.

[23] And Jesus said to his disciples: Verily I say to you, that a rich man shall hardly enter into the kingdom of heaven. [24] And again I say to you: It is easier for a camel to go through the eye of a needle, than for a rich man to enter into the kingdom of God. [25] And the disciples, hearing it, were exceedingly amazed, saying: Who then can be saved? [26] But Jesus, looking on them, said to them: With men this is impossible; but with God all things are possible. [27] Then Peter answering said to him: Behold, we forsook all, and followed thee; what then shall we have? [28] And Jesus said to them: Verily I say to you, that ye who followed me, in the renovation, when the Son of man shall sit on his throne of glory, shall also sit on twelve thrones, judging the twelve tribes of Israel. [29] And every one who forsook houses, or brothers, or sisters, or father, or mother, or wife, or children, or lands, for my name's sake, shall receive manifold more, and shall inherit everlasting life. [30] But many first will be last, and last first.

XX. For the kingdom of heaven is like to a householder, who went out early in the morning to hire laborers into his vineyard. [2] And having agreed with the laborers for a denáry a day, he sent them into his vineyard.

[3] And he went out about the third hour, and saw others standing idle in the market-place. [4] And to them he said: Go

---

V. 2. Denáry (*see* xviii., 28), *about one-third more than the daily pay of a Roman soldier.*

CHAPTER XX.

ye also into the vineyard, and whatever is right I will give you. And they went their way.

⁵ Again he went out about the sixth and ninth hour, and did likewise.

⁶ And about the eleventh he went out, and found others standing, and says to them: Why stand ye here all the day idle? ⁷ They say to him: Because no one hired us. He says to them: Go ye also into the vineyard.

⁸ And when evening was come, the lord of the vineyard says to his steward: Call the laborers, and pay them the hire, beginning from the last, unto the first. ⁹ And they of the eleventh hour came, and received every man a denáry. ¹⁰ But when the first came, they supposed that they should receive more; and they also received each one a denáry. ¹¹ And on receiving it, they murmured against the householder, ¹² saying: These last labored one hour, and thou madest them equal to us, who bore the burden of the day, and the burning heat.

¹³ But he answering said to one of them: Friend, I do thee no wrong. Didst thou not agree with me for a denáry? ¹⁴ Take what is thine, and go. But I will give to this last, even as to thee. ¹⁵ Is it not lawful for me to do what I will with my own? Is thine eye evil, because I am good?

¹⁶ So will the last be first, and the first last; for many are called, but few are chosen.

¹⁷ And Jesus, going up to Jerusalem, took the twelve disciples apart; and in the way he said to them: ¹⁸ Behold, we are going up to Jerusalem; and the Son of man will be delivered to the chief priests and scribes, and they will condemn him to death, ¹⁹ and will deliver him to the Gentiles to mock and scourge and crucify; and on the third day he will rise again.

²⁰ Then came to him the mother of the sons of Zebedee, with her sons, bowing down and asking a certain thing of him. ²¹ And he said to her: What wilt thou? She says to him: Command that these my two sons shall sit, one on thy right hand, and one on thy left, in thy kingdom. ²² But Jesus answering said: Ye know not what ye ask. Are ye able to drink of the cup that I shall drink of? They say to him: We

are able. ²³ And he says to them: Ye shall drink indeed of my cup; but to sit on my right hand, and on my left, is not mine to give, but is for them for whom it has been prepared by my Father. ²⁴ And the ten, hearing it, were much displeased with the two brothers. ²⁵ But Jesus, having called them to him, said: Ye know that the rulers of the Gentiles exercise lordship over them, and they that are great exercise authority over them. ²⁶ Not so shall it be among you; ²⁷ but whoever would become great among you, let him be your minister; and whoever would be first among you, let him be your servant; ²⁸ even as the Son of man came not to be ministered to, but to minister, and to give his life a ransom for many.

²⁹ And as they were going forth from Jericho, a great multitude followed him. ³⁰ And behold, two blind men sitting by the way-side, hearing that Jesus was passing by, cried, saying: Have mercy on us, O Lord, Son of David. ³¹ And the multitude rebuked them, that they should hold their peace. But they cried the more, saying: Have mercy on us, O Lord, Son of David. ³² And Jesus stood still, and called them, and said: What will ye that I shall do to you? ³³ They say to him: Lord, that our eyes may be opened. ³⁴ And Jesus, moved with compassion, touched their eyes; and immediately their eyes received sight; and they followed him.

XXI. And when they drew near to Jerusalem, and came to Bethphage, at the mount of the Olives, Jesus sent forth two disciples, ² saying to them: Go into the village over against you, and straightway ye will find an ass tied, and a colt with her; loose and bring them to me. ³ And if any one say aught to you, ye shall say: The Lord has need of them; and straightway he will send them.

⁴ Now all this has been done, that it might be fulfilled which was spoken through the prophet, saying:
⁵ Say to the daughter of Zion,
Behold, thy King comes to thee,
Meek, and mounted upon an ass,
And upon a colt, the foal of a beast of burden.

CHAPTER XXI.

⁶ And the disciples, having gone and done as Jesus commanded them, ⁷ brought the ass and the colt, and put on them their garments, and he sat thereon. ⁸ And most of the multitude spread their own garments in the way; and others cut down branches from the trees, and strewed in the way. ⁹ And the multitudes that went before, and that followed, cried, saying: Hosanna to the Son of David; Blessed is he who comes in the name of the Lord; Hosanna in the highest. ¹⁰ And as he entered into Jerusalem, all the city was moved, saying: Who is this? ¹¹ And the multitudes said: This is Jesus the prophet, from Nazareth of Galilee.

¹² And Jesus entered into the temple of God, and cast out all that sold and bought in the temple, and overturned the tables of the money-changers, and the seats of those who sold doves. ¹³ And he says to them: It is written,

My house shall be called a house of prayer;

But ye make it a den of robbers.

¹⁴ And the blind and the lame came to him in the temple, and he healed them. ¹⁵ But the chief priests and the scribes, seeing the wonders that he did, and the children crying in the temple, and saying, Hosanna to the Son of David, were much displeased, ¹⁶ and said to him: Dost thou hear what these say? And Jesus says to them: Yea; did ye never read: From the mouth of babes and sucklings thou preparedst praise?

¹⁷ And leaving them, he went forth out of the city into Bethany, and lodged there.

¹⁸ And in the morning, as he was returning into the city, he hungered. ¹⁹ And seeing a fig-tree by the way, he came to it, and found nothing thereon but leaves only. And he says to it: Let there be no fruit from thee henceforward, forever. And immediately the fig-tree withered away. ²⁰ And the disciples seeing it wondered, saying: How did the fig-tree immediately wither away? ²¹ And Jesus answering said to them: Verily I say to you, if ye have faith, and do not doubt, not

---

V. 9. Hosanna: *i. e.*, Save now!

only shall ye do what is done to the fig-tree, but even if ye say to this mountain, be thou taken up and cast into the sea, it shall be done. ²² And all things whatever ye ask in prayer, believing, ye shall receive.

²³ And when he had come into the temple, the chief priests and the elders of the people came to him as he was teaching, and said: By what authority doest thou these things; and who gave thee this authority? ²⁴ And Jesus answering said to them: I also will ask you one thing, which if ye tell me, I too will tell you by what authority I do these things. ²⁵ John's immersion, whence was it? From heaven, or from men? And they reasoned among themselves, saying: If we say, From heaven, he will say to us: Why then did ye not believe him? ²⁶ But if we say, From men, we fear the multitude; for all hold John as a prophet. ²⁷ And they answered Jesus, saying: We do not know. And he said to them: Neither do I say to you, by what authority I do these things.

²⁸ But what think ye? A man had two sons; and he came to the first, and said: Son, go work to-day in the vineyard. ²⁹ And he answering said: I will not; but afterward he repented, and went. ³⁰ And he came to the other, and said likewise. And he answering said: I will, sir; and went not. ³¹ Which of the two did the father's will? They say to him: The first. Jesus says to them: Verily I say to you, that the publicans and the harlots go into the kingdom of God before you. ³² For John came to you in the way of righteousness, and ye did not believe him; but the publicans and the harlots believed him; and ye, when ye had seen it, repented not afterward, that ye might believe him.

³³ Hear another parable. There was a householder, who planted a vineyard, and put a hedge around it, and dug a winepress in it, and built a tower, and let it out to husbandmen, and went abroad. ³⁴ And when the season of fruits drew near, he sent his servants to the husbandmen, to receive his fruits. ³⁵ And the husbandmen taking his servants, beat one,

---

V. 30. *In some ancient copies:* to the second
V. 31. *In the oldest copies:* They say to him: The tardier one

CHAPTER XXII.

and killed another, and stoned another. ³⁶ Again he sent other servants, more than the first; and they did to them likewise. ³⁷ And afterward he sent to them his son, saying: They will reverence my son. ³⁸ But the husbandmen, seeing the son, said among themselves: This is the heir; come, let us kill him, and have his inheritance. ³⁹ And taking him, they cast him out of the vineyard, and killed him. ⁴⁰ When therefore the lord of the vineyard comes, what will he do to those husbandmen? ⁴¹ They say to him: He will miserably destroy those wicked men, and will let out the vineyard to other husbandmen, who will deliver over to him the fruits in their seasons. ⁴² Jesus says to them: Did ye never read in the Scriptures:

>The stone which the builders disallowed,
>The same is become the head of the corner;
>This is from the Lord,
>And is wonderful in our eyes.

⁴³ Therefore I say to you, that the kingdom of God shall be taken from you, and given to a nation bringing forth the fruits thereof. ⁴⁴ And he that falls upon this stone will be broken; but on whomsoever it shall fall, it will grind him to powder.

⁴⁵ And the chief priests and Pharisees, hearing his parables, knew that he spoke of them. ⁴⁶ And they sought to lay hold of him, but feared the multitudes, since they held him as a prophet.

XXII. And Jesus answering spoke to them again in parables, saying:

² The kingdom of heaven is like to a certain king, who made a marriage for his son. ³ And he sent forth his servants to call those who were bidden to the wedding; and they would not come. ⁴ Again he sent forth other servants, saying: Tell those who are bidden, Behold, I have prepared my dinner; my oxen and my fatlings are killed, and all things are ready; come to the marriage. ⁵ But they made light of it, and went away, one to his farm, another to his merchandise. ⁶ And the rest laid hold of his servants, and ill-treated and slew them. ⁷ And the

MATTHEW.

king, hearing it, was angry; and sending forth his armies, he destroyed those murderers, and burned up their city. ⁸ Then he says to his servants: The wedding is ready, but they who were bidden were not worthy. ⁹ Go therefore into the thoroughfares, and as many as ye find, bid to the marriage. ¹⁰ And those servants went out into the highways, and gathered together all as many as they found, both bad and good; and the wedding was furnished with guests.

¹¹ And the king, coming in to view the guests, saw there a man not clothed with a wedding garment; ¹² and he says to him: Friend, how camest thou in hither, not having a wedding garment? And he was speechless. ¹³ Then the king said to the attendants: Bind him hand and foot, and cast him forth into the outer darkness. There will be the weeping, and the gnashing of teeth! ¹⁴ For many are called, but few are chosen.

¹⁵ Then the Pharisees went and took counsel, how they might ensnare him with a word. ¹⁶ And they send out to him their disciples, with the Herodians, saying: Teacher, we know that thou art true, and teachest the way of God in truth; neither carest thou for any one, for thou regardest not the person of men. ¹⁷ Tell us, therefore, what thinkest thou? Is it lawful to give tribute to Cæsar, or not? ¹⁸ But Jesus, knowing their wickedness, said: Why tempt ye me, hypocrites! ¹⁹ Show me the tribute money. And they brought to him a denáry. ²⁰ And he says to them: Whose is this image, and the inscription? ²¹ They say to him: Cæsar's. Then says he to them: Render therefore to Cæsar the things that are Cæsar's, and to God the things that are God's. ²² And hearing it they wondered, and left him and went away.

²³ On that day came to him Sadducees, who say that there is no resurrection, and asked him, ²⁴ saying: Teacher, Moses said, If any one die having no children, his brother shall marry his wife, and raise

---

V. 15. *Or,* ensnare him in discourse.
V. 19. Denáry, *a Roman coin.*

CHAPTER XXII.

up seed to his brother. ²⁵ Now there were with us seven brothers; and the first married and died, and having no seed left his wife to his brother. ²⁶ Likewise the second also, and the third, unto the seventh. ²⁷ And last of all the woman died also. ²⁸ In the resurrection therefore, of which of the seven shall she be wife? For they all had her.

²⁹ Jesus answering said to them: Ye err, not knowing the Scriptures, nor the power of God. ³⁰ For in the resurrection they neither marry, nor are given in marriage, but are as the angels of God in heaven. ³¹ But concerning the resurrection of the dead, have ye not read that which was spoken to you by God, saying: ³² I am the God of Abraham, and the God of Isaac, and the God of Jacob? God is not the God of the dead, but of the living. ³³ And the multitudes, hearing it, were astonished at his teaching.

³⁴ And the Pharisees, hearing that he had put the Sadducees to silence, collected together; ³⁵ and one of them, a lawyer, asked, tempting him and saying: ³⁶ Teacher, what commandment is great in the law? ³⁷ Jesus said to him: Thou shalt love the Lord thy God with all thy heart, and with all thy soul, and with all thy mind. ³⁸ This is the great and first commandment. ³⁹ And the second is like to it: Thou shalt love thy neighbor as thyself. ⁴⁰ On these two commandments hang all the law and the prophets.

⁴¹ While the Pharisees were collected together, Jesus asked them, ⁴² saying: What think ye concerning the Christ? Of whom is he the son? They say to him: Of David. ⁴³ He says to them: How then does David, in the Spirit, call him Lord, saying:

⁴⁴ The Lord said to my Lord,
   Sit on my right hand,
     Till I put thine enemies under thy feet.

⁴⁵ If then David calls him Lord, how is he his son? ⁴⁶ And no one was able to answer him a word; nor durst any one from that day question him any more.

XXIII. ¹Then Jesus spoke to the multitudes, and to his disciples, ²saying: The scribes and the Pharisees sat down in Moses' seat. ³All, therefore, whatever they bid you, do and observe; but do not according to their works, for they say and do not. ⁴For they bind heavy burdens and grievous to be borne, and lay them on men's shoulders, but will not move them with their finger. ⁵But all their works they do to be seen by men; they make broad their phylacteries, and enlarge the fringes; ⁶and love the first place at feasts, and the first seats in the synagogues, ⁷and the greetings in the markets, and to be called by men, Rabbi, Rabbi. ⁸But be not ye called Rabbi; for one is your Teacher, and all ye are brethren. ⁹And call not any your father on the earth; for one is your Father, he who is in heaven. ¹⁰Neither be called leaders; for one is your leader, the Christ. ¹¹But the greatest of you shall be your servant. ¹²And whoever shall exalt himself shall be humbled; and he that shall humble himself shall be exalted.

¹³But woe to you, scribes and Pharisees, hypocrites! because ye shut up the kingdom of heaven against men; for ye go not in, nor suffer those who are entering to go in.

¹⁵Woe to you, scribes and Pharisees, hypocrites! because ye traverse sea and land to make one proselyte, and when he is made, ye make him twofold more a child of hell than yourselves.

¹⁶Woe to you, blind guides, who say: Whoever shall swear by the temple, it is nothing; but whoever shall swear by the gold of the temple, he is bound. ¹⁷Fools and blind; for which is greater, the gold, or the temple that sanctifies the gold? ¹⁸And, Whoever shall swear by the altar, it is nothing; but whoever shall swear by the gift that is upon it, he is bound. ¹⁹Fools and blind; for which is greater, the gift, or the altar that sanctifies the gift?

V. 7. Rabbi *(my Master)*, *a Jewish title of respect, given to a teacher.*

V. 14 *is wanting here, in the oldest copies; it belongs to Mark* xii., 40, *and Luke* xx., 47.

CHAPTER XXIII.

²⁰ He therefore who swears by the altar, swears by it, and by all things thereon. ²¹ And he that swears by the temple, swears by it, and by him who dwells therein. ²² And he that swears by heaven, swears by the throne of God, and by him who sits thereon.

²³ Woe to you, scribes and Pharisees, hypocrites! because ye pay tithe of the mint and the dill and the cumin, and omitted the weightier things of the law, judgment, and mercy, and faith; these ought ye to have done, and not leave those undone.

²⁴ Blind guides! that strain out the gnat, and swallow the camel.

²⁵ Woe to you, scribes and Pharisees, hypocrites! because ye cleanse the outside of the cup and the platter, but within they are full of rapacity and excess. ²⁶ Blind Pharisee! Cleanse first the inside of the cup and the platter, that its outside also may become clean.

²⁷ Woe to you, scribes and Pharisees, hypocrites! because ye are like to whited sepulchres, which outwardly indeed appear beautiful, but within are full of bones of the dead, and of all uncleanness. ²⁸ So also ye outwardly indeed appear righteous to men, but within ye are full of hypocrisy and iniquity.

²⁹ Woe to you, scribes and Pharisees, hypocrites! because ye build the sepulchres of the prophets, and adorn the tombs of the righteous, and say: ³⁰ If we had been in the days of our fathers, we would not have been partakers with them in the blood of the prophets. ³¹ So that ye witness to yourselves, that ye are sons of those who killed the prophets; ³² and fill ye up the measure of your fathers!

³³ Serpents! Brood of vipers! How can ye escape the judgment of hell?

³⁴ Therefore, behold, I send forth to you prophets, and wise men, and scribes; and some of them ye will kill and crucify, and some of them ye will scourge in your synagogues, and persecute from city to city; ³⁵ that on you may come all the righteous blood shed upon the earth, from the blood of righteous Abel to the blood of Zechariah, son of Barachiah, whom

ye slew between the temple and the altar. ³⁶ Verily I say to you, all these things shall come upon this generation. ³⁷ Jerusalem! Jerusalem! that killest the prophets, and stonest those sent to her; how often would I have gathered thy children together, as a hen gathers her chickens under her wings, and ye would not! ³⁸ Behold, your house is left to you desolate. ³⁹ For I say to you, ye shall not see me henceforth, till ye shall say: Blessed is he that comes in the name of the Lord.

XXIV. And Jesus went out, and departed from the temple; and his disciples came to him, to show him the buildings of the temple. ² And he answering said to them: See ye not all these things? Verily I say to you, there shall not be left here one stone upon another, that shall not be thrown down.

³ And as he sat on the mount of the Olives, the disciples came to him privately, saying: Tell us, when will these things be, and what is the sign of thy coming and of the end of the world? ⁴ And Jesus answering said to them: Take heed, lest any one lead you astray. ⁵ For many will come in my name, saying: I am the Christ; and will lead astray many. ⁶ And ye will hear of wars, and rumors of wars. Take heed, be not troubled; for all must come to pass; but not yet is the end! ⁷ For nation will rise against nation, and kingdom against kingdom; and there will be famines, and pestilences, and earthquakes, in divers places. ⁸ But all these are the beginning of sorrows. ⁹ Then will they deliver you up unto affliction, and will kill you; and ye will be hated by all nations for my name's sake. ¹⁰ And then will many be offended, and will deliver up one another, and will hate one another. ¹¹ And many false prophets will arise, and will lead many astray. ¹² And because iniquity abounds, the love of the many will become cold. ¹³ But he that has endured to the end, the same shall be saved. ¹⁴ And this good news of the kingdom shall be

---

V. 6. *In some ancient copies:* for it must come to pass

CHAPTER XXIV.

preached in all the world, for a testimony to all nations; and then shall come the end.

¹⁵ When therefore ye see the abomination of desolation, spoken of through Daniel the prophet, standing in the holy place (let him that reads mark!) ¹⁶ then let those in Judæa flee to the mountains; he that is upon the house, ¹⁷ let him not come down to take the things out of his house; ¹⁸ and he that is in the field, let him not turn back to take his garments. ¹⁹ But woe to those who are with child, and to those who give suck in those days! ²⁰ And pray that your flight be not in winter, nor on a sabbath. ²¹ For then will be great affliction, such as has not been from the beginning of the world until now, no nor shall be. ²² And unless those days were shortened, no flesh would be saved; but for the sake of the chosen, those days shall be shortened. ²³ Then if any one say to you: Lo, here is the Christ, or, Here, believe it not. ²⁴ For there will arise false Christs, and false prophets, and will show great signs and wonders; so as, if possible, to lead even the chosen astray. ²⁵ Behold, I have told you before.

²⁶ If therefore they say to you: Behold, he is in the desert, go not forth; Behold, he is in the secret chambers, believe it not. ²⁷ For as the lightning comes forth from the east, and shines even unto the west, so shall be the coming of the Son of man. ²⁸ For wherever the carcass is, there will the eagles be gathered together.

²⁹ And immediately, after the affliction of those days, the sun shall be darkened, and the moon shall not give her light, and the stars shall fall from heaven, and the powers of heaven shall be shaken. ³⁰ And then shall appear the sign of the Son of man in heaven; and then shall all the tribes of the earth mourn, and shall see the Son of man coming on the clouds of heaven, with power and great glory.

³¹ And he will send forth his angels with a great sound of a trumpet, and they shall gather together his chosen from the four winds, from one end of heaven to the other.

V. 30. *Or*, tribes of the land

³² And learn the parable from the fig-tree: When its branch is already become tender, and puts forth leaves, ye know that the summer is near. ³³ So also ye, when ye see all these things, know that it is near, at the doors.

³⁴ Verily I say to you, this generation shall not pass, till all these things are done. ³⁵ Heaven and earth shall pass away; but my words shall not pass away.

³⁶ But of that day and hour no one knows, not even the angels of heaven, but my Father only. ³⁷ But as the days of Noah, so shall be also the coming of the Son of man. ³⁸ For as they were in the days before the flood, eating and drinking, marrying and giving in marriage, until the day that Noah entered into the ark, ³⁹ and knew not until the flood came, and took all away; so shall be also the coming of the Son of man. ⁴⁰ Then shall there be two men in the field, one is taken, and one is left; ⁴¹ two women grinding at the mill, one is taken, and one is left.

⁴² Watch therefore; for ye know not in what day your Lord comes. ⁴³ But know this, that if the master of the house had known in what watch the thief would come, he would have watched, and would not have suffered his house to be broken through. ⁴⁴ Therefore be ye also ready; for in such an hour as ye think not, the Son of man comes.

⁴⁵ Who then is the faithful and wise servant, whom his lord set over his household, to give them their food in due season? ⁴⁶ Happy that servant, whom his lord when he comes shall find so doing! ⁴⁷ Verily I say to you, that he will set him over all his goods. ⁴⁸ But if that evil servant shall say in his heart: My lord delays his coming; ⁴⁹ and shall begin to beat his fellow-servants, and shall eat and drink with the drunken; ⁵⁰ the lord of that servant will come in a day when he looks not for it, and in an hour when he is not aware; ⁵¹ and will cut him asunder, and appoint his portion with the hypocrites. There will be the weeping, and the gnashing of teeth!

V. 42. *In many ancient copies:* in what hour

CHAPTER XXV.

XXV. ¹ THEN shall the kingdom of heaven be likened to ten virgins, who took their lamps, and went out to meet the bridegroom. ² And five of them were wise, and five foolish. ³ The foolish, taking their lamps, took no oil with them; ⁴ but the wise took oil in their vessels with their lamps. ⁵ While the bridegroom tarried, they all slumbered and slept. ⁶ And at midnight a cry was made: Behold, the bridegroom! Go out to meet him. ⁷ Then all those virgins arose, and trimmed their lamps. ⁸ And the foolish said to the wise: Give us of your oil, for our lamps are going out. ⁹ But the wise answered, saying: Not so; there will not be enough for us and you. Go rather to those who sell, and buy for yourselves. ¹⁰ And while they went to buy, the bridegroom came; and they who were ready went in with him to the marriage; and the door was shut. ¹¹ And afterward come also the rest of the virgins, saying: Lord, Lord, open to us. ¹² But he answering said: Verily I say to you, I know you not.

¹³ Watch, therefore; because ye know not the day, nor the hour!

¹⁴ For as a man going abroad called his own servants, and delivered to them his goods; ¹⁵ and to one gave five talents, to another two, and to another one, to each according to his own ability; and straightway went abroad. ¹⁶ And he that received the five talents went and traded with them, and gained other five talents. ¹⁷ Likewise also he that received the two gained other two. ¹⁸ But he that received the one went away and digged in the earth, and hid his lord's money. ¹⁹ After a long time the lord of those servants comes, and reckons with them. ²⁰ And he that received the five talents came and brought other five talents, saying: Lord, thou deliveredst to me five talents; behold, I gained other five talents beside them. ²¹ His lord said to him: Well done, good and faithful servant; thou wast faithful over a little, I will set thee over much. Enter thou into the joy of thy lord. ²² And he also that received the two talents came and said: Lord, thou deliveredst to me two talents; behold, I gained other two talents beside them. ²³ His

lord said to him: Well done, good and faithful servant; thou wast faithful over a little, I will set thee over much. Enter thou into the joy of thy lord. ²⁴ And he also that received the one talent came and said: Lord, I knew thee that thou art a hard man, reaping where thou didst not sow, and gathering where thou strewedst not. ²⁵ And fearing, I went and hid thy talent in the earth. Lo, thou hast thine own. ²⁶ And his lord answering said to him: Wicked and slothful servant! Thou knewest that I reap where I did not sow, and gather where I strewed not? ²⁷ Thou oughtest therefore to have put my money to the exchangers; and when I came, I should have received my own with interest. ²⁸ Take therefore the talent from him, and give to him that has the ten talents. ²⁹ For to every one that has shall be given, and he shall have abundance; but from him that has not, even what he has shall be taken away. ³⁰ And cast forth the unprofitable servant into the outer darkness. There will be the weeping, and the gnashing of teeth!

³¹ And when the Son of man shall come in his glory, and all the angels with him, then will he sit on his throne of glory. ³² And before him shall be gathered all the nations; and he will divide them one from another, as the shepherd divides the sheep from the goats. ³³ And he will set the sheep on his right hand, but the goats on the left.

³⁴ Then will the King say to those on his right hand: Come, blessed of my Father, inherit the kingdom prepared for you from the foundation of the world. ³⁵ For I was hungry, and ye gave me to eat; I was thirsty, and ye gave me drink; I was a stranger and ye took me in, ³⁶ naked and ye clothed me; I was sick, and ye visited me; I was in prison, and ye came to me.

³⁷ Then will the righteous answer him, saying: Lord, when saw we thee hungering and fed thee, or thirsting and gave thee drink? ³⁸ And when saw we thee a stranger and took thee in, or naked and clothed thee? ³⁹ And when saw we thee sick, or in prison, and came to thee? ⁴⁰ And the King will answer and say to them: Verily I say to you, inasmuch as ye

did it to one of the least of these my brethren, ye did it to me.

⁴¹ Then will he say also to those on the left hand: Depart from me, accursed, into the everlasting fire, prepared for the Devil and his angels. ⁴² For I was hungry, and ye did not give me to eat; I was thirsty, and ye did not give me drink; ⁴³ I was a stranger, and ye did not take me in; naked, and ye did not clothe me; sick, and in prison, and ye did not visit me.

⁴⁴ Then will they also answer, saying: Lord, when saw we thee hungering, or thirsting, or a stranger, or naked, or sick, or in prison, and did not minister to thee? ⁴⁵ Then will he answer them, saying: Verily I say to you, inasmuch as ye did it not to one of the least of these, ye did it not to me.

⁴⁶ And these shall go away into everlasting punishment, but the righteous into everlasting life.

XXVI. And it came to pass, when Jesus finished all these sayings, he said to his disciples: ² Ye know that after two days comes the passover, and the Son of man is delivered up to be crucified.

³ Then assembled together the chief priests, and the elders of the people, in the court of the high priest, who was called Caiaphas, ⁴ and consulted together that they might take Jesus by craft, and put him to death. ⁵ But they said: Not at the feast, that there may not be a tumult among the people.

⁶ And Jesus being in Bethany, in the house of Simon the leper, ⁷ there came to him a woman having an alabaster box of very precious ointment, and poured it on his head as he reclined at table. ⁸ And his disciples seeing it were displeased, saying: To what purpose is this waste? ⁹ For this might have been sold for much, and given to the poor. ¹⁰ And Jesus knowing it, said to them: Why trouble ye the woman? For she wrought a good work upon me. ¹¹ For the poor ye have always with you; but me ye have not always. ¹² For she, in pouring this ointment on my body, did it to prepare me for burial. ¹³ Verily I say to you, wherever this good news shall

MATTHEW.

be preached in the whole world, this also that she did shall be told, for a memorial of her.

¹⁴ Then one of the twelve, called Judas Iscariot, went to the chief priests, ¹⁵ and said: What will ye give me, and I will deliver him to you? And they weighed out to him thirty pieces of silver. ¹⁶ And from that time he sought opportunity to deliver him up.

¹⁷ And on the first day of the feast of unleavened bread the disciples came to Jesus, saying to him: Where wilt thou that we prepare for thee to eat the passover? ¹⁸ And he said: Go into the city to such a man, and say to him: The Teacher says, my time is at hand; I will keep the passover at thy house with my disciples. ¹⁹ And the disciples did as Jesus directed them, and made ready the passover.

²⁰ And when evening was come, he reclined at table with the twelve. ²¹ And as they were eating, he said: Verily I say to you, that one of you will betray me. ²² And they were exceedingly sorrowful, and began to say to him, each one: Lord, is it I? ²³ And he answering said: He that dipped his hand with me in the dish, the same will betray me. ²⁴ The Son of man goes indeed, as it is written of him; but woe to that man through whom the Son of man is betrayed! It were good for him, if that man had not been born.

²⁵ And Judas, his betrayer, answering said: Rabbi, is it I? He says to him: Thou saidst it.

²⁶ And as they were eating, Jesus took the loaf, and blessed, and broke, and gave to the disciples, and said: Take, eat; this is my body. ²⁷ And he took the cup, and gave thanks, and gave to them, saying: Drink all ye of it. ²⁸ For this is my blood of the new covenant, which is shed for many, for remission of sins. ²⁹ And I say to you, that I will not drink henceforth of this fruit of the vine, until that day when I drink it new with you, in the kingdom of my Father.

³⁰ And having sung, they went out into the mount of the Olives.

V. 26. *In some ancient copies:* took a loaf
V. 28. *In some ancient copies:* of the covenant

CHAPTER XXVI.

³¹ Then Jesus says to them: All ye will be offended because of me this night. For it is written: I will smite the Shepherd, and the sheep of the flock shall be scattered abroad. ³² But after I have risen, I will go before you into Galilee.

³³ Peter answering said to him: Though all shall be offended because of thee, I will never be offended. ³⁴ Jesus said to him: Verily I say to thee, that this night, before a cock crows, thou wilt thrice deny me. ³⁵ Peter says to him: Even though I should die with thee, I will not deny thee. Likewise also said all the disciples.

³⁶ Then Jesus comes with them to a place called Gethsemane, and says to the disciples: Sit ye here, while I go yonder and pray. ³⁷ And taking with him Peter and the two sons of Zebedee, he began to be sorrowful, and to be troubled. ³⁸ Then says he to them: My soul is exceedingly sorrowful, unto death. Tarry ye here, and watch with me.

³⁹ And going forward a little, he fell on his face, praying, and saying: My Father, if it is possible, let this cup pass away from me. But yet, not as I will, but as thou wilt. ⁴⁰ And he comes to the disciples, and finds them sleeping; and he says to Peter: Were ye so unable to watch with me one hour? ⁴¹ Watch and pray, that ye enter not into temptation. The spirit indeed is willing, but the flesh is weak.

⁴² Again, a second time, he went away and prayed, saying: My Father, if this can not pass away from me, except I drink it, thy will be done. ⁴³ And coming he again found them sleeping; for their eyes were heavy.

⁴⁴ And leaving them, he went away again, and prayed the third time, saying the same words. ⁴⁵ Then he comes to his disciples, and says to them: Do ye sleep the remaining time, and take your rest! Behold, the hour is at hand, and the Son of man is betrayed into the hands of sinners. ⁴⁶ Rise, let us be going. Behold, he is at hand that betrays me.

⁴⁷ And while he was yet speaking, behold, Judas, one of the

V. 45. *Or*, Sleep on now, and take your rest!

twelve, came, and with him a great multitude with swords and staves, from the chief priests and elders of the people. ⁴⁸ And his betrayer gave them a sign, saying: Whom I shall kiss, that is he; hold him fast. ⁴⁹ And forthwith he came to Jesus, and said: Hail, Rabbi; and kissed him. ⁵⁰ And Jesus said to him: Friend, wherefore art thou come? Then they came, and laid hands on Jesus, and held him fast. ⁵¹ And, behold, one of those who were with Jesus stretched out his hand and drew his sword, and striking the servant of the high priest took off his ear. ⁵² Then says Jesus to him: Put back thy sword into its place; for all they who take the sword shall perish with the sword. ⁵³ Thinkest thou that I can not now pray to my Father, and he will send me more than twelve legions of angels? ⁵⁴ How then shall the Scriptures be fulfilled, that thus it must be?

⁵⁵ In that hour Jesus said to the multitudes: Are ye come out as against a robber, with swords and staves, to take me? I sat daily with you teaching in the temple, and ye did not lay hold of me. ⁵⁶ But all this has been done, that the scriptures of the prophets might be fulfilled. Then the disciples all forsook him, and fled.

⁵⁷ And they who laid hold of Jesus led him away to Caiaphas the high priest, where the scribes and the elders were assembled. ⁵⁸ And Peter followed him afar off, unto the court of the high priest; and entering in, he sat with the servants, to see the end.

⁵⁹ And the chief priests, and the elders, and all the council, sought false witness against Jesus, that they might put him to death; ⁶⁰ and found none, though many false witnesses came. But at last came two, ⁶¹ and said: This man said, I am able to destroy the temple of God, and to build it in three days. ⁶² And the high priest arose, and said to him: Answerest thou nothing? What do these witness against thee? ⁶³ But Jesus was silent. And the high priest answering said to him: I

V. 53. *In some ancient copies:* that I can not pray to my Father, and he will now send

CHAPTER XXVII.

adjure thee by the living God, that thou tell us whether thou art the Christ, the Son of God.' ⁶⁴ Jesus says to him: Thou saidst it. But I say to you, hereafter ye shall see the Son of man sitting on the right hand of power, and coming on the clouds of heaven. ⁶⁵ Then the high priest rent his clothes, saying: He blasphemed! What further need have we of witnesses? Behold, ye now heard his blasphemy. ⁶⁶ What think ye? They answering said: He is guilty of death. ⁶⁷ Then they spit in his face, and buffeted him; and others smote him, ⁶⁸ saying: Prophesy to us, O Christ, who is he that struck thee?

⁶⁹ And Peter was sitting without, in the court. And a damsel came to him, saying: Thou also wast with Jesus the Galilæan. ⁷⁰ But he denied before all, saying: I know not what thou sayest. ⁷¹ And he having gone out into the porch, another maid saw him, and said to those who were there: This man also was with Jesus the Nazarene. ⁷² And again he denied, with an oath: I do not know the man. ⁷³ And after a little while, they that stood by came and said to Peter: Surely thou also art one of them; for thy speech betrays thee. ⁷⁴ Then he began to invoke curses, and to swear: I do not know the man. And immediately a cock crowed. ⁷⁵ And Peter remembered the word of Jesus when he said: Before a cock crows, thou wilt thrice deny me. And he went out, and wept bitterly.

XXVII. And when morning came, all the chief priests and the elders of the people took counsel against Jesus, so as to put him to death. ² And having bound him, they led him away, and delivered him up to Pontius Pilate the governor.

³ Then Judas, who betrayed him, when he saw that he was condemned, repenting brought back the thirty pieces of silver to the chief priests and the elders, ⁴ saying: I sinned in betraying innocent blood. And they said: What is it to us? Look thou to it. ⁵ And casting down the pieces of silver in the temple, he departed; and he went away and hanged himself. ⁶ And the chief priests took the silver pieces, and said: It is not lawful to put them into the treasury, since it is the price of blood.

⁷ And they took counsel, and bought with them the potter's field, to bury strangers in. ⁸ Wherefore that field was called the field of blood, unto this day.

⁹ Then was fulfilled that which was spoken through Jeremiah the prophet, saying:

And they took the thirty pieces of silver,
The price of him that was priced,
Whom they of the sons of Israel did price,

¹⁰ And gave them for the potter's field, as the Lord appointed to me.

¹¹ And Jesus stood before the governor. And the governor questioned him, saying: Art thou the king of the Jews? And Jesus said to him: Thou sayest it. ¹² And when he was accused by the chief priests and the elders, he made no answer. ¹³ Then says Pilate to him: Hearest thou not what things they witness against thee? ¹⁴ And he made him no answer, not even to one word; so that the governor greatly wondered.

¹⁵ Now at the feast the governor was wont to release to the multitude one prisoner, whom they would. ¹⁶ And they had then a noted prisoner, called Barabbas. ¹⁷ When therefore they were assembled, Pilate said to them: Whom will ye that I release to you? Barabbas, or Jesus who is called Christ? ¹⁸ For he knew that through envy they delivered him up.

¹⁹ And as he sat on the judgment-seat, his wife sent to him, saying: Have nothing to do with that just man; for I suffered much this day, in a dream, because of him.

²⁰ And the chief priests and the elders persuaded the multitudes, that they should ask for Barabbas, and should destroy Jesus. ²¹ And the governor answering said to them: Which of the two will ye that I release to you? And they said: Barabbas. ²² Pilate says to them: What then shall I do with Jesus, who is called Christ? They all say to him: Let him be crucified. ²³ And the governor said: What evil then did he? But they cried the more, saying: Let him be crucified.

²⁴ And Pilate, seeing that it avails nothing, but rather that a tumult is made, took water and washed his hands before the multitude, saying: I am innocent of the blood of this just man.

CHAPTER XXVII.

Look ye to it. ²⁵ And all the people answering said: His blood be on us, and on our children. ²⁶ Then he released to them Barabbas; but Jesus, having scourged him, he delivered up to be crucified.

²⁷ Then the soldiers of the governor took Jesus into the Prætorium, and gathered to him the whole band. ²⁸ And they stripped him, and put on him a scarlet robe. ²⁹ And having platted a crown of thorns, they put it on his head, and a reed in his right hand; and bowing the knee before him, they mocked him, saying: Hail, King of the Jews! ³⁰ And they spit upon him, and took the reed, and smote him on the head. ³¹ And when they had mocked him, they took off the robe from him, and put on him his own garments, and led him away to crucify him. ³² And as they came out they found a man of Cyrene, Simon by name; him they compelled to bear his cross.

³³ And having come to a place called Golgotha (which is called, Place of a skull), ³⁴ they gave him vinegar to drink, mingled with gall; and tasting it, he would not drink. ³⁵ And having crucified him, they divided his garments among them, casting lots. ³⁶ And sitting down, they watched him there. ³⁷ And they set up over his head his accusation, written: THIS IS JESUS THE KING OF THE JEWS.

³⁸ Two robbers are then crucified with him, one on the right hand, and one on the left. ³⁹ And those passing by reviled him, wagging their heads, ⁴⁰ and saying: Thou that destroyest the temple, and buildest it in three days, save thyself. If thou art the Son of God, come down from the cross. ⁴¹ Likewise also the chief priests mocking, with the scribes and elders, said: ⁴² Others he saved, himself he can not save. If he is King of Israel, let him now come down from the cross, and we will believe on him. ⁴³ He trusts in God; let him now deliver him, if he desires him; for he said: I am the Son of God. ⁴⁴ And also the robbers, who were crucified with him, reproached him with the same thing.

V. 34. *In some ancient copies:* gave him wine to drink

MATTHEW.

⁴⁵ And from the sixth hour, there was darkness over all the land, unto the ninth hour. ⁴⁶ And about the ninth hour Jesus cried with a loud voice, saying: Eli, Eli, lema sabachthani? That is: My God, my God, why didst thou forsake me? ⁴⁷ Some of those standing there, hearing it, said: This man calls for Elijah. ⁴⁸ And straightway one of them ran and took a sponge, and having filled it with vinegar and put it on a reed, gave him to drink. ⁴⁹ But the rest said: Let alone; let us see whether Elijah comes to save him.

⁵⁰ And Jesus, again crying with a loud voice, yielded up his spirit. ⁵¹ And behold, the vail of the temple was rent in twain from the top to the bottom; and the earth quaked, and the rocks were rent; ⁵² and the tombs were opened, and many bodies of the saints who have fallen asleep arose, ⁵³ and coming out of the tombs, after his resurrection, went into the holy city, and appeared to many.

⁵⁴ And the centurion, and they that with him were watching Jesus, on seeing the earthquake, and the things that were done, were exceedingly afraid, saying: Truly this was the Son of God.

⁵⁵ And many women were there, beholding afar off, they who followed Jesus from Galilee, ministering to him; ⁵⁶ among whom was Mary the Magdalene, and Mary the mother of James and Joses, and the mother of the sons of Zebedee.

⁵⁷ And evening having come, there came a rich man from Arimathaea, named Joseph, who also himself was a disciple of Jesus. ⁵⁸ This man went to Pilate, and asked for the body of Jesus. Then Pilate commanded that the body should be given up. ⁵⁹ And taking the body, Joseph wrapped it in a clean linen cloth, ⁶⁰ and laid it in his own new tomb, which he hewed out in the rock. And having rolled a great stone to the door of the tomb, he departed. ⁶¹ And Mary the Magdalene was there, and the other Mary, sitting over against the sepulchre.

V. 47. Elijah; *in their form of address*, Elia.

CHAPTER XXVIII.

⁶² And on the morrow, which is after the preparation, the chief priests and the Pharisees came together to Pilate, ⁶³ saying: Sir, we remember that that deceiver said, while he was yet alive: After three days I will rise. ⁶⁴ Command, therefore, that the sepulchre be made secure until the third day; lest his disciples come and steal him away, and say to the people: He is risen from the dead; and the last error will be worse than the first. ⁶⁵ Pilate said to them: Ye have a watch; go, make secure, as ye know how. ⁶⁶ And they went, and made the sepulchre secure, sealing the stone, in connection with the watch.

XXVIII. And late in the sabbath, as it was dawning into the first day of the week, came Mary the Magdalene and the other Mary to view the sepulchre. ² And behold, there was a great earthquake. For an angel of the Lord, descending out of heaven, came and rolled away the stone, and sat upon it. ³ His countenance was like lightning, and his raiment white as snow; ⁴ and for fear of him the keepers shook, and became as dead men. ⁵ And the angel answering said to the women: Fear not ye; for I know that ye are seeking Jesus, who was crucified. ⁶ He is not here; for he is risen, as he said. Come hither, see the place where the Lord lay. ⁷ And go quickly, and tell his disciples that he is risen from the dead. And behold, he goes before you into Galilee; there ye shall see him. Behold, I told you.

⁸ And going out quickly from the sepulchre, with fear and great joy, they ran to bring his disciples word. ⁹ And behold, Jesus met them, saying: All hail! And they, coming to him, laid hold of his feet, and worshiped him. ¹⁰ Then Jesus says to them: Be not afraid; go, bear word to my brethren, to go away into Galilee, and there they shall see me.

¹¹ And as they were going, behold, some of the watch came into the city, and reported to the chief priests all the things that were done. ¹² And having assembled with the elders, and taken counsel, they gave much money to the soldiers, ¹³ saying: Say, that his disciples came by night, and stole him away while we

slept. ¹⁴And if this shall be heard by the governor, we will persuade him, and make you secure. ¹⁵And they, taking the money, did as they were taught. And this saying was reported abroad among the Jews, until this day.

¹⁶And the eleven disciples went away into Galilee, into the mountain where Jesus had appointed them: ¹⁷And seeing him, they worshiped him ; but some doubted.

¹⁸And Jesus came and spoke to them, saying: All power was given to me in heaven and on earth. ¹⁹Go therefore, and disciple all the nations, immersing them in the name of the Father, and of the Son, and of the Holy Spirit ; ²⁰teaching them to observe all things, whatever I commanded you. And, behold, I am with you alway, unto the end of the world.

THE GOSPEL ACCORDING TO MARK.

I. The beginning of the good news of Jesus Christ, Son of God, ²as it is written in Isaiah the prophet : Behold, I send forth my messenger before thy face, who shall prepare thy way; ³the voice of one crying in the wilderness, Prepare the way of the Lord, make straight his paths. ⁴John came immersing in the wilderness, and preaching the immersion of repentance unto remission of sins. ⁵And there went out to him all the country of Judæa, and all they of Jerusalem ; and they were immersed by him in the river Jordan, confessing their sins.

⁶And John was clothed with camel's hair, and with a leathern girdle about his loins, and ate locusts and wild honey. ⁷And he preached, saying : There comes after me he that is mightier than I, the latchet of whose sandals I am not worthy to stoop down and loose. ⁸I indeed immersed you in water ; but he will immerse you in the Holy Spirit.

⁹And it came to pass in those days, that Jesus came from Nazareth of Galilee, and was immersed by John in the Jordan. ¹⁰And straightway coming up out of the water, he saw

---

V. 14. *In some copies:* Shall be heard before the governor

CHAPTER I.

the heavens parted, and the Spirit as a dove descending upon him. ¹¹ And there came a voice out of heaven: Thou art my beloved son; in thee I am well pleased.

¹² And immediately the Spirit drives him forth into the wilderness. ¹³ And he was in the wilderness forty days, tempted by Satan, and was with the wild beasts; and the angels ministered to him.

¹⁴ And after John was delivered up, Jesus came into Galilee, publishing the good news of the kingdom of God, ¹⁵ and saying: The time is fulfilled, and the kingdom of God is at hand; repent, and believe in the good news.

¹⁶ And walking by the sea of Galilee, he saw Simon, and Andrew, Simon's brother, casting a net in the sea; for they were fishermen. ¹⁷ And Jesus said to them: Come after me, and I will cause you to become fishers of men. ¹⁸ And immediately leaving the nets, they followed him.

¹⁹ And going a little further, he saw James the son of Zebedee, and John his brother, who also were in the ship mending the nets. ²⁰ And straightway he called them; and leaving their father Zebedee in the ship with the hired servants, they went after him.

²¹ And they enter into Capernaum; and straightway on the sabbath he went into the synagogue, and taught. ²² And they were astonished at his teaching; for he taught them as having authority, and not as the scribes.

²³ And there was in their synagogue a man with an unclean spirit. And he cried out, ²⁴ saying: What have we to do with thee, Jesus, Nazarene! Didst thou come to destroy us? I know thee who thou art, the Holy One of God. ²⁵ And Jesus rebuked him, saying: Hold thy peace, and come out of him. ²⁶ And the unclean spirit, tearing him, and crying with a loud voice, came out of him. ²⁷ And they were all amazed; so that they questioned among themselves, saying: What is this? A

V. 14. *In some ancient copies:* the good news of God
V. 24. *In some ancient copies:* Hah! what have we to do with thee
V. 27. *In many ancient copies:* What new teaching is this? For with authority he commands even the unclean spirits

new teaching, with authority! And he commands the unclean spirits, and they obey him. ²⁸ And immediately his fame spread abroad into all the surrounding region of Galilee.

²⁹ And immediately, having come out of the synagogue, they entered into the house of Simon and Andrew, with James and John. ³⁰ And the mother-in-law of Simon was lying sick with fever; and immediately they tell him concerning her. ³¹ And he came and raised her up, taking hold of her hand; and immediately the fever left her, and she ministered to them.

³² And evening having come, when the sun set, they brought to him all that were sick, and those possessed with demons. ³³ And all the city was gathered together at the door. ³⁴ And he healed many that were sick with divers diseases, and cast out many demons; and suffered not the demons to speak, because they knew him.

³⁵ And rising very early, by night, he went out, and departed into a solitary place, and there prayed. ³⁶ And Simon, and they who were with him, followed after him. ³⁷ And having found him, they say to him: All are seeking thee. ³⁸ And he says to them: Let us go elsewhere, into the neighboring towns, that I may preach there also; for, for this I came forth. ³⁹ And he was preaching in their synagogues, throughout all Galilee, and casting out the demons.

⁴⁰ And there came a leper to him, beseeching him, and kneeling down to him, and saying to him: If thou wilt, thou canst cleanse me. ⁴¹ And Jesus, moved with compassion, stretched forth his hand and touched him, and says to him: I will; be thou cleansed. ⁴² And immediately the leprosy departed from him, and he was cleansed. ⁴³ And sternly charging him, he forthwith sent him away; ⁴⁴ and says to him: See thou say nothing to any one; but go, show thyself to the priest, and offer for thy cleansing what Moses commanded, for a testimony to them. ⁴⁵ But he, going forth, began to publish it much, and to spread abroad the report; so that he could no longer openly enter into a city, but was without in desert places. And they came to him from every quarter.

CHAPTER II.

II. AND again he entered into Capernaum after some days; and it was heard that he is in the house. ² And straightway many were gathered together, so that there was no longer room, not even at the door; and he spoke the word to them. ³ And they come to him, bringing one that was palsied, borne by four. ⁴ And not being able to come near him, on account of the multitude, they uncovered the roof where he was; and having broken it up, they let down the bed whereon the palsied man lay. ⁵ And Jesus, seeing their faith, says to the palsied man: Child, thy sins are forgiven. ⁶ But there were some of the scribes sitting there, and reasoning in their hearts: ⁷ Why does this man speak thus? He blasphemes. Who can forgive sins but one, God? ⁸ And Jesus, immediately perceiving in his spirit that they so reasoned within themselves, said to them: Why reason ye these things in your hearts? ⁹ Which is easier, to say to the palsied man, Thy sins are forgiven; or to say, Arise, and take up thy bed, and walk? ¹⁰ But that ye may know that the Son of man has power on earth to forgive sins, (he says to the palsied man,) ¹¹ I say to thee, arise, take up thy bed, and go to thy house. ¹² And he arose, and immediately taking up the bed went forth before all; so that all were amazed, and glorified God, saying: We never saw it thus.

¹³ And he went forth again by the sea-side; and all the multitude came to him, and he taught them.

¹⁴ And passing along, he saw Levi the son of Alpheus sitting at the place of receiving custom, and said to him: Follow me. And rising up he followed him. ¹⁵ And it came to pass, as he reclined at table in his house, that many publicans and sinners were reclining with Jesus and his disciples; for there were many, and they followed him. ¹⁶ And the scribes and the Pharisees, seeing him eating with the sinners and publicans, said to his disciples: How is it that he eats and drinks with the sinners and the publicans? ¹⁷ And Jesus, hearing it, says to them: They who are well need not a physician, but they who are sick. I came not to call righteous men, but sinners.

¹⁸ And the disciples of John, and the Pharisees, were fasting; and they come and say to him: Why do the disciples of John and the Pharisees fast, but thy disciples fast not? ¹⁹ And Jesus said to them: Can the sons of the bridechamber fast, while the bridegroom is with them? So long as they have the bridegroom with them, they can not fast. ²⁰ But days will come, when the bridegroom will be taken from them; and then they will fast in that day. ²¹ No one sews a piece of unfulled cloth upon an old garment; else the new filling up of the old takes from it, and a worse rent is made. ²² And no one puts new wine into old skins; else the wine bursts the skins, and the wine is destroyed, and the skins.

²³ And it came to pass, that he went through the grain-fields on the sabbath; and his disciples began to go forward, plucking the ears of grain. ²⁴ And the Pharisees said to him: Behold, why do they on the sabbath that which is not lawful? ²⁵ And he said to them: Did ye never read what David did, when he had need and hungered, himself and they who were with him; ²⁶ how he went into the house of God, in the days of Abiathar the high priest, and ate the show-bread, which it is not lawful to eat but for the priests, and gave also to those who were with him? ²⁷ And he said to them: The sabbath was made for man, and not man for the sabbath. ²⁸ So that the Son of man is Lord also of the sabbath.

III. And he entered again into the synagogue; and there was a man there, having his hand withered. ² And they watched him, whether he would heal him on the sabbath; that they might accuse him. ³ And he says to the man having the withered hand: Arise, and come into the midst. ⁴ And he says to them: Is it lawful to do good on the sabbath, or to do evil; to save life, or to kill? But they were silent. ⁵ And

---

V. 18. *Or*, used to fast
V. 19. *Or*, Can the bridemen fast
V. 22. *Some ancient copies add:* But new wine must be put into new skins.
V. 23. *Or*, began to make a way

CHAPTER III.

looking round on them with anger, being grieved for their hardness of heart, he says to the man: Stretch forth thy hand. And he stretched it forth; and his hand was restored.

⁶ And going out, the Pharisees immediately took counsel with the Herodians against him, how they might destroy him. ⁷ And Jesus withdrew with his disciples to the sea. And a great multitude from Galilee followed; and from Judæa, ⁸ and from Jerusalem, and from Idumæa, and from beyond the Jordan, and they about Tyre and Sidon, a great multitude, hearing what great things he did, came to him. ⁹ And he spoke to his disciples, that a small ship should wait on him because of the multitude, that they might not throng him. ¹⁰ For he healed many, so that they pressed upon him to touch him, as many as had plagues. ¹¹ And the unclean spirits, when they saw him, fell down before him, and cried, saying: Thou art the Son of God. ¹² And he strictly charged them that they should not make him known.

¹³ And he goes up into the mountain, and calls to him whom he would; and they went to him. ¹⁴ And he appointed twelve, that they should be with him, and that he might send them forth to preach, ¹⁵ and to have authority to heal sicknesses, and to cast out demons. ¹⁶ And Simon he surnamed Peter; ¹⁷ and James the son of Zebedee, and John the brother of James; and he surnamed them Boanerges, which is, Sons of thunder; ¹⁸ and Andrew, and Philip, and Bartholomew, and Matthew, and Thomas, and James the son of Alpheus, and Thaddeus, and Simon the Cananite, ¹⁹ and Judas Iscariot, who also betrayed him.

And they come into the house. ²⁰ And the multitude comes together again, so that they could not even eat bread. ²¹ And hearing of it, his kinsmen went out to lay hold of him; for they said: He is beside himself.

²² And the scribes who came down from Jerusalem said: He has Beelzebul, and through the prince of the demons he casts out the demons. ²³ And calling them to him, he said to them in

---

V.18. Cananite, (*as some suppose*) = Zelotes.

parables: How can Satan cast out Satan? ²⁴ And if a kingdom be divided against itself, that kingdom can not stand. ²⁵ And if a house be divided against itself, that house can not stand. ²⁶ And if Satan rose up against himself, and is divided, he can not stand, but has an end. ²⁷ No one can enter into a strong man's house, and plunder his goods, except he first bind the strong man; and then he will plunder his house. ²⁸ Verily I say to you, all sins will be forgiven the sons of men, and the blasphemies wherewith they shall blaspheme. ²⁹ But he that shall blaspheme against the Holy Spirit has no forgiveness forever, but is guilty of eternal sin; ³⁰ because they said: He has an unclean spirit.

³¹ And his brothers and his mother come; and standing without they sent to him, calling him. ³² And a crowd was sitting about him; and they say to him: Behold, thy mother and thy brothers without are seeking thee. ³³ And he answered them, saying: Who is my mother, or my brothers? ³⁴ And looking round on those who sat about him, he said: Behold my mother, and my brothers! ³⁵ For whoever shall do the will of God, he is my brother, and sister, and mother.

IV. And he began again to teach by the sea-side. And there was gathered to him a very great multitude, so that he entered into a ship, and sat down in the sea; and all the multitude was by the sea on the land. ² And he taught them many things in parables, and said to them in his teaching:

³ Hearken; behold, the sower went forth to sow. ⁴ And it came to pass, as he sowed, one fell by the way-side, and the birds came and devoured it. ⁵ And another fell on the rocky ground, where it had not much earth; and immediately it sprang up, because it had not depth of earth. ⁶ But when the sun was up, it was scorched; and because it had not root, it withered away. ⁷ And another fell among the thorns; and the thorns came up, and choked it, and it yielded no fruit. ⁸ And another fell into the good ground, and yielded fruit that sprang up and increased; and brought forth, thirty, and sixty, and a hundredfold. ⁹ And he said: He that has ears to hear, let him hear.

CHAPTER IV.

¹⁰ And when he was alone, they who were about him with the twelve asked him concerning the parables. ¹¹ And he said to them: To you is given the mystery of the kingdom of God, but to those who are without, all things are done in parables; ¹² that seeing they may see, and not perceive, and hearing they may hear, and not understand; lest haply they should turn, and be forgiven. ¹³ And he says to them: Know ye not this parable? And how will ye know all the parables?

¹⁴ The sower sows the word. ¹⁵ And these are they by the way-side; where the word is sown, and when they hear, Satan comes immediately and takes away the word that was sown in them. ¹⁶ And these are they likewise that are sown on the rocky places; who, when they hear the word, immediately receive it with gladness; ¹⁷ and have no root in themselves, but are only for a time. Afterward, when affliction or persecution arises because of the word, immediately they are offended. ¹⁸ And others are they that are sown among the thorns. These are they that hear the word, ¹⁹ and the cares of the world, and the deceitfulness of riches, and the lusts of other things, entering in choke the word, and it becomes unfruitful. ²⁰ And these are they that are sown on the good ground; such as hear the word, and receive it, and bring forth fruit, in thirty, and in sixty, and in a hundredfold.

²¹ And he said to them: Is the lamp brought that it may be put under the bushel, or under the bed? Is it not, that it may be put on the lamp-stand? ²² For nothing is hidden, but it shall be manifested; nor was done in secret, but that it should come abroad. ²³ If any one has ears to hear, let him hear.

²⁴ And he said to them: Take heed what ye hear. With what measure ye mete, it shall be measured to you, and there shall be added to you. ²⁵ For he that has, to him shall be given; and he that has not, even what he has shall be taken from him.

²⁶ And he said: So is the kingdom of God, as when a man has cast the seed upon the earth, ²⁷ and sleeps and rises night and day, and the seed sprouts and grows up, he knows not how. ²⁸ For the earth brings forth fruit of herself; first the

blade, then the ear, then the full grain in the ear. ²⁹ But when the fruit permits, immediately he puts forth the sickle, because the harvest is come.

³⁰ And he said: How shall we liken the kingdom of God, or in what comparison shall we set it forth? ³¹ As a grain of mustard; which, when it is sown in the earth, is less than all the seeds that are in the earth. ³² And when it is sown, it grows up, and becomes greater than all the herbs, and shoots out great branches; so that the birds of the air can lodge under its shadow.

³³ And with many such parables he spoke the word to them, as they were able to hear. ³⁴ But without a parable he spoke not to them; and in private he explained all things to his disciples.

³⁵ And on that day, when evening was come, he says to them: Let us pass over to the other side. ³⁶ And dismissing the multitude, they take him as he was in the ship. And there were also other ships with him. ³⁷ And there arose a great storm of wind, and the waves beat into the ship, so that the ship was already becoming filled. ³⁸ And he was in the stern, on the cushion, sleeping. And they awake him, and say to him: Teacher, carest thou not that we perish? ³⁹ And awaking, he rebuked the wind, and said to the sea: Peace, be still. And the wind ceased, and there was a great calm. ⁴⁰ And he said to them: Why are ye so fearful? How is it that ye have no faith? ⁴¹ And they feared exceedingly, and said one to another: Who then is this, that even the wind and the sea obey him?

V. And they came to the other side of the sea, into the country of the Gerasenes. ² And when he had come out of the ship, immediately there met him out of the tombs a man with an unclean spirit, ³ who had his dwelling in the tombs; and no one could any longer bind him, not even with chains. ⁴ Because he had often been bound with fetters and chains; and the chains had been torn asunder by him, and the fetters broken in pieces, and no one could tame him. ⁵ And

CHAPTER V.

always, night and day, he was in the tombs, and in the mountains, crying out, and cutting himself with stones. ⁶ But seeing Jesus afar off, he ran and bowed down to him, ⁷ and cried with a loud voice, and said: What have I to do with thee, Jesus, Son of the most high God? I adjure thee by God, do not torment me. ⁸ For he said to him: Come forth, unclean spirit, out of the man. ⁹ And he asked him: What is thy name? And he says to him: My name is Legion; because we are many. ¹⁰ And he besought him much that he would not send them away out of the country.

¹¹ And there was there, by the mountain, a great herd of swine feeding. ¹² And all the demons besought him, saying: Send us into the swine, that we may enter into them. ¹³ And immediately Jesus gave them leave. And coming out, the unclean spirits entered into the swine. And the herd rushed down the steep into the sea, about two thousand, and were choked in the sea. ¹⁴ And they who fed them fled, and reported it in the city and in the country. And they came to see what it was that was done. ¹⁵ And they come to Jesus, and see him who was possessed with demons, sitting, clothed and in his right mind, him who had the legion, and they were afraid. ¹⁶ And they who saw it related to them how it befell him who was possessed with demons, and concerning the swine. ¹⁷ And they began to beseech him to depart from their borders.

¹⁸ And as he was entering into the ship, he that had been possessed with demons besought him that he might be with him. ¹⁹ And he suffered him not; but says to him: Go into thy house, to thy friends, and announce to them how great things the Lord has done for thee, and had compassion on thee. ²⁰ And he departed, and began to publish in the Decapolis how great things Jesus did for him; and all wondered.

²¹ And Jesus having passed over again in the ship to the other side, a great multitude was gathered to him; and he was by the sea. ²² And there comes one of the rulers of the synagogue, Jairus by name. And seeing him, he fell at his feet, ²³ and besought him much, saying: My little daughter lies

at the point of death. I pray thee come, and lay thy hands on her, that she may be healed and live. ²⁴ And he went with him; and a great multitude was following him, and thronging him.

²⁵ And a certain woman, who had a flow of blood twelve years, ²⁶ and had suffered much by many physicians, and spent all that she had, and was not at all benefited but rather grew worse, ²⁷ hearing of Jesus, came in the crowd behind, and touched his garment. ²⁸ For she said: If I touch even his garments, I shall be made whole. ²⁹ And straightway the fountain of her blood was dried up; and she perceived in her body that she was healed of that plague. ³⁰ And immediately Jesus, perceiving in himself that power had gone forth from him, turned about in the crowd, and said: Who touched my garments? ³¹ And his disciples said to him: Thou seest the multitude thronging thee, and sayest thou: Who touched me? ³² And he looked around to see her who had done this. ³³ But the woman, fearing and trembling, knowing what was done to her, came and fell down before him, and told him all the truth. ³⁴ And he said to her: Daughter, thy faith has made thee whole; go in peace, and be healed of thy plague.

³⁵ While he was yet speaking, they come from the ruler of the synagogue's house, saying: Thy daughter is dead; why troublest thou the Teacher any further? ³⁶ And Jesus, overhearing the word that was spoken, says to the ruler of the synagogue: Be not afraid; only believe. ³⁷ And he suffered no one to follow with him, save Peter, and James, and John the brother of James. ³⁸ And they come to the house of the ruler of the synagogue; and he sees a tumult, and those who wept and wailed greatly. ³⁹ And entering in, he says to them: Why do ye make a tumult, and weep? The child is not dead, but is sleeping. ⁴⁰ And they laughed him to scorn. But he, putting them all out, takes the father of the child, and the mother, and those who were with him, and enters in where the child was. ⁴¹ And taking the hand of the child, he says to her: Talitha kumi; which is interpreted, Damsel, I say to thee, arise. ⁴² And straightway the damsel arose, and walked;

CHAPTER VI.

for she was of the age of twelve years. And they were astonished with a great astonishment. ⁴³ And he charged them strictly that no one should know this. And he commanded that something should be given her to eat.

VI. And he went out from thence, and came into his own country; and his disciples follow him. ² And when the sabbath was come, he began to teach in the synagogue. And many hearing were astonished, saying: From whence has this man these things? And what is the wisdom which is given him, and such miracles wrought by his hands? ³ Is not this the carpenter, the son of Mary, and brother of James, and Joses, and Judas, and Simon? And are not his sisters here with us? And they were offended at him. ⁴ And Jesus said to them: A prophet is not without honor, except in his own country, and among his own kindred, and in his own house. ⁵ And he was not able to do any miracle there, save that he laid his hands on a few sick, and healed them. ⁶ And he marveled because of their unbelief. And he went about the surrounding villages, teaching.

⁷ And he called to him the twelve, and began to send them forth by two and two; and gave them authority over the unclean spirits; ⁸ and commanded them that they should take nothing for the way, save a staff only; no bread, no bag, no money, in their girdle; ⁹ but that they be shod with sandals; and, Put not on two coats. ¹⁰ And he said to them: Wherever ye enter into a house, there abide till ye depart from thence. ¹¹ And whatever place shall not receive you, nor hear you, when ye depart thence, shake off the dust under your feet for a testimony to them.

¹² And they went out, and preached that men should repent. ¹³ And they cast out many demons, and anointed with oil many that were sick, and healed them.

¹⁴ And the king, Herod, heard of it, for his name was spread

V. 11. *The words omitted are not found here, in the oldest copies; they belong to Matt. x., 15.*

abroad; and he said: John the Immerser is risen from the dead, and therefore do these powers work in him. ¹⁵ Others said: It is Elijah. And others said: It is a prophet, like any one of the prophets. ¹⁶ But Herod hearing of it, said: John, whom I beheaded, is risen from the dead. ¹⁷ For he, Herod, sent forth and laid hold of John, and bound him in prison, for the sake of Herodias the wife of Philip, his brother; because he had married her. ¹⁸ For John said to Herod: It is not lawful for thee to have thy brother's wife. ¹⁹ And Herodias was angry with him, and desired to put him to death; and she could not, ²⁰ for Herod feared John, knowing that he was a just and holy man; and he observed him, and hearing him did many things, and heard him gladly.

²¹ And a convenient day having come, when Herod on his birthday made a supper for his nobles, and for the chief captains, and the first men of Galilee; ²² and the daughter of Herodias having come in and danced, it pleased Herod and those reclining at table with him; and the king said to the damsel: Ask of me whatever thou wilt, and I will give it thee. ²³ And he swore to her: Whatever thou shalt ask of me, I will give it thee, unto the half of my kingdom. ²⁴ And she, going out, said to her mother: What shall I ask? And she said: The head of John the Immerser. ²⁵ And straightway she came in with haste to the king, and asked, saying: I will that immediately thou give me, on a platter, the head of John the Immerser. ²⁶ And the king became very sorrowful; but for the sake of his oath, and of those reclining with him, he would not reject her. ²⁷ And immediately the king sent one of the guard, and commanded to bring his head. And he went and beheaded him in the prison, ²⁸ and brought his head on a platter, and gave it to the damsel; and the damsel gave it to her mother. ²⁹ And his disciples hearing of it came and took up his corpse, and laid it in a tomb.

³⁰ And the apostles gather together unto Jesus; and they reported to him all things, both what they did, and what they

---

V. 20. *Or*, and he kept him

CHAPTER VI.

taught. ³¹ And he said to them: Come ye yourselves apart into a desert place, and rest awhile; for there were many coming and going, and they had no leisure even to eat. ³² And they departed into a desert place by ship privately. ³³ And they saw them departing, and many knew them, and ran together there on foot from all the cities, and came before them. ³⁴ And going forth he saw a great multitude, and had compassion on them, because they were as sheep having no shepherd; and he began to teach them many things.

³⁵ And the day being now far spent, his disciples come to him, and say: The place is desert, and the time is now far passed. ³⁶ Dismiss them, that they may go away into the surrounding fields and villages, and buy themselves bread; for they have nothing to eat. ³⁷ He answering said to them: Give ye them to eat. And they say to him: Shall we go and buy two hundred denáries worth of bread, and give them to eat? ³⁸ He says to them: How many loaves have ye? Go and see. And when they knew, they say: Five, and two fishes. ³⁹ And he commanded them to make all lie down by companies on the green grass. ⁴⁰ And they lay down in ranks, by hundreds, and by fifties. ⁴¹ And taking the five loaves and the two fishes, he looked up to heaven, and blessed and broke the loaves, and gave to the disciples to set before them; and the two fishes he divided among them all. ⁴² And they all ate, and were filled. ⁴³ And they took up fragments filling twelve baskets, and part of the fishes. ⁴⁴ And they who ate of the loaves were five thousand men. ⁴⁵ And straightway he constrained his disciples to enter into the ship, and to go before to the other side to Bethsaida, while he dismissed the multitude. ⁴⁶ And having taken leave of them, he went away into the mountain to pray.

⁴⁷ And when evening was come, the ship was in the midst of the sea, and he was alone on the land. ⁴⁸ And he saw them distressed in rowing, for the wind was contrary to them. And about the fourth watch of the night he comes to them, walking on the sea, and would have passed by them. ⁴⁹ And they seeing him walking on the sea, supposed it was a spectre, and

cried out; ⁵⁰ for all saw him, and were troubled. And immediately he talked with them, and says to them: Be of good cheer; it is I, be not afraid. ⁵¹ And he went up to them into the ship; and the wind ceased. And they were sore amazed in themselves beyond measure, and wondered. ⁵² For they considered not the loaves; for their heart was hardened.

⁵³ And passing over, they came to the land of Gennesaret, and anchored there. ⁵⁴ And when they had come out of the ship, immediately recognizing him ⁵⁵ they ran through all that region, and began to carry about on beds those who were sick, where they heard he was. ⁵⁶ And wherever he entered, into villages, or cities, or fields, they laid the sick in the marketplaces, and besought him that they might touch if it were but the fringe of his garment. And as many as touched him were made whole.

VII. And there come together to him the Pharisees and certain of the scribes, who came from Jerusalem. ² And seeing some of his disciples eating bread with defiled (that is, unwashen) hands, they found fault. ³ For the Pharisees, and all the Jews, except they carefully wash their hands, do not eat, holding the tradition of the elders. ⁴ And coming from the market, except they immerse themselves, they do not eat. And there are many other things which they received to hold, immersions of cups, and pots, and brazen vessels, and couches. ⁵ And the Pharisees and the scribes ask him: Why do not thy disciples walk according to the tradition of the elders, but eat bread with defiled hands? ⁶ And he said to them: Well did Isaiah prophesy concerning you hypocrites; as it is written:

> This people honor me with their lips,
> But their heart is far from me.
> ⁷ But in vain they worship me,
> Teaching as doctrines commandments of men.

⁸ For laying aside the commandment of God, ye hold the tradition of men, immersions of pots and cups; and many other such things ye do. ⁹ And he said to them: Well do ye

CHAPTER VII.

reject the commandment of God, that ye may keep your own tradition! ¹⁰ For Moses said: Honor thy father and thy mother; and he that curses father or mother, let him surely die. ¹¹ But ye say: If a man say to his father or his mother, It is Corban (that is, a gift) whatever thou mightest be profited with from me —; ¹²and ye suffer him no more to do aught for his father or his mother, ¹³ annulling the word of God by your tradition, which ye handed down. And many such things ye do.

¹⁴ And again calling to him the multitude, he said to them: Hearken to me every one, and understand. ¹⁵ There is nothing from without a man, that entering into him can defile him; but the things that come out of him, these are they that defile the man. ¹⁶ If any one has ears to hear, let him hear.

¹⁷ And when he entered into the house from the multitude, his disciples asked him concerning the parable. ¹⁸ And he says to them: Are ye so without understanding also? Do ye not perceive, that whatever from without enters into the man can not defile him? ¹⁹Because it enters not into his heart, but into the belly, and goes out into the drain, cleansing all food. ²⁰ And he said: That which comes out of the man, that defiles the man. ²¹ For from within, out of the heart of men, come forth evil thoughts, adulteries, fornications, murders, ²² thefts, covetousness, wickedness, deceit, wantonness, an evil eye, blasphemy, pride, foolishness. ²³ All these evil things come forth from within, and defile the man.

²⁴ And rising up he departed thence into the borders of Tyre and Sidon; and entering into a house, he desired that no one should know it. And he could not be hidden. ²⁵ For a woman, whose little daughter had an unclean spirit, hearing of him, came and fell at his feet. ²⁶ The woman was a Greek, a Syrophenician by nation; and she besought him that he

---

V. 11. *The conclusion, "He is bound," (by his vow,) and so freed from the duty to his parents, is left to be inferred from the speaker's silence; compare the similar use of this figure of speech, in* Ex. xxxii., 32; Luke xiii., 9; Acts xxiii., 9.

would cast out the demon from her daughter. ²⁷ And he said to her: Let the children first be filled; for it is not good to take the children's bread and cast it to the dogs. ²⁸ And she answered and said to him: Yea, Lord; for the dogs under the table eat of the children's crumbs. ²⁹ And he said to her: For this saying go thy way; the demon has gone out of thy daughter. ³⁰ And departing to her house, she found the little child laid on the bed, and the demon gone out.

³¹ And again going forth out of the borders of Tyre, he came through Sidon to the sea of Galilee, through the midst of the borders of Decapolis. ³² And they bring to him one that was deaf, and had an impediment in his speech; and they beseech him to put his hand upon him. ³³ And taking him aside from the multitude he put his fingers into his ears, and spitting, touched his tongue, ³⁴ and looking up to heaven, he sighed, and says to him: Ephphatha, that is, Be opened. ³⁵ And straightway his ears were opened, and the bond of his tongue was loosed, and he spoke plainly. ³⁶ And he charged them that they should tell no one. But the more he charged them, the more abundantly they published it; ³⁷ and were beyond measure astonished, saying: He has done all things well; he makes both the deaf to hear, and the dumb to speak.

VIII. In those days, there being a very great multitude, and they having nothing to eat, he called to him his disciples, and says to them: ² I have compassion on the multitude, because they continue with me now three days, and have nothing to eat; ³ and if I dismiss them fasting to their own houses, they will faint by the way; and some of them have come from afar. ⁴ And his disciples answered him: From whence will one be able to satisfy these men with bread, here in a wilderness? ⁵ And he asked them: How many loaves have ye? And they said: Seven. ⁶ And he commanded the multitude to lie down on the ground. And he took the seven loaves, and gave thanks, and broke, and gave to his disciples to set before them; and they set them before the multitude. ⁷ And they had a few small fishes; and having blessed them,

CHAPTER VIII.

he commanded to set these also before them. ⁸ And they ate, and were filled ; and they took up of the fragments that were left seven baskets. ⁹ And they were about four thousand. And he dismissed them.

¹⁰ And straightway entering into the ship with his disciples, he came into the region of Dalmanutha. ¹¹ And the Pharisees came out, and began to question with him, seeking of him a sign from heaven, tempting him. ¹² And sighing deeply in his spirit, he says: Why does this generation seek a sign? Verily I say to you, there shall no sign be given to this generation. ¹³ And leaving them, he entered again into the ship, and departed to the other side.

¹⁴ And they forgot to take bread ; and they had none in the ship with them, except one loaf. ¹⁵ And he charged them, saying : Take heed, beware of the leaven of the Pharisees and the leaven of Herod. ¹⁶ And they reasoned among themselves, saying : It is because we have no bread. ¹⁷ And Jesus knowing it, says to them : Why reason ye, because ye have no bread? Do ye not yet perceive, nor understand? Have ye your heart yet hardened? ¹⁸ Having eyes, do ye not see? And having ears, do ye not hear? And do ye not remember? ¹⁹ When I broke the five loaves among the five thousand, how many baskets full of fragments did ye take up? They say to him : Twelve. ²⁰ And when the seven among the four thousand, how many baskets full of fragments did ye take up? And they said : Seven. ²¹ And he said to them : How is it that ye do not understand?

²² And they come to Bethsaida. And they bring to him a blind man, and beseech him to touch him. ²³ And taking the blind man by the hand, he led him forth out of the village ; and spitting in his eyes, and putting his hands on him, he asked him if he beheld anything. ²⁴ And looking up he said : I behold men ; for I see them as trees walking. ²⁵ Then again he put his hands on his eyes, and he saw clearly ; and he was restored, and saw all things distinctly. ²⁶ And he sent him away to his house, saying : Go not even into the village, nor tell it to any in the village.

²⁷ And Jesus went out, and his disciples, into the villages of Cæsarea Philippi. And in the way he asked his disciples, saying to them: Who do men say that I am? ²⁸ And they answered him saying: John the Immerser; and others, Elijah; and others, one of the prophets. ²⁹ And he asked them: But who do ye say that I am? And Peter answering says to him: Thou art the Christ. ³⁰ And he charged them that they should tell no one concerning him.

³¹ And he began to teach them, that the Son of man must suffer many things, and be rejected by the elders, and the chief priests, and the scribes, and be killed, and after three days rise again. ³² And he spoke that saying openly. And Peter, taking him aside, began to rebuke him. ³³ But he turning about, and seeing his disciples, rebuked Peter, saying: Get thee behind me, Satan; for thou thinkest not the things of God, but those of men.

³⁴ And calling to him the multitude, with his disciples, he said to them: Whoever desires to follow after me, let him deny himself, and take up his cross, and follow me. ³⁵ For whoever will save his life shall lose it; but whoever shall lose his life,.for the sake of me and of the glad tidings, shall save it. ³⁶ For what will it profit a man, to gain the whole world, and forfeit his soul? ³⁷ Or what shall a man give as an exchange for his soul? ³⁸ For whoever shall be ashamed of me and of my words, in this adulterous and sinful generation, of him will also the Son of man be ashamed, when he comes in the glory of his Father with the holy angels.

IX. And he said to them: Verily I say to you, that there are some of those standing here, who shall not taste of death, till they have seen the kingdom of God already come with power.

² And after six days Jesus takes with him Peter, and James, and John, and brings them up into a high mountain apart by themselves. And he was transfigured before them. ³ And his garments became shining, exceeding white as snow, such as no fuller on earth can whiten. ⁴ And there appeared to them

CHAPTER IX.

Elijah with Moses; and they were talking with Jesus. ⁵And Peter answering said to Jesus: Master, it is good for us to be here; and let us make three tents, one for thee, and one for Moses, and one for Elijah. ⁶For he knew not what to say; for they were sore afraid. ⁷And there came a cloud overshadowing them; and a voice came out of the cloud: This is my beloved Son; hear ye him. ⁸And suddenly, looking around, they no longer saw any one, but Jesus only with themselves.

⁹And as they came down from the mountain, he charged them that they should relate what they had seen to no one, except when the Son of man shall have risen from the dead. ¹⁰And they kept the saying, questioning among themselves, what is the rising from the dead.

¹¹And they asked him, saying: Why say the scribes that Elijah must first come? ¹²And he said to them: Elijah indeed comes first, and restores all things. And how is it written of the Son of man? That he must suffer many things, and be set at naught. ¹³But I say to you, that Elijah also has come, and they did to him whatever they would, as it is written of him.

¹⁴And coming to his disciples he saw a great multitude about them, and scribes questioning with them. ¹⁵And straightway all the multitude seeing him were greatly amazed, and running to him saluted him. ¹⁶And he asked them: What question ye with them? ¹⁷And one of the multitude answered him: Teacher, I brought to thee my son, having a dumb spirit. ¹⁸And wherever it lays hold of him, it tears him, and he foams, and gnashes his teeth, and he pines away. And I spoke to thy disciples, that they should cast it out; and they could not. ¹⁹And he answering, says to them: O faithless generation, how long shall I be with you? How long shall I bear with you? Bring him to me. ²⁰And they brought him to him. And seeing him, straightway the spirit rent him; and he fell on the ground, and wallowed foaming. ²¹And he asked his father: How long is it, since this came upon him? And he said: From a child. ²²And ofttimes it cast him both into the fire, and into the water, to destroy him. But if thou art able to do

anything, have compassion on us, and help us. ²³ Jesus said to him: If thou art able! All things are possible to the believing. ²⁴ And straightway the father of the child cried out, and said: I believe; help thou my unbelief. ²⁵ And Jesus, seeing that a multitude came running together, rebuked the unclean spirit, saying to him: Dumb and deaf spirit, I charge thee, come out of him, and enter into him no more. ²⁶ And crying out, and rending him sorely, it came out of him. And he became as one dead; so that many said: He is dead. ²⁷ But Jesus taking him by the hand, raised him, and he stood up.

²⁸ And when he had come into the house, his disciples asked him privately: Why could not we cast it out? ²⁹ And he said to them: This kind can go out by nothing, except by prayer and fasting.

³⁰ And going forth from thence, they passed through Galilee; and he would not that any one should know it. ³¹ For he taught his disciples, and said to them: The Son of man is delivered up into the hands of men, and they will kill him; and when he is killed, after three days he will rise again. ³² But they understood not the saying, and were afraid to ask him.

³³ And they came to Capernaum. And having come into the house he inquired of them: Of what were ye reasoning among yourselves by the way? ³⁴ But they were silent; for by the way they had disputed with one another, who was greatest. ³⁵ And sitting down, he called the twelve, and says to them: If any one desires to be first, he shall be last of all, and servant of all. ³⁶ And taking a child, he placed it in the midst of them; and folding it in his arms, he said to them: ³⁷ Whoever shall receive one of such children in my name, receives me; and whoever shall receive me, receives not me, but him who sent me.

³⁸ And John answered him, saying: Teacher, we saw one casting out demons in thy name, who follows not us; and we forbade him, because he follows not us. ³⁹ But Jesus said: Forbid him not; for there is no one who shall do a miracle in

CHAPTER X.

my name, and can lightly speak evil of me. ⁴⁰ For he that is not against us is for us. ⁴¹ For whoever shall give you a cup of water to drink in that name, that ye are Christ's, verily I say to you, he shall not lose his reward. ⁴² And whoever shall cause one of these little ones that believe on me to offend, it is better for him that an upper millstone were hanged about his neck, and he were cast into the sea. ⁴³ And if thy hand cause thee to offend, cut it off. It is better for thee to enter into life maimed, than having the two hands to go into hell, into the fire that is unquenchable; ⁴⁴ where their worm dies not, and the fire is not quenched. ⁴⁵ And if thy foot cause thee to offend, cut it off. It is better for thee to enter into life lame, than having the two feet to be cast into hell, into the fire that is unquenchable; ⁴⁶ where their worm dies not, and the fire is not quenched. ⁴⁷ And if thine eye cause thee to offend, pluck it out. It is better for thee to enter into the kingdom of God with one eye, than having two eyes to be cast into hell-fire; ⁴⁸ where their worm dies not, and the fire is not quenched. ⁴⁹ For every one shall be salted with fire, and every sacrifice shall be salted with salt. ⁵⁰ Salt is good; but if the salt become saltless, wherewith will ye season it? Have salt in yourselves, and be at peace with one another.

X. And rising up he goes thence into the borders of Judæa, and the further side of the Jordan. And again the multitudes come together to him; and as he was wont, he again taught them.

² And the Pharisees came to him, and asked him, if it is lawful for a man to put away a wife, tempting him. ³ And he answering said to them: What did Moses command you? ⁴ And they said: Moses permitted to write a bill of divorcement, and to put her away. ⁵ And Jesus answering said to them: For your hardness of heart he wrote you this command. ⁶ But from the beginning of the creation, God made them male and female. ⁷ For this cause shall a man leave his father and mother, and shall cleave to his wife; and the two shall be

one flesh. ⁸ So that they are no longer two, but one flesh. ⁹ What therefore God joined together, let not man put asunder.

¹⁰ And in the house his disciples asked him again concerning this. ¹¹ And he says to them: Whoever shall put away his wife, and marry another, commits adultery against her. ¹² And if a woman shall put away her husband, and be married to another, she commits adultery.

¹³ And they brought little children to him, that he might touch them; and the disciples rebuked those who brought them. ¹⁴ But Jesus seeing it, was much displeased, and said to them: Suffer the little children to come to me; forbid them not, for to such belongs the kingdom of God. ¹⁵ Verily I say to you, whoever shall not receive the kingdom of God as a little child, shall not enter therein. ¹⁶ And he folded them in his arms, put his hands on them, and blessed them.

¹⁷ And as he was going forth into the way, there came one running, and kneeling to him, and asked him: Good Teacher, what shall I do that I may inherit eternal life? ¹⁸ And Jesus said to him: Why callest thou me good? There is none good but one, God. ¹⁹ Thou knowest the commandments: Do not commit adultery, Do not kill, Do not steal, Do not bear false witness, Defraud not, Honor thy father and mother. ²⁰ And he answering said to him: Teacher, all these I kept from my youth. ²¹ And Jesus beholding him loved him, and said to him: One thing thou lackest; go, sell whatever thou hast, and give to the poor, and thou shalt have treasure in heaven; and come, take up the cross, and follow me. ²² And he became sad at that saying, and went away sorrowful; for he had great possessions.

²³ And looking around, Jesus says to his disciples: How hardly shall they that have riches enter into the kingdom of God! ²⁴ And the disciples were astonished at his words. But Jesus answering again says to them: Children, how hard it is for those who trust in riches to enter into the kingdom of God! ²⁵ It is easier for a camel to go through the eye of a

CHAPTER X.

needle, than for a rich man to enter into the kingdom of God. ²⁶ And they were exceedingly amazed, saying among themselves: Who then can be saved? ²⁷ And Jesus, looking on them, says: With men it is impossible, but not with God; for with God all things are possible.

²⁸ Peter began to say to him: Lo, we forsook all, and followed thee. ²⁹ And Jesus answering said: Verily I say to you, there is no one who forsook house, or brothers, or sisters, or father, or mother, or wife, or children, or lands, for the sake of me and of the glad tidings, ³⁰ but he shall receive a hundredfold now in this time, houses, and brothers, and sisters, and mothers, and children, and lands, with persecutions, and in the world to come eternal life. ³¹ But many first will be last, and the last first.

³² And they were in the way going up to Jerusalem. And Jesus was going before them; and they were amazed, and as they followed they were afraid. And again he took with him the twelve, and began to say to them what things should happen to him: ³³ Behold, we are going up to Jerusalem; and the Son of man will be delivered up to the chief priests, and to the scribes; and they will condemn him to death and will deliver him up to the Gentiles; ³⁴ and they will mock him, and scourge him, and spit upon him, and will kill him; and after three days he will rise again.

³⁵ And James and John, the sons of Zebedee, come to him saying: Teacher, we desire that thou shouldst do for us whatever we shall ask. ³⁶ And he said to them: What do ye desire that I should do for you? ³⁷ They said to him: Grant to us that we may sit, one on thy right hand, and the other on the left, in thy glory. ³⁸ And Jesus said to them: Ye know not what ye ask. Are ye able to drink the cup that I drink, or to endure the immersion which I endure? ³⁹ And they said to him: We are able. And Jesus said to them: Ye shall indeed drink the cup that I drink, and endure the immersion which I endure. ⁴⁰ But to sit on my right hand, or on the left, is not mine to give, but is for them for whom it has been prepared.

⁴¹ And the ten, hearing it, began to be much displeased with

James and John. ⁴²And Jesus, calling them to him, says to them: Ye know that they who are accounted to rule over the Gentiles exercise lordship over them; and their great ones exercise authority over them. ⁴³But it is not so among you. But whoever would become great among you, shall be your minister; ⁴⁴and whoever would become chiefest of you, shall be servant of all. ⁴⁵For even the Son of man came not to be ministered to, but to minister, and to give his life a ransom for many.

⁴⁶And they come to Jericho. And as he was going forth from Jericho with his disciples and a great multitude, the son of Timæus, Bartimæus, a blind beggar, was sitting by the way-side. ⁴⁷And hearing that it is Jesus the Nazarene, he began to cry out, and say: Son of David, Jesus, have mercy on me. ⁴⁸And many rebuked him, that he should hold his peace. But he cried all the more: Son of David, have mercy on me. ⁴⁹And Jesus stood still, and said: Call him. And they call the blind man, saying to him: Be of good cheer; rise, he calls thee. ⁵⁰And he, casting away his garment, leaped up, and came to Jesus. ⁵¹And Jesus answering said to him: What wilt thou that I should do to thee? The blind man said to him: Lord, that I may receive sight. ⁵²And Jesus said to him: Go thy way; thy faith has made thee whole. And immediately he received sight, and followed him in the way.

XI. AND when they come near to Jerusalem, to Bethphage and Bethany at the mount of the Olives, he sends forth two of his disciples, ²and says to them: Go into the village over against you; and immediately, on entering into it, ye will find a colt tied, whereon no man has sat; loose and bring him. ³And if any one say to you: Why do ye this? say: The Lord has need of him; and straightway he will send him hither. ⁴And they departed, and found a colt tied by the door without, on the street; and they loose him. ⁵And some of those standing there, said to them: What do ye, loosing the

---

V. 42. *Or*, they who claim to rule

CHAPTER XI.

colt? ⁶ And they said to them as Jesus commanded; and they let them go. ⁷ And they bring the colt to Jesus, and cast their garments on him; and he sat upon him. ⁸ And many spread their garments in the way, and others branches, cutting them from the fields. ⁹ And they that went before, and they that followed, cried: Hosanna! blessed is he that comes in the name of the Lord; ¹⁰ blessed is the coming kingdom of our father David; Hosanna in the highest! ¹¹ And he entered into Jerusalem, and into the temple; and having looked around on all things, the evening being now come, he went out to Bethany with the twelve.

¹² And on the morrow, when they had come out from Bethany, he was hungry. ¹³ And seeing a fig-tree afar off having leaves, he came, if haply he might find anything thereon. And coming to it, he found nothing but leaves; for it was not the season of figs. ¹⁴ And answering he said to it: Let no one eat fruit from thee, henceforth forever. And his disciples heard it.

¹⁵ And they come into Jerusalem. And entering into the temple, he began to cast out those who sold and bought in the temple, and overturned the tables of the money changers, and the seats of those who sold doves; ¹⁶ and suffered not that any one should carry a vessel through the temple. ¹⁷ And he taught, saying to them: Is it not written: M y   h o u s e   s h a l l   b e   c a l l e d   a   h o u s e   o f   p r a y e r   f o r   a l l   t h e   n a t i o n s ?   B u t   y e   h a v e   m a d e   i t   a   d e n   o f   r o b b e r s. ¹⁸ And the chief priests and the scribes heard it. And they sought how they might destroy him; for they feared him, for all the multitude was astonished at his teaching. ¹⁹ And when it became late, he went forth out of the city.

²⁰ And passing by in the morning, they saw the fig-tree dried up from the roots. ²¹ And Peter, calling to remembrance, says to him: Master, behold, the fig-tree which thou didst curse is withered away. ²² And Jesus answering says to them: Have

---

V. 8. *In the oldest copies:* and others branches, cutting them from the fields.

faith in God. ²³ Verily I say to you, that whoever shall say to this mountain: Be thou taken up and cast into the sea, and shall not doubt in his heart, but shall believe that what he says comes to pass, he shall have it. ²⁴ Therefore I say to you: All things whatever ye ask, when ye pray, believe that ye received, and ye shall have them. ²⁵ And when ye stand praying, forgive, if ye have aught against any one; that your Father also who is in heaven may forgive you your trespasses. ²⁶ But if ye do not forgive, neither will your Father who is in heaven forgive your trespasses.

²⁷ And they come again into Jerusalem. And as he was walking in the temple, there come to him the chief priests, and the scribes, and the elders. ²⁸ And they said to him: By what authority doest thou these things? And who gave thee this authority, to do these things? ²⁹ And Jesus answering said to them: I also will ask you one thing; and answer me, and I will tell you by what authority I do these things. ³⁰ John's immersion, was it from heaven, or from men? Answer me. ³¹ And they reasoned among themselves, saying: ³² If we say, from heaven; he will say, why then did ye not believe him? But shall we say from men? They feared the people; for all held that John was verily a prophet. ³³ And answering they say to Jesus: We do not know. And Jesus says to them: Neither do I say to you, by what authority I do these things.

XII. And he began to speak to them in parables. A man planted a vineyard, and set a hedge about it, and dug a wine-vat, and built a tower, and let it out to husbandmen, and went abroad. ²And at the season he sent to the husbandmen a servant, that he might receive from the husbandmen of the fruits of the vineyard. ³And they took him and beat him, and sent him away empty. ⁴And again he sent to them another servant; and at him they cast stones, and wounded him in the head, and sent him away shamefully treated. ⁵And he sent another; and him they killed, and many others; beating

V. 26 *is omitted in some ancient copies.*

CHAPTER XII.

some, and killing some. ⁶ Having yet therefore one beloved son, he sent him also to them last, saying: They will reverence my son. ⁷ But those husbandmen said among themselves: This is the heir; come, let us kill him, and the inheritance will be ours. ⁸ And they took, and killed him, and cast him out of the vineyard. ⁹ What therefore will the lord of the vineyard do? He will come and destroy the husbandmen, and will give the vineyard to others. ¹⁰ And have ye not read this scripture:

The stone which the builders disallowed,
The same is become the head of the corner;

¹¹ This is from the Lord, and is wonderful in our eyes.

¹² And they sought to lay hold of him, but feared the people; for they knew that he spoke the parable against them; and they left him, and went away.

¹³ And they send to him some of the Pharisees and of the Herodians, to entrap him with a word. ¹⁴ And they come and say to him: Teacher, we know that thou art true, and carest for no one; for thou regardest not the person of men, but teachest the way of God in truth. Is it lawful to give tribute to Cæsar, or not? ¹⁵ Shall we give, or shall we not give? But he, knowing their hypocrisy, said to them: Why tempt ye me? Bring me a denáry, that I may see it. ¹⁶ And they brought it. And he says to them: Whose is this image, and the inscription? And they said to him: Cæsar's. ¹⁷ And Jesus answering said to them: Render to Cæsar the things that are Cæsar's, and to God the things that are God's. And they marveled at him.

¹⁸ And there come to him Sadducees, who say there is no resurrection. And they asked him, saying: ¹⁹ Teacher, Moses wrote to us, that if one's brother die, and leave a wife behind, and leave no children, his brother should take the wife, and raise up seed to his brother. ²⁰ There were seven brothers; and the first took a wife, and dying left no seed. ²¹ And the second took her, and died, and he also left no seed; and the third likewise. ²² And the seven took her, and left no seed.

V. 15. Denáry, *a Roman coin.*

Last of all the woman died also. ²³ In the resurrection therefore, when they shall rise again, of which of them shall she be wife? For the seven had her for a wife. ²⁴ Jesus answering said to them: Do ye not therefore err, because ye know not the Scriptures, nor the power of God? ²⁵ For when they shall rise from the dead, they neither marry, nor are given in marriage; but are as angels who are in heaven. ²⁶ And concerning the dead, that they rise, have ye not read in the book of Moses, at The Bush, how God spoke to him, saying: I am the God of Abraham, and the God of Isaac, and the God of Jacob? ²⁷ He is not God of the dead, but of the living. Ye greatly err.

²⁸ And one of the scribes came to him, and having heard them reasoning together, and perceiving that he answered them well, asked him: Which commandment is first of all? ²⁹ And Jesus answered him: First is, Hear, O Israel; the Lord is our God, the Lord is one; ³⁰ and thou shalt love the Lord thy God with all thy heart, and with all thy soul, and with all thy mind, and with all thy strength. This is the first commandment. ³¹ Second is this: Thou shalt love thy neighbor as thyself. There is no other commandment greater than these. ³² And the scribe said to him: Well, Teacher; thou saidst truly that he is one, and there is no other beside him; ³³ and to love him with all the heart, and with all the understanding, and with all the soul, and with all the strength, and to love his neighbor as himself, is more than all the whole-burnt-offerings and sacrifices. ³⁴ And Jesus, seeing that he answered intelligently, said to him: Thou art not far from the kingdom of God. And no one dared any longer to question him. .

³⁵ And Jesus answering said, while teaching in the temple: How say the scribes that the Christ is son of David? ³⁶ For David himself said, in the Holy Spirit:

    The LORD said to my Lord,
    Sit on my right hand,
    Till I put thy enemies under thy feet.

CHAPTER XIII.

[37] David himself calls him Lord; and whence is he his son? And the great multitude heard him gladly.
[38] And he said to them in his teaching: Beware of the scribes, who love to go about in long robes, and love greetings in the markets, [39] and the first seats in the synagogues, and the first places at the feasts; [40] who devour widows' houses, and for a pretense make long prayers; these shall receive greater condemnation.
[41] And sitting over against the treasury, he beheld how the people cast money into the treasury; and many that were rich cast in much. [42] And one poor widow came, and cast in two mites, which are a farthing. [43] And calling to him his disciples, he said to them: Verily I say to you, that this poor widow cast in more than all who are casting into the treasury. [44] For all cast in out of their abundance; but she, out of her want, cast in all that she had, her whole living.

XIII. And as he went out of the temple, one of his disciples says to him: Teacher, see what manner of stones, and what manner of buildings! [2] And Jesus said to him: Seest thou these great buildings? There shall not be left one stone upon another, that shall not be thrown down.
[3] And as he was sitting on the mount of the Olives, over against the temple, Peter and James and John and Andrew asked him privately: [4] Tell us, when will these things be? And what is the sign when all these things are about to be accomplished.
[5] And Jesus began to say to them: Take heed lest any one lead you astray. [6] For many will come in my name, saying: I am he; and will lead many astray. [7] And when ye shall hear of wars and rumors of wars, be not troubled, for it must come to pass; but not yet is the end. [8] For nation will rise against nation, and kingdom against kingdom; and there will be earthquakes in divers places, and there will be famines and commotions; these are the beginning of sorrows.
[9] But do ye take heed to yourselves; for they will deliver you up to councils, and in the synagogues ye will be beaten;

and ye will be brought before governors and kings for my sake for a testimony to them. ¹⁰ And the good news must first be preached among all the nations.

¹¹ But when they lead you away to deliver you up, take not thought beforehand what ye shall speak nor premeditate; but whatever shall be given you in that hour, that speak; for it is not ye that speak, but the Holy Spirit. ¹² And the brother will deliver up the brother to death, and the father the child; and children will rise up against parents, and will put them to death. ¹³ And ye will be hated by all for my name's sake; but he that has endured unto the end, the same shall be saved.

¹⁴ But when ye see the abomination of desolation standing where it ought not, (let him that reads, mark!) then let those in Judæa flee to the mountains. ¹⁵ And he that is upon the house, let him not go down into the house, nor enter in to take anything out of his house. ¹⁶ And he that is in the field, let him not turn back to take his garment.

¹⁷ But woe to those who are with child, and to those who give suck in those days! ¹⁸ And pray that it be not in the winter. ¹⁹ For in those days will be affliction, such as has not been from the beginning of the creation which God created until now, neither shall be. ²⁰ And if the Lord had not shortened those days, no flesh would have been saved; but for the sake of the chosen, whom he chose, he shortened the days.

²¹ And then if any one say to you: Lo, here is the Christ, or Lo, there, believe not. ²² For false Christs and false prophets will arise, and will show signs and wonders, so as to lead, if possible, even the chosen astray. ²³ But do ye take heed; I have foretold you all.

²⁴ But in those days, after that affliction, the sun shall be darkened, and the moon shall not give her light; ²⁵ and the stars shall fall from heaven, and the powers that are in heaven shall be shaken. ²⁶ And then shall they see the Son of man coming in clouds, with great power and glory. ²⁷ And then will he send forth the angels, and gather together his chosen from the four winds, from the uttermost part of the earth to the uttermost part of heaven.

CHAPTER XIV.

²⁸ And learn the parable from the fig-tree. When its branch is already become tender, and puts forth leaves, ye know that summer is near. ²⁹ So also ye, when ye see these things come to pass, know that it is near, at the doors. ³⁰ Verily I say to you, that this generation shall not pass, till all these things are done. ³¹ Heaven and earth shall pass away; but my words shall not pass away.

³² But of that day or hour no one knows, not even the angels in heaven, nor the Son, but the Father. ³³ Take heed, watch; for ye know not when the time is. ³⁴ As a man who is abroad, having left his house, and given authority to his servants, to each one his work, also commanded the porter that he should watch; ³⁵ watch therefore, for ye know not when the master of the house comes, at evening, or at midnight, or at the cock-crowing, or in the morning; ³⁶ lest coming suddenly he find you sleeping. ³⁷ And what I say to you, I say to all, Watch.

XIV. Two days after, was the passover, and the feast of unleavened bread; and the chief priests and the scribes sought how they might take him by craft, and put him to death. ² For they said: Not at the feast, lest there shall be a tumult of the people.

³ And he being in Bethany, in the house of Simon the leper, as he was reclining at table, there came a woman having an alabaster box of ointment of pure spikenard, very precious; and she broke the box, and poured it on his head. ⁴ And there were some that were much displeased among themselves, and said: Why was this waste of the ointment made? ⁵ For this ointment could have been sold for more than three hundred denaries, and given to the poor. And they murmured at her. ⁶ And Jesus said: Let her alone; why do ye trouble her? She wrought a good work on me. ⁷ For the poor ye have always with you, and when ye will ye can do good to them; but me ye have not always. ⁸ She did what she could; she beforehand anointed my body for the preparation for burial. ⁹ Verily I say to you, wherever the good news shall be

preached in the whole world, this also that she did shall be told for a memorial of her.

¹⁰ And Judas Iscariot, one of the twelve, went to the chief priests, to deliver him up to them. ¹¹ And they, when they heard it, were glad, and promised to give him money. And he sought how he might conveniently deliver him up.

¹² And on the first day of the feast of unleavened bread, when they killed the passover, his disciples say to him: Where wilt thou that we go and prepare, that thou mayest eat the passover? ¹³ And he sends forth two of his disciples, and says to them: Go into the city, and there will meet you a man bearing a pitcher of water; follow him. ¹⁴ And where he shall go in, say to the master of the house: The Teacher says, Where is the guest-chamber, in which I may eat the passover with my disciples? ¹⁵ And he will show you a large upper room furnished, ready; there prepare for us. ¹⁶ And his disciples went forth, and came into the city, and found as he said to them; and they made ready the passover.

¹⁷ And at evening he comes with the twelve. ¹⁸ And as they were reclining at table, and eating, Jesus said: Verily I say to you, that one of you will betray me, one that eats with me! ¹⁹ And they began to be sorrowful, and to say to him one by one: Is it I? And another said: Is it I? ²⁰ And he answering said to them: It is one of the twelve, one that dips with me into the dish. ²¹ The Son of man indeed goes, as it is written of him; but woe to that man through whom the Son of man is betrayed! It were good for him if that man had not been born.

²² And as they were eating, Jesus, taking a loaf, blessed, and broke, and gave it to them, and said: Take it; this is my body. ²³ And taking the cup, he gave thanks, and gave it to them; and they all drank of it. ²⁴ And he said to them: This is my blood of the covenant, which is shed for many. ²⁵ Verily I say to you, I will drink no more of the fruit of the vine, until that day when I drink it new in the kingdom of God.

²⁶ And having sung, they went out into the mount of the

CHAPTER XIV.

Olives. ²⁷ And Jesus says to them: All ye will be offended; because it is written: I will smite the shepherd, and the sheep shall be scattered. ²⁸ But after I am risen, I will go before you into Galilee.

²⁹ And Peter said to him: Though all shall be offended, yet will not I. ³⁰ And Jesus says to him: Verily I say to thee, that thou this day, in this night, before a cock crows twice, wilt thrice deny me. ³¹ But he said the more vehemently: If I should die with thee, I will not deny thee. Likewise also said they all.

³² And they come to a place which was named Gethsemane. And he says to his disciples: Sit ye here, while I shall pray. ³³ And he takes with him Peter and James and John, and began to be sore amazed, and to be troubled. ³⁴ And he says to them: My soul is exceedingly sorrowful, unto death; tarry here, and watch. ³⁵ And going forward a little, he fell on the ground, and prayed that, if it were possible, the hour might pass from him. ³⁶ And he said: Abba, Father, all things are possible to thee; take away this cup from me; but not what I will, but what thou wilt.

³⁷ And he comes, and finds them sleeping. And he says to Peter: Simon, sleepest thou? Couldest thou not watch one hour? ³⁸ Watch and pray, that ye enter not into temptation. The spirit indeed is willing, but the flesh is weak.

³⁹ And again he went away and prayed, saying the same words. ⁴⁰ And returning, he found them again sleeping, for their eyes were heavy; and they knew not what to answer him.

⁴¹ And he comes the third time, and says to them: Do ye sleep the remaining time, and take your rest? It is enough, the hour is come; behold, the Son of man is betrayed into the hands of sinners. ⁴² Rise, let us go; behold, he that betrays me is at hand.

⁴³ And immediately, while he was yet speaking, comes Judas, one of the twelve, and with him a multitude with swords and

---

V. 41. *Or*, Sleep on now, and take your rest!

staves, from the chief priests and the scribes and the elders. ⁴⁴ And his betrayer had given them a signal, saying: Whom I shall kiss, that is he; lay hold of him, and lead him away securely. ⁴⁵ And coming, he goes straightway to him, and says: Master, Master; and kissed him.

⁴⁶ And they laid their hands on him, and held him fast. ⁴⁷ And one of those standing by drew his sword, and smote the servant of the high priest, and took off his ear. ⁴⁸ And Jesus answering said to them: Came ye out, as against a robber, with swords and staves to take me? ⁴⁹ I was daily with you in the temple teaching, and ye did not lay hold of me; but that the Scriptures might be fulfilled! ⁵⁰ And all forsook him, and fled.

⁵¹ And there followed him a certain young man, having a linen cloth cast about his naked body; and the young men lay hold of him. ⁵² And leaving behind the linen cloth, he fled from them naked.

⁵³ And they led Jesus away to the high priest; and with him assembled all the chief priests and the elders and the scribes. ⁵⁴ And Peter followed him afar off, even into the court of the high priest, and was sitting with the officers, and warming himself at the fire.

⁵⁵ And the chief priests and all the council sought for testimony against Jesus, in order to put him to death; and they found none. ⁵⁶ For many bore false witness against him; but their testimonies agreed not together. ⁵⁷ And certain ones rose up, and bore false witness against him, saying: ⁵⁸ We heard him say, I will destroy this temple that is made with hands, and in three days I will build another made without hands. ⁵⁹ And not even so did their testimony agree.

⁶⁰ And the high priest stood up in the midst, and asked Jesus, saying: Answerest thou nothing? What do these witness against thee? ⁶¹ But he was silent, and answered nothing. Again the high priest asked him, and said to him: Art thou the Christ, the Son of the Blessed? ⁶² And Jesus said: I am; and ye shall see the Son of man sitting on the right hand of power, and coming with the clouds of heaven. ⁶³ And the high

CHAPTER XV.

priest, rending his clothes, says: What further need have we of witnesses? ⁶⁴ Ye heard the blasphemy. What think ye? And they all condemned him to be guilty of death.

⁶⁵ And some began to spit on him, and to cover his face and buffet him, and say to him: Prophesy. And the officers, with blows, took him in charge.

⁶⁶ And Peter being below in the court, there comes one of the maid-servants of the high priest; ⁶⁷ and seeing Peter warming himself, she looked upon him, and said: Thou also wast with Jesus the Nazarene. ⁶⁸ But he denied, saying: I do not know, nor do I understand what thou sayest. And he went out into the fore-court; and a cock crowed.

⁶⁹ And the maid-servant, seeing him, began again to say to those standing by: This is one of them. ⁷⁰ And he again denied it.

And a little after, they that stood by said again to Peter: Surely thou art one of them; for thou art a Galilæan. ⁷¹ But he began to invoke curses, and to swear: I do not know this man of whom ye speak. ⁷² And a cock crowed a second time. And Peter remembered the word, how Jesus said to him: Before a cock crows twice, thou wilt thrice deny me. And as he thought thereon, he wept.

XV. And straightway, in the morning, the chief priests with the elders and scribes and the whole council, having held a consultation, bound Jesus and carried him away, and delivered him up to Pilate. ² And Pilate asked him: Art thou the King of the Jews? And he answering said to him: Thou sayest it. ³ And the chief priests accused him of many things.

⁴ And Pilate asked him again, saying: Answerest thou nothing? Behold what things they testify against thee. ⁵ But Jesus no longer made any answer; so that Pilate marveled.

⁶ And at the feast he released to them one prisoner, whomsoever they asked. ⁷ And there was the one called Barabbas, bound with his companions in sedition, who in the sedition had committed murder. ⁸ And coming up, the multitude began to

make request, according as he had always done for them. ⁹ And Pilate answered them, saying: Will ye that I release to you the King of the Jews? ¹⁰ For he knew that through envy the chief priests had delivered him up. ¹¹ But the chief priests stirred up the multitude, that he should rather release to them Barabbas. ¹² And Pilate answering, said again to them: What will ye then that I shall do to him whom ye call the King of the Jews? ¹³ And they cried again: Crucify him. ¹⁴ And Pilate said to them: What evil then has he done? And they cried the more exceedingly: Crucify him.

¹⁵ And Pilate, wishing to satisfy the multitude, released to them Barabbas; and he delivered up Jesus, after scourging him, to be crucified. ¹⁶ And the soldiers led him away into the court, which is Prætorium; and they call together the whole band. ¹⁷ And they clothe him with purple, and having platted a crown of thorns, they put it on him. ¹⁸ And they began to salute him: Hail, King of the Jews! ¹⁹ And they smote him on the head with a reed, and spit upon him, and kneeling down, did homage to him. ²⁰ And when they had mocked him, they took off the purple from him, and put on him his own garments.

And they lead him out to crucify him. ²¹ And they compel one Simon, a Cyrenian, who was passing by, coming from the country, the father of Alexander and Rufus, to bear his cross. ²² And they bring him to the place Golgotha, which is interpreted, Place of a skull. ²³ And they gave him wine mingled with myrrh; but he took it not. ²⁴ And having crucified him, they divide his garments, casting lots upon them, what any one should take. ²⁵ And it was the third hour; and they crucified him. ²⁶ And the inscription of the accusation against him was written over: THE KING OF THE JEWS.

²⁷ And with him they crucify two robbers; one on his right hand, and one on his left. ²⁸ And the scripture was fulfilled, which says: And he was reckoned with transgressors. ²⁹ And they that passed by railed at him, wagging their heads, and saying: Aha, thou that destroyest the temple, and buildest it in three days: ³⁰ save thyself, and come down

CHAPTER XV.

from the cross. ³¹ Likewise also the chief priests, mocking one with another, together with the scribes, said: Others he saved, himself he can not save. ³² Let the Christ, the King of Israel, come down now from the cross, that we may see and believe. And they that were crucified with him reproached him.
³³ And when the sixth hour was come, there was darkness over the whole land until the ninth hour. ³⁴ And at the ninth hour Jesus cried with a loud voice, saying: E l o i, E l o i, l a m a s a b a c h t h a n i? Which is interpreted: My God, my God, why didst thou forsake me? ³⁵ And some of those standing by, hearing it, said: Behold, he calls Elijah. ³⁶ And one ran and filled a sponge with vinegar, and put it on a reed, and gave him to drink, saying: Let alone; let us see whether Elijah comes to take him down. ³⁷ And Jesus, uttering a loud cry, expired. ³⁸ And the vail of the temple was rent in twain, from the top to the bottom. ³⁹ And the centurion who was standing near, over against him, seeing that he so cried out and expired, said: Truly this man was the Son of God.
⁴⁰ And there were also women looking on afar off; among whom was also Mary the Magdalene, and Mary the mother of James the younger and of Joses, and Salome; ⁴¹ who also, when he was in Galilee, followed him, and ministered to him; and many other women who came up with him to Jerusalem.
⁴² And evening having now come, since it was the preparation (which is the day before the sabbath), ⁴³ Joseph from Arimathæa, an honorable counselor, who also was himself waiting for the kingdom of God, came and went in boldly to Pilate, and asked for the body of Jesus. ⁴⁴ And Pilate marveled, if he were already dead; and calling to him the centurion, he asked him if he had been long dead. ⁴⁵ And having learned it from the centurion, he gave the dead body to Joseph. ⁴⁶ And having bought fine linen, and taken him down, he wrapped him in the linen, and laid him in a sepulchre which was hewn out of a rock, and rolled a stone to the door of the sepulchre. ⁴⁷ And Mary the Magdalene, and Mary the mother of Joses, beheld where he was laid.

V. 42. *Gr.* which is the ante-sabbath

XVI. And the sabbath being past, Mary the Magdalene, and Mary the mother of James, and Salome, bought spices, that they might come and anoint him.

² And very early, on the first day of the week, they come to the sepulchre, when the sun was risen. ³ And they said to one another: Who will roll away the stone for us, out of the door of the sepulchre? ⁴ And looking up, they see that the stone has been rolled away. For it was very great. ⁵ And entering into the sepulchre, they saw a young man sitting on the right side, clothed in a white robe; and they were affrighted. ⁶ And he says to them: Be not affrighted. Ye are seeking Jesus the Nazarene, who was crucified. He is risen; he is not here. Behold the place where they laid him. ⁷ But go, say to his disciples, and to Peter; that he goes before you into Galilee. There shall ye see him, as he said to you. ⁸ And they went out, and fled from the sepulchre; for trembling and astonishment seized them. And they said nothing to any one; for they were afraid.

⁹ And having risen early, on the first day of the week, he appeared first to Mary the Magdalene, from whom he had cast out seven demons. ¹⁰ She went and reported it to those who had been with him, as they mourned and wept. ¹¹ And they, hearing that he is alive, and was seen by her, believed not.

¹² After that he appeared in another form to two of them, as they walked, going into the country. ¹³ They also went and reported it to the rest; nor did they believe them.

¹⁴ Afterward he appeared to the eleven themselves as they reclined at table, and upbraided their unbelief and hardness of heart, because they believed not those who saw him after he was risen. ¹⁵ And he said to them: Go into all the world, and preach the good news to every creature. ¹⁶ He that believes and is immersed shall be saved; but he that believes not shall be condemned. ¹⁷ And these signs shall accompany those who have believed; in my name they shall cast out demons; they shall speak with new tongues: ¹⁸ they shall take up serpents;

CHAPTER I.

and if they drink any deadly thing, it shall not hurt them, they shall lay hands on the sick, and they shall recover.

¹⁹ The Lord therefore, after he had spoken to them, was taken up into heaven, and sat down on the right hand of God; ²⁰ and they went forth, and preached everywhere, the Lord working with them, and confirming the word by the signs that followed.

THE GOSPEL ACCORDING TO LUKE.

I. Forasmuch as many have taken in hand to set forth in order a narration concerning the things fully believed among us, ² as they, who from the beginning were eyewitnesses and ministers of the word, delivered them to us; ³ it seemed good to me also, having accurately traced all from the very first, to write to thee in order, most excellent Theophilus; ⁴ that thou mightest know the certainty concerning those things wherein thou wast instructed.

⁵ There was in the days of Herod, the king of Judæa, a certain priest, Zachariah by name, of the course of Abijah; and his wife was of the daughters of Aaron, and her name was Elisabeth. ⁶ And they were both righteous before God, walking in all the commandments and ordinances of the Lord blameless. ⁷ And they had no child, because Elisabeth was barren; and they both were now far advanced in years.

⁸ And it came to pass, that while he executed the priest's office before God, in the order of his course, ⁹ it fell to his lot, according to the custom of the priest's office, to burn incense, going into the temple of the Lord. ¹⁰ And the whole multitude of the people were praying without, at the hour of incense. ¹¹ And there appeared to him an angel of the Lord, standing on the right side of the altar of incense. ¹² And Zachariah seeing him was troubled, and fear fell upon him. ¹³ But the angel said to him: Fear not, Zachariah; for thy prayer was

---

V. 1. *Or*, the things accomplished among us
V. 4. *Or*, those words

heard, and thy wife Elisabeth shall bear thee a son, and thou shalt call his name John. ¹⁴ And thou shalt have joy and gladness; and many shall rejoice at his birth. ¹⁵ For he shall be great before the Lord; and he shall not drink wine nor strong drink; and he shall be filled with the Holy Spirit, even from his mother's womb. ¹⁶ And many of the sons of Israel shall he turn to the Lord their God. ¹⁷ And he shall go before him in the spirit and power of Elijah, to turn the hearts of the fathers to the children, and the disobedient to the wisdom of the just; to make ready a prepared people for the Lord.

¹⁸ And Zachariah said to the angel: Whereby shall I know this? For I am an old man, and my wife is far advanced in years. ¹⁹ And the angel answering said to him: I am Gabriel, that stands in the presence of God; and I was sent to speak to thee, and to bring thee these glad tidings. ²⁰ And, behold, thou shalt be dumb, and not able to speak, until the day that these things shall be performed, because thou didst not believe my words, which shall be fulfilled in their season.

²¹ And the people were waiting for Zachariah; and they were wondering at his long tarrying in the temple. ²² And when he came out he was not able to speak to them, and they perceived that he had seen a vision in the temple; and he was making signs to them, and remained speechless.

²³ And it came to pass, when the days of his ministration were completed, that he departed to his own house.

²⁴ And after those days his wife Elisabeth conceived; and she hid herself five months, saying: ²⁵ Thus has the Lord dealt with me, in the days wherein he looked on me to take away my reproach among men.

²⁶ And in the sixth month the angel Gabriel was sent from God to a city of Galilee, named Nazareth, ²⁷ to a virgin betrothed to a man whose name was Joseph, of the house of David; and the virgin's name was Mary. ²⁸ And the angel coming in to her, said: Hail, highly favored! The Lord is with thee. Blessed art thou among women. ²⁹ And she was troubled at the saying; and was considering what manner of salutation this might be. ³⁰ And the angel said to her: Fear not, Mary;

CHAPTER I.

for thou didst find favor with God. ³¹ And, behold, thou shalt conceive in thy womb, and bring forth a son, and shalt call his name Jesus. ³² He shall be great, and shall be called Son of the Highest; and the Lord God will give to him the throne of David his father; ³³ and he shall reign over the house of Jacob forever; and of his kingdom there shall be no end.

³⁴ Then said Mary to the angel: How shall this be, seeing that I know not a man? ³⁵ And the angel answering said to her: The Holy Spirit will come upon thee, and the power of the Highest will overshadow thee; therefore also the Holy One that is born shall be called the Son of God. ³⁶ And, behold, Elisabeth thy kinswoman, she also has conceived a son in her old age; and this is the sixth month with her who is called barren. ³⁷ For with God nothing shall be impossible.

³⁸ And Mary said: Behold the handmaid of the Lord; let it be to me according to thy word. And the angel departed from her.

³⁹ And Mary arose in those days, and went into the hill-country with haste, into a city of Judah; ⁴⁰ and entered into the house of Zachariah, and saluted Elisabeth. ⁴¹ And it came to pass, as Elisabeth heard the salutation of Mary, that the babe leaped in her womb; and Elisabeth was filled with the Holy Spirit. ⁴² And she spoke out with a loud voice and said: Blessed art thou among women, and blessed is the fruit of thy womb. ⁴³ And whence is this to me, that the mother of my Lord should come to me? ⁴⁴ For, behold, as the voice of thy salutation came into my ears, the babe leaped in my womb for joy. ⁴⁵ And happy is she, who believed that there shall be a fulfillment of the things told her from the Lord.

⁴⁶ And Mary said: My soul magnifies the Lord; ⁴⁷ and my spirit rejoiced in God my Savior. ⁴⁸ Because he looked upon the low estate of his handmaid; for, behold, henceforth all generations will call me happy. ⁴⁹ Because the Mighty One did great things for me; and holy is his name. ⁵⁰ And his mercy is from generation to generation, to those who fear him.

V. 37. *Or*, no word shall be   V. 45. *Or*, for there shall be

⁵¹ He wrought might with his arm ; he scattered the proud in the imagination of their hearts. ⁵² He cast down princes from thrones, and exalted those of low degree. ⁵³ The hungry he filled with good, and the rich he sent empty away. ⁵⁴ He helped Israel, his servant ; to remember mercy, ⁵⁵ as he spoke to our fathers, for Abraham and for his seed forever.

⁵⁶ And Mary abode with her about three months, and returned to her own house.

⁵⁷ Now Elisabeth's full time came that she should be delivered ; and she brought forth a son. ⁵⁸ And her neighbors and her kindred heard that the Lord showed great mercy toward her ; and they rejoiced with her.

⁵⁹ And it came to pass, that on the eighth day they came to circumcise the child ; and they called him Zachariah, after the name of his father. ⁶⁰ And his mother answered and said : Nay ; but he shall be called John. ⁶¹ And they said to her : There is none of thy kindred that is called by this name. ⁶² And they made signs to his father, how he would have him called. ⁶³ And asking for a writing-tablet, he wrote, saying : His name is John. And they all wondered. ⁶⁴ And his mouth was opened immediately, and his tongue was loosed ; and he spoke, blessing God. ⁶⁵ And fear came on all that dwelt around them. And all these things were told abroad in all the hill-country of Judæa. ⁶⁶ And all who heard laid them up in their hearts, saying : What then will this child be ! And the hand of the Lord was with him.

⁶⁷ And Zachariah his father was filled with the Holy Spirit, and prophesied, saying : ⁶⁸ Blessed be the Lord, the God of Israel, that he visited and wrought redemption for his people ; ⁶⁹ and raised up a horn of salvation for us, in the house of David his servant, ⁷⁰ (as he spoke by the mouth of his holy prophets of old,) ⁷¹ salvation from our enemies, and from the hand of all that hate us ; ⁷² to show mercy to our fathers, and to remember his holy covenant ; ⁷³ the oath which he swore to Abraham our father, ⁷⁴ to grant to us, that without fear, being

---

V. 65. *Or*, all these words

CHAPTER II.

rescued from the hand of our enemies, we should serve him, ⁷⁵ in holiness and righteousness before him all our days. ⁷⁶ And also thou, O child, shalt be called Prophet of the Highest; for thou shalt go before the face of the Lord, to prepare his ways, ⁷⁷ in order to give knowledge of salvation to his people in remission of their sins; ⁷⁸ through the tender mercies of our God, whereby the dayspring from on high visited us, ⁷⁹ to give light to those sitting in darkness and the shadow of death, in order to guide our feet into the way of peace.
⁸⁰ And the child grew, and became strong in spirit, and was in the deserts till the day of his manifestation to Israel.

II. And it came to pass in those days, that there went out a decree from Cæsar Augustus, that all the world should be registered. ² This registering was the first made when Cyrenius was governor of Syria. ³ And all went to be registered, each one to his own city. ⁴ And Joseph also went up from Galilee, out of the city of Nazareth, into Judæa, to the city of David which is called Bethlehem (because he was of the house and family of David), ⁵ to be registered with Mary his betrothed wife, who was with child. ⁶ And so it was, that, while they were there, the days were completed that she should bring forth. ⁷ And she brought forth her first-born son, and wrapped him in swathing bands, and laid him in a manger; because there was no room for them in the inn.
⁸ And there were in the same country shepherds abiding in the field, and keeping watch over their flock by night. ⁹ And, behold, an angel of the Lord came upon them, and the glory of the Lord shone around them; and they were sore afraid. ¹⁰ And the angel said to them: Fear not; for, behold, I bring you good tidings of great joy, which shall be to all the people. ¹¹ For to you is born this day in the city of David a Savior, who is Christ the Lord. ¹² And this shall be to you the sign: Ye will find a babe wrapped in swathing bands, lying in a manger. ¹³ And suddenly there was with the angel a multitude of the heavenly host, praising God and saying: ¹⁴ Glory to God in the highest, and on earth peace, good will among men.

¹⁵ And it came to pass, when the angels were gone away from them into heaven, that the shepherds said one to another: Let us go now unto Bethlehem, and see this thing that is come to pass, which the Lord made known to us. ¹⁶ And they came with haste, and found both Mary and Joseph, and the babe lying in the manger. ¹⁷ And having seen it, they made known abroad the saying which was told them concerning this child. ¹⁸ And all that heard wondered at the things which were told them by the shepherds. ¹⁹ And Mary kept all these things, pondering them in her heart. ²⁰ And the shepherds returned, glorifying and praising God for all that they heard and saw, as it was told to them.

²¹ And when eight days were completed for circumcising him, his name was called Jesus; the name given by the angel before he was conceived in the womb.

²² And when the days of their purification, according to the law of Moses, were completed, they brought him up to Jerusalem, to present him to the Lord, ²³ (as it is written in the law of the Lord: Every male that opens the womb shall be called holy to the Lord;) ²⁴ and to offer a sacrifice according to what is said in the law of the Lord: A pair of turtle-doves, or two young pigeons.

²⁵ And, behold, there was a man in Jerusalem, whose name was Simeon; and this man was just and devout, waiting for the consolation of Israel; and the Holy Spirit was upon him. ²⁶ And it was revealed to him by the Holy Spirit, that he should not see death, before he had seen the Christ of the Lord. ²⁷ And he came by the Spirit into the temple; and when the parents brought in the child Jesus, to do for him after the custom of the law, ²⁸ then he took him into his arms, and blessed God, and said: ²⁹ Now, Lord, thou lettest thy servant depart in peace, according to thy word; ³⁰ because my eyes saw thy salvation, ³¹ which thou preparedst before the face

---

V. 19. *Or,* all these words

CHAPTER II.

of all the peoples, ³²a light for a revelation to the Gentiles, and the glory of thy people Israel.

³³ And his father and mother wondered at the things spoken of him. ³⁴ And Simeon blessed them, and said to Mary his mother: Behold, this child is set for the fall and rising of many in Israel, and for a sign that shall be spoken against, (³⁵and a sword shall pierce through thine own soul also), that thoughts from many hearts may be revealed.

³⁶ And there was Anna, a prophetess, daughter of Phanuel, of the tribe of Asher. She was of great age, and had lived with a husband seven years from her virginity; ³⁷ and she was a widow of about fourscore and four years, who departed not from the temple, serving day and night with fastings and prayers. ³⁸ And she, coming up at that very time, likewise gave thanks to the Lord, and spoke of him to all that were looking for the redemption of Jerusalem.

³⁹ And when they had performed all things according to the law of the Lord, they returned into Galilee, to their own city Nazareth. ⁴⁰ And the child grew, and became strong, being filled with wisdom; and the favor of God was upon him.

⁴¹ And his parents went to Jerusalem every year at the feast of the passover. ⁴² And when he was twelve years old, they having gone up according to the custom of the feast, ⁴³ and completed the days, as they returned, Jesus the child remained behind in Jerusalem. And his parents knew it not, ⁴⁴ but supposing that he was in the company, went a day's journey, and sought him among their kindred and acquaintance; ⁴⁵ and not finding him, they returned to Jerusalem, seeking him.

⁴⁶ And it came to pass, that after three days they found him in the temple, sitting in the midst of the teachers, both hearing them, and asking them questions. ⁴⁷ And all that heard him, were astonished at his understanding and answers. ⁴⁸ And seeing him they were amazed. And his mother said to him: Child, why didst thou thus deal with us? Behold, thy father and I sought thee, sorrowing. ⁴⁹ And he said to them: How is it that ye sought me? Did ye not know, that I must

be in my Father's house? ⁵⁰ And they understood not the saying which he spoke to them.

⁵¹ And he went down with them, and came to Nazareth, and was subject to them. And his mother kept all these sayings in her heart.

⁵² And Jesus increased in wisdom and stature, and in favor with God and men.

III. Now in the fifteenth year of the reign of Tiberius Cæsar, when Pontius Pilate was governor of Judæa, and Herod tetrarch of Galilee, and his brother Philip tetrarch of Iturea and of the region of Trachonitis, and Lysanias tetrarch of Abilene, ² when Annas was high priest and Caiaphas, the word of God came to John, the son of Zachariah, in the wilderness. ³ And he came into all the country about the Jordan, preaching the immersion of repentance, unto remission of sins, ⁴ as it is written in the book of the words of Isaiah the prophet:

  The voice of one crying in the wilderness,
  Prepare the way of the Lord,
  Make straight his paths.
⁵ Every valley shall be filled,
  And every mountain and hill shall be brought low;
  And the crooked shall be straight,
  And the rough ways smooth;
⁶ And all flesh shall see the salvation of God.

⁷ He said therefore to the multitudes that came out to be immersed by him: Brood of vipers, who warned you to flee from the coming wrath? ⁸ Bring forth therefore fruits worthy of repentance; and begin not to say within yourselves, We have Abraham for our father; for I say to you, that God is able of these stones to raise up children to Abraham. ⁹ And now also the axe is laid to the root of the trees. Every tree therefore, that brings not forth good fruit, is cut down and cast into the fire.

¹⁰ And the multitudes asked him, saying: What then shall

V. 49. *Or*, must be in my Father's business

CHAPTER III.

we do? ¹¹ He answering says to them: He that has two coats, let him impart to him that has none; and he that has food, let him do likewise.

¹² And there came also publicans to be immersed; and they said to him: Teacher, what shall we do? ¹³ And he said to them: Exact no more than that which is appointed you. ¹⁴ And soldiers also asked him, saying: What shall we also do? And he said to them: Do violence to no one, neither accuse any falsely; and be content with your wages.

¹⁵ And while the people were in expectation, and all were reasoning in their hearts concerning John, whether he himself were not the Christ, ¹⁶ John answered them all, saying: I indeed immerse you in water; but there comes he that is mightier than I, the latchet of whose sandals I am not worthy to loose; he will immerse you in the Holy Spirit and fire; ¹⁷ whose fan is in his hand, and he will thoroughly cleanse his threshing-floor, and will gather the wheat into his garner; but the chaff he will burn up with fire unquenchable.

¹⁸ And with many other exhortations he published the good tidings to the people.

¹⁹ But Herod the tetrarch, being reproved by him on account of Herodias, the wife of his brother, and for all the evils which Herod did, ²⁰ added to all this also, that he shut up John in prison.

²¹ Now it came to pass, when all the people had been immersed, that as Jesus, having also been immersed, was praying, the heaven was opened, ²² and the Holy Spirit descended in a bodily shape as a dove upon him; and there came a voice out of heaven: Thou art my beloved Son; in thee I am well pleased.

²³ And Jesus himself was, when he began, about thirty years of age; being the son (as was supposed) of Joseph, the son of Heli, ²⁴ the son of Matthat, the son of Levi, the son of Melchi, the son of Janna, the son of Joseph, ²⁵ the son of Matthias, the son of Amos, the son of Nahum, the son of Esli, the son of

---

V 14 *Or*, with your allowance   V. 23. *Or*, was beginning to be

Naggai, ²⁶ the son of Maath, the son of Mattathias, the son of Shimei, the son of Joseph, the son of Judah, ²⁷ the son of Joanna, the son of Reza, the son of Zerubbabel, the son of Salathiel, the son of Neri, ²⁸ the son of Melchi, the son of Addi, the son of Cosam, the son of Elmodam, the son of Er, ²⁹ the son of Joses, the son of Eliezer, the son of Jorim, the son of Matthat, the son of Levi, ³⁰ the son of Simeon, the son of Judah, the son of Joseph, the son of Jonan, the son of Eliakim, ³¹ the son of Meleah, the son of Mainan, the son of Mattatha, the son of Nathan, the son of David, ³² the son of Jesse, the son of Obed, the son of Boaz, the son of Salmon, the son of Nahon, ³³ the son of Amminadab, the son of Ram, the son of Hezron, the son of Pharez, the son of Judah, ³⁴ the son of Jacob, the son of Isaac, the son of Abraham, the son of Terah, the son of Nahor, ³⁵ the son of Serug, the son of Reu, the son of Peleg, the son of Eber, the son of Salah, ³⁶ the son of Cainan, the son of Arphaxad, the son of Shem, the son of Noah, the son of Lamech, ³⁷ the son of Methuselah, the son of Enoch, the son of Jared, the son of Mehalaleel, the son of Cainan, ³⁸ the son of Enos, the son of Seth, the son of Adam, the son of God.

IV. And Jesus, full of the Holy Spirit, returned from the Jordan; and he was led in the Spirit into the wilderness ² forty days, tempted by the Devil. And he ate nothing in those days; and when they were ended, he hungered.

³ And the Devil said to him: If thou art the Son of God, command this stone that it become bread. ⁴ And Jesus answered him, saying: It is written, M a n s h a l l n o t l i v e o n b r e a d a l o n e.

⁵ And the Devil, leading him up into a high mountain, showed him all the kingdoms of the world in a moment of time. ⁶ And the Devil said to him: All this power will I give thee, and the glory of them; because it has been delivered to me, and I give it to whomsoever I will. ⁷ If thou therefore wilt worship me, all shall be thine. ⁸ And Jesus answering said to him: It is written, T h o u s h a l t w o r s h i p t h e L o r d t h y G o d, a n d h i m o n l y s h a l t t h o u s e r v e.

CHAPTER IV.

⁹ And he brought him to Jerusalem, and set him on the pinnacle of the temple, and said to him: If thou art the Son of God, cast thyself down from hence. ¹⁰ For it is written: He will give his angels command concerning thee, to keep thee; ¹¹ and on their hands they shall bear thee up, lest haply thou dash thy foot against a stone. ¹² And Jesus answering said to him: It is said, Thou shalt not tempt the Lord thy God.

¹³ And having finished every temptation, the Devil departed from him for a season.

¹⁴ And Jesus returned in the power of the Spirit into Galilee; and there went out a report concerning him through all the surrounding country. ¹⁵ And he taught in their synagogues, being honored by all.

¹⁶ And he came to Nazareth, where he had been brought up. And, as his custom was, he went into the synagogue on the sabbath day; and he stood up to read. ¹⁷ And there was delivered to him the book of the prophet Isaiah. And unrolling the book, he found the place where it was written:

¹⁸ The Spirit of the Lord is upon me;
Because he anointed me to publish good tidings to the poor;
He has sent me to proclaim deliverance to the captives,
And recovering of sight to the blind,
To send the oppressed away free,
¹⁹ To proclaim the acceptable year of the Lord.

²⁰ And rolling up the book he gave it again to the servant, and sat down. And the eyes of all in the synagogue were fastened on him. ²¹ And he began to say to them: To-day is this scripture fulfilled in your ears. ²² And all bore witness to him, and wondered at the words of grace which proceeded out of his mouth. And they said: Is not this Joseph's son? ²³ And he said to them: Ye will surely say to me this proverb, Physician, heal thyself. Whatever we heard done in Capernaum, do also here in thy country. ²⁴ And he said: Verily I say to you, no prophet is accepted in his own country. ²⁵ But I tell you of a truth, there were many widows in Israel in the

days of Elijah, when the heaven was shut up three years and six months, when there was a great famine throughout all the land; ²⁶ and to none of them was Elijah sent, but unto Zarephath of Sidonia, to a woman that was a widow. ²⁷ And there were many lepers in Israel, in the time of Elisha the prophet; and none of them was cleansed, but only Naaman the Syrian. ²⁸ And all in the synagogue, when they heard these things, were filled with wrath. ²⁹ And they rose up, and thrust him out of the city, and led him to the brow of the hill whereon their city was built, to cast him down headlong. ³⁰ But he, passing through the midst of them, went away.

³¹ And he came down to Capernaum, a city of Galilee. And he was teaching them on the sabbath; ³² and they were astonished at his teaching, because his word was with power.

³³ And in the synagogue there was a man having a spirit of an unclean demon; and he cried out with a loud voice, ³⁴ saying: Ah! what have we to do with thee, Jesus of Nazareth? Didst thou come to destroy us? I know thee who thou art, the Holy One of God. ³⁵ And Jesus rebuked him, saying: Hold thy peace, and come out from him. And the demon throwing him in the midst came out from him, doing him no harm. ³⁶ And amazement came on all; and they spoke with one another, saying: What is this word, that with authority and power he commands the unclean spirits, and they come out? ³⁷ And there went out a rumor concerning him into every place of the country around.

³⁸ And he rose up and went from the synagogue, and entered into the house of Simon. And the mother-in-law of Simon was seized with a violent fever: and they besought him for her. ³⁹ And standing over her he rebuked the fever, and it left her; and immediately she arose and ministered to them.

⁴⁰ Now when the sun was setting, all that had any sick with divers diseases brought them to him; and he laid his hands on each one of them, and healed them. ⁴¹ And demons also came out from many, crying out, and saying: Thou art the Son of

---

V. 38. *Gr.* with a great fever

CHAPTER V.

God. And he, rebuking them, suffered them not to speak, because they knew that he was the Christ.
⁴² And when it was day he went out, and went into a desert place. And the multitudes sought him, and came to him, and stayed him, that he should not depart from them. ⁴³ And he said to them: I must publish the good news of the kingdom of God to other cities also; because for this I was sent forth. ⁴⁴ And he preached in the synagogues of Galilee.

V. And it came to pass, as the multitude pressed upon him to hear the word of God, and he was standing by the lake of Gennesaret, ² that he saw two ships standing by the lake; but the fishermen had gone out of them, and were washing the nets. ³ And entering into one of the ships, which was Simon's, he asked him to put out a little from the land. And sitting down, he taught the multitudes out of the ship.

⁴ And when he ceased speaking, he said to Simon: Put out into the deep; and do ye let down your nets for a draught. ⁵ And Simon answering said to him: Master, we toiled all night and took nothing; but at thy word I will let down the net. ⁶ And having done this, they inclosed a great multitude of fishes; and their net began to break. ⁷ And they beckoned to their partners in the other ship, to come and help them. And they came, and filled both the ships, so that they began to sink. ⁸ And Simon Peter, seeing it, fell down at the knees of Jesus, saying: Depart from me; for I am a sinful man, O Lord. ⁹ For astonishment had seized him, and all that were with him, at the draught of the fishes which they had taken; ¹⁰ and likewise also James and John, sons of Zebedee, who were partners with Simon.

And Jesus said to Simon: Fear not; from henceforth thou shalt catch men. ¹¹ And having brought their ships to land, they forsook all, and followed him.

¹² And it came to pass, when he was in one of the cities, that there was a man full of leprosy. And seeing Jesus he fell on his face, and besought him, saying: Lord, if thou wilt, thou canst cleanse me. ¹³ And stretching forth his hand he touched

him, saying: I will; be thou cleansed. And immediately the leprosy departed from him. ¹⁴ And he charged him to tell no one: But go, and show thyself to the priest, and offer for thy cleansing as Moses commanded, for a testimony to them.

¹⁵ But all the more went abroad the report concerning him; and great multitudes came together to hear, and to be healed of their infirmities. ¹⁶ And he was wont to retire into the solitary places, and pray.

¹⁷ And it came to pass, on a certain day, that he was teaching; and there were Pharisees and teachers of the law sitting by, who had come out of every village of Galilee, and Judæa, and Jerusalem; and there was power of the Lord for healing them. ¹⁸ And, behold, men brought on a bed a man who was palsied; and they sought to bring him in, and to lay him before him. ¹⁹ And not finding by what way they might bring him in, because of the multitude, they went upon the housetop, and let him down through the tiling with the couch into the midst before Jesus. ²⁰ And seeing their faith he said: Man, thy sins are forgiven thee. ²¹ And the scribes and the Pharisees began to reason, saying: Who is this that speaks blasphemies? Who can forgive sins, but God alone? ²² But Jesus, perceiving their thoughts, answering said to them: What reason ye in your hearts? ²³ Which is easier, to say, Thy sins are forgiven thee; or to say, Arise and walk? ²⁴ But that ye may know that the Son of man has power on the earth to forgive sins, (he said to the palsied man,) I say to thee, arise, and taking up thy couch go to thy house. ²⁵ And immediately standing up before them, he took up that whereon he lay, and departed to his house, glorifying God. ²⁶ And they were all amazed; and they glorified God, and were filled with fear, saying: We have seen strange things to-day.

²⁷ And after these things he went forth, and saw a publican, named Levi, sitting at the place of receiving custom; and he said to him: Follow me. ²⁸ And leaving all, he arose and followed him.

²⁹ And Levi made him a great feast in his own house; and there was a great company of publicans and of others who

CHAPTER VI.

reclined at the table with them. ³⁰ And the Pharisees, and their scribes, murmured against his disciples, saying: Why do ye eat and drink with the publicans and sinners? ³¹ And Jesus answering said to them: They who are well need not a physician, but they who are sick. ³² I have not come to call righteous men, but sinners to repentance.

³³ And they said to him: Why do the disciples of John fast often, and make prayers, and likewise those of the Pharisees, but thine eat and drink? ³⁴ And he said to them: Can ye make the sons of the bridechamber fast, while the bridegroom is with them? ³⁵ But days will come, when the bridegroom will be taken away from them; then shall they fast in those days. ³⁶ And he spoke also a parable to them: No one rends a piece from a new garment, and puts it on an old garment; else both the new will make a rent, and the piece from the new agrees not with the old. ³⁷ And no one puts new wine into old skins; else the new wine will burst the skins, and will itself be poured out, and the skins will perish. ³⁸ But new wine must be put into new skins, and both are preserved together. ³⁹ And no one having drunk old wine straightway desires new; for he says: The old is better.

VI. And it came to pass on the second sabbath after the first, that he was going through grain-fields; and his disciples plucked and ate the ears of grain, rubbing them with their hands. ² And some of the Pharisees said: Why do ye that which it is not lawful to do on the sabbath? ³ And Jesus answering them said: And have ye not read this, what David did when he hungered, himself and they who were with him; ⁴ how he went into the house of God, and took and ate the show-bread, and gave to those who were with him, which it is

---

V. 30. *Or,* the scribes and Pharisees among them
V. 34. *Or,* Can ye make the bridemen fast
V. 38. *Some ancient copies omit,* and both are preserved together.
V. 39. *In the oldest copies:* is good (*or,* is mild).
V. 1. *Or,* on the second-first sabbath (*omitted in some ancient copies*).

not lawful to eat except for the priests alone? ⁵ And he said to them : The Son of man is Lord also of the sabbath.

⁶ And it came to pass also on another sabbath, that he entered into the synagogue and taught. And there was a man whose right hand was withered. ⁷ And the scribes and Pharisees were watching, whether he would heal on the sabbath ; that they might find an accusation against him. ⁸ But he knew their thoughts, and said to the man having the withered hand : Arise, and stand forth in the midst. And he rose up, and stood. ⁹ Then said Jesus to them : I will ask you what is lawful on the sabbath, to do good, or to do evil ; to save life, or to destroy it? ¹⁰ And looking round on them all, he said to him : Stretch forth thy hand. And he did so, and his hand was restored. ¹¹ And they were filled with madness, and conferred one with another, as to what they should do to Jesus.

¹² And it came to pass in those days, that he went out into the mountain to pray, and continued all night in prayer to God. ¹³ And when it was day, he called to him his disciples. And having chosen from them twelve (whom he named also apostles) ; ¹⁴ Simon, whom he also named Peter, and Andrew his brother, and James and John, and Philip and Bartholomew, ¹⁵ and Matthew and Thomas, James the son of Alpheus, and Simon called Zelotes, ¹⁶ and Judas brother of James, and Judas Iscariot, who became a betrayer ; ¹⁷ and having come down with them, he stood on a plain, and a company of his disciples, and a great multitude of people from all Judæa and Jerusalem and the sea-coast of Tyre and Sidon, who came to hear him, and to be healed of their diseases ; ¹⁸ and those vexed by unclean spirits were healed ; ¹⁹ and all the multitude sought to touch him, because power went out from him and healed them all.

²⁰ And he, lifting up his eyes on his disciples, said : Happy are ye poor ; for yours is the kingdom of God. ²¹ Happy are ye that hunger now ; for ye shall be filled. Happy are ye that weep now ; for ye shall laugh.

V 9. *In some ancient copies:* whether it is lawful

CHAPTER VI.

²² Happy are ye, when men shall hate you, and when they shall separate you from them, and shall reproach you, and cast out your name as evil, for the sake of the Son of man. ²³ Rejoice in that day, and leap for joy; for, behold, your reward is great in heaven; for in the same manner did their fathers to the prophets.

²⁴ But woe to you that are rich; for ye have received your consolation. ²⁵ Woe to you that are full; for ye shall hunger. Woe to you that laugh now; for ye shall mourn and weep. ²⁶ Woe! when all men shall speak well of you; for in the same manner did their fathers to the false prophets.

²⁷ But I say to you who hear: Love your enemies, do good to those who hate you, ²⁸ bless those who curse you, pray for those who abuse you. ²⁹ To him who smites thee on the cheek offer also the other; and him who takes away thy cloak forbid not to take thy coat also.

³⁰ Give to every one that asks of thee; and of him who takes away thy goods demand them not again. ³¹ And as ye would that men should do to you, do ye also in like manner to them.

³² For if ye love those who love you, what thanks have ye? For even the sinners love those who love them. ³³ And if ye do good to those who do good to you, what thanks have ye? For even the sinners do the same. ³⁴ And if ye lend to those of whom ye hope to receive, what thanks have ye? And sinners lend to sinners, that they may receive as much in return.

³⁵ But love your enemies, and do good, and lend, hoping for nothing in return; and your reward shall be great, and ye shall be sons of the Highest; for he is kind to the unthankful and evil. ³⁶ Be ye merciful, as your Father also is merciful.

³⁷ And judge not, and ye shall not be judged; condemn not, and ye shall not be condemned; acquit, and ye shall be acquitted.

³⁸ Give, and it shall be given to you; good measure, pressed down, shaken together, running over, shall they give into your

---

V. 28. *Or,* for those who falsely accuse you

bosom. For with the same measure with which ye mete it shall be measured to you again.

³⁹ And he spoke also a parable to them: Can the blind lead the blind? Shall they not both fall into the ditch? ⁴⁰ A disciple is not above the teacher; but every one shall be perfected as his teacher.

⁴¹ And why beholdest thou the mote that is in thy brother's eye, but perceivest not the beam that is in thine own eye? ⁴² How canst thou say to thy brother: Brother, let me cast out the mote that is in thine eye, when thou thyself beholdest not the beam that is in thine own eye? Hypocrite! cast out first the beam out of thine eye, and then thou shalt see clearly to cast out the mote that is in thy brother's eye.

⁴³ For there is no good tree that bears corrupt fruit, nor corrupt tree that bears good fruit. ⁴⁴ For every tree is known from its own fruit. For from thorns they do not gather figs, nor from a bramble bush do they harvest grapes. ⁴⁵ The good man out of the good treasure of his heart brings forth that which is good; and the evil, out of the evil, brings forth that which is evil; for out of the abundance of the heart his mouth speaks.

⁴⁶ And why call ye me, Lord, Lord, and do not the things which I say? ⁴⁷ Every one that comes to me, and hears my sayings, and does them, I will show you to whom he is like. ⁴⁸ He is like a man building a house, who digged deep, and laid a foundation on the rock. And when a flood arose, the stream burst upon that house, and could not shake it; because it was well builded. ⁴⁹ But he that hears, and does not, is like a man that built a house upon the earth without a foundation; on which the stream burst, and immediately it fell; and the ruin of that house was great.

VII. When he completed all his sayings in the hearing of the people, he entered into Capernaum. ² And a certain centurion's servant, who was dear to him, was sick and

---

V. 49. *Gr.* it fell together

CHAPTER VII.

about to die. ³ And having heard concerning Jesus, he sent to him elders of the Jews, asking him that he would come and heal his servant. ⁴ And they, coming to Jesus, besought him earnestly, saying: He is worthy that thou shouldst do this for him; ⁵ for he loves our nation, and himself built our synagogue.

⁶ And Jesus went with them. And when he was now not far from the house, the centurion sent friends to him, saying to him: Lord, trouble not thyself; for I am not worthy that thou shouldst enter under my roof. ⁷ Wherefore neither thought I myself worthy to come to thee; but say with a word, and my servant will be healed. ⁸ For I am a man placed under authority, having soldiers under me, and I say to this one, Go, and he goes, and to another, Come, and he comes; and to my servant, Do this, and he does it. ⁹ And Jesus hearing these things, marveled at him; and turning said to the multitude that followed him: I say to you, I found not so great faith, even in Israel.

¹⁰ And they who were sent, returning to the house, found the servant whole that had been sick.

¹¹ And it came to pass the day after, that he went into a city called Nain; and many of his disciples went with him, and a great multitude. ¹² And as he came near to the gate of the city, behold, a dead man was carried out, the only son of his mother, and she was a widow; and a great multitude of the city was with her. ¹³ And seeing her, the Lord had compassion on her, and said to her: Weep not. ¹⁴ And he came and touched the bier; and they who bore it stood still. And he said: Young man, I say to thee, arise. ¹⁵ And the dead sat up, and began to speak. And he gave him to his mother. ¹⁶ And fear seized on all; and they glorified God, saying: A great prophet has arisen among us; and, God has visited his people. ¹⁷ And this report went forth in all Judaea concerning him, and in all the country around.

¹⁸ And the disciples of John reported to him concerning all these things. ¹⁹ And John calling to him two of his disciples sent them to Jesus, saying: Art thou he that comes, or look

we for another? ²⁰ And coming to him, the men said: John the Immerser has sent us to thee, saying: Art thou he that comes, or look we for another? ²¹ And in that very hour he cured many, of diseases and plagues, and evil spirits; and on many blind he bestowed sight. ²² And answering he said to them: Go, and report to John what ye saw and heard; that the blind receive sight, the lame walk, the lepers are cleansed, the deaf hear, the dead are raised, to the poor good tidings are published. ²³ And happy is he, whoever shall not be offended at me.

²⁴ And when the messengers of John had departed, he began to say to the multitudes concerning John: What went ye out into the wilderness to behold? A reed shaken by the wind? ²⁵ But what went ye out to see? A man clothed in soft raiment? Behold, they who are gorgeously appareled, and live delicately, are in kings' palaces. ²⁶ But what went ye out to see? A prophet? Yea, I say to you, and much more than a prophet. ²⁷ This is he, of whom it is written:

Behold, I send forth my messenger before thy face,
Who shall prepare thy way before thee.

²⁸ For I say to you, among those born of women, no one is a greater prophet than John; but he that is least in the kingdom of God is greater than he. ²⁹ And all the people, hearing it, and the publicans, justified God, having been immersed with John's immersion. ³⁰ But the Pharisees and the lawyers rejected the counsel of God toward themselves, not having been immersed by him.

³¹ To what then shall I liken the men of this generation? And to what are they like? ³² They are like to children sitting in the market, and calling to one another, saying: We piped to you, and ye danced not; we sang the lament to you, and ye wept not. ³³ For John the Immerser has come, neither eating bread nor drinking wine; and ye say: He has a demon. ³⁴ The Son of man has come eating and drinking; and ye say: Behold a glutton, and a wine-drinker, a friend of publicans and sinners. ³⁵ But wisdom was justified on the part of all her children.

CHAPTER VIII.

[36] And one of the Pharisees asked him to eat with him. And entering into the house of the Pharisee, he reclined at table. [37] And, behold, a woman who was a sinner in the city, learning that he is reclining at table in the house of the Pharisee, brought an alabaster box of ointment; [38] and standing behind at his feet weeping, began to wet his feet with tears, and wipe them with the hairs of her head, and kissed his feet, and anointed them with the ointment.

[39] And seeing it, the Pharisee who had bidden him spoke within himself, saying: This man, if he were a prophet, would know who and what sort of woman this is that touches him; for she is a sinner. [40] And Jesus answering said to him: Simon, I have somewhat to say to thee. And he says: Teacher, say on. [41] A certain money-lender had two debtors. The one owed five hundred denáries, and the other fifty. [42] And they having nothing to pay, he forgave them both. Which of them therefore, tell me, will love him most? [43] Simon answering said: I suppose he to whom he forgave most. And he said to him: Thou didst rightly judge. [44] And turning to the woman, he said to Simon: Seest thou this woman? I entered into thy house, thou gavest me no water for my feet; but she has wet my feet with tears, and wiped them with her hair. [45] Thou gavest me no kiss; but she, from the time I came in, ceased not to kiss my feet. [46] My head with oil thou didst not anoint; but she anointed my feet with ointment. [47] Wherefore I say to thee, her many sins are forgiven; for she loved much. But to whom little is forgiven, the same loves little. [48] And he said to her: Thy sins are forgiven. [49] And they who reclined with him began to say within themselves: Who is this that also forgives sins? [50] And he said to the woman: Thy faith has saved thee; go in peace.

VIII. AND it came to pass afterward, that he journeyed through every city and village, preaching, and publishing the good news of the kingdom of God; and with him

---

V. 41. Denáry, *about seven and a half pence sterling, or fifteen cents.*

the twelve, ²and certain women who had been healed of evil spirits and infirmities, Mary called the Magdalene, from whom had gone out seven demons, ³and Joanna wife of Chuza, Herod's steward, and Susanna, and many others, who ministered to them of their substance.

⁴And a great multitude coming together, of those also who came to him out of every city, he spoke by a parable: ⁵The sower went forth to sow his seed. And as he sowed, one fell by the way-side; and it was trodden down, and the fowls of the air devoured it. ⁶And another fell upon the rock; and springing up, it withered away, because it had no moisture. ⁷And another fell among the thorns; and the thorns sprang up with it, and choked it. ⁸And another fell into the good ground, and sprang up, and bore fruit a hundredfold.

And saying these things, he cried: He that has ears to hear, let him hear.

⁹And his disciples asked him, what this parable was. ¹⁰And he said: To you it is given to know the mysteries of the kingdom of God; but to the rest in parables, that seeing they may not see, and hearing they may not understand.

¹¹Now the parable is this: The seed is the word of God. ¹²Those by the way-side are they that hear; after that comes the Devil, and takes away the word from their heart, that they may not believe and be saved. ¹³Those on the rock are they who, when they hear, with joy receive the word; and these have no root, who for a while believe, and in time of temptation fall away. ¹⁴And that which fell among the thorns, these are they who have heard, and going forth are choked with the cares and riches and pleasures of life, and bring no fruit to perfection. ¹⁵But that in the good ground, these are they who, in an honest and good heart, having heard, hold fast the word, and bring forth fruit with patience.

¹⁶No one, having lighted a lamp, covers it with a vessel, or puts it under a bed; but puts it on a lamp-stand, that they who enter in may behold the light. ¹⁷For nothing is secret, that shall not be made manifest, nor hidden, that shall not be known and come abroad. ¹⁸Take heed therefore how ye hear.

CHAPTER VIII.

For whoever has, to him shall be given; and whoever has not, even what he seems to have shall be taken from him.

¹⁹ And his mother and his brothers came to him; and they could not come near him on account of the multitude. ²⁰ And it was told him, saying: Thy mother and thy brothers are standing without, desiring to see thee. ²¹ And he answering, said to them: My mother and my brothers are these, who hear and do the word of God.

²² And it came to pass on a certain day, that he went into a ship with his disciples. And he said to them: Let us go over to the other side of the lake. And they launched forth. ²³ And as they were sailing, he fell asleep. And there came down a storm of wind on the lake; and they began to be filled, and were in jeopardy. ²⁴ And coming to him, they awoke him, saying: Master, Master, we perish. And he, rising, rebuked the wind and the raging of the water; and they ceased, and there was a calm. ²⁵ And he said to them: Where is your faith? And they, fearing, wondered; saying one to another: Who then is this, that he commands even the winds and the water, and they obey him!

²⁶ And they sailed to the country of the Gerasenes, which is over against Galilee. ²⁷ And when he had gone forth upon the land, there met him a certain man out of the city, who had demons a long time, and wore no clothing, and abode not in a house, but in the tombs. ²⁸ And seeing Jesus, he cried out, and fell down before him, and with a loud voice said: What have I to do with thee, Jesus, Son of the most high God? I beseech thee, do not torment me. ²⁹ For he commanded the unclean spirit to come out from the man. For of a long time it had seized him, and he was bound, being secured with chains and fetters; and bursting the bands, he was driven by the demon into the deserts.

³⁰ And Jesus asked him, saying: What is thy name? And he said, Legion; because many demons had entered into him. ³¹ And he besought him that he would not command them to go away into the abyss. ³² And there was a herd of many swine feeding in the mountain; and they besought him that he

would permit them to enter into them. And he permitted them. ³³ And going out of the man, the demons entered into the swine; and the herd rushed down the steep into the lake, and were choked. ³⁴ And seeing what was done the herdsmen fled, and reported it in the city and in the country. ³⁵ And they went out to see what was done. And they came to Jesus, and found the man from whom the demons had gone out, sitting at the feet of Jesus, clothed and in his right mind; and they were afraid. ³⁶ They also who saw it reported to them how he that was possessed by demons was healed. ³⁷ And the whole multitude of the surrounding country of the Gerasenes besought him to depart from them; for they were seized with great fear.

And he, entering into the ship, returned. ³⁸ And the man, out of whom the demons had gone, besought him that he might be with him. But he sent him away, saying: ³⁹ Return into thy house, and relate how great things God did for thee. And he departed, and published through the whole city how great things Jesus did for him.

⁴⁰ And it came to pass, when Jesus returned, that the multitude received him; for they were all waiting for him. ⁴¹ And, behold, there came a man whose name was Jairus, and he was a ruler of the synagogue; and falling at the feet of Jesus, he besought him that he would come into his house; ⁴² for he had an only daughter, about twelve years of age, and she was dying. And as he went the multitudes thronged him.

⁴³ And a woman having a flow of blood twelve years, who had spent all her living on physicians, and could not be healed by any one, ⁴⁴ came up behind, and touched the fringe of his garment; and immediately her flow of blood ceased. ⁴⁵ And Jesus said: Who is it that touched me? And when all denied it, Peter and those with him said: Master, the multitudes throng thee and press thee, and sayest thou: Who is it that touched me? ⁴⁶ And Jesus said: Some one touched me; for I perceived that power has gone out from me.

⁴⁷ And the woman, seeing that she was not concealed, came trembling, and falling down before him, declared before all the

CHAPTER IX.

people for what cause she touched him, and how she was healed immediately. ⁴⁸ And he said to her: Daughter, thy faith has made thee whole; go in peace.

⁴⁹ While he was yet speaking, there comes one from the ruler of the synagogue's house, saying to him: Thy daughter is dead; trouble not the Teacher. ⁵⁰ But Jesus hearing it, answered him: Fear not; only believe, and she shall be restored.

⁵¹ And entering into the house, he suffered no one to go in with him, save Peter and James and John, and the father of the maiden, and the mother. ⁵² And all were weeping and bewailing her. And he said: Weep not; she is not dead, but is sleeping. ⁵³ And they laughed him to scorn, knowing that she was dead. ⁵⁴ And he, taking hold of her by the hand, called, saying: Maiden, arise. ⁵⁵ And her spirit returned, and she immediately arose; and he commanded that food should be given her. ⁵⁶ And her parents were astonished. But he charged them to tell no one what was done.

IX. And having called the twelve together, he gave them power and authority over all the demons, and to cure diseases. ² And he sent them to preach the kingdom of God, and to heal the sick. ³ And he said to them: Take nothing for the journey, neither staff, nor bag, nor bread, nor money, nor have two coats apiece. ⁴ And into whatever house ye enter, there abide, and thence depart. ⁵ And whoever will not receive you, when ye go out from that city, shake off even the dust from your feet for a testimony against them.

⁶ And going forth, they went through the villages, publishing the good news, and healing everywhere.

⁷ And Herod the tetrarch heard of all the things that were done. And he was perplexed, because it was said by some: John has risen from the dead; ⁸ and by some: Elijah has appeared; and by others: One of the old prophets has risen again. ⁹ And Herod said: John I beheaded; but who is this, of whom I hear such things? And he desired to see him.

¹⁰ And the apostles, returning, related to him all that they did. And taking them with him, he retired privately to a city

called Bethsaida. ¹¹ And the multitudes, when they knew it, followed him. And receiving them, he spoke to them concerning the kingdom of God, and healed those who had need of healing.

¹² And the day began to decline. And the twelve came, and said to him: Dismiss the multitude, that they may go into the villages around, and the fields, and lodge, and find food; for here we are in a desert place. ¹³ And he said to them: Do ye give them to eat. And they said: We have not more than five loaves and two fishes; except we should go and buy food for all this people. ¹⁴ For they were about five thousand men. And he said to his disciples: Make them lie down in companies of fifty. ¹⁵ And they did so, and made them all lie down. ¹⁶ And taking the five loaves and the two fishes, he looked up to heaven and blessed them, and broke, and gave to the disciples to set before the multitude. ¹⁷ And they ate, and were all filled. And there were taken up of fragments that remained to them twelve baskets.

¹⁸ And it came to pass, as he was alone praying, that his disciples were with him; and he asked them, saying: Who do the multitudes say that I am? ¹⁹ They answering said: John the Immerser; and others, Elijah; and others, that one of the old prophets has risen again. ²⁰ And he said to them: But who do ye say that I am? Peter answering said: The Christ of God. ²¹ And strictly charging them, he commanded them to say this to no one; ²² saying: The Son of man must suffer many things, and be rejected on the part of the elders and chief priests and scribes, and be killed, and rise on the third day.

²³ And he said to all: If any one will come after me, let him deny himself, and take up his cross daily, and follow me. ²⁴ For whoever will save his life shall lose it; and whoever may lose his life for my sake, the same shall save it ²⁵ For what is a man profited, when he has gained the whole world, and lost or forfeited himself? ²⁶ For whoever is ashamed of me and of my words, of him will the Son of man be ashamed, when he shall come in his glory, and in that of the Father and of the

CHAPTER IX.

holy angels. ²⁷ And I say to you of a truth, there are some of those standing here, who shall not taste of death, till they see the kingdom of God.

²⁸ And it came to pass, about eight days after these sayings, that he took with him Peter and John and James, and went up into the mountain to pray. ²⁹ And it came to pass, while he was praying, that the appearance of his countenance became changed, and his raiment white and glistening. ³⁰ And, behold, two men were talking with him, who were Moses and Elijah; ³¹ who appeared in glory, and spoke of his departure, which he was about to fulfill in Jerusalem.

³² But Peter and they who were with him were heavy with sleep ; and awaking, they saw his glory, and the two men that stood with him. ³³ And it came to pass, that, as they were departing from him, Peter said to Jesus: Master, it is good for us to be here ; and let us make three tents, one for thee, and one for Moses, and one for Elijah ; not knowing what he said. ³⁴ While he said this, there came a cloud, and overshadowed them ; and they feared as they entered into the cloud. ³⁵ And there came a voice out of the cloud, saying: This is my chosen Son ; hear ye him.

³⁶ And when the voice had come, Jesus was found alone. And they kept silent, and told no one in those days any of the things which they had seen.

³⁷ And it came to pass, on the next day, when they had come down from the mountain, that a great multitude met him. ³⁸ And, behold, a man from the multitude cried, saying: Teacher, I beseech thee, look upon my son ; for he is my only child. ³⁹ And, behold, a spirit takes him, and he suddenly cries out ; and it tears him with foaming, and hardly departs from him, bruising him. ⁴⁰ And I entreated thy disciples to cast him out ; and they could not.

⁴¹ And Jesus answering said : O faithless and perverse generation, how long shall I be with you, and bear with you? Bring hither thy son. ⁴² And while he was yet coming, the demon threw him down, and tore him. And Jesus rebuked the unclean spirit, and healed the child, and gave him back to

his father. ⁴³ And all were amazed at the mighty power of God.

But while all were wondering at all things which Jesus did, he said to his disciples: ⁴⁴ Do ye let these words sink into your ears, for the Son of man will be delivered into the hands of men. ⁴⁵ But they understood not this saying, and it was hidden from them, that they perceived it not; and they feared to ask him concerning that saying.

⁴⁶ And there arose in them the thought, which of them was greatest. ⁴⁷ And Jesus, perceiving the thought of their heart, took a child and placed it by him, ⁴⁸ and said to them: Whoever shall receive this child in my name, receives me; and whoever shall receive me, receives him who sent me; for he that is least among you all, the same is great.

⁴⁹ And John answering said: Master, we saw one casting out demons in thy name; and we forbade him, because he follows not with us. ⁵⁰ And Jesus said to him: Forbid him not; for he that is not against us is for us.

⁵¹ And it came to pass, when the days were being completed that he should be received up, he steadfastly set his face to go to Jerusalem. ⁵² And he sent messengers before his face; and they went and entered into a village of the Samaritans, to make ready for him. ⁵³ And they did not receive him, because his face was directed toward Jerusalem. ⁵⁴ And his disciples, James and John, seeing it, said: Lord, wilt thou that we command fire to come down from heaven, and consume them, as also Elijah did? ⁵⁵ And he turned, and rebuked them, and said: Ye know not of what spirit ye are. ⁵⁶ And they went to another village.

⁵⁷ And as they were going in the way, a certain one said to him: I will follow thee whithersoever thou goest. ⁵⁸ And Jesus said to him: The foxes have holes, and the birds of the air have nests; but the Son of man has not where to lay his head.

⁵⁹ And he said to another: Follow me. But he said: Lord,

V. 46. *Or*, there arose a dispute among them

V. 55. *Or*, Know ye not

CHAPTER X.

permit me first to go and bury my father. ⁶⁰ And he said to him: Let the dead bury their own dead; but do thou go and announce the kingdom of God.
⁶¹ And another also said; I will follow thee, Lord; but first permit me to bid farewell to those in my house. ⁶² And Jesus said to him: No one, having put his hand to the plow, and looking back, is fit for the kingdom of God.

X. AFTER these things the Lord appointed also seventy others, and sent them two and two before his face, into every city and place, whither he himself was about to come. ² And he said to them: The harvest indeed is great, but the laborers are few. Pray therefore the Lord of the harvest, that he will send forth laborers into his harvest ³ Go your ways; behold, I send you forth as lambs among wolves. ⁴ Carry neither purse, nor bag, nor sandals; and salute no one by the way. ⁵ And into whatever house ye enter, first say: Peace be to this house. ⁶ And if a son of peace be there, your peace shall rest upon it; and if not, it shall return to you. ⁷ And in that house remain, eating and drinking such things as they give; for the laborer is worthy of his hire. Go not from house to house. ⁸ And into whatever city ye enter and they receive you, eat what is set before you; ⁹ and heal the sick that are therein, and say to them: The kingdom of God has come nigh unto you. ¹⁰ But into whatever city ye enter and they receive you not, go out into the streets of the same, and say: ¹¹ Even the dust of your city that cleaves to our feet, we wipe off to you; yet know this, that the kingdom of God has come nigh. ¹² I say to you, that it will be more tolerable in that day for Sodom, than for that city.
¹³ Woe to thee, Chorazin! Woe to thee, Bethsaida! For if the miracles had been done in Tyre and Sidon, which were done in you, they would long ago have repented, sitting in sackcloth and ashes. ¹⁴ But it will be more tolerable for Tyre and Sidon in the judgment, than for you. ¹⁵ And thou, Caper-

---

V. 7. *Or*, as they have . V. 11. *Or*, against you

naum, that art exalted to heaven, shalt be brought down to the underworld. ¹⁶ He that hears you, hears me; and he that rejects you, rejects me; and he that rejects me, rejects him who sent me.

¹⁷ And the seventy returned with joy, saying: Lord, even the demons are subjected to us in thy name. ¹⁸ And he said to them: I beheld Satan fall as lightning from heaven. ¹⁹ Behold, I have given you power to tread on serpents and scorpions, and over all the power of the enemy; and nothing shall hurt you. ²⁰ But yet, rejoice not in this, that the spirits are subjected to you; but rejoice, that your names are written in heaven.

²¹ In that hour he rejoiced in spirit, and said: I thank thee, O Father, Lord of heaven and earth, that thou didst hide these things from the wise and discerning, and reveal them to babes; yea, O Father, that so it seemed good in thy sight. ²² All things were delivered to me by my Father; and no one knows who the Son is but the Father, and who the Father is but the Son, and he to whom the Son is pleased to reveal him.

²³ And turning to the disciples, he said privately: Happy are the eyes that behold what ye are beholding. ²⁴ For I say to you, that many prophets and kings desired to see what ye are beholding, and saw not, and to hear what ye are hearing, and heard not.

²⁵ And, behold, a certain lawyer stood up, tempting him, saying: Teacher, what shall I do to inherit eternal life? ²⁶ He said to him: What is written in the law? How readest thou? ²⁷ And he answering said: Thou shalt love the Lord thy God with all thy heart, and with all thy soul, and with all thy strength, and with all thy mind; and thy neighbor as thyself. ²⁸ And he said to him: Thou answeredst rightly. This do, and thou shalt live. ²⁹ But he, desiring to justify himself, said to Jesus: Who then is my neighbor?

³⁰ And Jesus answering said: A certain man was going down from Jerusalem to Jericho, and fell among robbers, who stripped him of his raiment, and wounded him, and departed,

CHAPTER XI.

leaving him half dead. ³¹ And by chance a certain priest was going down that way; and seeing him, he passed by on the other side. ³² And in like manner also a Levite, arriving at the place, came and saw, and passed by on the other side.

³³ And a certain Samaritan, as he was journeying, came where he was, and seeing him had compassion; ³⁴ and coming to him, bound up his wounds, pouring in oil and wine; and setting him on his own beast, he brought him to an inn, and took care of him. ³⁵ And on the morrow when he departed, he took out two denáries and gave to the host, and said: Take care of him; and whatever thou spendest more, when I come again, I will repay thee.

³⁶ Which now of these three, thinkest thou, was neighbor to him that fell among the robbers? ³⁷ And he said: He that had mercy on him. And Jesus said to him: Go, and do thou likewise.

³⁸ And it came to pass, as they were going, that he entered into a certain village; and a certain woman named Martha received him into her house. ³⁹ And she had a sister called Mary, who also sat at the feet of Jesus, and heard his word. ⁴⁰ But Martha was encumbered with much serving; and she came to him, and said: Lord, dost thou not care that my sister left me to serve alone? Bid her therefore that she help me. ⁴¹ And Jesus answering said to her: Martha, Martha, thou art anxious and troubled about many things. ⁴² But one thing is needful; and Mary chose the good part, which shall not be taken away from her.

XI. And it came to pass that, as he was in a certain place praying, when he ceased, one of his disciples said to him: Lord, teach us to pray, as also John taught his disciples. ² And he said to them: When ye pray, say; Father, hallowed be thy name. Thy kingdom come. ³ Give us day by day our daily bread. ⁴ And forgive us our sins; for we ourselves

---

V. 35. *Denáry, seven and a half pence sterling, or fifteen cents (one third more than the daily pay of a Roman soldier).*

V. 3. *Or, our needful bread*

forgive every one indebted to us. And bring us not into temptation.

⁵ And he said to them: Who of you shall have a friend, and shall go to him at midnight, and say to him: ⁶ Friend, lend me three loaves; for a friend of mine is come to me from a journey, and I have nothing to set before him; ⁷ and he from within shall answer and say, Trouble me not; the door is already shut, and my children with me are in bed; I can not rise and give thee? ⁸ I say to you, though he will not rise and give him because he is his friend, yet because of his importunity he will rise and give him as many as he needs. ⁹ I also say to you: Ask, and it shall be given you; seek, and ye shall find; knock, and it shall be opened to you. ¹⁰ For every one that asks receives; and he that seeks finds; and to him that knocks it shall be opened.

¹¹ And what father is there among you, of whom if his son ask bread, he will give him a stone; or a fish, will instead of a fish give him a serpent? ¹² Or if he shall ask an egg, will he give him a scorpion? ¹³ If ye then, being evil, know how to give good gifts to your children, how much more will your heavenly Father give the Holy Spirit to those who ask him?

¹⁴ And he was casting out a demon, and it was dumb. And it came to pass, when the demon was gone out, that the dumb man spoke; and the multitudes wondered. ¹⁵ But some of them said: He casts out the demons through Beelzebul, the prince of the demons. ¹⁶ And others, tempting, sought of him a sign from heaven. ¹⁷ But he, knowing their thoughts, said to them: Every kingdom divided against itself is brought to desolation, and a house divided against a house falls. ¹⁸ And if Satan also is divided against himself, how shall his kingdom stand? because ye say that I cast out the demons through Beelzebul. ¹⁹ And if I through Beelzebul cast out the demons, through whom do your sons cast them out? Therefore they shall be your judges. ²⁰ But if with the finger of God I cast out the demons, then is the kingdom of God come near to you.

V. 17. *Or*, and house falls upon house

CHAPTER XI.

²¹ When a strong man armed keeps his palace, his goods are in peace. ²² But when a stronger than he shall come upon him and overcome him, he takes away his whole armor, wherein he trusted, and divides his spoils.

²³ He that is not with me is against me; and he that gathers not with me scatters abroad.

²⁴ When the unclean spirit is gone out from the man, he goes through dry places, seeking rest; and not finding it, he says, I will return into my house whence I came out. ²⁵ And coming, he finds it swept and set in order. ²⁶ Then he goes, and takes with him seven other spirits more wicked than himself, and they enter in and dwell there; and the last state of that man becomes worse than the first.

²⁷ And it came to pass, as he was saying these things, that a certain woman lifting up her voice from the multitude, said to him: Happy the womb that bore thee, and breasts which thou didst suck! ²⁸ And he said: Yea, rather, Happy they who hear the word of God, and keep it!

²⁹ And the multitudes gathering more and more, he began to say: This generation is an evil generation. It seeks a sign; and no sign shall be given it, but the sign of Jonah. ³⁰ For as Jonah became a sign to the Ninevites, so shall also the Son of man be to this generation.

³¹ A queen of the south will rise up in the judgment with the men of this generation, and will condemn them; because she came from the utmost parts of the earth to hear the wisdom of Solomon; and, behold, a greater than Solomon is here. ³² Men of Nineveh will rise in the judgment with this generation, and will condemn it; because they repented at the preaching of Jonah; and behold, a greater than Jonah is here.

³³ No one, having lighted a lamp, puts it in a secret place, or under the bushel, but on the lamp-stand, that they who come in may see the light. ³⁴ The lamp of the body is thine eye. When thine eye is single, thy whole body also is light; but when it is evil, thy body also is dark. ³⁵ Take heed therefore,

---

V. 35. *Or*, whether the light that is in thee is darkness

lest the light that is in thee is darkness. ³⁶ If therefore thy whole body is light, having no part dark, it shall be all light as when the lamp, with its bright shining, gives thee light.

³⁷ And as he was speaking, a Pharisee asked him to dine with him; and he went in, and reclined at table. ³⁸ And the Pharisee, seeing it, wondered that he did not first immerse himself before dinner. ³⁹ And the Lord said to him: Now ye Pharisees cleanse the outside of the cup and the platter; but your inward part is full of rapacity and wickedness. ⁴⁰ Fools! Did not he, who made the outside, make the inside also? ⁴¹ But give that which ye have in alms; and, behold, all things are clean to you.

⁴² But woe to you, Pharisees! because ye pay tithe of mint and rue and every herb, and pass by judgment and the love of God. These ought ye to have done, and not leave those undone.

⁴³ Woe to you, Pharisees! because ye love the first seat in the synagogues, and the greetings in the markets.

⁴⁴ Woe to you! because ye are as tombs that appear not, and men walking over them know it not.

⁴⁵ And a certain one of the lawyers answering says to him: Teacher, in saying these things thou reproachest us also. ⁴⁶ And he said: Woe to you lawyers also! because ye load men with burdens grievous to be borne, and ye yourselves touch not the burdens with one of your fingers.

⁴⁷ Woe to you! because ye build the sepulchres of the prophets, and your fathers killed them. ⁴⁸ So then ye bear witness to and approve the deeds of your fathers; because they indeed killed them, and ye build their sepulchres. ⁴⁹ Therefore also said the wisdom of God: I will send them prophets and apostles, and some of them they will slay and persecute; ⁵⁰ that the blood of all the prophets, which was shed from the foundation of the world, may be required of this generation, ⁵¹ from the blood of Abel unto the blood of Zachariah, who

---

V. 41. *Or,* give that which is within in alms
V. 48. *In some ancient copies,* and ye build !

CHAPTER XII.

perished between the altar and the temple. Verily I say to you, it shall be required of this generation.
⁵² Woe to you lawyers! because ye took away the key of knowledge; ye entered not in yourselves, and those who were entering in ye hindered.
⁵³ And as he said these things to them, the scribes and the Pharisees began to urge him vehemently, and to provoke him to speak of many things; ⁵⁴ lying in wait for him, seeking to catch something out of his mouth, that they might accuse him.

XII. In the mean time, the multitude having gathered together in tens of thousands, so that they trod one upon another, he began first to say to his disciples: Beware of the leaven of the Pharisees, which is hypocrisy. ² For there is nothing covered, that shall not be revealed, nor hidden, that shall not be known. ³ Wherefore, whatever ye said in the darkness, shall be heard in the light; and what ye spoke in the ear in closets, shall be proclaimed on the house-tops.
⁴ And I say to you, my friends, be not afraid of those who kill the body, and after that have no more that they can do. ⁵ But I will warn you whom ye shall fear; fear him, who after he has killed has power to cast into hell; yea, I say to you, fear him. ⁶ Are not five sparrows sold for two pence? And not one of them is forgotten before God. ⁷ But even the hairs of your head are all numbered. Fear not; ye are of more value than many sparrows.
⁸ And I say to you: Every one that shall acknowledge me before men, him will the Son of man also acknowledge before the angels of God; ⁹ but he that denied me before men shall be denied before the angels of God. ¹⁰ And every one that shall speak a word against the Son of man, it will be forgiven him; but to him that blasphemes against the Holy Spirit, it shall not be forgiven.
¹¹ And when they bring you to the synagogues, and magistrates, and authorities, take not thought how or what ye shall

---

V. 53 *Gr.* to answer off-hand concerning many things

answer, or what ye shall say. ¹² For the Holy Spirit will teach you in that very hour what ye ought to say.

¹³ And a certain one of the multitude said to him: Teacher, speak to my brother, that he divide the inheritance with me. ¹⁴ And he said to him: Man, who made me a judge or a divider over you? ¹⁵ And he said to them: Take heed, and beware of all covetousness; because a man's life consists not in the abundance of his possessions.

¹⁶ And he spoke a parable to them, saying: The ground of a certain rich man brought forth plentifully. ¹⁷ And he thought within himself, saying: What shall I do, because I have not where to store my fruits? ¹⁸ And he said: This will I do; I will pull down my barns, and will build greater; and there I will store all my fruits and my goods. ¹⁹ And I will say to my soul: Soul, thou hast many goods laid up for many years; take thine ease, eat, drink, be merry. ²⁰ But God said to him: Fool! this night thy soul shall be required of thee; and whose shall those things be, which thou didst provide? ²¹ So is he that lays up treasure for himself, and is not rich toward God.

²² And he said to his disciples: Therefore I say to you, take not thought for the life, what ye shall eat, nor for the body, what ye shall put on. ²³ The life is more than food, and the body than raiment. ²⁴ Consider the ravens, that they sow not nor reap; which have neither storehouse nor barn; and God feeds them. How much better are ye than the birds! ²⁵ And which of you by taking thought can add a cubit to his stature? ²⁶ If therefore ye can not do even that which is least, why take ye thought for the rest?

²⁷ Consider the lilies, how they grow; they toil not, nor spin; and I say to you, that even Solomon, in all his glory, was not arrayed like one of these. ²⁸ And if God so clothes the grass, which to-day is in the field, and to-morrow is cast into the oven, how much more you, ye of little faith? ²⁹ And ye, seek not what ye shall eat, or what ye shall drink, and be not of a

---

V. 25. *Or,* to his age

CHAPTER XII.

doubtful mind. ³⁰ For all these things do the nations of the world seek after; and your Father knows that ye have need of these. ³¹ But seek his kingdom, and these things shall be added to you.

³² Fear not, little flock; for it is your Father's good pleasure to give you the kingdom. ³³ Sell what ye have, and give alms; provide yourselves purses that wax not old, a treasure unfailing in the heavens, where a thief approaches not, nor moth corrupts. ³⁴ For where your treasure is, there will your heart be also.

³⁵ Let your loins be girded about, and your lamps burning; ³⁶ and ye like men waiting for their lord, when he shall return from the wedding; that, when he comes and knocks, they may open to him immediately. ³⁷ Happy those servants, whom their lord when he comes shall find watching! Verily I say to you, that he will gird himself, and make them recline at table, and will come forth and serve them. ³⁸ And if he shall come in the second watch, or in the third watch, and find it so, happy are those servants. ³⁹ And this know, that if the master of the house had known at what hour the thief is coming, he would have watched, and not have suffered his house to be broken through. ⁴⁰ Be ye also ready; for at an hour when ye think not, the Son of man comes.

⁴¹ And Peter said to him: Lord, speakest thou this parable to us, or also to all? ⁴² And the Lord said: Who then is the faithful, the wise steward, whom his lord will set over his household, to give the portion of food in due season? ⁴³ Happy that servant, whom his lord when he comes shall find so doing! ⁴⁴ Of a truth I say to you, that he will make him ruler over all his goods.

⁴⁵ But if that servant say in his heart: My lord delays his coming; and shall begin to beat the men-servants and maid-servants, and to eat and drink, and to be drunken; ⁴⁶ the lord of that servant will come in a day when he looks not for it, and in an hour when he is not aware, and will cut him asunder, and appoint his portion with the faithless.

⁴⁷ And that servant, who knew his lord's will, and prepared

not, nor did according to his will, shall be beaten with many stripes; ⁴⁸ but he that knew not, and did things worthy of stripes, shall be beaten with few. For to whomsoever much was given, of him much will be required; and to whom they committed much, of him they will require the more.

⁴⁹ I came to send fire upon the earth; and what will I, if it is already kindled? ⁵⁰ But I have an immersion to undergo; and how am I straitened till it be accomplished! ⁵¹ Suppose ye that I came to give peace in the earth? I tell you, nay; but only division. ⁵² For from this time forth, five in one house will be divided, three against two, and two against three. ⁵³ They will be divided, father against son, and son against father; mother against the daughter, and daughter against the mother; mother-in-law against her daughter-in-law, and daughter-in-law against the mother-in-law.

⁵⁴ And he said also to the multitudes: When ye see the cloud rising from the west, straightway ye say: A shower is coming; and so it comes to pass. ⁵⁵ And when ye see a south wind blowing, ye say: There will be heat; and it comes to pass. ⁵⁶ Hypocrites! Ye know how to judge of the face of the earth and the sky; but how is it that ye know not how to judge of this time? ⁵⁷ And why even of yourselves do ye not judge what is right? ⁵⁸ For when thou art going with thine adversary to the magistrate, on the way give diligence that thou mayest be delivered from him; lest he drag thee to the judge, and the judge deliver thee to the exactor, and the exactor cast thee into prison. ⁵⁹ I say to thee, thou shalt not depart thence, till thou hast paid the very last mite.

XIII. There were present at that season some who brought him word concerning the Galilæans, whose blood Pilate mingled with their sacrifices. ² And answering he said to them: Suppose ye that these Galilæans were sinners above all the Galilæans, because they have suffered such things? ³ I tell you, nay; but, except ye repent, ye shall all

---

V. 49. *Or,* and how I would it were already kindled!

CHAPTER XIII.

in like manner perish. ⁴ Or those eighteen, on whom the tower in Siloam fell, and slew them, suppose ye that they were sinners above all the men who dwell in Jerusalem? ⁵ I tell you, nay; but, except ye repent, ye shall all in like manner perish.

⁶ He spoke also this parable: A certain man had a fig-tree planted in his vineyard; and he came seeking fruit thereon, and found none. ⁷ And he said to the vine-dresser: Behold, three years I come seeking fruit on this fig-tree, and find none. Cut it down; why does it also encumber the ground? ⁸ And he answering says to him: Lord, let it alone this year also, till I shall dig about it, and cast in manure. ⁹ And if it bear fruit —; and if not, hereafter thou shalt cut it down.

¹⁰ And he was teaching in one of the synagogues on the sabbath. ¹¹ And, behold, there was a woman who had a spirit of infirmity eighteen years, and was bowed together, and wholly unable to raise herself up. ¹² And Jesus seeing her, called her to him, and said to her: Woman, thou art loosed from thine infirmity. ¹³ And he laid his hands on her; and immediately she was made straight, and glorified God. ¹⁴ And the ruler of the synagogue answering (being indignant because Jesus healed on the sabbath), said to the multitude: There are six days in which it is proper to work; in them therefore come and be healed, and not on the sabbath. ¹⁵ And the Lord answered him, and said: Hypocrites! Does not each of you on the sabbath loose his ox or ass from the manger, and lead him away to water him? ¹⁶ And ought not this woman, being a daughter of Abraham, whom Satan bound, lo, eighteen years, to be loosed from this bond on the sabbath? ¹⁷ And as he said these things, all his adversaries were ashamed; and all the multitude rejoiced for all the glorious things that were done by him.

¹⁸ He said therefore: To what is the kingdom of God like? And to what shall I liken it? ¹⁹ It is like to a grain of mustard, which a man took, and cast into his garden; and it grew,

---

V. 7. *Or*, impoverish the ground   V. 9. *Compare Mark* vii., 11.

and became a great tree, and the birds of the air lodged in its branches.

²⁰ And again he said: To what shall I liken the kingdom of God? ²¹ It is like to leaven, which a woman took and hid in three measures of meal, till the whole was leavened.

²² And he went through cities and villages, teaching, and journeying toward Jerusalem.

²³ And a certain one said to him: Lord, are there few that are saved? ²⁴ And he said to them: Strive to enter in through the strait gate; for many, I say to you, will seek to enter in, and will not be able. ²⁵ When once the master of the house has risen and shut the door, and ye begin to stand without, and to knock at the door, saying, Lord, open to us, and he answering shall say to you, I know you not whence ye are; ²⁶ then will ye begin to say, We ate and drank in thy presence, and thou didst teach in our streets. ²⁷ And he will say, I tell you, I know not whence ye are; depart from me, all workers of unrighteousness. ²⁸ There will be the weeping, and the gnashing of teeth, when ye shall see Abraham, and Isaac, and Jacob, and all the prophets, in the kingdom of God, and yourselves thrust out. ²⁹ And they will come from east and west, and from north and south, and will recline at table in the kingdom of God. ³⁰ And, behold, there are last who will be first, and there are first who will be last.

³¹ On that day there came certain Pharisees, saying to him: Depart, and go hence; for Herod desires to kill thee. ³² And he said to them: Go, tell that fox, Behold, I cast out demons and perform cures to-day and to-morrow, and the third day I am perfected. ³³ But yet, I must go to-day, and to-morrow, and the day following; because it may not be that a prophet perish out of Jerusalem.

³⁴ Jerusalem! Jerusalem! that kills the prophets, and stones those sent to her; how often would I have gathered thy children together, as a hen her brood under her wings, and ye would not! ³⁵ Behold, your house is left to you desolate. And I say to you: Ye shall not see me, until the time come when ye shall say, Blessed is he that comes in the name of the Lord.

CHAPTER XIV.

XIV. And it came to pass, as he went into the house of one of the chief of the Pharisees to eat bread on the sabbath, that they watched him. ² And, behold, there was a certain man before him who had the dropsy. ³ And Jesus answering spoke to the lawyers and Pharisees, saying: Is it lawful to heal on the sabbath, or not? And they were silent. ⁴ And taking hold of him, he healed him, and let him go. ⁵ And to them he said: Who is there of you, whose ox or ass shall fall into a pit, and he will not straightway draw him up on the sabbath day? ⁶ And they could not answer him again to these things.

⁷ And he spoke a parable to those who were bidden, when he marked how they chose out the first places; saying to them: ⁸ When thou art bidden by any one to a wedding, recline not in the first place at table, lest one more honorable than thou may have been bidden by him; ⁹ and he that bade thee and him shall come and say to thee, Give place to this man; and then thou shalt begin with shame to take the lowest place. ¹⁰ But when thou art bidden, go and recline in the lowest place; that when he that bade thee comes, he may say to thee, Friend, go up higher. Then shalt thou have honor in the presence of those who recline at table with thee. ¹¹ For every one that exalts himself shall be humbled; and he that humbles himself shall be exalted.

¹² And he said also to him who bade him: When thou makest a dinner or a supper, call not thy friends, nor thy brothers, nor thy kinsmen, nor rich neighbors; lest they also bid thee again, and a recompense be made thee. ¹³ But when thou makest a feast, call the poor, the maimed, the lame, the blind. ¹⁴ And happy shalt thou be, because they can not recompense thee; for thou shalt be recompensed at the resurrection of the righteous.

¹⁵ And a certain one of those who reclined at table with him, hearing these things, said to him: Happy is he, who shall eat

---

V. 5. *In the oldest copies:* whose son, or ox

bread in the kingdom of God! ¹⁶ And he said to him: A certain man made a great supper, and bade many. ¹⁷ And he sent his servant, at the hour of the supper, to say to those who were bidden: Come, for all things are now ready. ¹⁸ And they all, with one mind, began to excuse themselves. The first said to him: I bought a piece of ground, and I must needs go out and see it; I pray thee let me be excused. ¹⁹ And another said: I bought five yoke of oxen, and I am going to make trial of them; I pray thee let me be excused. ²⁰ And another said: I married a wife; and therefore I can not come.

²¹ And the servant came, and reported these things to his lord. Then the master of the house, being angry, said to his servant: Go out quickly into the streets and lanes of the city, and bring in hither the poor, and maimed, and lame, and blind. ²² And the servant said: Lord, it is done as thou didst command, and yet there is room. ²³ And the Lord said to the servant: Go out into the highways and hedges, and compel them to come in, that my house may be filled; ²⁴ for I say to you, that none of those men who were bidden shall taste of my supper.

²⁵ And great multitudes were going with him; and turning, he said to them: ²⁶ If any one comes to me, and hates not his father, and mother, and wife, and children, and brothers, and sisters, and even his own life besides, he can not be my disciple. ²⁷ And whoever does not bear his cross, and come after me, can not be my disciple. ²⁸ For who of you, intending to build a tower, does not first sit down, and count the cost, whether he has sufficient to finish it? ²⁹ Lest haply, when he has laid a foundation, and is not able to finish, all that behold begin to mock him, ³⁰ saying: This man began to build, and was not able to finish. ³¹ Or what king, going to make war against another king, does not first sit down and consult, whether he is able, with ten thousand, to meet him who comes against him with twenty thousand? ³² Else, while he is yet a great way off, he sends an embassy, and desires conditions of peace.

V. 18. *Or*, they all, at once, began   V. 23. *Or*, and constrain them

CHAPTER XV.

[33] So then, whoever of you forsakes not all that he has can not be my disciple. [34] Salt therefore is good; but if even the salt has become tasteless, wherewith shall it be seasoned? [35] It is fit neither for the land, nor for the dunghill; they cast it out. He that has ears to hear, let him hear.

XV. And there were drawing near to him all the publicans and the sinners to hear him. [2] And the Pharisees and the scribes murmured, saying: This man receives sinners, and eats with them.

[3] And he spoke this parable to them, saying: [4] What man of you, having a hundred sheep, and having lost one of them, does not leave the ninety and nine in the wilderness, and go after that which is lost, until he finds it? [5] And having found it, he lays it on his shoulders, rejoicing. [6] And coming home, he calls together his friends and neighbors, saying to them: Rejoice with me; because I found my sheep which was lost. [7] I say to you, that so there will be joy in heaven over one sinner that repents, more than over ninety and nine just persons, who have no need of repentance.

[8] Or what woman having ten pieces of silver, if she lose one piece, does not light a lamp, and sweep the house, and seek carefully till she finds it? [9] And having found it, she calls her friends and neighbors together, saying: Rejoice with me; because I found the piece which I lost. [10] So, I say to you, there is joy in the presence of the angels of God over one sinner that repents.

[11] And he said: A certain man had two sons. [12] And the younger of them said to his father: Father, give me the portion of the property that falls to me. And he divided to them his living. [13] And not many days after, the younger son gathered all together, and went abroad into a far country, and there wasted his substance in riotous living. [14] And when he had spent all, there arose a grievous famine in that country; and he began to be in want. [15] And he went and joined himself to one of the citizens of that country; and he sent him into his fields to feed swine. [16] And he would fain have fill-

ed his belly with the husks which the swine ate; and no one gave to him. ¹⁷ And coming to himself, he said: How many hired servants of my father have bread enough and to spare, and I perish here with hunger! ¹⁸ I will arise and go to my father, and will say to him: Father, I sinned against heaven, and before thee. ¹⁹ I am no longer worthy to be called thy son; make me as one of thy hired servants.

²⁰ And he arose, and came to his father. But when he was yet a great way off, his father saw him and had compassion, and ran and fell on his neck, and kissed him. ²¹ And the son said to him: Father, I sinned against heaven, and before thee; I am no longer worthy to be called thy son. ²² But the father said to his servants: Bring forth a robe, the best, and put it on him; and put a ring on his hand, and sandals on his feet; ²³ and bring the fatted calf; and kill it; and let us eat and be merry. ²⁴ Because this my son was dead and is alive again, was lost and is found. And they began to be merry.

²⁵ Now his elder son was in the field. And as he came, and drew near to the house, he heard music and dancing. ²⁶ And calling to him one of the servants, he inquired what these things meant. ²⁷ And he said to him: Thy brother is come; and thy father killed the fatted calf, because he received him back, safe and sound. ²⁸ And he was angry, and would not go in; and his father came out, and entreated him. ²⁹ And he answering said to his father: Lo, so many years do I serve thee, and never transgressed thy command; and to me thou never gavest a kid, that I might make merry with my friends. ³⁰ But when this thy son came, who devoured thy living with harlots, thou didst kill for him the fatted calf. ³¹ And he said to him: Child, thou art ever with me, and all that I have is thine. ³² It was meet that we should make merry, and be glad; because this thy brother was dead and is alive again; and was lost, and is found.

XVI. And he said also to the disciples: There was a certain rich man, who had a steward; and the same was accused to him as wasting his goods. ² And having called

CHAPTER XVI.

him, he said to him: What is this that I hear of thee? Give account of thy stewardship; for thou canst be no longer steward. ³ And the steward said within himself: What shall I do? for my master takes away from me the stewardship. I am not able to dig; to beg I am ashamed. ⁴ I am resolved what to do, that, when I am put out of the stewardship, they may receive me into their houses. ⁵ And having called to him each one of his master's debtors, he said to the first: How much owest thou to my master? ⁶ And he said: A hundred measures of oil. And he said to him: Take thy bill, and sit down quickly, and write fifty. ⁷ Then he said to another: And how much owest thou? And he said: A hundred measures of wheat. And he said to him: Take thy bill, and write fourscore. ⁸ And the master commended the unjust steward, because he had done wisely; because the sons of this world are, in their generation, wiser than the sons of light. ⁹ And I say to you: Make to yourselves friends of the mammon of unrighteousness; that, when it fails, they may receive you into the everlasting habitations. ¹⁰ He that is faithful in that which is least is faithful also in much; and he that is unjust in the least is unjust also in much. ¹¹ If therefore ye were not faithful in the unrighteous mammon, who will entrust to you the true riches? ¹² And if ye were not faithful in that which is another's, who will give to you your own? ¹³ No servant can serve two masters; for either he will hate the one, and love the other, or he will hold to one, and despise the other. Ye can not serve God and Mammon.

¹⁴ And the Pharisees also, who were covetous, heard all these things; and they derided him. ¹⁵ And he said to them: Ye are they who justify themselves before men; but God knows your hearts; for that which is highly esteemed among men is abomination before God.

¹⁶ The law and the prophets were until John; from that time the good news of the kingdom of God is published, and every man presses into it. ¹⁷ And it is easier that heaven and earth should pass away, than that one tittle of the law should fail.

¹⁸ Every one who puts away his wife, and marries another, commits adultery; and he who marries her when put away from a husband commits adultery.

¹⁹ There was a certain rich man, who was clothed in purple and fine linen, and fared sumptuously every day. ²⁰ And there was a certain beggar named Lazarus, who was laid at his gate, full of sores, ²¹ and desiring to be fed with the crumbs that fell from the rich man's table. Moreover the dogs came and licked his sores. ²² And it came to pass, that the beggar died; and he was borne away by the angels into Abraham's bosom. The rich man also died, and was buried; ²³ and in the underworld, lifting up his eyes, being in torments, he sees Abraham afar off, and Lazarus in his bosom. ²⁴ And he cried and said: Father Abraham, have mercy on me, and send Lazarus, that he may dip the tip of his finger in water, and cool my tongue; for I am tormented in this flame. ²⁵ But Abraham said: Child, remember that in thy lifetime thou receivedst thy good things in full, and Lazarus in like manner his evil things; but now here, he is comforted and thou art tormented. ²⁶ And besides all this, between us and you a great gulf is fixed; that they who would pass from hence to you may not be able, nor those from thence pass over to us. ²⁷ And he said: I pray thee therefore, father, that thou wouldst send him to my father's house. ²⁸ For I have five brothers; that he may testify to them, that they may not also come into this place of torment. ²⁹ Abraham says to him: They have Moses and the prophets; let them hear them. ³⁰ And he said: Nay, father Abraham; but if one should go to them from the dead, they will repent. ³¹ And he said to him: If they hear not Moses and the prophets, neither will they be persuaded, though one should rise from the dead.

XVII.

And he said to his disciples: It is impossible that causes of offense should not come; but woe to him through whom they come! ² It were better for him that a millstone were placed about his neck, and he were thrown into the sea, than that he should cause one of these little ones to offend.

CHAPTER XVII.

³ Take heed to yourselves. If thy brother sin, rebuke him; and if he repent, forgive him. ⁴ And if he sin against thee seven times in the day, and seven times turn to thee saying, I repent, thou shalt forgive him.

⁵ And the apostles said to the Lord: Increase our faith. ⁶ And the Lord said: If ye had faith as a grain of mustard, ye would say to this sycamine-tree, Be thou plucked up by the root, and planted in the sea; and it would have obeyed you.

⁷ And who of you, having a servant plowing, or feeding cattle, will say to him immediately, when he has come in from the field, Come and recline at table; ⁸ and will not rather say to him, Make ready wherewith I may sup, and gird thyself and serve me, till I have eaten and drunken, and afterward thou shalt eat and drink? ⁹ Does he thank that servant, because he did the things that were commanded? I think not. ¹⁰ So also ye, when ye shall have done all the things that were commanded you, say, We are unprofitable servants; we have done that which was our duty to do.

¹¹ And it came to pass, as he was going to Jerusalem, that he went through the midst of Samaria and Galilee. ¹² And as he was entering into a certain village, there met him ten leprous men, who stood afar off. ¹³ And they lifted up their voice, saying: Jesus, Master, have mercy on us. ¹⁴ And seeing it, he said to them: Go, show yourselves to the priests. And it came to pass that, as they went, they were cleansed. ¹⁵ And one of them, seeing that he was healed, turned back, with a loud voice glorifying God, ¹⁶ and fell down on his face at his feet, giving thanks to him; and he was a Samaritan. ¹⁷ And Jesus answering said: Were not the ten cleansed? And where are the nine? ¹⁸ Were none found returning to give glory to God, except this stranger? ¹⁹ And he said to him: Arise, and go; thy faith has made thee whole.

²⁰ And being asked by the Pharisees, when the kingdom of God would come, he answered them and said: The kingdom of God comes not with observation; ²¹ nor shall they say, Lo

---

V. 21. *Or*, is among you

here! or, Lo there! for, behold, the kingdom of God is within you. ²² And he said to the disciples: Days will come, when ye will desire to see one of the days of the Son of man, and ye will not see it. ²³ And they will say to you, See here; or, See there; go not away, and follow not. ²⁴ For as the lightning, that lightens out of the one part under heaven, shines unto the other part under heaven, so will the Son of man be in his day. ²⁵ But first he must suffer many things, and be rejected on the part of this generation.

²⁶ And as it was in the days of Noah, so will it be also in the days of the Son of man. ²⁷ They ate, they drank, they married, they were given in marriage, until the day that Noah entered into the ark, and the flood came and destroyed all. ²⁸ In like manner also as it was in the days of Lot; they ate, they drank, they bought, they sold, they planted, they builded; ²⁹ but the same day that Lot went out from Sodom, it rained fire and brimstone from heaven, and destroyed all. ³⁰ After the same manner will it be, in the day when the Son of man is revealed.

³¹ In that day, he who shall be on the house-top, and his goods in the house, let him not come down to take them away; and he that is in the field, let him likewise not turn back. ³² Remember Lot's wife. ³³ Whoever shall seek to save his life shall lose it; and whoever may lose his life shall preserve it.

³⁴ I say to you, in that night there will be two men in one bed; one will be taken, and the other will be left. ³⁵ Two women will be grinding together; one will be taken, and the other left. ³⁷ And they answering say to him: Where, Lord? And he said to them: Where the body is, there also will the eagles be gathered together.

XVIII. And he spoke also a parable to them, to the end that they ought always to pray, and not to faint; ² saying: There was in a certain city a certain judge, who

---

V. 36 *belongs in Matt.* xxiv., 40; *it is omitted here in the oldest copies.*

CHAPTER XVIII.

feared not God, nor regarded man. ³ And there was a widow in that city; and she came to him, saying: Avenge me of my adversary. ⁴ And he would not for a while; but afterward he said within himself: Though I fear not God, nor regard man, ⁵ yet because this widow troubles me, I will avenge her, lest continually coming she weary me.

⁶ And the Lord said: Hear what the unjust judge says. ⁷ And will not God avenge his chosen, who cry to him day and night, though he is long suffering in respect to them? ⁸ I say to you, that he will avenge them speedily. But yet, when the Son of man comes, will he find faith on the earth?

⁹ And he spoke this parable to some who trust in themselves that they are righteous, and despise others. ¹⁰ Two men went up into the temple to pray; one a Pharisee, and the other a publican. ¹¹ The Pharisee stood, and prayed thus with himself: God, I thank thee, that I am not as other men, extortioners, unjust, adulterers, or even as this publican. ¹² I fast twice in the week; I give tithes of all that I possess. ¹³ And the publican, standing afar off, would not even lift up his eyes to heaven, but smote upon his breast, saying: God be merciful to me, the sinner. ¹⁴ I say to you, this man went down to his house justified, rather than the other. For every one that exalts himself shall be humbled; and he that humbles himself shall be exalted.

¹⁵ And they brought to him also infants, that he might touch them; and the disciples seeing it rebuked them. ¹⁶ But Jesus calling them to him, said: Suffer the little children to come to me, and forbid them not; for to such belongs the kingdom of God. ¹⁷ Verily I say to you, whoever shall not receive the kingdom of God as a little child, shall not enter therein.

¹⁸ And a certain ruler asked him, saying: Good Teacher, what shall I do to inherit eternal life? ¹⁹ And Jesus said to him: Why dost thou call me good? None is good save one, God. ²⁰ Thou knowest the commandments: Do not commit adultery, Do not kill, Do not steal, Do

---

V. 12. *Or*, of all that I gain

not bear false witness, Honor thy father and thy mother. ²¹ And he said: All these I kept from my youth. ²² And Jesus hearing it said to him: Yet lackest thou one thing; sell all that thou hast, and distribute to the poor, and thou shalt have treasure in heaven; and come, follow me. ²³ And hearing this, he became very sorrowful; for he was exceedingly rich. ²⁴ And Jesus seeing him become very sorrowful, said: How hardly shall they that have riches enter into the kingdom of God! ²⁵ For it is easier for a camel to go through the eye of a needle, than for a rich man to enter into the kingdom of God. ²⁶ And they who heard it said: And who can be saved? ²⁷ And he said: The things that are impossible with men are possible with God.

²⁸ And Peter said: Lo, we forsook all, and followed thee. ²⁹ And he said to them: Verily I say to you, there is no one that forsook house, or parents, or brothers, or wife, or children, for the sake of the kingdom of God, ³⁰ who shall not receive manifold more in this present time, and in the world to come life everlasting.

³¹ And taking with him the twelve, he said to them: Behold, we are going up to Jerusalem, and all the things written by the prophets for the Son of man shall be accomplished. ³² For he will be delivered to the Gentiles, and will be mocked, and insulted, and spit upon, ³³ and they will scourge him, and put him to death; and on the third day he will rise again. ³⁴ And they understood none of these things; and this saying was hidden from them, and they knew not the things that were said.

³⁵ And it came to pass, that as he came near to Jericho, a certain blind man was sitting by the way-side, begging. ³⁶ And hearing a multitude passing by, he inquired what this was. ³⁷ And they told him, that Jesus of Nazareth is passing by. ³⁸ And he called aloud, saying: Jesus, Son of David, have mercy on me. ³⁹ And they who went before rebuked him, that he should hold his peace. But he cried much the more: Son of David, have mercy on me. ⁴⁰ And Jesus stood still, and commanded him to be brought to him. And when he was

CHAPTER XIX.

come near, he asked him, ⁴¹saying: What wilt thou that I shall do to thee? And he said: Lord, that I may receive sight. ⁴²And Jesus said to him: Receive sight; thy faith has made thee whole. ⁴³And immediately he received sight, and followed him, glorifying God. And all the people, seeing it, gave praise to God.

XIX. And having entered in, he was passing through Jericho. ²And behold, there was a man named Zaccheus, and he was a chief publican; and this man was rich. ³And he sought to see Jesus, who he was; and he could not on account of the multitude, because he was small in stature. ⁴And running before, he climbed up into a sycamore-tree to see him; because by that way he was to pass through. ⁵And Jesus, when he came to the place, looked up and saw him, and said to him: Zaccheus, make haste and come down; for to-day I must abide at thy house. ⁶And he made haste, and came down, and received him joyfully. ⁷And seeing it, they all murmured, saying that he went in to be a guest with a sinner.

⁸And Zaccheus stood up, and said to the Lord: Behold, Lord, the half of my goods I give to the poor; and if I took aught from any one by false accusation, I restore fourfold. ⁹And Jesus said to him: This day is salvation come to this house, inasmuch as he also is a son of Abraham. ¹⁰For the Son of man came to seek and to save that which was lost.

¹¹And as they were hearing these things, he added and spoke a parable, because he was nigh to Jerusalem, and because they thought that the kingdom of God would immediately appear. ¹²He said therefore: A certain nobleman went into a far country to receive for himself a kingdom, and to return. ¹³And having called his ten servants, he gave them ten pounds, and said to them: Traffic, till I come.

¹⁴But his citizens hated him, and sent an embassy after him, saying: We will not have this man to reign over us.

¹⁵And it came to pass, when he had returned, having received the kingdom, that he commanded these servants to be called to him, to whom he gave the money, that he might

know what each gained by trading. ¹⁶ And the first came, saying: Lord, thy pound gained ten pounds. ¹⁷ And he said to him: Well done, good servant; because thou wast faithful in a very little, have thou authority over ten cities. ¹⁸ And the second came, saying: Lord, thy pound made five pounds. ¹⁹ And he said also to this man: And be thou over five cities. ²⁰ And another came, saying: Lord, behold thy pound, which I kept laid up in a napkin. ²¹ For I feared thee, because thou art an austere man; thou takest up what thou layedst not down, and reapest what thou didst not sow. ²² And he says to him: Out of thy mouth will I judge thee, wicked servant. Thou knewest that I was an austere man, taking up what I laid not down, and reaping what I did not sow? ²³ Why then didst thou not put my money into the bank? and I, at my coming, should have required it with interest. ²⁴ And he said to those standing by: Take from him the pound, and give it to him that has the ten pounds. ²⁵ And they said to him: Lord, he has ten pounds. ²⁶ For I say to you, that to every one that has shall be given; and from him that has not, even what he has shall be taken away.

²⁷ But those my enemies, who would not that I should reign over them, bring hither, and slay them before me.

²⁸ And having spoken these things, he went before, going up to Jerusalem. ²⁹ And it came to pass, as he drew near to Bethphage and Bethany, at the mount called Olivet, that he sent forth two of his disciples, ³⁰ saying: Go into the opposite village, in which as ye are entering ye will find a colt tied, whereon no man ever sat; loose and bring him. ³¹ And if any one ask you, why do ye loose him? thus shall ye say to him: Because the Lord has need of him. ³² And they that were sent forth departed, and found even as he said to them. ³³ And as they were loosing the colt, its owners said to them: Why loose ye the colt? ³⁴ And they said: The Lord has need of him. ³⁵ And they brought him to Jesus; and having cast their garments upon the colt, they set Jesus thereon. ³⁶ And as he went, they spread their garments in the way. ³⁷ And as he was drawing near, just at the descent of the mount of the

CHAPTER XX.

Olives, the whole multitude of the disciples began to rejoice, and praise God with a loud voice for all the miracles which they saw; ³⁸ saying: Blessed be the King who comes in the name of the Lord! Peace in heaven, and glory in the highest!
³⁹ And some of the Pharisees from the multitude said to him: Teacher, rebuke thy disciples. ⁴⁰ And answering he said to them: I tell you that if these shall hold their peace, the stones will cry out.

⁴¹ And when he came near, as he saw the city, he wept over it, ⁴² saying: If even thou hadst known, at least in this thy day, the things that belong to thy peace! But now they are hidden from thine eyes. ⁴³ For days will come upon thee, that thine enemies will cast up a mound about thee, and compass thee round, and shut thee in on every side, ⁴⁴ and will level thee with the ground, and thy children within thee, and will not leave in thee one stone upon another; because thou knewest not the time of thy visitation.

⁴⁵ And entering into the temple, he began to cast out those who sold; ⁴⁶ saying to them: It is written, A n d m y h o u s e s h a l l b e a h o u s e o f p r a y e r; but ye made it a den of robbers.

⁴⁷ And he was teaching daily in the temple; and the chief priests and the scribes and the chief of the people were seeking to destroy him, ⁴⁸ and could not find what they might do; for all the people hung, listening, upon him.

XX. And it came to pass, on one of the days, as he was teaching the people in the temple, and publishing the good news, that the chief priests and the scribes came to him with the elders, ² and spoke to him, saying: Tell us, by what authority doest thou these things? Or who is he that gave thee this authority? ³ And he answering said to them: I also will ask you one thing; and tell it me. ⁴ John's immersion, was it from heaven, or from men? ⁵ And they reasoned with themselves, saying: If we say, From heaven, he will say, Why, then did ye not believe him? ⁶ But if we say, From men, all the people will stone us; for they are persuaded that

John was a prophet. ⁷ And they answered, that they knew not whence it was. ⁸ And Jesus said to them: Neither do I say to you, by what authority I do these things.

⁹ And he began to speak to the people this parable: A man planted a vineyard, and let it out to husbandmen, and went abroad for a long time. ¹⁰ And at the season he sent a servant to the husbandmen, that they should give him of the fruit of the vineyard; but the husbandmen beat him, and sent him away empty. ¹¹ And again he sent another servant; and him also, having beaten and treated him shamefully, they sent away empty. ¹² And again he sent a third; and they wounded him also, and cast him out.

¹³ And the lord of the vineyard said: What shall I do? I will send my beloved son; perhaps, seeing him, they will reverence him. ¹⁴ But when the husbandmen saw him, they reasoned among themselves, saying: This is the heir; come, let us kill him, that the inheritance may become ours. ¹⁵ So they cast him out of the vineyard, and killed him. What therefore will the lord of the vineyard do to them? ¹⁶ He will come and destroy these husbandmen, and will give the vineyard to others. And hearing it, they said: Far be it! ¹⁷ And he, looking on them, said: What then is this that is written,

> The stone which the builders disallowed,
> The same is become the head of the corner.

¹⁸ Every one that falls upon that stone shall be broken; but on whomsoever it shall fall, it will grind him to powder.

¹⁹ And the scribes and the chief priests sought to lay hands on him in that hour; and they feared the people; for they knew that he spoke this parable against them.

²⁰ And watching him, they sent forth spies, feigning themselves to be just men, that they might take hold of his words, in order to deliver him up to the magistracy, and to the authority of the governor. ²¹ And they asked him, saying: Teacher, we know that thou sayest and teachest rightly, and regardest not the person of any, but teachest the way of God

---

V 20. *Or,* And having kept watch,

CHAPTER XX.

truly. ²² Is it lawful that we should give tribute to Cæsar, or not? ²³ And perceiving their craftiness, he said to them: ²⁴ Show me a denáry. Whose image and inscription has it? And answering they said: Cæsar's. ²⁵ And he said to them: Render therefore to Cæsar the things that are Cæsar's, and to God the things that are God's. ²⁶ And they could not take hold of his words before the people; and they marveled at his answer, and held their peace.

²⁷ And some of the Sadducees, who deny that there is a resurrection, coming to him, asked him, ²⁸ saying: Teacher, Moses wrote to us, if a man's brother die, having a wife, and he die childless, that his brother should take his wife, and raise up seed to his brother.

²⁹ There were therefore seven brothers; and the first took a wife, and died childless; ³⁰ and the second and the third took her; ³¹ and in like manner also the seven left no children, and died. ³² At last the woman also died. ³³ In the resurrection, therefore, of which of them is she wife? For the seven had her for a wife.

³⁴ And Jesus answering said to them: The sons of this world marry, and are given in marriage. ³⁵ But they who are accounted worthy to obtain that world, and the resurrection from the dead, neither marry, nor are given in marriage; ³⁶ for neither can they die any more; for they are equal to the angels, and are sons of God, being sons of the resurrection.

³⁷ Now that the dead are raised, even Moses showed, at The Bush, when he calls the Lord the God of Abraham, and the God of Isaac, and the God of Jacob. ³⁸ For he is not a God of the dead, but of the living; for to him all live.

³⁹ And some of the scribes answering said: Teacher, thou saidst well. ⁴⁰ For they no longer dared to ask him any question.

⁴¹ And he said to them: How say they that the Christ is son of David? ⁴² And David himself says in the book of Psalms:
The LORD said to my Lord,
Sit on my right hand,
⁴³ Till I make thine enemies thy footstool.

V. 24. Denáry, *a Roman coin.*

⁴⁴ David therefore calls him Lord, and how is he his son?

⁴⁵ And in the hearing of all the multitude, he said to his disciples: ⁴⁶ Beware of the scribes, who desire to go about in long robes, and love greetings in the markets, and the first seats in the synagogues, and the first places at feasts; ⁴⁷ who devour widows' houses, and for a pretense make long prayers. These shall receive greater condemnation.

XXI. And looking up, he saw the rich men casting their gifts into the treasury. ² And he saw also a certain poor widow casting in thither two mites. ³ And he said: Of a truth I say to you, that this poor widow cast in more than all. ⁴ For all these, out of their abundance, cast into the offerings; but she, out of her want, cast in all the living that she had.

⁵ And as some were saying of the temple, that it has been adorned with beautiful stones and offerings, he said: ⁶ As for these things which ye behold, days will come in which there shall not be left one stone upon another, that shall not be thrown down. ⁷ And they asked him, saying: Teacher, when therefore will these things be, and what will be the sign when these things are about to come to pass?

⁸ And he said: Take heed that ye be not led astray. For many will come in my name, saying: I am he, and the time is at hand. Go not after them. ⁹ And when ye shall hear of wars and commotions, be not terrified; for these things must first come to pass; but the end is not immediately.

¹⁰ Then said he to them: Nation will rise against nation, and kingdom against kingdom; ¹¹ and there will be great earthquakes, and in divers places famines and pestilences: and there will be great portents and signs from heaven. ¹² And before all these, they will lay their hands on you, and persecute you, delivering you up into synagogues and prisons, being brought before kings and rulers for my name's sake. ¹³ And it shall turn out to you for a testimony.

¹⁴ Settle it therefore in your hearts, not to meditate before what ye shall answer. ¹⁵ For I will give you a mouth and wisdom, which all your adversaries shall not be able to gain-

CHAPTER XXI.

say or withstand. [16] And ye will be delivered up both by parents, and brothers, and kindred, and friends; and some of you they will cause to be put to death. [17] And ye will be hated by all for my name's sake. [18] And there shall not a hair of your head perish. [19] In your patience possess your souls.

[20] And when ye shall see Jerusalem encompassed by armies, then know that its desolation is at hand. [21] Then let those in Judæa flee into the mountains; and let those in the midst of it depart out; and let those in the fields not enter into it. [22] Because these are the days of vengeance, that all the things which are written may be fulfilled.

[23] Woe to those who are with child, and to those who give suck, in those days! For there shall be great distress upon the land, and wrath to this people. [24] And they shall fall by the edge of the sword, and shall be led away captive into all the nations; and Jerusalem shall be trodden down by the Gentiles, until the times of the Gentiles shall be fulfilled.

[25] And there shall be signs in the sun, and moon, and stars; and on the earth distress of nations, in perplexity for the roaring of the sea and waves; [26] men's hearts failing them for fear, and for looking for those things that are coming on the world; for the powers of heaven shall be shaken. [27] And then shall they see the Son of man coming in a cloud, with power and great glory. [28] And when these things begin to come to pass, then look up, and lift up your heads; for your redemption is drawing nigh.

[29] And he spoke to them a parable: Behold the fig-tree, and all the trees. [30] When they already shoot forth, seeing it ye know of yourselves that the summer is already near. [31] So also ye, when ye see these things coming to pass, know that the kingdom of God is near. [32] Verily I say to you, this generation shall not pass away, till all shall have come to pass. [33] Heaven and earth shall pass away; but my words shall not pass away.

[34] And take heed to yourselves, lest at any time your hearts

---

V. 19. *Or*, By your patience preserve your souls.

be overcharged with surfeiting, and drunkenness, and cares of this life, and that day come upon you unawares. ³⁵ For as a snare shall it come on all that dwell on the face of the whole earth. ³⁶ And watch, in every time praying that ye may be accounted worthy to escape all these things that shall come to pass, and to stand before the Son of man.

³⁷ And in the daytime he was teaching in the temple; and at night he went out, and abode in the mount that is called Olivet. ³⁸ And all the people came early in the morning to him in the temple, to hear him.

XXII. Now the feast of unleavened bread was drawing near, which is called the Passover; ² and the chief priests and the scribes were seeking how they might kill him; for they feared the people.

³ And Satan entered into Judas called Iscariot, being of the number of the twelve. ⁴ And he went away, and consulted with the chief priests and captains, how he might deliver him up to them. ⁵ And they were glad, and covenanted to give him money. ⁶ And he promised, and sought opportunity to deliver him up to them in the absence of the multitude.

⁷ And the day of unleavened bread came, when the passover must be killed. ⁸ And he sent away Peter and John, saying: Go, and prepare us the passover, that we may eat it. ⁹ And they said to him: Where wilt thou that we prepare? ¹⁰ And he said to them: Behold, when ye have entered into the city, there will meet you a man bearing a pitcher of water; follow him into the house where he enters in. ¹¹ And ye shall say to the master of the house: The Teacher says to thee, Where is the guestchamber, where I may eat the passover with my disciples? ¹² And he will show you a large upper room furnished; there make ready. ¹³ And they went away, and found as he had said to them. And they made ready the passover.

¹⁴ And when the hour came, he reclined at table, and the apostles with him. ¹⁵ And he said to them: I earnestly desired to eat this passover with you before I suffer. ¹⁶ For I say to you, I shall eat of it no more, until it be fulfilled in the king-

CHAPTER XXII.

dom of God. ¹⁷ And having received a cup, he gave thanks and said: Take this, and divide it among yourselves. ¹⁸ For I say to you, I will not drink of the fruit of the vine, until the kingdom of God shall come.

¹⁹ And taking a loaf, he gave thanks, and broke it, and gave to them, saying: This is my body which is given for you; this do in remembrance of me. ²⁰ And the cup in like manner after supper, saying: This cup is the new covenant in my blood, which is shed for you.

²¹ But, behold, the hand of him that betrays me is with me on the table. ²² For the Son of man indeed goes, as it was determined; but woe to that man by whom he is betrayed! ²³ And they began to inquire among themselves, who then it might be that should do this thing?

²⁴ And there arose also a contention among them, which of them should be accounted the greatest. ²⁵ And he said to them: The kings of the Gentiles exercise lordship over them; and they who exercise authority over them are called benefactors. ²⁶ But ye are not so; but let the greatest among you become as the younger, and he that is chief as he that serves. ²⁷ For which is greater, he that reclines at table, or he that serves? Is not he that reclines at table? But I am in the midst of you as he that serves. ²⁸ Ye are they who have continued with me in my temptations; ²⁹ and I appoint to you a kingdom, as my Father appointed to me, ³⁰ that ye may eat and drink at my table in my kingdom; and ye shall sit on thrones, judging the twelve tribes of Israel.

³¹ And the Lord said: Simon, Simon, behold, Satan asked for you, to sift as the wheat. ³² But I prayed for thee, that thy faith fail not; and thou, when thou hast turned, strengthen thy brethren.

³³ And he said to him: Lord, I am ready to go with thee, both to prison and to death. ³⁴ And he said: I say to thee, Peter, a cock will not crow this day, till thou shalt thrice deny that thou knowest me.

³⁵ And he said to them: When I sent you without purse, and bag, and sandals, lacked ye anything? And they said:

Nothing. ⁵⁶ Therefore said he to them: But now, he that has a purse let him take it, and likewise a bag; and he that has not, let him sell his garment and buy a sword. ³⁷ For I say to you, that yet this which is written must be accomplished in me: And he was reckoned among transgressors; for the things concerning me have an end.

³⁸ And they said: Lord, behold, here are two swords. And he said: It is enough!

³⁹ And going out, he went as he was wont to the mount of the Olives; and his disciples also followed him. ⁴⁰ And when he was at the place, he said to them: Pray that ye enter not into temptation. ⁴¹ And he withdrew from them about a stone's throw; and kneeling down, he prayed, ⁴²saying: Father, if thou art willing to remove this cup from me! Yet, not my will but thine be done.

⁴³ And there appeared to him an angel from heaven, strengthening him. ⁴⁴ And being in an agony he prayed more earnestly; and his sweat became as it were great drops of blood falling down to the ground. ⁴⁵ And rising up from prayer, and coming to the disciples, he found them sleeping, from sorrow. ⁴⁶ And he said to them: Why sleep ye? Arise and pray, that ye enter not into temptation.

⁴⁷ While he was yet speaking, behold a multitude, and he that was called Judas, one of the twelve, went before them and drew near to Jesus to kiss him. ⁴⁸ But Jesus said to him: Judas, betrayest thou the Son of man with a kiss? ⁴⁹ And they who were about him, seeing what would follow, said to him: Lord, shall we smite with the sword? ⁵⁰ And a certain one of them smote the servant of the high priest, and took off his right ear. ⁵¹ And Jesus answering said: Suffer thus far. And he touched his ear, and healed him.

⁵² And Jesus said to the chief priests and captains of the temple and elders, who were come to him: Have ye come out as against a robber, with swords and staves? ⁵³ When I was daily with you in the temple, ye stretched not forth your

---

V. 37. *Or*, are having an end.

CHAPTER XXII.

hands against me. But this is your hour, and the power of darkness.

⁵⁴ And they took him, and led him away, and brought him into the house of the high priest. And Peter followed afar off. ⁵⁵ And they having kindled a fire in the midst of the court, and sat down together, Peter sat down among them. ⁵⁶ And a certain maid seeing him as he sat by the fire, and looking intently upon him, said: This man also was with him. ⁵⁷ And he denied him, saying: Woman, I do not know him.

⁵⁸ And after a little while, another seeing him said: Thou also art of them. And Peter said: Man, I am not.

⁵⁹ And about the space of one hour after, another confidently affirmed, saying: Of a truth this one also was with him; for he is a Galilæan. ⁶⁰ And Peter said: Man, I know not what thou sayest. And immediately, while he was yet speaking, a cock crowed.

⁶¹ And the Lord turning looked upon Peter. And Peter remembered the word of the Lord, how he said to him: Before a cock crows this day, thou wilt deny me thrice. ⁶² And Peter went out, and wept bitterly.

⁶³ And the men who held Jesus mocked him, beating him; ⁶⁴ and having blindfolded him they asked him, saying: Prophesy, who is it that smote thee? ⁶⁵ And many other things they said, reviling him.

⁶⁶ And when it was day, the elders of the people, and the chief priests and scribes, came together; and they brought him up into their council, saying: ⁶⁷ If thou art the Christ, tell us. And he said to them: If I tell you, ye will not believe. ⁶⁸ And if I ask, ye will not answer. ⁶⁹ But henceforth shall the Son of man sit on the right hand of the power of God. ⁷⁰ And they all said: Art thou then the Son of God? And he said to them: Ye say it; for I am. ⁷¹ And they said: Why need we any further witness? For we ourselves heard it from his own mouth.

V. 66. *Gr.* the eldership of the people

XXIII. ¹And the whole multitude of them arose, and led him unto Pilate. ²And they began to accuse him, saying: We found this man perverting our nation, and forbidding to give tribute to Cæsar, saying that he himself is Christ, a king. ³And Pilate asked him, saying: Art thou the King of the Jews? And he answering said to him: Thou sayest it. ⁴And Pilate said to the chief priests and the multitudes: I find no fault in this man. ⁵And they were the more violent, saying: He stirs up the people, teaching throughout all Judæa, beginning from Galilee, unto this place.

⁶When Pilate heard of Galilee, he asked if the man is a Galilæan. ⁷And learning that he belonged to Herod's jurisdiction, he sent him up to Herod, who also was himself in Jerusalem at that time.

⁸And Herod, when he saw Jesus, rejoiced greatly; for he had desired for a long time to see him, because he had heard concerning him; and he hoped to see some sign wrought by him. ⁹And he questioned him in many words; but he answered him nothing. ¹⁰And the chief priests and scribes stood, vehemently accusing him. ¹¹And Herod with his men of war set him at naught, and mocked him, and arraying him in a gorgeous robe sent him back to Pilate. ¹²And Pilate and Herod on that day became friends with each other; for before they were at enmity between themselves.

¹³And Pilate, having called together the chief priests and the rulers and the people, ¹⁴said to them: Ye brought to me this man, as one perverting the people; and, behold, I, having examined him before you, found no fault in this man, touching those things whereof ye accuse him. ¹⁵No, nor yet Herod; for I sent you up to him; and behold, nothing worthy of death has been done by him. ¹⁶I will therefore chastise, and release him. ¹⁷And they cried out all at once, saying: Away with this man, and release to us Barabbas! (¹⁹who for a certain sedition made in the city, and for murder, was cast into prison.)

V. 17 *is omitted in all the oldest and best copies.*

CHAPTER XXIII.

[20] Again, therefore, Pilate spoke to them, desiring to release Jesus. [21] But they cried, saying: Crucify, crucify him. [22] And a third time he said to them: What evil then has this man done? I found no cause of death in him. I will therefore chastise, and release him. [23] And they were urgent with loud voices, requiring that he should be crucified. And their voices and those of the chief priests prevailed. [24] And Pilate gave sentence, that what they required should be done. [25] And he released him who for sedition and murder was cast into prison, whom they required; but Jesus he delivered up to their will.

[26] And as they led him away, they laid hold of one Simon a Cyrenian, coming from the country, and on him they laid the cross, that he might bear it after Jesus. [27] And there followed him a great company of the people, and of women who also bewailed and lamented him. [28] But Jesus turning to them said: Daughters of Jerusalem, weep not for me, but weep for yourselves, and for your children. [29] For, behold, days are coming in which they shall say: Happy the barren, and wombs that never bore, and breasts that never gave suck. [30] Then shall they begin to say to the mountains: Fall on us; and to the hills: Cover us. [31] For if they do these things in the green tree, what shall be done in the dry?

[32] And there were also two others, malefactors, led with him to be put to death. [33] And when they had gone away to the place which is called A Skull, there they crucified him, and the malefactors, one on the right hand, and the other on the left. [34] And Jesus said: Father, forgive them; for they know not what they do. And they divided his garments, casting lots.

[35] And the people stood beholding. And the rulers also scoffed, saying: Others he saved; let him save himself, if he is the Christ, the chosen of God. [36] And the soldiers also coming to him mocked him, offering him vinegar, [37] and saying: If thou art the King of the Jews, save thyself.

[38] And there was an inscription written over him: THIS IS THE KING OF THE JEWS.

⁳⁹ And one of the malefactors who were hanged railed at him, saying: If thou art the Christ, save thyself and us. ⁴⁰ But the other answering rebuked him, saying: Dost thou not even fear God, seeing thou art in the same condemnation? ⁴¹ And we indeed justly; for we are receiving the due reward of our deeds; but this man did nothing amiss. ⁴² And he said to Jesus: Remember me, when thou comest in thy kingdom. ⁴³ And Jesus said to him: Verily I say to thee, to-day thou shalt be with me in paradise.

⁴⁴ And it was about the sixth hour; and darkness came over the whole land until the ninth hour. ⁴⁵ And the sun was darkened; and the vail of the temple was rent in the midst. ⁴⁶ And Jesus, crying with a loud voice, said: Father, into thy hands I commit my spirit. And having said this, he expired.

⁴⁷ And the centurion, seeing what was done, glorified God, saying: Verily, this man was righteous! ⁴⁸ And all the multitudes who had come together to that sight, having beheld the things that were done, returned, beating their breasts. ⁴⁹ And all his acquaintance were standing afar off, and women who had followed him from Galilee, beholding these things.

⁵⁰ And, behold, a man named Joseph, a counselor, a good and just man, ⁵¹ (he had not consented to their counsel and deed), from Arimathaea a city of the Jews, who was waiting for the kingdom of God, ⁵² this man went to Pilate, and asked for the body of Jesus. ⁵³ And taking it down, he wrapped it in linen, and laid it in a sepulchre that was hewn in the rock, where no one was yet laid. ⁵⁴ And it was the day of preparation, and the sabbath drew on. ⁵⁵ And the women also, who had come with him out of Galilee, followed after, and viewed the sepulchre, and how his body was laid. ⁵⁶ And returning, they prepared spices and ointments; and on the sabbath they rested, according to the commandment.

XXIV. Now on the first day of the week, very early in the morning, they came to the sepulchre, bringing the spices which they prepared. ² And they found the stone rolled away from the sepulchre. ³ And entering in, they found

CHAPTER XXIV.

not the body of the Lord Jesus. ⁴ And it came to pass, that as they were much perplexed concerning this, behold two men stood by them in shining garments. ⁵ And they being afraid and bowing their faces to the earth, they said to them: Why seek ye the living among the dead? ⁶ He is not here, but is risen. Remember how he spoke to you when he was yet in Galilee, saying: The Son of man must be delivered into the hands of sinful men, and be crucified, and on the third day rise again. ⁸ And they remembered his words.

⁹ And returning from the sepulchre, they reported all these things to the eleven, and to all the rest. ¹⁰ And it was Mary the Magdalene, and Joanna, and Mary the mother of James, and the other women with them, who said these things to the apostles. ¹¹ And their words seemed to them as idle talk, and they believed them not.

¹² But Peter rose up, and ran to the sepulchre; and stooping down, he beholds the linen cloths lying by themselves; and he departed to his home, wondering at that which was come to pass.

¹³ And, behold, two of them were going on that same day to a village called Emmaus, distant sixty furlongs from Jerusalem. ¹⁴ And they were conversing together concerning all these things that had taken place. ¹⁵ And it came to pass, that while they were conversing and reasoning, Jesus himself drew near, and went with them. ¹⁶ But their eyes were holden that they should not know him.

¹⁷ And he said to them: What communications are these, that ye have one with another, as ye walk, and are sad? ¹⁸ And one, whose name was Cleopas, answering said to him: Dost thou alone sojourn in Jerusalem and not know the things that have come to pass there in these days? ¹⁹ And he said to them: What things? And they said to him: The things concerning Jesus of Nazareth, who was a prophet mighty in deed and word before God and all the people; ²⁰ and how the chief priests and our rulers delivered him up to be condemned to death, and crucified him. ²¹ But we were hoping that it was he who was to redeem Israel. But indeed, beside

all this,. to-day is the third day since these things were done. ²²Yea, and certain women also of our company made us astonished, who were early at the sepulchre; ²³and not finding his body, came saying, that they had also seen a vision of angels, who say that he is alive. ²⁴And some of those who were with us went away to the sepulchre, and found it even so as the women said; but him they saw not.

²⁵Then he said to them: O foolish, and slow of heart to believe all that the prophets have spoken! ²⁶Was it not necessary, that the Christ should suffer these things, and enter into his glory? ²⁷And beginning from Moses, and all the prophets, he explained to them in all the Scriptures the things concerning himself.

²⁸And they drew near to the village, whither they were going; and he made as though he would go further. ²⁹But they constrained him, saying: Abide with us; for it is toward evening, and the day has declined. And he went in to abide with them.

³⁰And it came to pass, that as he was reclining at table with them, he took bread, and blessed it, and breaking, gave to them. ³¹And their eyes were opened, and they knew him; and he vanished out of their sight. ³²And they said one to another: Did not our heart burn within us, while he talked to us in the way, and while he opened to us the Scriptures?

³³And rising up in the same hour, they returned to Jerusalem; and they found the eleven and those who were with them gathered together, ³⁴saying: The Lord is risen indeed, and he appeared to Simon. ³⁵And they related what things were done in the way, and how he became known by them in the breaking of bread.

³⁶And while they were speaking these things, he himself stood in the midst of them, and says to them: Peace be to you. ³⁷But they were terrified and affrighted, and supposed that they beheld a spirit. ³⁸And he said to them: Why are ye troubled? And wherefore do thoughts arise in your hearts? ³⁹See my hands and my feet, that it is I myself. Handle me, and see; for a spirit has not flesh and bones, as

CHAPTER I.

ye see me have. ⁴⁰ And having said this, he showed them his hands and his feet. ⁴¹ And while they yet believed not for joy, and wondered, he said to them: Have ye here anything to eat? ⁴² And they gave him a piece of a broiled fish, and of a honeycomb. ⁴³ And he took, and ate it before them. ⁴⁴ And he said to them: These are my words which I spoke to you, while I was yet with you, that all things must be fulfilled, which are written in the law of Moses, and the prophets, and psalms, concerning me. ⁴⁵ Then he opened their understanding, that they might understand the Scriptures. ⁴⁶ And he said to them: Thus it is written, that the Christ should suffer, and should rise from the dead on the third day; ⁴⁷ and that repentance and remission of sins should be preached in his name among all the nations, beginning at Jerusalem. ⁴⁸ Ye are witnesses of these things.

⁴⁹ And, behold, I send forth the promise of my Father upon you. But do ye tarry in the city, until ye are endued with power from on high.

⁵⁰ And he led them out as far as to Bethany; and lifting up his hands, he blessed them. ⁵¹ And it came to pass, while he blessed them, that he parted from them, and was borne up into heaven. ⁵² And they, having worshiped him, returned to Jerusalem with great joy: ⁵³ and were continually in the temple, praising and blessing God.

THE GOSPEL ACCORDING TO JOHN.

I. In the beginning was the Word, and the Word was with God, and the Word was God. ² The same was in the beginning with God. ³ All things were made by him; and without him was nothing made that has been made. ⁴ In him was life; and the life was the light of men. ⁵ And the light shines in the darkness; and the darkness comprehended it not.

V. 3. *Or,* were made through him

JOHN.

⁶ There was a man sent from God, whose name was John. ⁷ The same came for witness, to bear witness of the light, that through him all might believe. ⁸ He was not the light; but [came] to bear witness of the light. ⁹ There was the true light, which lights every man that comes into the world. ¹⁰ He was in the world, and the world was made by him, and the world knew him not. ¹¹ He came to his own, and his own received him not. ¹² But as many as received him, to them he gave power to become children of God, to those who believe on his name; ¹³ who were born, not of blood, nor of the will of the flesh, nor of the will of man, but of God.

¹⁴ And the Word became flesh, and dwelt among us; and we beheld his glory, a glory as of the only begotten from the Father, full of grace and truth.

¹⁵ John bore witness of him; and cried, saying: This was he of whom I said, He that comes after me is preferred before me, because he was before me. ¹⁶ Because out of his fullness we all received, and grace for grace. ¹⁷ For the law was given through Moses; grace and truth came through Jesus Christ. ¹⁸ No one has ever seen God; the only begotten Son, who is in the bosom of the Father, he declared him.

¹⁹ And this is the witness of John, when the Jews sent priests and Levites from Jerusalem to ask him: Who art thou? ²⁰ And he confessed, and denied not; and he confessed: I am not the Christ. ²¹ And they asked him: What then? Art thou Elijah? And he says: I am not. Art thou the Prophet? And he answered: No. ²² They said therefore to him: Who art thou? that we may give an answer to those who sent us. What sayest thou of thyself? ²³ He said: I am the voice of one crying in the wilderness: M a k e s t r a i g h t t h e w a y o f t h e L o r d, as said Isaiah the prophet.

²⁴ And they who were sent were of the Pharisees. ²⁵ And they asked him, and said to him: Why then dost thou immerse, if thou art not the Christ, nor Elijah, nor the Prophet? ²⁶ John answered them, saying: I immerse in water. There

---

V. 14. *Gr.* tabernacled among us
V. 15. *Gr.* is become before me; because he was prior to me.

CHAPTER I.

stands one in the midst of you, whom ye know not ; ²⁷ he who comes after me, the latchet of whose sandal I am not worthy to loose.

²⁸ These things took place in Bethany beyond the Jordan, where John was immersing.

²⁹ On the morrow, he sees Jesus coming to him, and says: Behold the Lamb of God, that takes away the sin of the world ! ³⁰ This is he of whom I said : After me comes a man who is preferred before me ; because he was before me. ³¹ And I knew him not ; but that he might be made manifest to Israel, for this I came immersing in water.

³² And John bore witness, saying : I have seen the Spirit descending as a dove out of heaven, and it abode upon him. ³³ And I knew him not ; but he who sent me to immerse in water, the same said to me : Upon whom thou shalt see the Spirit descending, and abiding on him, the same is he who immerses in the Holy Spirit. ³⁴ And I have seen, and have borne witness, that this is the Son of God.

³⁵ Again, on the morrow, John was standing, and two of his disciples ; ³⁶ and looking upon Jesus as he walked, he says : Behold the Lamb of God ! ³⁷ And the two disciples heard him speak, and they followed Jesus. ³⁸ And Jesus turning, and beholding them following, says to them : What seek ye ? They said to him : Rabbi (which interpreted means, Teacher), where dost thou abide ? ³⁹ He says to them : Come, and ye shall see. They came and saw where he abode ; and they abode with him that day. It was about the tenth hour.

⁴⁰ Andrew, the brother of Simon Peter, was one of the two who heard it from John, and followed him. ⁴¹ He first finds his brother Simon, and says to him : We have found the Messiah, which is interpreted, Christ. ⁴² And he brought him to Jesus. Jesus, beholding him, said : Thou art Simon the son of Jonah ; thou shalt be called Cephas, which is interpreted, Peter.

⁴³ On the morrow he would go forth into Galilee. And he

V. 30. *Gr., as in verse* 15.   V. 42. Peter : *that is*, Rock.

finds Philip; and Jesus says to him: Follow me. ⁴⁴ Now Philip was from Bethsaida, of the city of Andrew and Peter. ⁴⁵ Philip finds Nathanael, and says to him: We have found him of whom Moses, in the law, and the prophets wrote, Jesus the son of Joseph, who is from Nazareth. ⁴⁶ And Nathanael said to him: Can any good thing come out of Nazareth? Philip says to him: Come and see. ⁴⁷ Jesus saw Nathanael coming to him, and says of him: Behold an Israelite indeed, in whom is no guile! ⁴⁸ Nathanael says to him: Whence knowest thou me? Jesus answered and said to him: Before Philip called thee, when thou wast under the fig-tree, I saw thee. ⁴⁹ Nathanael answered: Rabbi, thou art the Son of God, thou art the King of Israel. ⁵⁰ Jesus answered and said to him: Because I said to thee, I saw thee under the fig-tree, believest thou? Thou shalt see greater things than these. ⁵¹ And he says to him: Verily, verily, I say to you, henceforth ye shall see heaven opened, and the angels of God ascending and descending upon the Son of man.

II. And on the third day there was a marriage in Cana of Galilee; and the mother of Jesus was there. ² And Jesus also was bidden, and his disciples, to the marriage. ³ And wine having failed, the mother of Jesus says to him: They have no wine. ⁴ Jesus says to her: Woman, what have I to do with thee? My hour is not yet come. ⁵ His mother says to the servants: Whatever he says to you, do it. ⁶ Now there were set there six water-pots of stone, after the Jewish custom of purifying, containing two or three firkins apiece. ⁷ Jesus says to them: Fill the water-pots with water. And they filled them up to the brim. ⁸ And he says to them: Draw out now, and bear to the ruler of the feast. And they bore it. ⁹ When the ruler of the feast tasted the water that was made wine (and he knew not whence it was, but the servants who had drawn the water knew), the ruler of the feast called

---

V. 51. *Some ancient copies omit:* henceforth.
V. 6. Firkin: *holding nine gallons.*

CHAPTER III.

the bridegroom, ¹⁰ and says to him: Every man sets forth the good wine first; and when they have drunk freely, then that which is worse. Thou hast kept the good wine until now. ¹¹ This beginning of the signs Jesus wrought in Cana of Galilee, and manifested his glory; and his disciples believed on him.

¹² After this he went down to Capernaum, he, and his mother, and his brothers, and his disciples; and they abode there not many days.

¹³ And the passover of the Jews was at hand; and Jesus went up to Jerusalem. ¹⁴ And he found in the temple those who sold oxen and sheep and doves, and the money-changers sitting. ¹⁵ And having made a scourge of small cords, he drove all out of the temple, both the sheep and the oxen; and poured out the changers' money, and overthrew the tables; ¹⁶ and to those who sold doves he said: Take these things hence; make not my Father's house a house of merchandise. ¹⁷ And his disciples remembered that it is written: Zeal for thy house consumes me.

¹⁸ The Jews therefore answered and said to him: What sign dost thou show to us, seeing that thou doest these things? ¹⁹ Jesus answered and said to them: Destroy this temple, and in three days I will raise it up. ²⁰ Therefore said the Jews: Forty and six years was this temple in building, and wilt thou raise it up in three days? ²¹ But he said it of the temple of his body. ²² When therefore he was risen from the dead, his disciples remembered that he said this; and they believed the Scripture, and the word which Jesus spoke.

²³ And when he was in Jerusalem at the passover, on the feast-day, many believed on his name, beholding his signs which he wrought. ²⁴ But Jesus did not trust himself to them, because he knew all men, ²⁵ and had no need that any one should testify of man; for he himself knew what was in man.

III. THERE was a man of the Pharisees, named Nicodemus, a ruler of the Jews. ² The same came to him by night, and said to him: Rabbi, we know that thou hast come a teacher from God; for no one can do these signs which thou doest, except God be with him.

³ Jesus answered and said to him: Verily, verily, I say to thee, except a man be born again, he can not see the kingdom of God. ⁴ Nicodemus says to him: How can a man be born when he is old? Can he enter the second time into his mother's womb, and be born?

⁵ Jesus answered: Verily, verily, I say to thee, except a man be born of water and the Spirit, he can not enter into the kingdom of God. ⁶ That which is born of the flesh is flesh; and that which is born of the Spirit is spirit. ⁷ Marvel not that I said to thee: Ye must be born again.

⁸ The wind blows where it will, and thou hearest the sound thereof, but knowest not whence it comes, and whither it goes. So is every one that is born of the Spirit.

⁹ Nicodemus answered and said to him: How can these things be? ¹⁰ Jesus answered and said to him: Art thou the teacher of Israel, and knowest not these things? ¹¹ Verily, verily, I say to thee, we speak that which we know, and testify that which we have seen; and ye receive not our testimony. ¹² If I told you the earthly things, and ye believe not, how shall ye believe, if I tell you the heavenly things? ¹³ And no one has ascended up into heaven, but he who came down out of heaven, the Son of man who is in heaven. ¹⁴ And as Moses lifted up the serpent in the wilderness, so must the Son of man be lifted up; ¹⁵ that every one who believes on him may have everlasting life. ¹⁶ For God so loved the world, that he gave his only-begotten Son, that whoever believes on him, should not perish, but may have everlasting life. ¹⁷ For God sent not his Son into the world to judge the world; but that the world through him might be saved. ¹⁸ He that believes on him is not judged; but he that believes not has already been judged, because he has not believed on the name of the only-begotten Son of God. ¹⁹ And this is the judgment, that light has come into the world, and men loved

---

V. 3. *Or*, born from above

CHAPTER III.

the darkness rather than the light; for their deeds were evil. ²⁰ For every one that does evil hates the light, and comes not to the light, lest his deeds should be reproved. ²¹ But he that does the truth comes to the light, that his deeds may be made manifest, that they are wrought in God.

²² After these things came Jesus and his disciples into the land of Judæa; and there he remained with them, and immersed. ²³ And John also was immersing in Ænon near to Salim, because there was much water there; and they came, and were immersed. ²⁴ For John was not yet cast into prison.

²⁵ There arose therefore a question, on the part of John's disciples with a Jew, about purification. ²⁶ And they came to John and said to him: Rabbi, he who was with thee beyond the Jordan, to whom thou hast borne witness, behold, he immerses, and all come to him.

²⁷ John answered and said: A man can receive nothing, except it be given him from heaven. ²⁸ Ye yourselves bear me witness, that I said, I am not the Christ, but I am sent before him. ²⁹ He that has the bride is the bridegroom. But the friend of the bridegroom, who stands and hears him, rejoices greatly because of the bridegroom's voice. This my joy therefore is made full. ³⁰ He must increase, but I must decrease. ³¹ He that comes from above is above all; he that is from the earth is of the earth, and speaks of the earth; he that comes from heaven is above all. ³² And what he has seen and heard, that he testifies; and his testimony no one receives. ³³ He that received his testimony has set his seal, That God is true. ³⁴ For he whom God sent forth speaks the words of God; for he gives not the Spirit by measure. ³⁵ The Father loves the Son, and has given all things into his hand. ³⁶ He that believes on the Son has everlasting life; and he that believes not the Son shall not see life, but the wrath of God abides on him.

V. 34. *In some ancient copies:* God gives not

JOHN.

IV. When therefore the Lord knew that the Pharisees heard, that Jesus made and immersed more disciples than John (²though Jesus himself immersed not, but his disciples), ³ he left Judæa, and departed again into Galilee. ⁴ And he must go through Samaria. ⁵ He comes therefore to a city of Samaria, called Sychar, near to the parcel of ground that Jacob gave to his son Joseph. ⁶ And Jacob's well was there. Jesus therefore, being wearied with the journey, sat down thus on the well. It was about the sixth hour.

⁷ There comes a woman of Samaria to draw water. Jesus says to her: Give me to drink. ⁸ For his disciples had gone away into the city to buy food. ⁹ The Samaritan woman therefore says to him: How is it that thou, being a Jew, askest drink of me, being a Samaritan woman? For Jews do not associate with Samaritans. ¹⁰ Jesus answered and said to her: If thou knewest the gift of God, and who it is that says to thee, Give me to drink, thou wouldest have asked of him, and he would have given thee living water. ¹¹ The woman says to him: Sir, thou hast nothing to draw with, and the well is deep. From whence then hast thou the living water. ¹² Art thou greater than our father Jacob, who gave us the well, and drank thereof himself, and his children, and his cattle? ¹³ Jesus answered and said to her: Every one that drinks of this water shall thirst again. ¹⁴ But whoever drinks of the water that I shall give him shall never thirst; but the water that I shall give him shall become in him a well of water, springing up into everlasting life. ¹⁵ The woman says to him: Sir, give me this water, that I may not thirst, nor come hither to draw.

¹⁶ Jesus says to her: Go, call thy husband, and come hither. ¹⁷ The woman answered and said: I have no husband. Jesus says to her: Thou saidst well, I have no husband. ¹⁸ For thou hast had five husbands; and he whom thou now hast is not thy husband. That thou hast spoken truly.

¹⁹ The woman says to him: Sir, I perceive that thou art a

V. 5. Sychar: *also called Shechem.*

CHAPTER IV.

prophet. ²⁰ Our fathers worshiped in this mountain; and ye say, that in Jerusalem is the place where men ought to worship. ²¹ Jesus says to her: Woman, believe me, an hour is coming, when ye shall neither in this mountain nor in Jerusalem worship the Father. ²² Ye worship that which ye know not; we worship that which we know; because salvation is of the Jews. ²³ But an hour is coming, and now is, when the true worshipers shall worship the Father in spirit and in truth; for such the Father seeks to worship him. ²⁴ God is spirit; and they that worship him, must worship in spirit and in truth.
²⁵ The woman says to him: I know that Messiah comes (who is called Christ); when he is come, he will tell us all things. ²⁶ Jesus says to her: I that speak to thee am he. ²⁷ And upon this came his disciples; and they marveled that he talked with the woman. Yet no one said: What seekest thou? or, Why talkest thou with her? ²⁸ The woman then left her water-pot, and went away into the city; and she says to the men: ²⁹ Come, see a man who told me all things that ever I did. Is this the Christ? ³⁰ Then they went out of the city, and came to him.
³¹ In the mean while the disciples prayed him, saying: Master, eat. ³² But he said to them: I have food to eat that ye know not of. ³³ Therefore said the disciples one to another: Has any one brought him aught to eat? ³⁴ Jesus says to them: My food is to do the will of him who sent me, and to finish his work. ³⁵ Do ye not say, that there are yet four months, and then comes the harvest? Behold, I say to you, lift up your eyes and look on the fields, that they are already white for harvest. ³⁶ And he that reaps receives wages, and gathers fruit unto life eternal; that both he that sows and he that reaps may rejoice together. ³⁷ And herein is the true saying: One sows, and another reaps. ³⁸ I sent you to reap that whereon ye have not labored. Other men have labored, and ye have entered into their labor.
³⁹ And many of the Samaritans of that city believed on him for the saying of the woman, who testified: He told me all

---

V. 27. *Or*, was talking with a woman.

that ever I did. ⁴⁰ When therefore the Samaritans came to him, they besought him to remain with them. And he remained there two days. ⁴¹ And far more believed because of his word; ⁴² and said to the woman: We no longer believe because of thy saying; for we ourselves have heard, and know that this is in truth the Savior of the world.

⁴³ And after the two days he departed thence, and went into Galilee. ⁴⁴ For Jesus himself testified, that a prophet has no honor in his own country.

⁴⁵ When therefore he came into Galilee, the Galilæans received him, having seen all that he did in Jerusalem at the feast; for they also went to the feast. ⁴⁶ So he came again into Cana of Galilee, where he made the water wine.

And there was a certain nobleman, whose son was sick, in Capernaum. ⁴⁷ He, having heard that Jesus is come out of Judæa into Galilee, went to him, and besought him that he would come down and heal his son; for he was about to die. ⁴⁸ Jesus therefore said to him: Except ye see signs and wonders, ye will not believe. ⁴⁹ The nobleman says to him: Sir, come down ere my child die. ⁵⁰ Jesus says to him: Go thy way; thy son lives. And the man believed the word that Jesus spoke to him, and he went his way. ⁵¹ And as he was now going down, his servants met him, and brought word saying: Thy child lives. ⁵² He inquired of them, therefore, the hour when he began to amend. And they said to him: Yesterday, at the seventh hour, the fever left him. ⁵³ The father knew, therefore, that it was in the same hour in which Jesus said to him: Thy son lives. And he himself believed, and his whole house. ⁵⁴ This second sign Jesus wrought, when he had come out of Judæa into Galilee.

V. AFTER these things there was a feast of the Jews; and Jesus went up to Jerusalem. ² And there is in Jerusalem by the sheep-gate a pool, which is called in the Hebrew tongue Bethesda, having five porches. ³ In these lay a multitude of

---

VV. 3, 4. *The words in brackets are wanting in the oldest and best copies.*

CHAPTER V.

the infirm, of blind, lame, withered [waiting for the moving of the water. ⁴ For an angel went down at a certain season into the pool, and troubled the water. He therefore, who first went in after the troubling of the water, was made whole of whatever disease he had]. ⁵ And a certain man was there, who had an infirmity thirty and eight years. ⁶ Jesus seeing this man lying, and knowing that he had been already a long time thus, says to him : Dost thou desire to be made whole ? ⁷ The infirm man answered him : Sir, I have no man, when the water is troubled, to put me into the pool; but while I am coming, another goes down before me. ⁸ Jesus says to him : Rise, take up thy bed, and walk. ⁹ And immediately the man was made whole, and took up his bed and walked.

And on that day was the sabbath. ¹⁰ The Jews therefore said to him that was cured : It is the sabbath ; it is not lawful for thee to carry the bed. ¹¹ He answered them : He who made me whole, the same said to me : Take up thy bed, and walk. ¹² They asked him therefore : Who is the man that said to thee : Take up thy bed and walk ? ¹³ And he who was healed knew not who it was ; for Jesus conveyed himself away, there being a multitude in the place.

¹⁴ Afterward Jesus finds him in the temple. And he said to him : Behold, thou hast been made whole ; sin no more, lest something worse befall thee. ¹⁵ The man departed, and told the Jews that it was Jesus who made him whole. ¹⁶ And for this the Jews persecuted Jesus, because he did these things on the sabbath. ¹⁷ But Jesus answered them : My Father works hitherto, and I work. ¹⁸ For this therefore the Jews sought the more to kill him, because he not only broke the sabbath, but also called God his Father, making himself equal with God.

¹⁹ Jesus therefore, answered and said to them : Verily, verily, I say to you, the Son can do nothing of himself, but what he sees the Father do ; for what things soever he does, these also does the Son in like manner. ²⁰ For the Father loves the Son, and shows him all things that he himself does ; and greater works than these will he show him, that ye may marvel. ²¹ For as the Father raises up the dead, and quickens them ; so

also the Son quickens whom he will. ²²For neither does the Father judge any one; but all judgment he has given to the Son; ²³that all may honor the Son, as they honor the Father. He that honors not the Son, honors not the Father who sent him.

²⁴Verily, verily, I say to you, he that hears my word, and believes him who sent me, has everlasting life, and comes not into judgment, but has passed out of death into life. ²⁵Verily, verily, I say to you, an hour is coming, and now is, when the dead shall hear the voice of the Son of God; and they that hear shall live. ²⁶For as the Father has life in himself, so he gave also to the Son to have life in himself. ²⁷And he gave him authority to execute judgment also, because he is a son of man. ²⁸Marvel not at this; for an hour is coming, in which all that are in the graves shall hear his voice, ²⁹and shall come forth; they that did good, to the resurrection of life, and they that did evil, to the resurrection of judgment.

³⁰I can of myself do nothing. As I hear, I judge; and my judgment is just; because I seek not my own will, but the will of him who sent me.

³¹If I bear witness of myself, my witness is not true. ³²There is another that bears witness of me; and I know that the witness which he witnesses of me is true. ³³Ye have sent to John, and he has borne witness to the truth. ³⁴But I receive the witness not from man; but these things I say, that ye might be saved. ³⁵He was the burning and shining lamp; and ye were willing for a season to rejoice in his light. ³⁶But I have greater witness than that of John; for the works which the Father gave me to finish, the works themselves that I do bear witness of me, that the Father has sent me. ³⁷And the Father, who sent me, he has borne witness of me. Ye have neither heard his voice at any time, nor have ye seen his shape. ³⁸And ye have not his word abiding in you; for whom he sent, him ye believe not.

³⁹Search the Scriptures; because in them ye think ye have eternal life, and these are they that testify of me; ⁴⁰and ye will not come to me, that ye may have life. ⁴¹I receive not

---

V. 39. *Or*, Ye search

CHAPTER VI.

honor from men. [42] But I know you, that ye have not the love of God in you. [43] I have come in my Father's name, and ye receive me not; if another shall come in his own name, him ye will receive. [44] How can ye believe, receiving honor from one another, and the honor that is from God alone ye seek not? [45] Do not think that I will accuse you to the Father; there is one that accuses you, Moses in whom ye have placed your hope. [46] For if ye believed Moses, ye would believe me; for he wrote of me. [47] But if ye believe not his writings, how shall ye believe my words?

VI. After these things Jesus went away, beyond the sea of Galilee, which is the sea of Tiberias. [2] And a great multitude followed him, because they saw the signs which he wrought on the sick. [3] And Jesus went up into the mountain, and there he sat with his disciples. [4] And the passover, the feast of the Jews, was near. [5] Jesus therefore lifting up his eyes, and seeing that a great multitude is coming to him, says to Philip: Whence shall we buy bread that these may eat? [6] And this he said to try him; for he himself knew what he was about to do. [7] Philip answered him: Two hundred denaries worth of bread is not sufficient for them, that each one may take a little. [8] One of his disciples, Andrew, the brother of Simon Peter, says to him: [9] There is a lad here, who has five barley loaves and two small fishes; but what are they among so many? [10] Jesus said: Make the men lie down. Now there was much grass in the place. So the men lay down, in number about five thousand. [11] And Jesus took the loaves; and having given thanks, he distributed to those who were lying down; and likewise of the fishes as much as they desired. [12] When they were filled, he said to his disciples: Gather up the fragments that remain, that nothing be lost. [13] Therefore they gathered them together, and filled twelve baskets with fragments of the five barley loaves, which remained over and above to those who had eaten. [14] The men therefore, seeing the sign that Jesus wrought, said: This is of a truth the Prophet that comes into the world.

¹⁵ Jesus therefore, knowing that they were about to come and take him by force, to make him a king, withdrew again into the mountain, himself alone. ¹⁶ And when evening came, his disciples went down to the sea, ¹⁷ and entering into the ship, were going over the sea to Capernaum. And it was now dark, and Jesus had not come to them; ¹⁸ and as a strong wind was blowing, the sea began to rise. ¹⁹ When therefore they had rowed about twenty-five or thirty furlongs, they see Jesus walking on the sea, and drawing near to the ship; and they were afraid. ²⁰ But he says to them: It is I, be not afraid. ²¹ They therefore willingly received him into the ship; and immediately the ship was at the land whither they were going.

²² On the morrow, the multitude that stood on the other side of the sea, seeing that there was no other boat there but one, and that Jesus went not with his disciples into the ship, but his disciples went away alone (²³ but there came other boats from Tiberias near to the place where they ate bread, when the Lord had given thanks); ²⁴ when therefore the multitude saw that Jesus was not there, nor his disciples, they themselves entered into the boats, and came to Capernaum, seeking for Jesus. ²⁵ And having found him on the other side of the sea, they said to him: Rabbi, when camest thou hither? ²⁶ Jesus answered them and said: Verily, verily, I say to you, ye seek me, not because ye saw signs, but because ye ate of the loaves and were filled. ²⁷ Work not for the food that perishes, but for the food that endures unto everlasting life, which the Son of man will give to you; for him the Father, God, has sealed. ²⁸ Therefore they said to him: What shall we do, that we may work the works of God? ²⁹ Jesus answered and said to them: This is the work of God, that ye believe on him whom he sent. ³⁰ They therefore said to him: What sign doest thou then, that we may see, and believe thee? What dost thou work? ³¹ Our fathers ate the manna in the wilderness; as it is written: He gave them bread from heaven to eat. ³² Jesus therefore said to them: Verily, verily, I say to you, Moses has not given you the bread from heaven; but my Father gives you the true bread from heaven. ³³ For the

CHAPTER VI.

bread of God is that which comes down out of heaven, and gives life to the world.

³⁴ They therefore said to him: Lord, evermore give us this bread. ³⁵ Jesus said to them: I am the bread of life. He that comes to me shall never hunger, and he that believes on me shall never thirst. ³⁶ But I said to you, that ye have also seen me, and do not believe. ³⁷ All that the Father gives me will come to me; and him that comes to me I will not cast out. ³⁸ Because I have come down from heaven, not to do my own will, but the will of him who sent me. ³⁹ And this is the will of him who sent me, that of all which he has given me I should lose nothing, but should raise it up at the last day. ⁴⁰ For this is the will of my Father, that every one who sees the Son, and believes on him, may have everlasting life; and I will raise him up at the last day.

⁴¹ The Jews therefore murmured at him, because he said: I am the bread that came down out of heaven. ⁴² And they said: Is not this Jesus, the son of Joseph, whose father and mother we know? How then does this man say: I have come down out of heaven?

⁴³ Jesus answered and said to them: Murmur not among yourselves. ⁴⁴ No one can come to me, except the Father who sent me draw him; and I will raise him up at the last day. ⁴⁵ It is written in the prophets: And they shall all be taught of God. Every one that has heard from the Father, and has learned, comes to me. ⁴⁶ Not that any one has seen the Father, save he who is from God; he has seen the Father.

⁴⁷ Verily, verily, I say to you, he that believes on me has everlasting life. ⁴⁸ I am the bread of life. ⁴⁹ Your fathers ate the manna in the wilderness, and are dead. ⁵⁰ This is the bread that comes down out of heaven, that one may eat thereof, and not die. ⁵¹ I am the living bread that came down out of heaven. If any one eat of this bread, he shall live forever; yea, and the bread that I will give is my flesh, which I will give for the life of the world.

V. 33. *Or*, is he who

⁵² The Jews therefore contended with one another, saying: How can this man give us his flesh to eat? ⁵³ Jesus therefore said to them: Verily, verily, I say to you, except ye eat the flesh of the Son of man, and drink his blood, ye have no life in you. ⁵⁴ He that eats my flesh, and drinks my blood, has eternal life; and I will raise him up at the last day. ⁵⁵ For my flesh is true food, and my blood is true drink. ⁵⁶ He that eats my flesh, and drinks my blood, abides in me, and I in him. ⁵⁷ As the living Father has sent me, and I live because of the Father; so he that eats me, he also shall live because of me. ⁵⁸ This is the bread that came down out of heaven. Not as your fathers ate the manna, and are dead; he that eats of this bread shall live forever.

⁵⁹ These things he said in the synagogue, while teaching in Capernaum.

⁶⁰ Many therefore of his disciples, when they heard it, said: This is a hard saying; who can hear it? ⁶¹ But Jesus, knowing in himself that his disciples murmured at this, said to them: Does this offend you? ⁶² What then if ye behold the Son of man ascending up where he was before? ⁶³ It is the spirit that makes alive, the flesh profits nothing; the words which I have spoken to you are spirit, and are life. ⁶⁴ But there are some of you that believe not. For Jesus knew from the beginning who they were that believed not, and who it was that should betray him. ⁶⁵ And he said: For this cause I have said to you, that no one can come to me, except it be given him from the Father.

⁶⁶ From this time many of his disciples went back, and walked no more with him.

⁶⁷ Jesus said therefore to the twelve: Will ye also go away? ⁶⁸ Simon Peter answered him: Lord, to whom shall we go? Thou hast words of eternal life. ⁶⁹ And we believe and know, that thou art the Holy One of God. ⁷⁰ Jesus answered them: Did I not choose you, the twelve, and one of you is a devil? ⁷¹ He spoke of Judas Iscariot, son of Simon; for he it was that would betray him, being one of the twelve.

CHAPTER VII.

VII. ¹ AND after these things Jesus walked in Galilee; for he would not walk in Judæa, because the Jews were seeking to kill him. ² Now the feast of the Jews, the feast of tabernacles, was at hand. ³ His brothers therefore said to him: Depart hence, and go into Judæa, that thy disciples also may behold thy works that thou doest. ⁴ For no one does anything in secret, and he himself seeks to be known openly. If thou doest these things, manifest thyself to the world. ⁵ For neither did his brothers believe on him. ⁶ Jesus therefore says to them: My time is not yet come; but your time is always ready. ⁷ The world can not hate you; but me it hates, because I testify of it, that its works are evil. ⁸ Go ye up to the feast. I go not up to this feast; because my time is not yet fully come.

⁹ Having said these things to them, he remained in Galilee. ¹⁰ But when his brothers were gone up to the feast, then he also went up, not openly, but as it were in secret.

¹¹ The Jews therefore sought him at the feast, and said: Where is he? ¹² And there was much murmuring among the multitudes concerning him. Some said: He is a good man; others said: Nay, but he misleads the multitude. ¹³ No one, however, spoke openly of him, for fear of the Jews.

¹⁴ But when it was already the midst of the feast, Jesus went up into the temple and taught. ¹⁵ And the Jews wondered, saying: How knows this man letters, having never learned? ¹⁶ Jesus therefore answered them, and said: My teaching is not mine, but his who sent me. ¹⁷ If any one desires to do his will, he shall know of the teaching, whether it is of God, or whether I speak from myself. ¹⁸ He that speaks from himself seeks his own glory; but he that seeks the glory of him who sent him, the same is true, and there is no unrighteousness in him.

¹⁹ Has not Moses given you the law, and none of you keeps the law? Why do ye seek to kill me? ²⁰ The multitude answered and said: Thou hast a demon; who seeks to kill thee? ²¹ Jesus answered and said to them: I did one work, and ye all marvel. ²² Moses has for this cause given you circumcision,

not that it is of Moses, but of the fathers; and on the sabbath ye circumcise a man. ²³ If a man receives circumcision on the sabbath, that the law of Moses may not be broken; are ye angry at me, because I made a man altogether whole on the sabbath? ²⁴ Judge not according to appearance, but judge the righteous judgment.

²⁵ Then said some of those of Jerusalem: Is not this he whom they seek to kill? ²⁶ But, lo, he speaks boldly, and they say nothing to him. Did the rulers know in truth that this is the Christ? ²⁷ But we know this man, whence he is; but when the Christ comes, no one knows whence he is.

²⁸ Jesus therefore cried, teaching in the temple and saying: Ye both know me, and ye know whence I am; and I have not come of myself, but he that sent me is true, whom ye know not. ²⁹ I know him; because I am from him, and he sent me. ³⁰ Therefore they sought to seize him; and no one laid hands on him, because his hour had not yet come.

³¹ But of the multitude many believed on him, and said: When the Christ comes, will he work more signs than these which this man wrought? ³² The Pharisees heard the multitude murmuring these things concerning him; and the chief priests and the Pharisees sent officers to seize him. ³³ Jesus therefore said: Yet a little while I am with you, and I go to him who sent me. ³⁴ Ye will seek me, and shall not find me; and where I am, ye can not come. ³⁵ The Jews said therefore among themselves: Whither will this man go, that we shall not find him? Will he go to those dispersed among the Greeks, and teach the Greeks? ³⁶ What is this saying that he said: Ye will seek me, and shall not find me; and where I am, ye can not come?

³⁷ In the last day, the great day of the feast, Jesus stood and cried, saying: If any one thirst, let him come to me and drink. ³⁸ He that believes on me, as said the Scripture, out of his belly shall flow rivers of living water. ³⁹ And this he spoke concerning the Spirit, which they that believe on him should receive;

V. 26. *Or,* Have the rulers come to know

CHAPTER VIII.

for the Holy Spirit was not yet [given], because Jesus was not yet glorified. ⁴⁰ Some of the multitude therefore, hearing the words, said: Of a truth this is the Prophet. ⁴¹ Others said: This is the Christ. But some said: Does the Christ then come out of Galilee? ⁴² Did not the Scripture say, that the Christ comes of the seed of David, and from the town of Bethlehem, where David was? ⁴³ A division therefore arose among the multitude because of him. ⁴⁴ And some of them desired to seize him; but no one laid hands on him.

⁴⁵ The officers therefore came to the chief priests and Pharisees; and they said to them: Why did ye not bring him? ⁴⁶ The officers answered: Never man spoke like this man. ⁴⁷ The Pharisees answered them: Are ye also led astray? ⁴⁸ Did any of the rulers believe on him, or of the Pharisees? ⁴⁹ But this multitude, that know not the law, are accursed. ⁵⁰ Nicodemus says to them (he who came to him by night, being one of them): ⁵¹ Does our law judge a man, except it first hear from him, and know what he does? ⁵² They answered and said to him: Art thou also of Galilee? Search, and see, that out of Galilee arises no prophet. ⁵³ [And each one went to his house. ¹ Jesus went to the mount of the Olives.

² And early in the morning he came again into the temple, and all the people came to him; and having sat down, he was teaching them. ³ And the scribes and the Pharisees bring to him a woman taken in adultery; and having placed her in the midst, ⁴ they say to him: Teacher, this woman was taken in adultery, in the very act. ⁵ Now in the law Moses commanded us, that such should be stoned; what then dost thou say? ⁶ This they said, tempting him, that they might have whereof to accuse him. But Jesus, having stooped down, was writing with his finger in the ground. ⁷ And as they continued asking him, raising himself up, he said to them: He that is without

---

V. 46. *In the oldest copies:* Never man spoke thus.
V. 52. *Or,* has arisen no prophet.
Ch. vii., 53—viii., 11. *The words in brackets are wanting in most of the ancient copies.*

sin among you, let him first cast the stone at her. ⁸ And again stooping down, he wrote in the ground. ⁹ And they hearing it, and being convicted by their conscience, went out one by one, beginning at the eldest, unto the last; and Jesus was left alone, and the woman standing in the midst. ¹⁰ And Jesus raising himself up, and seeing none but the woman, said to her: Woman, where are they, thine accusers? Did no one condemn thee? ¹¹ She said: No one, Lord. And Jesus said to her: Neither do I condemn thee; go, and sin no more.]

¹² Again therefore Jesus spoke to them, saying: I am the light of the world; he that follows me shall not walk in the darkness, but shall have the light of life. ¹³ The Pharisees therefore said to him: Thou bearest witness of thyself; thy witness is not true. ¹⁴ Jesus answered and said to them: Though I bear witness of myself, my witness is true; because I know whence I came, and whither I go; but ye know not whence I come, or whither I go. ¹⁵ Ye judge according to the flesh; I judge no one. ¹⁶ And even if I judge, my judgment is true; because I am not alone, but I and the Father who sent me. ¹⁷ It is written also in your law, that the witness of two men is true. ¹⁸ I am one that bear witness of myself, and the Father who sent me bears witness of me. ¹⁹ They said therefore to him: Where is thy Father? Jesus answered: Ye know neither me, nor my Father. If ye knew me, ye would know my Father also.

²⁰ These words he spoke in the treasury, while teaching in the temple; and no one laid hands on him, because his hour had not yet come.

²¹ Again therefore he said to them: I go away, and ye will seek me, and shall die in your sin. Whither I go, ye can not come. ²² The Jews therefore said: Will he kill himself? because he says: Whither I go, ye can not come. ²³ And he said to them: Ye are from beneath: I am from above. Ye are of this world; I am not of this world. ²⁴ I said therefore to you, that ye shall die in your sins; for if ye believe not that I am he, ye shall die in your sins. ²⁵ Therefore they said to him: Who art thou? And Jesus said to them: That which I

CHAPTER VIII.

also say to you from the beginning. [26] I have many things to say and to judge concerning you. But he who sent me is true; and the things which I heard from him, these I speak to the world. [27] They understood not that he spoke to them of the Father.

[28] Therefore Jesus said to them: When ye shall have lifted up the Son of man, then ye shall know that I am he; and of myself I do nothing, but as the Father taught me, those things I speak. [29] And he who sent me is with me. He has not left me alone; because I do always the things that please him. [30] As he spoke these words many believed on him.

[31] Jesus therefore said to those Jews who have believed him: If ye continue in my word, ye are truly my disciples; [32] and ye shall know the truth, and the truth will make you free. [33] They answered him: We are Abraham's seed, and have never been in bondage to any one. How sayest thou: Ye shall be made free? [34] Jesus answered them: Verily, verily, I say to you, every one who commits sin is a servant of sin. [35] And the servant abides not in the house forever. [36] The Son abides forever; if therefore the Son shall make you free, ye will be free indeed. [37] I know that ye are Abraham's seed; but ye seek to kill me, because my word has no place in you. [38] I speak what I have seen with my Father; and ye therefore do what ye have heard from your father.

[39] They answered and said to him: Our father is Abraham. Jesus says to them: If ye were children of Abraham, ye would do the works of Abraham. [40] But now ye seek to kill me, a man who has spoken to you the truth, which I heard from God. This Abraham did not. [41] Ye do the works of your father. They said to him: We were not born of fornication; we have one father, God. [42] Jesus said to them: If God were your father, ye would love me; for from God I came forth, and am come; neither have I come of myself, but he sent me. [43] Why do ye not understand my speech? Because ye can not hear my word. [44] Ye are of your father the Devil, and the lusts of your father ye will do. He was a murderer from the beginning, and abides not in the truth, because truth is not in him.

When he speaks a lie, he speaks of his own; because he is a liar, and the father of it. ⁴⁵ And because I speak the truth, ye believe me not.

⁴⁶ Which of you convicts me of sin? If I speak truth, why do ye not believe me? ⁴⁷ He that is of God hears God's words; ye therefore hear not, because ye are not of God.

⁴⁸ The Jews answered and said to him: Say we not well, that thou art a Samaritan, and hast a demon? ⁴⁹ Jesus answered: I have not a demon; but I honor my Father, and ye dishonor me. ⁵⁰ And I seek not my own glory; there is one that seeks, and judges. ⁵¹ Verily, verily, I say to you, if any one keep my saying, he shall not see death, forever. ⁵² The Jews said to him: Now we know that thou hast a demon. Abraham is dead, and the prophets; and thou sayest: If a man keep my saying, he shall not taste of death, forever. ⁵³ Art thou greater than our father Abraham, who is dead? And the prophets are dead. Whom makest thou thyself? ⁵⁴ Jesus answered: If I honor myself, my honor is nothing. It is my Father that honors me, of whom ye say, that he is your God. ⁵⁵ And ye know him not; but I know him. And if I say, I know him not, I shall be a liar like to you. But I know him, and I keep his word. ⁵⁶ Abraham, your father, rejoiced to see my day; and he saw it, and was glad. ⁵⁷ The Jews therefore said to him: Thou art not yet fifty years old, and hast thou seen Abraham? ⁵⁸ Jesus said to them: Verily, verily, I say to you, before Abraham was, I am. ⁵⁹ They took up stones therefore to cast at him. But Jesus hid himself, and went out of the temple.

IX. And passing along, he saw a man blind from his birth. ² And his disciples asked him, saying: Master, who sinned, this man or his parents, that he should be born blind? ³ Jesus answered: Neither this man sinned, nor his parents; but that the works of God should be made manifest in him. ⁴ I must work the works of him who sent me, while it is day. Night is coming, when none can work. ⁵ As long as I am in the world, I am the light of the world.

CHAPTER IX.

⁶ Having thus spoken, he spit on the ground, and made clay of the spittle, and anointed the eyes of the blind man with the clay, ⁷ and said to him: Go, wash in the pool of Siloam (which is interpreted, Sent). He went away therefore, and washed, and came seeing.

⁸ The neighbors therefore, and they who before had seen him that he was a beggar, said: Is not this he that sits and begs? ⁹ Some said: This is he; and others: He is like him; he said: I am he. ¹⁰ Therefore they said to him: How were thine eyes opened? ¹¹ He answered: A man called Jesus made clay, and anointed mine eyes, and said to me: Go to the pool of Siloam, and wash. And I went away and washed, and received sight. ¹² They said to him: Where is he? He said: I know not.

¹³ They bring to the Pharisees him who before was blind. ¹⁴ And it was the sabbath when Jesus made the clay, and opened his eyes. ¹⁵ Again therefore the Pharisees also asked him, how he received sight. He said to them: He put clay upon mine eyes, and I washed, and do see. ¹⁶ Therefore some of the Pharisees said: This man is not from God, because he keeps not the sabbath. Others said: How can a man that is a sinner do such signs? And there was a division among them. ¹⁷ They say to the blind man again: What sayest thou of him, seeing that he opened thine eyes? He said: He is a Prophet.

¹⁸ The Jews therefore did not believe concerning him, that he was blind and received sight, until they called the parents of him that received sight. ¹⁹ And they asked them, saying: Is this your son, who ye say was born blind? How then does he now see? ²⁰ His parents answered them and said: We know that this is our son, and that he was born blind. ²¹ But by what means he now sees, we know not; or who opened his eyes, we know not. He is of age; ask him. He shall speak for himself. ²² These words spoke his parents, because they feared the Jews; for the Jews had agreed already, that if any one acknowledged him as Christ, he should be put out of the synagogue. ²³ Therefore his parents said: He is of age; ask him.

²⁴ They therefore called a second time the man that was blind, and said to him: Give glory to God; we know that this man is a sinner. ²⁵ He answered therefore: Whether he is a sinner, I know not; one thing I know, that, whereas I was blind, now I see. ²⁶ They therefore said to him: What did he to thee? How opened he thine eyes? ²⁷ He answered them: I told you already, and ye did not hear. Wherefore would ye hear again? Will ye also become his disciples? ²⁸ They reviled him, and said: Thou art his disciple; but we are Moses' disciples. ²⁹ We know that God has spoken to Moses; but this man we know not, whence he is. ³⁰ The man answered and said to them: Why herein is a marvelous thing, that ye know not whence he is, and he opened mine eyes. ³¹ Now we know that God hears not sinners. But if any one is a worshiper of God, and does his will, him he hears. ³² Since the world began, it was not heard that any one opened the eyes of one born blind. ³³ If this man were not from God, he could do nothing. ³⁴ They answered and said to him: Thou wast altogether born in sins, and dost thou teach us? And they cast him out.

³⁵ Jesus heard that they cast him out; and finding him, he said to him: Dost thou believe on the Son of God? ³⁶ He answered and said: Who then is he, Lord, that I may believe on him? ³⁷ And Jesus said to him: Thou hast both seen him, and he it is that talks with thee. ³⁸ And he said: Lord, I believe. And he worshiped him.

³⁹ And Jesus said: For judgment came I into this world; that they who see not may see, and that they who see may become blind. ⁴⁰ And some of the Pharisees who were with him heard these words, and said to him: Are we also blind? ⁴¹ Jesus said to them: If ye were blind, ye would not have sin. But now ye say: We see. Your sin remains!

X. Verily, verily, I say to you: He that enters not through the door into the sheepfold, but climbs up some other way, the same is a thief and a robber. ² But he that enters in through the door is a shepherd of the sheep. ³ To him the

CHAPTER X.

porter opens, and the sheep hear his voice; and he calls his own sheep by name, and leads them out. ⁴ And when he has put forth all his own, he goes before them; and the sheep follow him, for they know his voice. ⁵ And a stranger they will not follow, but will flee from him; because they know not the voice of strangers.

⁶ This parable spoke Jesus to them; but they understood not what things they were which he spoke to them.

⁷ Therefore said Jesus to them again: Verily, verily, I say to you, I am the door of the sheep. ⁸ All who came before me are thieves and robbers; but the sheep did not hear them. ⁹ I am the door. If any one enter in through me, he shall be saved, and shall go in and out and find pasture. ¹⁰ The thief comes not but to steal, and to kill, and to destroy. I came that they may have life, and that they may have it abundantly.

¹¹ I am the good shepherd. The good shepherd lays down his life for the sheep. ¹² But he that is a hireling, and not a shepherd, whose own the sheep are not, sees the wolf coming, and leaves the sheep, and flees; and the wolf catches them, and scatters the sheep. ¹³ The hireling flees, because he is a hireling, and cares not for the sheep. ¹⁴ I am the good shepherd; and I know mine, and am known by mine, ¹⁵ as the Father knows me, and I know the Father; and I lay down my life for the sheep. ¹⁶ And other sheep I have, which are not of this fold. Them also I must bring, and they shall hear my voice; and there shall be one flock, one shepherd. ¹⁷ For this the Father loves me, because I lay down my life, that I may take it again. ¹⁸ No one takes it from me, but I lay it down of myself. I have authority to lay it down, and I have authority to take it again. This commandment I received from my Father.

¹⁹ Again there arose a division among the Jews because of these words. ²⁰ And many of them said: He has a demon, and is mad, why do ye hear him? ²¹ Others said: These are not the words of one that has a demon. Can a demon open the eyes of the blind?

²² And there came the feast of the dedication, in Jerusalem;

and it was winter. ²³ And Jesus was walking in the temple, in the porch of Solomon. ²⁴ The Jews therefore came around him, and said to him: How long dost thou hold us in doubt? If thou art the Christ, tell us plainly.

²⁵ Jesus answered them: I told you, and ye do not believe. The works that I do in my Father's name, these bear witness of me. ²⁶ But ye do not believe; for ye are not of my sheep, as I said to you. ²⁷ My sheep hear my voice, and I know them, and they follow me; ²⁸ and I give to them eternal life; and they shall never perish, nor shall any one pluck them out of my hand. ²⁹ My Father, who has given them to me, is greater than all; and no one is able to pluck them out of my Father's hand. ³⁰ I and the Father are one.

³¹ The Jews therefore took up stones again to stone him. ³² Jesus answered them: Many good works have I showed you from my Father; for which of those works do ye stone me? ³³ The Jews answered him: For a good work we stone thee not, but for blasphemy, and because thou, being man, makest thyself God. ³⁴ Jesus answered them: Is it not written in your law, I said, Ye are gods? ³⁵ If he called them gods to whom the word of God came, and the Scripture can not be broken, ³⁶ say ye of him, whom the Father sanctified, and sent into the world, Thou blasphemest, because I said, I am the Son of God? ³⁷ If I do not the works of my Father, believe me not. ³⁸ But if I do, though ye believe not me, believe the works; that ye may learn and know, that the Father is in me, and I in the Father. ³⁹ Therefore they sought again to seize him; and he went forth, out of their hand.

⁴⁰ And he went away again beyond the Jordan, to the place where John was at first immersing; and there he abode. ⁴¹ And many came to him, and said: John indeed wrought no sign; but all things that John spoke of this man were true. ⁴² And many believed on him there.

V. 24. *Or*, hold us in expectation?

CHAPTER XI.

XI. Now a certain one was sick, Lazarus of Bethany, from the village of Mary and Martha her sister. ² It was the Mary who anointed the Lord with ointment, and wiped his feet with her hair, whose brother Lazarus was sick. ³ The sisters therefore sent to him, saying: Lord, behold, he whom thou lovest is sick. ⁴ And Jesus hearing it, said: This sickness is not for death, but for the sake of the glory of God, that the Son of God may be glorified thereby.

⁵ Now Jesus loved Martha, and her sister, and Lazarus. ⁶ When therefore he heard that he was sick, he then abode two days in the place where he was. ⁷ Then after this he says to the disciples: Let us go into Judæa again. ⁸ The disciples say to him: Master, the Jews of late sought to stone thee; and goest thou thither again? ⁹ Jesus answered: Are there not twelve hours in the day? If any one walk in the day, he stumbles not, because he sees the light of this world. ¹⁰ But if any one walk in the night, he stumbles, because the light is not in him.

¹¹ These things said he; and after this he says to them: Lazarus our friend has fallen asleep; but I go, that I may awake him out of sleep. ¹² Therefore his disciples said: Lord if he has fallen asleep, he will be restored. ¹³ But Jesus had spoken of his death; but they thought that he said it of taking rest in sleep. ¹⁴ Then therefore Jesus said to them plainly: Lazarus is dead. ¹⁵ And I am glad for your sakes that I was not there, that ye may believe. But let us go to him. ¹⁶ Therefore said Thomas, who is called Didymus, to his fellow disciples: Let us also go, that we may die with him.

¹⁷ Having come therefore, Jesus found that he had already been four days in the tomb.

¹⁸ Now Bethany was nigh to Jerusalem, about fifteen furlongs off. ¹⁹ And many of the Jews had come to Martha and Mary, to comfort them concerning their brother.

²⁰ Therefore Martha, when she heard that Jesus is coming, went and met him; but Mary sat in the house. ²¹ Then said Martha to Jesus: Lord, if thou hadst been here, my brother

had not died. ²²But even now, I know that whatever thou shalt ask of God, God will give it thee. ²³Jesus says to her: Thy brother will rise again. ²⁴Martha says to him: I know that he will rise again, in the resurrection at the last day. ²⁵Jesus said to her: I am the resurrection, and the life; he that believes on me, though he be dead, yet shall he live; ²⁶and whoever lives and believes on me, shall never die. Believest thou this? ²⁷She says to him: Yea, Lord; I believe that thou art the Christ, the Son of God, who comes into the world.

²⁸And having said this, she went away, and called Mary her sister secretly, saying: The Teacher is come, and calls for thee. ²⁹And she, when she heard it, rises quickly and comes to him.

³⁰Now Jesus had not yet come into the village, but was in the place where Martha met him. ³¹The Jews therefore who were with her in the house and comforting her, when they saw that Mary rose up hastily and went out, followed her, saying: She goes to the tomb to weep there.

³²Mary therefore, when she came where Jesus was, seeing him, fell down at his feet, saying to him: Lord, if thou hadst been here, my brother had not died.

³³Jesus therefore, when he saw her weeping, and the Jews weeping who came with her, groaned in spirit, and was troubled. ³⁴And he said: Where have ye laid him? They say to him: Lord, come and see. ³⁵Jesus wept.

³⁶The Jews therefore said: Behold how he loved him! ³⁷And some of them said: Could not this man, who opened the eyes of the blind, have caused even that this man should not have died? ³⁸Jesus therefore, again groaning in himself, comes to the tomb. It was a cave, and a stone lay upon it.

³⁹Jesus says: Take away the stone. The sister of him that was dead, Martha, says to him: Lord, by this time he is offensive; for he has been dead four days. ⁴⁰Jesus says to her: Said I not to thee, that, if thou believe, thou shalt see the glory of God?

⁴¹So they took away the stone. And Jesus raised his eyes upward, and said: Father, I thank thee that thou didst hear

CHAPTER XI.

me. ⁴² And I know that thou always hearest me; but for the sake of the multitude standing around I said it, that they might believe that thou didst send me. ⁴³ And having thus spoken, he cried with a loud voice: Lazarus, come forth. ⁴⁴ And he that was dead came forth, bound hand and foot with grave clothes; and his face was bound about with a napkin. Jesus says to them: Loose him, and let him go.

⁴⁵ Many therefore of the Jews who came to Mary, and saw what he did, believed on him. ⁴⁶ But some of them went away to the Pharisees, and told them what Jesus did.

⁴⁷ Therefore the chief priests and the Pharisees gathered a council, and said: What do we, seeing that this man works many signs? ⁴⁸ If we let him thus alone, all will believe on him; and the Romans will come and take away both our place and nation. ⁴⁹ And a certain one of them, Caiaphas, being high priest that year, said to them: Ye know nothing; ⁵⁰ nor do ye consider that it is expedient for us, that one man die for the people, and not the whole nation perish. ⁵¹ And this he spoke not of himself; but being high priest that year, he prophesied that Jesus should die for the nation; ⁵² and not for the nation only, but that also he should gather together into one the children of God that were scattered abroad.

⁵³ Therefore from that day forth they took counsel together to put him to death. ⁵⁴ Jesus therefore no longer walked openly among the Jews; but departed thence to the country near to the wilderness, to a city called Ephraim, and there continued with his disciples.

⁵⁵ And the passover of the Jews was at hand; and many went up to Jerusalem out of the country, before the passover, that they might purify themselves. ⁵⁶ They sought therefore for Jesus, and said among themselves, as they stood in the temple: What think ye, that he will not come to the feast? ⁵⁷ Now the chief priests and the Pharisees had given a commandment, that, if any one knew where he was, he should make it known, that they might seize him.

XII. Therefore Jesus, six days before the passover, came to Bethany, where Lazarus was who had been dead, whom Jesus raised from the dead. ² They therefore made him a supper there, and Martha served; and Lazarus was one of those who reclined at table with him.

³ Then Mary took a pound of ointment of pure spikenard, very costly, and anointed the feet of Jesus, and wiped his feet with her hair; and the house was filled with the odor of the ointment. ⁴ Then says one of his disciples, Judas Iscariot, Simon's son, who was about to betray him: ⁵ Why was not this ointment sold for three hundred denaries, and given to the poor? ⁶ This he said, not because he cared for the poor; but because he was a thief, and had the bag, and bore what was put therein. ⁷ Then said Jesus: Let her alone; she has kept it to the day of my preparation for burial. ⁸ For the poor ye have always with you; but me ye have not always.

⁹ A great multitude of the Jews therefore knew that he was there. And they came, not because of Jesus only, but that they might see Lazarus also, whom he raised from the dead. ¹⁰ But the chief priests consulted that they might put Lazarus also to death; ¹¹ because by reason of him many of the Jews went away, and believed on Jesus.

¹² On the morrow a great multitude that had come to the feast, hearing that Jesus is coming to Jerusalem, ¹³ took branches of the palm-trees and went forth to meet him, and cried: Hosanna; blessed is he who comes in the name of the Lord, the King of Israel. ¹⁴ And Jesus, having found a young ass, sat thereon; as it is written:

¹⁵ Fear not, daughter of Zion;
Behold, thy King comes,
Sitting on an ass's colt.

¹⁶ These things his disciples understood not at the first. But when Jesus was glorified, then they remembered that these

V. 5. Denary, *seven and a half pence sterling, or fifteen cents.*
V. 6. *Or, and bore off*
V. 7. *In the oldest copies:* that she may keep it

CHAPTER XII.

things were written of him, and that they did these things to him.

[17] The multitude therefore that was with him when he called Lazarus out of the tomb, and raised him from the dead, bore witness. [18] For this the multitude also met him, because they heard that he had wrought this sign. [19] The Pharisees therefore said among themselves: Perceive ye that ye avail nothing? Behold, the world is gone after him.

[20] And there were certain Greeks, of those who come up to worship at the feast. [21] These came therefore to Philip, who was from Bethsaida of Galilee, and desired him, saying: Sir, we would see Jesus. [22] Philip comes and tells Andrew; Andrew and Philip come and tell Jesus.

[23] And Jesus answered them, saying: The hour has come, that the Son of man should be glorified. [24] Verily, verily, I say to you, except the grain of wheat fall into the ground and die, it abides alone; but if it die, it brings forth much fruit. [25] He that loves his life shall lose it; and he that hates his life in this world shall keep it unto life eternal. [26] If any one serve me, let him follow me; and where I am, there shall also my servant be. If any one serve me, him will the Father honor.

[27] Now is my soul troubled; and what shall I say? Father, save me from this hour! But for this cause came I unto this hour. [28] Father, glorify thy name. Then there came a voice out of heaven: I both have glorified it, and will glorify it again.

[29] The multitude therefore that stood by and heard, said that it thundered; others said: An angel has spoken to him. [30] Jesus answered and said: This voice came not for my sake, but for your sakes. [31] Now is the judgment of this world; now shall the prince of this world be cast out. [32] And I, if I be lifted up from the earth, will draw all men to me. [33] This he said, signifying by what manner of death he should die.

[34] The multitude answered him: We heard out of the law

V. 27. *Or,* save me from this hour?

that the Christ abides forever; and how sayest thou: The Son of man must be lifted up? Who is this Son of man? ³⁵ Jesus therefore said to them: Yet a little while is the light among you. Walk while ye have the light, that darkness may not overtake you; and he that walks in the darkness knows not whither he goes. ³⁶ While ye have the light, believe on the light, that ye may become sons of light.

These things spoke Jesus, and departed, and hid himself from them.

³⁷ But though he had wrought so many signs before them, they did not believe on him; ³⁸ that the saying of Isaiah the prophet might be fulfilled, which he spoke:

Lord, who believed our report,
And to whom was the arm of the Lord revealed?

³⁹ Therefore they could not believe, because Isaiah said again:

⁴⁰ He has blinded their eyes,
And has hardened their heart;
That they should not see with their eyes,
And understand with their heart,
And turn, and I should heal them.

⁴¹ These things said Isaiah, because he saw his glory, and spoke of him. ⁴² Yet, even of the rulers many believed on him; but because of the Pharisees they did not acknowledge him, lest they should be put out of the synagogue; ⁴³ for they loved the glory of men more than the glory of God.

⁴⁴ And Jesus cried and said: He that believes on me, believes not on me but on him who sent me. ⁴⁵ And he that beholds me beholds him who sent me. ⁴⁶ I have come a light into the world, that whoever believes on me may not abide in the darkness. ⁴⁷ And if any one hear my words, and keep them not, I do not judge him; for I came not to judge the world, but to save the world. ⁴⁸ He that rejects me, and receives not my words, has one that judges him. The word that I spoke, that shall judge him in the last day. ⁴⁹ Because I spoke not from myself; but the Father who sent me, he has given me a commandment, what I should say, and what I should speak.

CHAPTER XIII.

⁵⁰ And I know that his commandment is everlasting life. What things I speak therefore, as the Father has said to me, so I speak.

XIII. AND before the feast of the passover, Jesus knowing that his hour has come that he should depart out of this world to the Father, having loved his own who were in the world, loved them to the end. ² And supper being served, the Devil having already put into the heart of Judas Iscariot, Simon's son, to betray him; ³ knowing that the Father has given all things into his hands, and that he came out from God, and is going to God, ⁴ he rises from the supper, and lays aside his garments, and taking a towel he girded himself. ⁵ After that he pours water into the basin, and began to wash the feet of his disciples, and to wipe them with the towel with which he was girded.

⁶ He comes therefore to Simon Peter; and Peter says to him: Lord, dost thou wash my feet? ⁷ Jesus answered and said to him: What I do thou knowest not now; but thou shalt know hereafter. ⁸ Peter says to him: Never shalt thou wash my feet. Jesus answered him: If I wash thee not, thou hast no part with me. ⁹ Simon Peter says to him: Lord, not my feet only, but also my hands and my head. ¹⁰ Jesus says to him: He that has bathed has no need save to wash the feet, but is wholly clean. And ye are clean; but not all. ¹¹ For he knew his betrayer; therefore he said: Ye are not all clean.

¹² When therefore he had washed their feet, he took his garments, and reclining again at table, said to them: Know ye what I have done to you? ¹³ Ye call me the Teacher, and the Master; and ye say well, for so I am. ¹⁴ If I then, the Master and the Teacher, washed your feet, ye also ought to wash one another's feet. ¹⁵ For I gave you an example, that as I did to you, ye also should do. ¹⁶ Verily, verily, I say to you, a servant is not greater than his lord, nor one that is sent greater than he who sent him. ¹⁷ If ye know these things, happy are ye if ye do them.

V. 16. *Or,* nor an apostle *(i. e., one that is sent).*

JOHN.

¹⁸ I speak not of you all; I know whom I chose; but that the scripture might be fulfilled, He that eats the loaf with me lifted up his heel against me. ¹⁹ Even now I tell you, before it comes to pass, that when it comes to pass, ye may believe that I am he. ²⁰ Verily, verily, I say to you, he that receives whomsoever I send receives me; and he that receives me receives him who sent me.

²¹ Having said this, Jesus was troubled in spirit, and testified and said: Verily, verily, I say to you, that one of you will betray me. ²² The disciples therefore looked one on another, doubting of whom he spoke. ²³ And there was reclining in Jesus' bosom one of his disciples, whom Jesus loved. ²⁴ To him therefore Simon Peter beckons, and says to him: Say who it is of whom he speaks. ²⁵ And he, leaning back on Jesus' breast, says to him: Lord, who is it? ²⁶ Jesus answers: He it is, to whom I shall give the morsel, when I have dipped it. And having dipped the morsel, he gives it to Judas Iscariot, son of Simon. ²⁷ And after the morsel, then entered Satan into him. Jesus therefore says to him: What thou doest, do quickly.

²⁸ And no one at the table knew for what intent he spoke this to him. ²⁹ For some thought, because Judas had the bag, that Jesus said to him: Buy what we need for the feast; or, that he should give something to the poor.

³⁰ He then, having received the morsel, went immediately out; and it was night.

³¹ When therefore he was gone out, Jesus says: Now is the Son of man glorified, and God is glorified in him. ³² If God is glorified in him, God will also glorify him in himself, and will straightway glorify him. ³³ Children, yet a little while I am with you. Ye will seek me; and as I said to the Jews, whither I go ye can not come, so now I say to you. ³⁴ A new commandment I give to you, that ye love one another; as I loved you, that ye also love one another. ³⁵ By this shall all know that ye are my disciples, if ye have love one toward another.

CHAPTER XIV.

³⁶ Simon Peter says to him: Lord, whither goest thou? Jesus answered him: Whither I go, thou canst not follow me now; but thou shalt follow me afterward. ³⁷ Peter says to him: Lord, why can not I follow thee now? I will lay down my life for thee. ³⁸ Jesus answers: Wilt thou lay down thy life for me? Verily, verily, I say to thee, a cock will not crow, till thou hast denied me thrice.

XIV. Let not your heart be troubled. Believe on God, and believe on me. ² In my Father's house are many mansions; if it were not so, I would have told you; because I go to prepare a place for you. ³ And if I go and prepare a place for you, I will come again, and will receive you to myself; that where I am ye may be also. ⁴ And ye know the way whither I go.

⁵ Thomas says to him: Lord, we know not whither thou goest; and how do we know the way? ⁶ Jesus says to him: I am the way, the truth, and the life. No one comes to the Father, but by me. ⁷ If ye knew me, ye would know my Father also; and from henceforth ye know him, and have seen him.

⁸ Philip says to him: Lord, show us the Father, and it suffices us. ⁹ Jesus says to him: Am I so long time with you, and dost thou not know me, Philip? He that has seen me has seen the Father; and how sayest thou: Show us the Father? ¹⁰ Believest thou not that I am in the Father, and the Father in me? The words that I speak to you I speak not of myself; but the Father who dwells in me, he does the works. ¹¹ Believe me, that I am in the Father, and the Father in me; or else believe for the very works' sake.

¹² Verily, verily, I say to you, he that believes on me, the works that I do he shall do also, and greater than these shall he do. because I go to the Father. ¹³ And whatever ye shall ask in my name, that I will do, that the Father may be glorified in the Son. ¹⁴ If ye shall ask anything in my name, I will do it.

V. 1. *Or*, Ye believe on God, believe also on me.

¹⁵ If ye love me, keep my commandments. ¹⁶ And I will ask of the Father, and he will give you another Comforter, that he may be with you forever; ¹⁷ the Spirit of truth, whom the world can not receive, because it sees him not, neither knows him; but ye know him, because he abides with you, and shall be in you. ¹⁸ I will not leave you bereaved; I will come to you.

¹⁹ Yet a little while, and the world sees me no more; but ye see me; because I live, ye shall live also. ²⁰ In that day ye shall know that I am in my Father, and ye in me, and I in you. ²¹ He that has my commandments, and keeps them, he it is that loves me; and he that loves me shall be loved by my Father, and I will love him, and will manifest myself to him.

²² Judas says to him (not Iscariot): Lord, how is it that thou wilt manifest thyself to us, and not to the world? ²³ Jesus answered and said to him: If any one loves me, he will keep my word; and my Father will love him, and we will come to him, and make our abode with him. ²⁴ He that loves me not, keeps not my words; and the word which ye hear is not mine, but the Father's who sent me.

²⁵ These things have I spoken to you, while abiding with you. ²⁶ But the Comforter, the Holy Spirit, whom the Father will send in my name, he will teach you all things, and bring to your remembrance all things which I said to you.

²⁷ Peace I leave with you, my peace I give to you; not as the world gives, give I to you. Let not your heart be troubled, neither let it be afraid. ²⁸ Ye heard how I said to you: I go away; and I come to you. If ye loved me, ye would have rejoiced that I go to the Father; because the Father is greater than I. ²⁹ And now I have told you before it comes to pass, that, when it is come to pass, ye may believe.

³⁰ I will no longer talk much with you; for the prince of the world comes, and in me he has nothing. ³¹ But that the world may know that I love the Father, and as the Father gave me commandment, so I do. Arise, let us go hence.

V. 18. *Gr.* I will not leave you orphans

CHAPTER XV.

XV. I am the true vine, and my Father is the husbandman. ² Every branch in me that bears not fruit, he takes it away; and every one that bears fruit, he cleanses it, that it may bear more fruit. ³ Ye are already clean, through the word which I have spoken to you.
⁴ Abide in me, and I in you. As the branch can not bear fruit of itself, if it abide not in the vine, so neither can ye, if ye abide not in me. ⁵ I am the vine, ye are the branches. He that abides in me and I in him, the same bears much fruit; because without me ye can do nothing. ⁶ If any one abide not in me, he is cast forth as the branch, and is withered; and they gather them, and cast them into the fire, and they are burned. ⁷ If ye abide in me, and my words abide in you, ask whatever ye will, and it shall be done to you.
⁸ Herein is my Father glorified, that ye bear much fruit; and ye shall become my disciples. ⁹ As the Father loved me, I also loved you; abide in my love. ¹⁰ If ye keep my commandments, ye shall abide in my love; as I have kept my Father's commandments, and abide in his love.
¹¹ These things I have spoken to you, that my joy may be in you, and your joy be made full. ¹² This is my commandment, that ye love one another, as I loved you. ¹³ Greater love has no one than this, that one lay down his life for his friends. ¹⁴ Ye are my friends, if ye do whatever I command you.
¹⁵ No longer do I call you servants; because the servant knows not what his lord does. But I have called you friends; because all things that I heard from my Father I made known to you. ¹⁶ Ye did not choose me, but I chose you, and appointed you that ye may go and bear fruit, and that your fruit may remain; that whatever ye shall ask of the Father in my name, he may give it you.
¹⁷ These things I command you, that ye love one another. ¹⁸ If the world hates you, ye know that it has hated me before it hated you. ¹⁹ If ye were of the world, the world would love its own; but because ye are not of the world, but I chose you out of the world, for this the world hates you. ²⁰ Remember

the word that I said to you: A servant is not greater than his lord. If they persecuted me, they will also persecute you; if they kept my saying, they will keep yours also. ²¹ But all these things they will do to you for my name's sake, because they know not him who sent me.

²² If I had not come and spoken to them, they would not have sin; but now they have no cloak for their sin. ²³ He that hates me hates my Father also. ²⁴ If I had not done among them the works which no other one has done, they would not have sin; but now they have both seen and hated both me and my Father. ²⁵ But this comes to pass, that the word might be fulfilled that is written in their law: T h e y h a t e d m e w i t h o u t a c a u s e.

²⁶ But when the Comforter is come, whom I will send to you from the Father, the Spirit of truth, which proceeds from the Father, he will bear witness of me. ²⁷ And ye also shall bear witness, because ye are with me from the beginning.

XVI. These things I have spoken to you, that ye should not be offended. ² They will put you out of the synagogues; yea, a time is coming, that every one who kills you will think he makes an offering to God. ³ And these things they will do to you, because they have not known the Father, nor me. ⁴ But these things I have spoken to you, that when the time shall come, ye may remember that I told you. And these things I told you not from the beginning, because I was with you.

⁵ And now I go to him who sent me; and none of you asks me: Whither goest thou? ⁶ But because I have spoken these things to you, sorrow has filled your heart. ⁷ But I tell you the truth, it is expedient for you that I depart; for if I depart not, the Comforter will not come to you; but if I go, I will send him to you. ⁸ And when he is come, he will convict the world, in respect of sin, and of righteousness, and of judgment; ⁹ of sin, in that they believe not on me; ¹⁰ of righteousness, in that I go to my Father, and ye behold me no more; ¹¹ of judgment, in that the prince of this world has been judged.

CHAPTER XVI.

[12] I have yet many things to say to you, but ye can not bear them now. [13] But when he, the Spirit of truth is come, he will guide you into all the truth; for he will not speak from himself, but whatever he shall hear, that will he speak, and he will tell you the things to come. [14] He will glorify me; because he will receive of mine, and will tell it to you. [15] All things that the Father has are mine. Therefore, I said, that he will receive of mine, and will tell it to you. [16] A little while, and ye behold me not; and again a little while, and ye shall see me.

[17] Therefore some of his disciples said to one another: What is this that he says to us, A little while, and ye behold me not; and again a little while, and ye shall see me; and, I go to the Father? [18] They said therefore: What is this that he says, A little while? We know not what he says.

[19] Jesus knew that they were desirous to ask him, and said to them: Do ye inquire of this with one another, that I said, A little while, and ye behold me not; and again a little while, and ye shall see me? [20] Verily, verily, I say to you, that ye will weep and lament, but the world will rejoice; and ye will be sorrowful, but your sorrow shall be turned into joy. [21] A woman when she is in travail has sorrow, because her hour is come; but when she has borne the child, she remembers no more the anguish, for joy that a man is born into the world. [22] And so ye now have sorrow; but I will see you again, and your heart shall rejoice, and your joy no one takes from you.

[23] And in that day ye shall ask nothing of me. Verily, verily, I say to you: Whatever ye shall ask of the Father, he will give it you in my name. [24] Hitherto ye asked nothing in my name. Ask, and ye shall receive, that your joy may be made full.

[25] These things I have spoken to you in parables. A time is coming, when I will no more speak to you in parables, but I will tell you plainly of the Father. [26] In that day ye shall ask in my name. And I say not to you, that I will pray the Father for you; [27] for the Father himself loves you, because ye have loved me, and have believed that I came forth from God. [28] I came forth from the Father, and have come into the world; again, I leave the world, and go to the Father.

²⁹ His disciples say to him: Lo, now thou speakest plainly, and speakest no parable. ³⁰ Now we know that thou knowest all things, and needest not that any one should ask thee. By this we believe that thou camest forth from God. ³¹ Jesus answered them: Do ye now believe? ³² Behold, an hour is coming, and has come, that ye will be scattered, each one to his own, and will leave me alone; and I am not alone, because the Father is with me. ³³ These things I have spoken to you, that in me ye may have peace. In the world ye have tribulation; but be of good cheer, I have overcome the world.

XVII. These words spoke Jesus, and lifted up his eyes to heaven, and said: Father, the hour has come; glorify thy Son, that thy Son may glorify thee; ² as thou gavest him authority over all flesh, that as many as thou hast given to him, to them he should give eternal life. ³ And this is the eternal life, that they know thee the only true God, and Jesus Christ, whom thou didst send. ⁴ I glorified thee on the earth; I finished the work which thou hast given me to do. ⁵ And now, O Father, glorify thou me with thine own self, with the glory which I had with thee before the world was. ⁶ I manifested thy name to the men whom thou hast given me out of the world. Thine they were, and thou hast given them to me; and they have kept thy word. ⁷ Now they know that all things whatever thou hast given me are from thee; ⁸ because the words which thou gavest me I have given to them, and they received them, and knew in truth that I came forth from thee, and believed that thou didst send me. ⁹ I pray for them; I pray not for the world, but for those whom thou hast given me: because they are thine. ¹⁰ And all things that are mine are thine, and thine are mine; and I am glorified in them.

¹¹ And I am no longer in the world; and these are in the world, and I come to thee. Holy Father, keep those in thy name whom thou hast given me, that they may be one, as we are. ¹² While I was with them, I kept them in thy name.

CHAPTER XVIII.

Those whom thou hast given me I watched over and none of them perished, except the son of perdition, that the scripture might be fulfilled. [13] And now I come to thee; and these things I speak in the world, that they may have my joy made full in them. [14] I have given them thy word; and the world hated them, because they are not of the world, as I am not of the world. [15] I pray not that thou shouldest take them out of the world, but that thou shouldest keep them from the evil. [16] They are not of the world, as I am not of the world. [17] Sanctify them in the truth; thy word is truth. [18] As thou didst send me into the world, I also sent them into the world. [19] And for their sakes I sanctify myself, that they also may be sanctified in the truth. [20] And I pray not for these only, but also for those who believe on me through their word; [21] that all may be one; as thou, Father, in me and I in thee, that they also may be in us; that the world may believe that thou didst send me. [22] And the glory which thou hast given to me I have given to them, that they may be one, as we are one; [23] I in them, and thou in me, that they may be perfected into one; that the world may know that thou didst send me, and lovedst them as thou lovedst me.

[24] Father, those whom thou hast given me, I will that where I am they also be with me; that they may behold my glory, which thou hast given me; because thou lovedst me before the foundation of the world. [25] Righteous Father! And the world knew thee not! But I knew thee, and these knew that thou didst send me; [26] and I made known to them thy name, and will make it known; that the love wherewith thou lovedst me may be in them, and I in them.

XVIII. Having spoken these words, Jesus went out with his disciples beyond the brook Kedron, where was a garden, into which he entered and his disciples. [2] And Judas also, his betrayer knew the place; because Jesus ofttimes resorted thither with his disciples.

[3] Judas therefore, having received the band and officers from the chief priests and Pharisees, comes thither with torches and

JOHN.

lamps and weapons. ⁴ Jesus therefore, knowing all the things that were coming upon him, went forth and said to them: Whom do ye seek? ⁵ They answered him: Jesus the Nazarene. Jesus says to them: I am he. And Judas also, his betrayer, was standing with them.

⁶ When therefore he said to them, I am he, they went backward, and fell to the ground.

⁷ Again therefore he asked them: Whom do ye seek? And they said: Jesus the Nazarene. ⁸ Jesus answered: I told you that I am he; if therefore ye seek me, let these go their way; ⁹ that the saying might be fulfilled, which he spoke: Of those whom thou hast given me, I lost none.

¹⁰ Then Simon Peter, having a sword, drew it and smote the servant of the high priest, and cut off his right ear. The servant's name was Malchus. ¹¹ Jesus therefore said to Peter: Put up thy sword into the sheath. The cup which my Father has given me, shall I not drink it?

¹² So the band, and the captain, and the officers of the Jews, took Jesus and bound him, ¹³ and led him away to Annas first; for he was father-in-law of Caiaphas, who was high priest that year. ¹⁴ And it was Caiaphas who counseled the Jews, that it is expedient that one man should die for the people.

¹⁵ And Simon Peter and the other disciple followed Jesus. That disciple was known to the high priest, and went in with Jesus into the court of the high priest. ¹⁶ But Peter was standing at the door without. Therefore the other disciple, who was known to the high priest, went out and spoke to her that kept the door, and brought in Peter. ¹⁷ Then the damsel that kept the door says to Peter: Art not thou also one of this man's disciples? He says: I am not.

¹⁸ And the servants and the officers were standing there, having made a fire of coals, because it was cold, and were warming themselves; and Peter was standing with them, and warming himself.

¹⁹ The high priest therefore asked Jesus concerning his disciples, and concerning his teaching. ²⁰ Jesus answered him: I have spoken openly to the world; I ever taught in the syna-

CHAPTER XVIII.

gogue, and in the temple, where all the Jews assemble; and I spoke nothing in secret. [21] Why askest thou me? Ask those who have heard, what I spoke to them. Behold, these know what things I said.

[22] And when he had said this, one of the officers who was standing by gave Jesus a blow on the face, saying: Answerest thou the high priest so? [23] Jesus answered him: If I spoke evil, bear witness of the evil; but if well, why dost thou smite me?

[24] Annas sent him bound to Caiaphas the high priest. [25] And Simon Peter was standing and warming himself. They said therefore to him: Art thou also one of his disciples? He denied, and said: I am not. [26] One of the servants of the high priest, being a kinsman of him whose ear Peter cut off, says: Did not I see thee in the garden with him? [27] Again therefore Peter denied; and immediately a cock crowed.

[28] Then they lead Jesus from Caiaphas into the Governor's palace; and it was early; and they themselves went not into the palace, that they might not be defiled, but might eat the passover. [29] Pilate therefore went out to them, and said: What accusation do ye bring against this man? [30] They answered and said to him: If this man were not a malefactor, we would not have delivered him up to thee. [31] Pilate therefore said to them: Do ye take him, and judge him according to your law. The Jews therefore said to him: It is not lawful for us to put any one to death; [32] that the saying of Jesus might be fulfilled, which he spoke, signifying by what manner of death he should die.

[33] Pilate therefore entered into the palace again, and called Jesus, and said to him: Art thou the King of the Jews? [34] Jesus answered: Dost thou say this of thyself, or did others tell thee concerning me? [35] Pilate answered: Am I a Jew? Thine own nation, and the chief priests, delivered thee up to me. What didst thou? [36] Jesus answered: My kingdom is not of this world. If my kingdom were of this world, my servants would fight, that I might not be delivered up to the Jews; but now is my kingdom not from hence. [37] Pilate therefore said to

him: Art thou a king then? Jesus answered: Thou sayest it; because I am a king. To this end have I been born, and to this end have I come into the world, that I may bear witness to the truth. Every one that is of the truth hears my voice. ⁲⁸ Pilate says to him: What is truth? And having said this, he went out again to the Jews, and says to them: I find no fault in him. ³⁹ But ye have a custom, that I should release to you one at the passover. Do ye desire therefore that I release to you the King of the Jews? ⁴⁰ They all therefore cried out again, saying: Not this one, but Barabbas. Now Barabbas was a robber.

XIX. Then therefore Pilate took Jesus, and scourged him. ² And the soldiers platted a crown of thorns, and put it on his head, and put on him a purple robe; and they came to him, ³ and said: Hail, King of the Jews! And they gave him blows on the face.

⁴ Pilate went forth again, and says to them: Behold, I bring him forth to you, that ye may know that I find no fault in him. ⁵ Jesus therefore came forth, wearing the crown of thorns, and the purple robe. And he says to them: Behold the man!

⁶ When therefore the chief priests and the officers saw him, they cried out, saying: Crucify him, crucify him. Pilate says to them: Do ye take him, and crucify him; for I find no fault in him. ⁷ The Jews answered him: We have a law, and by our law he ought to die, because he made himself the Son of God.

⁸ When therefore Pilate heard this saying, he was the more afraid. ⁹ And he went again into the palace, and says to Jesus: Whence art thou? But Jesus gave him no answer. ¹⁰ Then says Pilate to him: Dost thou not speak to me? Knowest thou not that I have power to release thee, and have power to crucify thee? ¹¹ Jesus answered: Thou wouldst have no power against me, except it were given thee from above. Therefore he that delivers me to thee has the greater sin.

CHAPTER XIX.

¹² Thenceforth Pilate sought to release him. But the Jews cried out, saying: If thou let this man go, thou art not a friend of Cæsar. Whoever makes himself a king speaks against Cæsar.
¹³ When therefore Pilate heard these words, he brought Jesus forth, and sat down on the judgment-seat in a place called the Pavement, and in Hebrew, Gabbatha. ¹⁴ And it was the preparation of the passover, and about the sixth hour. And he says to the Jews: Behold your king! ¹⁵ But they cried out: Away with him, away with him, crucify him. Pilate says to them: Shall I crucify your king? The chief priests answered: We have no king but Cæsar. ¹⁶ Then therefore he delivered him to them to be crucified. And they took Jesus, and led him away.
¹⁷ And bearing his cross he went forth into the place called Place of a skull, which in Hebrew is called Golgotha; ¹⁸ where they crucified him, and two others with him, on either side one, and Jesus in the midst. ¹⁹ And Pilate wrote also a title, and put it on the cross. And the writing was: JESUS THE NAZARENE THE KING OF THE JEWS.
²⁰ This title therefore many of the Jews read; because the place where Jesus was crucified was nigh to the city, and it was written in Hebrew, and Greek, and Latin. ²¹ Therefore said the chief priests of the Jews to Pilate: Write not, The King of the Jews; but that he said, I am King of the Jews. ²² Pilate answered: What I have written, I have written.
²³ Then the soldiers, when they crucified Jesus, took his garments, and made four parts, to every soldier a part, and also his coat. And the coat was without a seam, woven from the top throughout. ²⁴ They said therefore to one another: Let us not rend it, but cast lots for it, whose it shall be; that the scripture might be fulfilled which says:

> They parted my garments among them.
> And for my vesture they cast lots.

These things the soldiers did. ²⁵ And there were standing by the cross of Jesus his mother, and his mother's sister, Mary the wife of Clopas, and Mary the Magdalene. ²⁶ Jesus therefore seeing his mother, and the disciple whom he loved standing by, says to his mother: Woman, behold thy son! ²⁷ Then he says to the disciple: Behold thy mother! And from that hour the disciple took her to his own home.

²⁸ After this, Jesus knowing that all things were now finished, that the ·scripture might be accomplished, says: I thirst. ²⁹ Now there was set a vessel full of vinegar; and they, having filled a sponge with vinegar, and put it on a hyssop-stalk, bore it to his mouth. ³⁰ When Jesus therefore received the vinegar, he said: It is finished; and he bowed his head, and gave up his spirit.

³¹ The Jews therefore, since it was the preparation, that the bodies might not remain upon the cross on the sabbath (for that sabbath day was a great day), besought Pilate that their legs might be broken, and they be taken away. ³² The soldiers came, therefore, and broke the legs of the first, and of the other who was crucified with him. ³³ But when they came to Jesus, and saw that he was already dead, they broke not his legs. ³⁴ But one of the soldiers with a spear pierced his side, and forthwith there came out blood and water.

³⁵ And he that has seen has borne witness, and his witness is true, and he knows that he says what is true, that ye also might believe. ³⁶ For these things came to pass, that the scripture might be fulfilled: A bone of him shall not be broken. ³⁷ And again another scripture says: They shall look on him whom they pierced.

³⁸ And after this, Joseph from Arimathaea, being a disciple of Jesus, but secretly for fear of the Jews, besought Pilate that he might take away the body of Jesus; and Pilate gave him leave. He came therefore, and took away the body of Jesus. ³⁹ And there came also Nicodemus, who at the first came to Jesus by night, bringing a mixture of myrrh and aloes, about a hundred pounds weight. ⁴⁰ They took therefore the body of Jesus, and wound it in linen cloths with the spices, as is the custom of the Jews to prepare for burial.

⁴¹ And in the place where he was crucified there was a garden, and in the garden a new sepulchre, wherein no one was

CHAPTER XX.

yet laid. ⁴²There they laid Jesus therefore, on account of the preparation of the Jews, because the sepulchre was nigh at hand.

XX. AND on the first day of the week Mary the Magdalene comes early, while it is yet dark, to the sepulchre, and sees the stone taken away out of the sepulchre. ²She runs therefore and comes to Simon Peter, and to the other disciple, whom Jesus loved, and says to them: They took away the Lord out of the sepulchre, and we know not where they laid him.
³Peter therefore went forth, and the other disciple, and they went to the sepulchre. ⁴And the two ran together; and the other disciple outran Peter, and came first to the sepulchre. ⁵And stooping down he sees the linen cloths lying; yet he went not in. ⁶Then comes Simon Peter following him; and he went into the sepulchre, and sees the linen cloths lying, ⁷and the napkin that was about his head not lying with the linen cloths, but wrapped together in a place by itself. ⁸Then therefore the other disciple, who came first to the sepulchre, went in also; and he saw, and believed. ⁹For not even yet did they know the scripture, that he must rise from the dead.
¹⁰The disciples therefore went away again to their own home. ¹¹And Mary was standing by the sepulchre without, weeping. So, as she wept, she stooped down into the sepulchre, ¹²and beholds two angels in white, sitting the one at the head and the other at the feet, where the body of Jesus lay. ¹³And they say to her: Woman, why weepest thou? She says to them: Because they took away my Lord, and I know not where they laid him.
¹⁴Having said this, she turned back and beholds Jesus standing, and knew not that it was Jesus. ¹⁵Jesus says to her: Woman, why weepest thou? Whom dost thou seek? She, supposing that it was the gardener, says to him: Sir, if thou didst bear him hence, tell me where thou laidest him, and I will take him away. ¹⁶Jesus says to her: Mary! Turning, she says to him in Hebrew: Rabboni! (which is to say,

Teacher!) ¹⁷ Jesus says to her: Touch me not; for I have not yet ascended to my Father; but go to my brethren, and say to them: I ascend to my Father and your Father, and my God and your God.

¹⁸ Mary the Magdalene comes bringing word to the disciples, that she has seen the Lord, and that he spoke these things to her.

¹⁹ When therefore it was evening on that day, the first day of the week, the doors having been shut, where the disciples were assembled, for fear of the Jews, Jesus came and stood in the midst; and he says to them: Peace be to you. ²⁰ And having said this, he showed them his hands and his side. The disciples rejoiced therefore, when they saw the Lord.

²¹ Jesus therefore said to them again: Peace be to you. As the Father has sent me, I also send you. ²² And having said this, he breathed on them, and says to them: Receive the Holy Spirit. ²³ Whosesoever sins ye remit, they are remitted to them; and whosesoever ye retain, they are retained.

²⁴ But Thomas, one of the twelve, called Didymus, was not with them when Jesus came. ²⁵ The other disciples therefore said to him: We have seen the Lord. But he said to them: Except I see in his hands the print of the nails, and thrust my finger into the print of the nails, and thrust my hand into his side, I will not believe.

²⁶ And after eight days, again his disciples were within, and Thomas with them. Jesus comes, the doors being shut, and stood in the midst, and said: Peace be to you. ²⁷ After that, he says to Thomas: Reach hither thy finger, and see my hands; and reach thy hand, and thrust it into my side; and be not faithless, but believing. ²⁸ Thomas answered and said to him: My Lord, and my God. ²⁹ Jesus says to him: Because thou hast seen me, thou hast believed. Happy they who saw not, and have believed!

³⁰ Many other signs also did Jesus in the presence of his disciples, which are not written in this book. ³¹ But these are written, that ye might believe that Jesus is the Christ, the Son of God, and that believing ye may have life in his name.

CHAPTER XXI.

XXI. After these things Jesus manifested himself again to the disciples at the sea of Tiberias; and he manifested himself in this manner. ² There were together Simon Peter, and Thomas called Didymus, and Nathanael from Cana of Galilee, and the sons of Zebedee, and two others of his disciples. ³ Simon Peter says to them: I go a fishing. They say to him: We also go with thee. They went forth, and entered into the ship; and in that night they caught nothing.

⁴ But when morning was now come, Jesus stood on the beach; yet the disciples knew not that it was Jesus. ⁵ Jesus therefore says to them: Children, have ye anything to eat? They answered him: No. ⁶ And he said to them: Cast the net on the right side of the ship, and ye shall find. They cast it therefore; and now they were not able to draw it, for the multitude of the fishes.

⁷ Therefore that disciple whom Jesus loved says to Peter: It is the Lord. Simon Peter therefore, hearing that it is the Lord, girded on his outer garment (for he was naked), and cast himself into the sea. ⁸ And the other disciples came in the boat (for they were not far from land, but about two hundred cubits off), dragging the net with the fishes.

⁹ When therefore they went out upon the land, they see a fire of coals there, and a fish lying thereon, and bread. ¹⁰ Jesus says to them: Bring of the fishes which ye just now caught. ¹¹ Simon Peter went on board, and drew the net to land full of great fishes, a hundred and fifty and three; and though there were so many, the net was not broken.

¹² Jesus says to them: Come hither, and break your fast. And none of the disciples durst ask him, Who art thou? knowing that it is the Lord. ¹³ Jesus comes, and takes the bread and gives to them, and the fish likewise. ¹⁴ This the third time already, Jesus manifested himself to his disciples, after he was risen from the dead.

¹⁵ When therefore they had broken their fast, Jesus says to Simon Peter: Simon, son of Jonah, lovest thou me more than

these? He says to him: Yea, Lord; thou knowest that I love thee. He says to him: Feed my lambs.

[16] He says to him again a second time: Simon, son of Jonah, lovest thou me? He says to him: Yea, Lord; thou knowest that I love thee. He says to him: Tend my sheep.

[17] He says to him the third time: Simon, son of Jonah, lovest thou me? Peter was grieved because he said to him the third time, Lovest thou me? And he said to him: Lord, thou knowest all things; thou knowest that I love thee. Jesus says to him: Feed my sheep.

[18] Verily, verily, I say to thee, when thou wast young, thou didst gird thyself, and walk whither thou wouldst; but when thou shalt be old, thou shalt stretch forth thy hands, and another shall gird thee, and lead thee whither thou wouldst not. [19] And this he spoke, signifying by what manner of death he should glorify God.

And having spoken this, he says to him: Follow me. [20] Peter, turning about, sees the disciple whom Jesus loved following; who also at the supper leaned back on his breast, and said: Lord, who is he that betrays thee? [21] Peter seeing him says to Jesus: Lord, and what shall this man do? [22] Jesus says to him: If I will that he remain till I come, what is it to thee? Do thou follow me.

[23] This saying therefore went abroad among the brethren, that that disciple should not die. And Jesus said not to him, that he should not die; but, If I will that he tarry till I come, what is it to thee?

[24] This is the disciple who testifies of these things, and wrote these things; and we know that his testimony is true. [25] And there are also many other things which Jesus did; and if they should be written every one, I suppose that even the world itself would not contain the books that should be written.

CHAPTER I.

THE ACTS OF THE APOSTLES.

1. The former narration I made, O Theophilus, concerning all things that Jesus began both to do and to teach, ² until the day when he was taken up, after he had given commandment, through the Holy Spirit, to the apostles whom he chose ; ³ to whom also he showed himself living, after he had suffered, by many infallible proofs, during forty days appearing to them, and speaking the things concerning the kingdom of God.

⁴ And, being assembled together with them, he commanded them not to depart from Jerusalem, but to wait for the promise of the Father, which ye heard from me; ⁵ for John indeed immersed in water; but ye shall be immersed in the Holy Spirit, not many days hence.

⁶ They therefore, having come together, asked him, saying : Lord, wilt thou at this time restore again the kingdom to Israel? ⁷ And he said to them: It is not yours to know times or seasons, which the Father appointed by his own authority. ⁸ But ye shall receive power, when the Holy Spirit is come upon you; and ye shall be my witnesses both in Jerusalem, and in all Judæa, and Samaria, and unto the utmost part of the earth.

⁹ And having spoken these things, while they beheld he was borne up, and a cloud received him out of their sight. ¹⁰ And while they were looking intently into heaven as he went, behold, two men stood by them in white apparel; ¹¹ who also said: Men of Galilee, why stand ye looking into heaven? This Jesus, who was taken up from you into heaven, shall so come in like manner as ye saw him going into heaven.

¹² Then they returned to Jerusalem from the mount called Olivet, which is near Jerusalem, a sabbath day's journey. ¹³ And when they came in, they went up into the upper room, where were abiding both Peter, and James, and John, and

---

V. 6. *Or*, They therefore who came together
V. 7. *Or*, put in his own power.

THE ACTS.

Andrew, Philip and Thomas, Bartholomew and Matthew, James the son of Alpheus, and Simon Zelotes, and Judas the brother of James. ¹⁴ These all continued with one accord in prayer, with women, and Mary the mother of Jesus, and his brothers.

¹⁵ And in those days Peter stood up in the midst of the brethren, and said (the number of names together was about a hundred and twenty): ¹⁶ Men, brethren, it was necessary that the scripture should be fulfilled, which the Holy Spirit by the mouth of David spoke before concerning Judas, who became guide to those who took Jesus. ¹⁷ Because he was numbered with us, and obtained the office of this ministry.—¹⁸ Now this man purchased a field with the wages of iniquity; and falling headlong, he burst asunder in the midst, and all his bowels gushed out. ¹⁹ And it became known to all who dwell at Jerusalem; so that that field was called, in their own tongue, Aceldama, that is, Field of blood.—²⁰ For it is written in the book of Psalms:

Let his habitation be made desolate,
And let no one dwell therein.

And:

Let another take his office.

²¹ Therefore, of these men, who accompanied us all the time that the Lord Jesus went in and out among us, ²² beginning from John's immersion, unto the day when he was taken up from us, must one be made a witness with us of his resurrection.

²³ And they appointed two, Joseph called Barsabas, who was surnamed Justus, and Matthias. ²⁴ And they prayed, saying: Thou, Lord, who knowest the hearts of all, show which of these two thou didst choose, ²⁵ that he may take part in this ministry and apostleship, from which Judas by transgression fell away, that he might go to his own place. ²⁶ And they gave their lots; and the lot fell upon Matthias; and he was numbered with the eleven apostles.

V. 20. *Or*, his charge.
V. 26. *In some ancient copies:* gave lots for them;

CHAPTER II.

II. And when the day of Pentecost was fully come, they were all with one accord in one place. ²And suddenly there came a sound out of heaven as of a rushing mighty wind, and it filled all the house where they were sitting. ³And there appeared to them tongues as of fire, distributed among them; and it sat upon each of them. ⁴And they were all filled with the Holy Spirit, and began to speak with other tongues, as the Spirit gave them utterance.

⁵Now there were dwelling in Jerusalem, Jews, devout men, from every nation under heaven. ⁶And this being noised abroad, the multitude came together, and were confounded, because every man heard them speak in his own language. ⁷And all were amazed, and wondered, saying one to another: Behold, are not all these who speak Galilæans? ⁸And how do we hear, every man in our own tongue, wherein we were born, ⁹Parthians and Medes and Elamites, and those who inhabit Mesopotamia, Judæa and Cappadocia, Pontus and Asia, ¹⁰Phrygia and Pamphylia, Egypt and the parts of Libya about Cyrene, and strangers of Rome, both Jews and proselytes, ¹¹Cretes and Arabians, hear them speak in our tongues the wonderful works of God? ¹²And all were amazed, and were in doubt, saying one to another: What may this mean? ¹³But others mocking said: They are filled with sweet wine.

¹⁴But Peter, standing up with the eleven, lifted up his voice, and said to them: Men of Judæa, and all that dwell in Jerusalem, be this known to you, and hearken to my words. ¹⁵For these are not drunken, as ye suppose, for it is the third hour of the day. ¹⁶But this is what was spoken through the prophet Joel:

¹⁷And it shall be in the last days, saith God,
That I will pour out of my Spirit upon all flesh;
And your sons and your daughters shall prophesy,
And your young men shall see visions,
And your old men shall dream dreams;

V. 6. *Or*, when this sound occurred

¹⁸ And even on my servants and on my handmaids,
I will pour out of my Spirit in those days,
And they shall prophesy.
¹⁹ And I will show wonders in heaven above,
And signs in the earth beneath,
Blood, and fire, and vapor of smoke.
²⁰ The sun shall be turned into darkness,
And the moon into blood,
Before the great and notable day of the Lord shall come.
²¹ And it shall be, that every one who shall call on the name of the Lord shall be saved.

²² Men of Israel, hear these words! Jesus the Nazarene, a man accredited to you from God by miracles, and wonders, and signs, which God wrought by him in the midst of you, as ye yourselves know; ²³ this man, delivered up according to the established counsel and foreknowledge of God, ye slew, crucifying him by the hand of lawless ones; ²⁴ whom God raised up, having loosed the pains of death; because it was not possible that he should be held by it. ²⁵ For David says concerning him:

I saw the Lord always before me;
Because he is on my right hand, that I should not be moved.
²⁶ For this my heart rejoiced, and my tongue exulted;
Moreover also my flesh shall rest in hope;
²⁷ Because thou wilt not abandon my soul to the underworld,
Nor wilt thou suffer thy Holy One to see corruption.
²⁸ Thou didst make known to me the ways of life;
Thou wilt make me full of joy with thy presence.

²⁹ Men, brethren, I may speak freely to you of the patriarch David, that he both died and was buried, and his sepulchre is among us unto this day. ³⁰ Being a prophet, therefore, and knowing that God swore to him, with an oath, that of the fruit of his loins one should sit on his throne, ³¹ he, foreseeing, spoke of the resurrection of the Christ, that neither was his soul abandoned to the underworld, nor did his flesh see corruption.

³² This Jesus God raised up, whereof we all are witnesses.

CHAPTER II.

³³ Being therefore exalted to the right hand of God, and having received from the Father the promise of the Holy Spirit, he poured forth this, which ye now see and hear. ³⁴ For David did not ascend into heaven; but he says himself:

The Lord said to my Lord,
Sit on my right hand,
³⁵ Until I make thy foes thy footstool.

³⁶ Therefore let all the house of Israel know assuredly, that God made him, this Jesus whom ye crucified, both Lord and Christ.

³⁷ And hearing this, they were pierced to the heart, and said to Peter and the rest of the apostles: Men, brethren, what shall we do? ³⁸ And Peter said to them: Repent, and be each of you immersed, upon the name of Jesus Christ, unto remission of sins, and ye shall receive the gift of the Holy Spirit. ³⁹ For the promise is to you, and to your children, and to all those afar off, as many as the Lord our God shall have called.

⁴⁰ And with many other words did he bear witness and exhort, saying: Save yourselves from this perverse generation.

⁴¹ They therefore, having received his word, were immersed; and on that day there were added about three thousand souls. ⁴² And they were constantly attending on the teaching of the apostles, and the distribution, and the breaking of bread, and prayers. ⁴³ And fear came upon every soul; and many wonders and signs were wrought through the apostles. ⁴⁴ And all that believed were together, and had all things common; ⁴⁵ and sold their possessions and goods, and divided them among all, as any one had need. ⁴⁶ And daily attending with one accord in the temple, and breaking bread from house to house, they partook of food with gladness and singleness of heart, ⁴⁷ praising God, and having favor with all the people. And the Lord added to the church daily those who are saved.

V. 41. *Or*, They therefore who received
V. 47. *Or*, who are being saved.

THE ACTS.

III. ² And Peter and John were going up together into the temple at the hour of prayer, being the ninth hour. ² And a certain man lame from his mother's womb was carried along, whom they laid daily at the gate of the temple, the one called Beautiful, to ask alms of those entering into the temple; ³ who, seeing Peter and John about to go into the temple, asked alms. ⁴ And Peter, looking intently upon him, with John, said: Look upon us. ⁵ And he gave heed to them, expecting to receive something from them. ⁶ And Peter said: Silver and gold have I none; but what I have, that I give thee. In the name of Jesus Christ, the Nazarene, rise up and walk. ⁷ And seizing him by the right hand, he raised him up. And immediately his feet and ankles received strength; ⁸ and leaping forth, he stood, and walked, and entered with them into the temple, walking, and leaping, and praising God. ⁹ And all the people saw him walking and praising God; ¹⁰ and they recognized him, that this was he who sat for alms at the beautiful gate of the temple; and they were filled with wonder and amazement at that which had happened to him.

¹¹ And as he held fast to Peter and John, all the people ran together to them in the porch that is called Solomon's, greatly wondering. ¹² And Peter, seeing it, answered to the people: Men of Israel, why wonder ye at this? Or why look ye so intently on us, as though by our own power or godliness we had made this man to walk? ¹³ The God of Abraham, and of Isaac, and of Jacob, the God of our fathers, glorified his servant Jesus; whom ye delivered up, and denied him in the presence of Pilate, when he decided to release him. ¹⁴ But ye denied the Holy and Just, and demanded that a murderer should be granted to you. ¹⁵ But the Author of life ye killed; whom God raised from the dead, whereof we are witnesses. ¹⁶ And his name, upon the faith in his name, made this man strong, whom ye see and know; and the faith, which is through Him, gave him this perfect soundness in the presence of you all.

V. 15. *Or,* whose witnesses we are.

CHAPTER IV.

¹⁷ And now, brethren, I know that ye acted in ignorance, as also your rulers. ¹⁸ But thus God fulfilled what he before announced by the mouth of all his prophets, that the Christ should suffer. ¹⁹ Repent therefore, and turn, that your sins may be blotted out, in order that the times of refreshing may come from the presence of the Lord; ²⁰ and that he may send forth Jesus Christ, before appointed for you; ²¹ whom the heavens, indeed, must receive, until the times of the restoration of all things, which God spoke of by the mouth of all his holy prophets from the beginning. ²² Moses said: A Prophet will the Lord your God raise up to you of your brethren, like unto me; him shall ye hear in all things whatever he shall say to you. ²³ And it shall be that every soul, that will not hear that Prophet, shall be utterly destroyed from among the people. ²⁴ And also all the prophets from Samuel, both he and they who followed, as many as spoke, also foretold these days.

²⁵ Ye are sons of the prophets, and of the covenant which God made with our fathers, saying to Abraham: And in thy seed shall all the nations of the earth be blessed. ²⁶ Unto you first, God, having raised up his servant Jesus, sent him to bless you, in turning away every one of you from your iniquities.

IV. And while they were speaking to the people, the priests, and the captain of the temple, and the Sadducees, came upon them, ² being indignant because they taught the people, and announced in Jesus the resurrection from the dead. ³ And they laid hands on them, and put them in prison unto the morrow; for it was now evening.

⁴ But many of those who heard the word believed; and the number of the men became about five thousand.

⁵ And it came to pass on the morrow, that their rulers, and elders, and scribes, ⁶ and Annas the high priest, and Caiaphas, and John, and Alexander, and as many as were of the kindred

of the high priest, were gathered together unto Jerusalem. ⁷And having set them in the midst, they asked: By what power, or by what name, did ye do this?

⁸Then Peter, filled with the Holy Spirit, said to them: Rulers of the people, and elders of Israel; ⁹if we are this day examined in respect to a good deed done to an impotent man, by what means this person has been made whole; ¹⁰be it known to you all, and to all the people of Israel, that by the name of Jesus Christ the Nazarene, whom ye crucified, whom God raised from the dead, by him does this man stand here before you whole. ¹¹He is the stone that was set at naught by you the builders, which is become the head of the corner. ¹²And there is salvation in no other; for neither is there any other name under heaven, that is given among men, in which we must be saved.

¹³And seeing the boldness of Peter and John, and perceiving that they were unlearned and obscure men, they wondered; and they recognized them, that they were with Jesus. ¹⁴And beholding the man who had been healed standing with them, they had nothing to say against it. ¹⁵But having commanded them to go aside out of the council, they conferred among themselves, ¹⁶saying: What shall we do to these men? For that a notorious miracle has been done by them is manifest to all that dwell in Jerusalem, and we are not able to deny it. ¹⁷But that it spread no further among the people, let us strictly threaten them, that they speak henceforth to no man in this name. ¹⁸And having called them, they commanded them not to speak at all, nor teach, in the name of Jesus.

¹⁹But Peter and John answering said to them: Whether it is right in the sight of God to hearken to you rather than to God, judge ye. ²⁰For we can not but speak the things which we saw and heard.

²¹And they, having further threatened them, let them go, finding no way to punish them, on account of the people, because all glorified God for that which was done; ²²for the man was above forty years old, on whom this sign of the healing had been wrought.

CHAPTER IV.

²³ And being dismissed, they went to their own company, and reported all that the chief priests and elders said to them. ²⁴ And they, hearing it, lifted up their voice to God with one accord, and said: Lord, thou art he who made heaven, and earth, and the sea, and all things in them; ²⁵ who by the mouth of thy servant David said:

Why did the heathen rage,
And the peoples imagine vain things?
²⁶ The kings of the earth stood near,
And the rulers assembled together,
Against the Lord, and against his Christ.

²⁷ For in truth there assembled in this city, against thy holy servant Jesus, whom thou didst anoint, both Herod, and Pontius Pilate, with the Gentiles, and the peoples of Israel, ²⁸ to do whatever thy hand and thy counsel before determined to be done. ²⁹ And now, Lord, behold their threatenings; and grant to thy servants, that with all boldness they may speak thy word, ³⁰ by stretching forth thy hand for healing, and that signs and wonders may be wrought through the name of thy holy servant Jesus.

³¹ And when they had prayed, the place was shaken where they were assembled; and they were all filled with the Holy Spirit, and they spoke the word of God with boldness.

³² And the multitude of those who believed were of one heart and of one soul; and not one said that aught of the things which he possessed was his own, but they had all things common. ³³ And with great power the apostles gave the testimony to the resurrection of the Lord Jesus; and great grace was upon them all. ³⁴ For there was no one among them that lacked; for as many as were possessors of lands or houses sold them, and brought the prices of the things sold, ³⁵ and laid them at the feet of the apostles; and distribution was made to each one, according as he had need.

³⁶ And Joseph, who by the apostles was surnamed Barnabas (which is interpreted, Son of consolation), a Levite, born in

---

V. 25. *Or*, Why rage the heathen

Cyprus, ³⁷ having land sold it, and brought the money, and laid it at the feet of the apostles.

V. But a certain man named Ananias, with Sapphira his wife, sold a possession, ²and kept back part of the price, his wife also being aware of it, and brought a certain part, and laid it at the feet of the apostles. ³But Peter said: Ananias, why did Satan fill thy heart, that thou shouldst lie to the Holy Spirit, and keep back part of the price of the land? ⁴While it remained, was it not thine own? And after it was sold, was it not in thine own power? Why didst thou conceive this thing in thy heart? Thou didst not lie to men, but to God. ⁵And Ananias hearing these words fell down, and expired; and great fear came on all that heard these things. ⁶And the young men arose, wrapt him up, and carried him out, and buried him.

⁷And it was about the space of three hours after, when his wife, not knowing what was done, came in. ⁸And Peter answered her: Tell me, whether ye sold the land for so much? And she said: Yes, for so much. ⁹And Peter said to her: Why is it that ye agreed together to tempt the Spirit of the Lord? Behold, the feet of those who buried thy husband are at the door, and shall carry thee out. ¹⁰And immediately she fell at his feet, and expired; and coming in, the young men found her dead, and carried her forth, and buried her by her husband. ¹¹And great fear came upon all the church, and upon all that heard these things.

¹²And by the hands of the apostles were many signs and wonders wrought among the people; and they were all with one accord in Solomon's porch. ¹³But of the rest no one dared to join himself to them; but the people honored them; (¹⁴and still more were believers added to the Lord, multitudes both of men and women); ¹⁵so that along the streets they brought forth the sick, and laid them on beds and pallets, that, as Peter was passing, the shadow at least might overshadow

---

V. 6. *(Second clause)* or, laid him out

CHAPTER V.

some one of them. ¹⁶ And the multitude also of the cities around came together to Jerusalem, bringing sick persons, and those who were vexed by unclean spirits; and they were all healed.

¹⁷ But the high priest rose up, and all that were with him, which is the sect of the Sadducees, and were filled with indignation, ¹⁸ and laid their hands on the apostles, and put them in the public prison.

¹⁹ But an angel of the Lord by night opened the prison doors; and having brought them forth, he said: ²⁰ Go, stand and speak in the temple to the people all the words of this life. ²¹ And hearing it, they went into the temple at early dawn, and taught.

And the high priest came, and they that were with him, and called the council together, and all the eldership of the children of Israel, and sent to the prison to have them brought. ²² But the officers, when they came, found them not in the prison; and returning, they reported, ²³ saying: The prison indeed we found shut with all security, and the keepers standing without before the doors; but when we opened them, we found no one within.

²⁴ And when the priest and the captain of the temple and the chief priests heard these things, they were at a loss concerning them, to what this might grow. ²⁵ But one came and told them, saying: Behold, the men whom ye put in the prison are in the temple, standing and teaching the people. ²⁶ Then went the captain with the officers, and brought them, not with violence (for they feared the people), that they might not be stoned. ²⁷ And having brought them, they set them before the council. And the high priest asked them, ²⁸ saying: Did we not strictly command you not to teach in this name? And, behold, ye have filled Jerusalem with your teaching, and intend to bring this man's blood upon us.

²⁹ And Peter answering, and the apostles, said: We ought to obey God rather than men. ³⁰ The God of our fathers raised up Jesus, whom ye slew, hanging him on a tree. ³¹ Him, as a prince and a Savior, did God exalt to his right hand, to give

repentance to Israel, and remission of sins. ³²And we are his witnesses of these things, and the Holy Spirit also, which God gave to those who obey him.

³³And they, hearing it, were convulsed with rage, and took counsel to slay them. ³⁴But there stood up one in the council, a Pharisee, named Gamaliel, a teacher of the law, honored by all the people, and commanded to put the men forth a little while; ³⁵and said to them: Men of Israel, take heed to yourselves, what ye are about to do in respect to these men. ³⁶For before these days arose Theudas, boasting himself to be somebody; to whom a number of men, about four hundred, joined themselves; who was slain, and all, as many as obeyed him, were scattered and brought to naught. ³⁷After this man arose Judas the Galilæan, in the days of the registering, and drew away much people after him; he also perished, and all, as many as obeyed him, were dispersed. ³⁸And now I say to you, refrain from these men, and let them alone: for if this counsel or this work be of men, it will come to naught; ³⁹but if it is of God ye can not overthrow them; lest haply ye be found also fighting against God.

⁴⁰And to him they assented; and having called the apostles, they scourged them, and commanded them not to speak in the name of Jesus, and let them go.

⁴¹They therefore went rejoicing from the presence of the council, because for that name they were counted worthy to suffer shame. ⁴²And every day, in the temple, and from house to house, they ceased not to teach, and to publish the glad tidings of Jesus the Christ.

VI. And in these days, when the number of the disciples was multiplied, there arose a murmuring of the Grecian Jews against the Hebrews, because their widows were neglected in the daily ministration. ²And the twelve called the multitude of the disciples to them, and said: It is not proper that we should leave the word of God, and serve tables. ³Therefore, brethren, look ye out among you seven men of good repute, full of the Holy Spirit and of wisdom, whom we

CHAPTER VII.

will appoint over this business. ⁴ But we will give ourselves to prayer, and to the ministry of the word.

⁵ And the saying pleased the whole multitude. And they chose Stephen, a man full of faith and of the Holy Spirit, and Philip, and Prochorus, and Nicanor, and Timon, and Parmenas, and Nicolas a proselyte of Antioch, ⁶ whom they set before the apostles; and having prayed, they laid their hands on them.

⁷ And the word of God increased; and the number of the disciples multiplied in Jerusalem greatly; and a great company of the priests were obedient to the faith.

⁸ And Stephen, full of grace and of power, did great wonders and signs among the people. ⁹ And there arose certain ones of the synagogue so called of the Freedmen, and Cyrenians, and Alexandrians, and of those from Cilicia and Asia, disputing with Stephen. ¹⁰ And they were not able to resist the wisdom and the spirit with which he spoke. ¹¹ Then they suborned men, who said: We have heard him speak blasphemous words against Moses, and against God.

¹² And they stirred up the people, and the elders, and the scribes; and coming upon him, they seized him, and brought him to the council, ¹³ and set up false witnesses, who said: This man ceases not to speak words against this holy place, and the law. ¹⁴ For we have heard him say, that this Jesus the Nazarene will destroy this place, and will change the customs which Moses delivered to us. ¹⁵ And all that sat in the council, looking intently upon him, saw his face as the face of an angel.

VII. ¹ AND the high priest said: Are then these things so? ² And he said: Brethren, and fathers, hearken. The God of glory appeared to our father Abraham, when he was in Mesopotamia, before he dwelt in Haran, ³ and said to him: Go forth from thy country, and from thy kindred, and come into the land which I

V. 9. Freedmen: *captive Jews, carried to Rome as slaves, who (or their offspring) had been freed, and allowed to return.*

shall show thee. ⁴Then he went forth from the land of the Chaldæans, and dwelt in Haran; and from thence, after his father was dead, he caused him to remove into this land, wherein ye now dwell. ⁵And he gave him no inheritance in it, not even a foot-breadth; and he promised to give it to him for a possession, and to his seed after him, when he had no child. ⁶And God spoke after this manner, that his seed shall be a sojourner in a strange land, and they will bring them into bondage, and afflict them four hundred years. ⁷And the nation to whom they shall be in bondage I will judge, said God; and after that they shall come forth, and shall serve me in this place. ⁸And he gave him the covenant of circumcision; and thus he begot Isaac, and circumcised him the eighth day, and Isaac, Jacob, and Jacob the twelve patriarchs. ⁹And the patriarchs, moved with envy, sold Joseph into Egypt. And God was with him, ¹⁰and delivered him out of all his afflictions, and gave him favor and wisdom in the sight of Pharaoh king of Egypt; and he made him governor over Egypt and all his house.

¹¹And there came a famine over all the land of Egypt and Canaan, and a great affliction; and our fathers found no sustenance. ¹²But Jacob, hearing that there was grain in Egypt, first sent out our fathers. ¹³And at the second time, Joseph was recognized by his brothers; and the race of Joseph was made known to Pharaoh. ¹⁴Then Joseph sent, and called for Jacob his father, and all his kindred, threescore and fifteen souls. ¹⁵And Jacob went down into Egypt, and died, he and our fathers, ¹⁶and were removed to Shechem, and laid in the tomb that Abraham bought for a sum of money of the sons of Hamor, the father of Shechem.

¹⁷But as the time of the promise drew near, which God declared to Abraham, the people grew and multiplied in Egypt, ¹⁸until another king arose who knew not Joseph. ¹⁹He, dealing subtly with our race, afflicted our fathers, so that they should cast out their infants, that they might not be preserved alive. ²⁰In which time Moses was born, and was

CHAPTER VII.

exceeding fair, who was nourished three months in his father's house. ²¹ And when he was cast out, Pharaoh's daughter took him up, and nourished him for herself as a son. ²² And Moses was instructed in all the wisdom of the Egyptians, and was mighty in words and in deeds. ²³ And when he was forty years old, it came into his heart to visit his brethren the sons of Israel. ²⁴ And seeing one of them suffer wrong, he defended him, and avenged the one oppressed by smiting the Egyptian. ²⁵ For he supposed his brethren would understand, that God by his hand would deliver them; but they understood not. ²⁶ And on the following day he showed himself to them as they were contending, and urged them to peace, saying: Ye are brethren; why wrong ye one another? ²⁷ But he who was wronging his neighbor thrust him away, saying: Who made thee a ruler and a judge over us? ²⁸ Wilt thou kill me, as thou didst kill the Egyptian yesterday? ²⁹ And Moses fled at this saying, and became a sojourner in the land of Midian, where he begot two sons. ³⁰ And when forty years were completed, there appeared to him in the wilderness of the mount Sinai an angel in a flame of fire, in a bush. ³¹ And Moses, seeing it, wondered at the sight; and as he drew near to behold it, the voice of the Lord came to him, saying: ³² I am the God of thy fathers, the God of Abraham, and the God of Isaac, and the God of Jacob. And Moses trembled, and durst not behold. ³³ And the Lord said to him: Loose the sandals from thy feet; for the place where thou standest is holy ground. ³⁴ Truly, I saw the affliction of my people in Egypt, and I heard their groaning, and came down to deliver them. And now come, I will send thee into Egypt. ³⁵ This Moses whom they denied, saying: Who made thee a ruler and a judge? him did God send as a ruler

---

V. 20. *Gr.* was beautiful before God

and a redeemer by the hand of the angel who appeared to him in the bush. ³⁶ He brought them out, working wonders and signs in the land of Egypt, and in the Red sea, and in the wilderness forty years.

³⁷ This is the Moses who said to the children of Israel: A Prophet will God raise up to you of your brethren, like unto me. ³⁸ This is he who was in the congregation in the wilderness with the angel who spoke to him in the mount Sinai, and with our fathers; who received the living oracles to give to us; ³⁹ to whom our fathers would not be obedient, but thrust him from them, and in their hearts turned back again into Egypt, ⁴⁰ saying to Aaron: Make us gods who shall go before us: for as for this Moses, who brought us out of the land of Egypt, we know not what is become of him.

⁴¹ And they made a calf in those days, and offered sacrifice to the idol, and rejoiced in the works of their own hands. ⁴² And God turned away, and gave them up to worship the host of heaven; as it is written in the book of the prophets:

Did ye offer to me slain beasts and sacrifices,
Forty years in the wilderness, O house of Israel?
⁴³ And ye took up the tabernacle of Moloch,
And the star of the god Remphan,
The figures which ye made to worship them;
And I will carry you away beyond Babylon.

⁴⁴ Our fathers had the tabernacle of the testimony in the wilderness, as he who spoke to Moses commanded, that he should make it according to the pattern that he had seen; ⁴⁵ which also our fathers received, and brought in with Joshua into the possession of the heathen, whom God drove out before our fathers, unto the days of David; ⁴⁶ who found favor before God, and asked that he might find a habitation for the God of Jacob. ⁴⁷ But Solomon built a house for him. ⁴⁸ Yet the Most High dwells not in temples made with hands; as says the prophet:

V. 35. *In some ancient copies:* with the hand

CHAPTER VIII.

⁴⁹ Heaven is my throne,
And the earth is my footstool.
What house will ye build for me, saith the Lord;
Or what is my place of rest?
⁵⁰ Did not my hand make all these things?
⁵¹ Stiff-necked, and uncircumcised in heart and ears! Ye always resist the Holy Spirit; as your fathers did, so do ye. ⁵² Which of the prophets did not your fathers persecute? And they slew those who announced beforehand concerning the coming of the Just One; of whom ye have now become the betrayers and murderers; ⁵³ who received the law as the ordinances of angels, and kept it not.

⁵⁴ Hearing these things, they were enraged in their hearts, and gnashed their teeth against him. ⁵⁵ But, being full of the Holy Spirit, he looked intently into heaven, and saw the glory of God, and Jesus standing on the right hand of God, and said: ⁵⁶ Behold, I see the heavens opened, and the Son of man standing on the right hand of God. ⁵⁷ And crying out with a loud voice, they stopped their ears, and rushed upon him with one accord; ⁵⁸ and having cast him out of the city, they stoned him. And the witnesses laid off their garments at the feet of a young man named Saul, ⁵⁹ and stoned Stephen, calling and saying: Lord Jesus, receive my spirit. ⁶⁰ And kneeling down, he cried with a loud voice: Lord, lay not this sin to their charge. And saying this, he fell asleep.

VIII. And Saul was consenting to his death. And on that day there arose a great persecution against the church which was at Jerusalem; and all were scattered abroad throughout the regions of Judæa and Samaria, except the apostles. ² And devout men carried Stephen to his burial, and made great lamentation over him. ³ But Saul laid waste the church, entering house after house, and dragging both men and women, committed them to prison.

⁴ They, therefore, that were scattered, went abroad, preaching the word. ⁵ And Philip went down to the city of Samaria, and

---

V. 5. *Or,* to a city

preached to them the Christ. ⁶And the multitudes with one accord gave heed to the things said by Philip, when they heard, and saw the signs which he wrought. ⁷For out of many who had unclean spirits they went forth, crying with loud voice; and many that were palsied, and that were lame, were healed. ⁸And there was great joy in that city.

⁹But a certain man, named Simon, was in the city before, using sorcery, and bewitching the people of Samaria, saying that he was some great one; ¹⁰to whom all gave heed, from the least to the greatest, saying: This man is the great power of God. ¹¹And to him they gave heed, because for a long time they were bewitched by his sorceries. ¹²But when they believed Philip publishing the good news concerning the kingdom of God and the name of Jesus Christ, they were immersed, both men and women. ¹³And Simon also himself believed; and having been immersed, he continued with Philip, and wondered, beholding the miracles and signs which were wrought.

¹⁴And the apostles in Jerusalem, hearing that Samaria has received the word of God, sent to them Peter and John; ¹⁵who, having come down, prayed for them, that they might receive the Holy Spirit; ¹⁶for he had not yet fallen upon any of them; but they had only been immersed in the name of the Lord Jesus. ¹⁷Then they laid their hands on them, and they received the Holy Spirit.

¹⁸And Simon, seeing that through the laying on of the apostles' hands the Holy Spirit was given, offered them money, ¹⁹saying: Give me also this power, that on whomsoever I lay hands, he may receive the Holy Spirit. ²⁰But Peter said to him: Thy money perish with thee; because thou didst think to obtain the gift of God with money. ²¹Thou hast no part nor lot in this matter; for thy heart is not right in the sight of God. ²²Repent therefore of this thy wickedness, and pray the Lord, if perhaps the thought of thy heart shall be forgiven thee. ²³For I perceive that thou art in the gall of bitterness, and the bond of iniquity.

V. 10. *In many ancient copies:* is the power of God, which is called great.
V. 21. *Or,* in this word

CHAPTER VIII.

²⁴ And Simon answering, said: Pray ye to the Lord for me, that none of the things which ye have spoken come upon me.
²⁵ They, therefore, having testified and spoken the word of the Lord, were returning to Jerusalem, and publishing the good news to many villages of the Samaritans. ²⁶ But an angel of the Lord spoke to Philip, saying: Arise, and go down to the south, to the way that goes down from Jerusalem to Gaza. This is desert.
²⁷ And he arose and went. And behold, a man of Ethiopia, a eunuch, an officer of state of Candace queen of the Ethiopians, who was over all her treasure, and had come to Jerusalem to worship, ²⁸ was returning, and sitting in his chariot; and he was reading the prophet Isaiah. ²⁹ And the Spirit said to Philip: Go near, and join thyself to this chariot. ³⁰ And Philip ran thither, and heard him reading Isaiah the prophet. And he said: Understandest thou then what thou art reading? ³¹ And he said: How could I, except some one should guide me? And he entreated Philip to come up, and sit with him.
³² And the contents of the Scripture which he was reading was this:

He was led as a sheep to the slaughter;
And as a lamb dumb before his shearer,
So he opens not his mouth.
³³ In his humiliation his judgment was taken away;
And his generation who shall fully declare?
For his life is taken away from the earth.

³⁴ And the eunuch answering said to Philip: I pray thee, of whom does the prophet speak this? Of himself, or of some other man? ³⁵ And Philip opened his mouth, and beginning from this Scripture, made known to him the good news of Jesus. ³⁶ And as they went along the way, they came to a certain water. And the eunuch said: See, here is water; what hinders that I should be immersed? ³⁷ And Philip said: If thou believest with all thy heart, thou mayest. And an-

---

V. 33. *Or, and his posterity*
V. 37 *is wanting in the best ancient copies.*

swering he said : I believe that Jesus Christ is the Son of God. ³⁸ And he commanded that the chariot should stop. And they went down both into the water, both Philip and the eunuch : and he immersed him. ³⁹ And when they came up out of the water, the Spirit of the Lord caught away Philip ; and the eunuch saw him no more, for he went on his way rejoicing. ⁴⁰ But Philip was found at Azotus ; and passing through, he published the good news to all the cities, till he came to Cæsarea.

IX. But Saul, yet breathing threatening and slaughter against the disciples of the Lord, went to the high priest, ² and asked of him letters to Damascus to the synagogues, that if he found any of this way, whether they were men or women, he might bring them bound to Jerusalem.

³ And as he journeyed, he came near Damascus. And suddenly there flashed around him a light from heaven ; ⁴ and he fell to the earth, and heard a voice saying to him : Saul, Saul, why persecutest thou me ? ⁵ And he said : Who art thou, Lord ? And the Lord said : I am Jesus, whom thou persecutest. ⁶ But arise, and go into the city, and it shall be told thee what thou must do.

⁷ And the men who journeyed with him were standing speechless, hearing the voice, but seeing no one. ⁸ And Saul arose from the earth ; and his eyes being opened, he saw nothing ; and leading him by the hand, they brought him into Damascus. ⁹ And he was three days without sight, and neither ate nor drank.

¹⁰ And there was a certain disciple at Damascus, named Ananias ; and to him the Lord said, in a vision, Ananias ! And he said, Behold, I am here, Lord. ¹¹ And the Lord said to him : Arise, and go into the street which is called Straight, and inquire in the house of Judas for one called Saul of Tarsus. For, behold, he prays ; ¹² and in a vision he saw a man named Ananias coming in, and putting his hand on him, that he might receive sight.

¹³ And Ananias answered : Lord, I have heard from many

CHAPTER IX.

concerning this man, how great evils he did to thy saints at Jerusalem. ¹⁴ And here he has authority from the chief priests to bind all that call on thy name. ¹⁵ But the Lord said to him: Go ; for he is to me a chosen vessel, to bear my name before Gentiles, and kings, and the sons of Israel ; ¹⁶ for I will show him how great things he must suffer for my name's sake. ¹⁷ And Ananias went, and entered into the house ; and putting his hands on him, he said : Brother Saul, the Lord has sent me, Jesus who appeared to thee in the way thou camest, that thou mayest receive sight, and be filled with the Holy Spirit. ¹⁸ And immediately there fell off from his eyes as it were scales ; and he received sight, and arose, and was immersed ; ¹⁹ and having taken food, he was strengthened.

And Saul was certain days with the disciples at Damascus. ²⁰ And straightway he preached Jesus, in the synagogues, that he is the Son of God. ²¹ And all that heard him were amazed, and said : Is not this he who destroyed in Jerusalem those who call on this name? And he came hither for this purpose, that he might bring them bound to the chief priests.

²² But Saul was more strengthened, and confounded the Jews who dwelt at Damascus, proving that this is the Christ.

²³ And when many days were completed, the Jews took counsel to kill him. ²⁴ But their lying in wait became known to Saul. And they were watching the gates day and night to kill him. ²⁵ But the disciples took him by night, and let him down through the wall, lowering him in a basket.

²⁶ And Saul, having come to Jerusalem, attempted to join himself to the disciples; and all were afraid of him, not believing that he was a disciple. ²⁷ But Barnabas took him, and brought him to the apostles, and related fully to them how he saw the Lord in the way, and that he spoke to him, and how he preached boldly at Damascus in the name of Jesus. ²⁸ And he was with them, going in and out at Jerusalem. ²⁹ and speaking boldly in the name of the Lord Jesus; and was speaking and disputing against the Grecian Jews; but they were attempting to slay him. ³⁰ And the brethren, learning it, brought him down to Cæsarea, and sent him forth to Tarsus.

³¹ The church therefore, throughout all Judæa and Galilee and Samaria, had peace, being built up, and walking in the fear of the Lord, and in the consolation of the Holy Spirit, was multiplied. ³² And it came to pass that Peter, going through them all, came down also to the saints who dwelt at Lydda. ³³ And there he found a certain man named Æneas, who had lain upon a pallet eight years, who was palsied. ³⁴ And Peter said to him: Æneas, Jesus the Christ makes thee whole; arise, and make thy bed. And immediately he arose. ³⁵ And all that dwelt at Lydda and Saron saw him; and they turned to the Lord.

³⁶ And there was at Joppa a certain disciple named Tabitha, which interpreted is called Dorcas. This woman was full of good works, and of alms, which she did. ³⁷ And it came to pass in those days, that she was sick, and died. And having washed her, they laid her in an upper chamber. ³⁸ And as Lydda was near to Joppa, the disciples, having heard that Peter was there, sent to him two men, entreating that he would not delay to come to them.

³⁹ And Peter arose and went with them. When he was come, they brought him into the upper chamber; and all the widows stood by him weeping, and showing coats and garments which Dorcas made, while she was with them. ⁴⁰ But Peter put them all forth, and kneeled down, and prayed; and turning to the body, he said: Tabitha, arise. And she opened her eyes; and seeing Peter, she sat up. ⁴¹ And he gave her his hand, and raised her up; and calling the saints and widows, he presented her alive. ⁴² And it became known throughout all Joppa; and many believed on the Lord.

⁴³ And it came to pass, that he remained many days in Joppa, with one Simon, a tanner.

X. There was a certain man in Cæsarea named Cornelius, a centurion of the band called the Italian band: ² devout, and one that feared God with all his house, giving many alms to the people, and praying to God always. ³ He saw in a vis-

CHAPTER X.

ion distinctly, about the ninth hour of the day, an angel of God coming in to him, and saying to him: Cornelius! ⁴ And fixing his eyes on him, he was afraid, and said: What is it, Lord? And he said to him: Thy prayers and thine alms are come up for a memorial before God. ⁵ And now send men to Joppa, and call for Simon, who is surnamed Peter. ⁶ He lodges with one Simon a tanner, whose house is by the seaside.

⁷ And when the angel who spoke to Cornelius was gone, he called two of his household servants, and a devout soldier of those who waited on him ; ⁸ and having told them all these things, he sent them to Joppa.

⁹ On the morrow, as they were journeying, and drawing near to the city, Peter went up upon the house-top to pray, about the sixth hour. ¹⁰ And he became very hungry, and desired to eat. While they now were making ready, there fell upon him a trance ; ¹¹ and he beholds heaven opened, and a certain vessel descending upon him, as a great sheet, bound by four corners, and let down upon the earth ; ¹² wherein were all the fourfooted beasts and creeping things of the earth, and birds of the air. ¹³ And there came a voice to him: Arise, Peter ; slay, and eat. ¹⁴ But Peter said: Not so, Lord ; for I never ate anything common or unclean. ¹⁵ And a voice came to him again, the second time: What God cleansed, call not thou common. ¹⁶ This was done thrice ; and the vessel was taken up again into heaven.

¹⁷ And while Peter was doubting in himself what the vision might be which he saw, behold, the men who were sent from Cornelius, having made inquiry for Simon's house, came and stood before the gate ; ¹⁸ and calling they asked, whether Simon, who is surnamed Peter, lodges here.

¹⁹ While Peter was earnestly considering the vision, the Spirit said to him: Behold, men are seeking thee. ²⁰ But arise, and go down, and go with them, making no scruple ; because I have sent them.

²¹ Peter went down to the men, and said: Behold, I am he whom ye seek. What is the cause for which ye are here?

²² And they said: Cornelius, a centurion, a just man, and one that fears God, and of good report among all the nation of the Jews, was warned from God by a holy angel to send for thee to his house, and to hear words from thee. ²³ He called them in, therefore, and lodged them. And on the morrow Peter went forth with them, and certain brethren from Joppa went with him. ²⁴ And on the morrow after, they entered into Cæsarea. And Cornelius was expecting them, having called together his kinsmen and near friends. ²⁵ And as Peter was coming in, Cornelius met him, and fell down at his feet, and did reverence to him. ²⁶ But Peter raised him, saying: Stand up; I myself also am a man. ²⁷ And while talking with him, he went in, and found many that were come together. ²⁸ And he said to them: Ye know that it is unlawful for a Jew to keep company with, or come to, one of another nation; but God showed me that I should not call any man common or unclean. ²⁹ Wherefore I also came without delay, when sent for. I ask therefore for what reason did ye send for me?

³⁰ And Cornelius said: Four days ago I was fasting unto this hour, and at the ninth hour was praying in my house; and, behold, a man stood before me in bright clothing, ³¹ and said: Cornelius, thy prayer was heard, and thine alms were remembered before God. ³² Send therefore to Joppa, and call for Simon, who is surnamed Peter; he lodges in the house of Simon a tanner, by the sea-side; who, when he comes will speak to thee. ³³ Immediately therefore I sent to thee; and thou didst well in coming hither. Now therefore we are all present before God, to hear all things that are commanded thee from the Lord.

³⁴ And Peter opened his mouth, and said: Of a truth I perceive that God is not a respecter of persons; ³⁵ but in every nation he that fears him, and works righteousness, is acceptable to him. ³⁶ The word which he sent to the sons of Israel, publishing glad tidings of peace through Jesus Christ (he is

---

V. 28. *Or*, how unlawful it is

CHAPTER XI.

Lord of all), ³⁷ ye know; the thing which was done throughout all Judæa, beginning from Galilee, after the immersion which John preached; Jesus of Nazareth, ³⁸ how God anointed him with the Holy Spirit and with power; who went about doing good, and healing all that were oppressed by the Devil; because God was with him. ³⁹ And we are witnesses of all things which he did both in the country of the Jews, and in Jerusalem; whom they slew, hanging him on a tree. ⁴⁰ Him God raised on the third day, and showed him openly; ⁴¹ not to all the people, but to witnesses before appointed by God, to us, who ate and drank with him after he rose from the dead. ⁴² And he commanded us to preach to the people, and to testify that it is he who has been appointed by God to be Judge of the living and dead. ⁴³ To him all the prophets bear witness, that through his name every one who believes on him shall receive remission of sins.

⁴⁴ While Peter was yet speaking these words, the Holy Spirit fell on all who heard the word. ⁴⁵ And those of the circumcision who believed, as many as came with Peter, were astonished, that on the Gentiles also was poured out the gift of the Holy Spirit. ⁴⁶ For they heard them speaking with tongues, and magnifying God.

Then answered Peter: ⁴⁷ Can any one forbid the water, that these should not be immersed, who received the Holy Spirit even as we also? ⁴⁸ And he commanded that they should be immersed in the name of the Lord. Then they entreated him to remain certain days.

XI. AND the apostles, and the brethren throughout Judæa, heard that the Gentiles also received the word of God. ² And when Peter went up to Jerusalem, they that were of the circumcision contended with him, ³ saying: Thou wentest in to men uncircumcised, and didst eat with them.

⁴ But Peter rehearsed the matter to them in order, from the beginning, saying: ⁵ I was in the city of Joppa praying; and in a trance I saw a vision, a certain vessel descending, as a great sheet, let down out of heaven by four corners; and it

came even to me. ⁶ On which fixing my eyes, I considered, and saw fourfooted beasts of the earth, and wild beasts, and creeping things, and birds of the air. ⁷ And I heard a voice saying to me: Arise, Peter; slay and eat. ⁸ But I said: Not so, Lord; for nothing common or unclean ever entered into my mouth. ⁹ But a voice answered me a second time out of heaven: What God cleansed, regard not thou as common. ¹⁰ And this was done three times; and all were drawn up again into heaven.

¹¹ And, behold, immediately there stood three men at the house where I was, having been sent to me from Cæsarea. ¹² And the Spirit bade me go with them, making no scruple. And these six brethren also went with me, and we entered into the man's house. ¹³ And he told us how he saw the angel in his house, standing and saying to him: Send to Joppa, and call for Simon who is surnamed Peter; ¹⁴ who will speak to thee words, whereby thou shalt be saved, and all thy house.

¹⁵ And as I began to speak, the Holy Spirit fell on them, as also on us at the beginning; ¹⁶ and I remembered the word of the Lord, how he said: John indeed immersed in water, but ye shall be immersed in the Holy Spirit. ¹⁷ If therefore God gave the like gift to them as to us, having believed on the Lord Jesus Christ, who then was I, that I could withstand God?

¹⁸ When they heard these things, they held their peace, and glorified God, saying: So then, to the Gentiles also God gave repentance unto life.

¹⁹ Now they who were scattered abroad by the persecution that arose on account of Stephen, went as far as Phœnicia, and Cyprus, and Antioch, speaking the word to none but Jews. ²⁰ But some of them were men of Cyprus and Cyrene, who, having come to Antioch, spoke to the Greeks, publishing the good news of the Lord Jesus. ²¹ And the hand of the Lord was with them; and a great number believed, and turned to the Lord.

²² But the report concerning them came to the ears of the church which was in Jerusalem; and they sent forth Barnabas,

CHAPTER XII.

to go as far as Antioch. ²³ Who having come, and seen the grace of God, rejoiced; and he exhorted all, that with purpose of heart they should cleave to the Lord. ²⁴ For he was a good man, and full of the Holy Spirit and of faith. And a great multitude was added to the Lord.

²⁵ And Barnabas departed to Tarsus, to seek for Saul; ²⁶ and having found him, he brought him to Antioch. And it came to pass, that a whole year they came together in the church, and taught a great multitude; and the disciples were first called Christians in Antioch.

²⁷ And in these days prophets came down from Jerusalem to Antioch. ²⁸ And there stood up one of them named Agabus, and signified by the Spirit that there should be a great dearth over all the world; which came to pass in the days of Claudius Cæsar. ²⁹ And the disciples, according as any one was prospered, determined each of them to send relief to the brethren dwelling in Judæa; ³⁰ which also they did, sending it to the elders by the hands of Barnabas and Saul.

XII. AND about that time, Herod the king stretched forth his hands to oppress certain of the church. ² And he slew James the brother of John with the sword. ³ And seeing that it pleased the Jews, he proceeded further to take Peter also; (then were the days of unleavened bread;) ⁴ whom he also seized and put in prison, delivering him to four quaternions of soldiers to keep him; intending after the passover to bring him forth to the people.

⁵ Peter therefore was kept guarded in the prison; but earnest prayer was made by the church to God on his behalf.

⁶ And when Herod was about to bring him forth, in that night Peter was sleeping between two soldiers, bound with two chains; and keepers before the door were guarding the prison. ⁷ And, behold, an angel of the Lord stood by him, and a light shined in the prison; and he smote Peter on the side, and raised him, saying: Rise up quickly. And his chains fell from

---

V. 1. *Gr.* laid hands on, to oppress

off his hands. ⁸And the angel said to him: Gird thyself, and bind on thy sandals; and he did so. And he said to him: Cast thy garment about thee, and follow me. ⁹And he went out, and followed him; and knew not that what was done by the angel was true, but thought he saw a vision.

¹⁰ And having passed the first and the second watch, they came to the iron gate that leads into the city, which opened to them of its own accord; and they went out, and passed on through one street, and immediately the angel departed from him.

¹¹ And Peter, having come to himself, said: Now I know truly, that the Lord sent forth his angel, and delivered me out of the hand of Herod, and from all the expectation of the people of the Jews. ¹² And becoming fully conscious of it, he went to the house of Mary the mother of John, who was surnamed Mark, where many were gathered together, and praying.

¹³ And as Peter knocked at the door of the gate, a maid-servant came to hearken, named Rhoda.

¹⁴ And recognizing Peter's voice, she opened not the gate for gladness, but ran in, and told that Peter was standing before the gate. ¹⁵ And they said to her: Thou art mad. But she confidently affirmed that it was even so. And they said: It is his angel.

¹⁶ But Peter continued knocking; and opening the door they saw him, and were amazed. ¹⁷ And beckoning to them with the hand to be silent, he related to them how the Lord brought him out of the prison. And he said: Go tell these things to James, and to the brethren. And he departed, and went to another place.

¹⁸ And when it was day, there was no small commotion among the soldiers, as to what was become of Peter. ¹⁹ And Herod, when he had sought for him, and found him not, after examining the keepers, commanded that they should be led away to death. And he went down from Judæa to Cæsarea, and there abode.

²⁰ And Herod was highly displeased with the Tyrians and

CHAPTER XIII.

Sidonians. But they came with one accord to him, and, having made Blastus the king's chamberlain their friend, desired peace; because their country was nourished by that of the king.

21 And on a set day Herod, arrayed in royal apparel, sat upon his throne, and made a speech to them. 22 And thereupon the people shouted: The voice of a god, and not of a man! 23 And immediately an angel of the Lord smote him, because he gave not glory to God; and he was eaten by worms, and expired.

24 But the word of God grew and multiplied. 25 And Barnabas and Saul returned from Jerusalem, having performed the service, taking with them also John, who was surnamed Mark.

XIII. AND there were at Antioch, in the church that was there, prophets and teachers; Barnabas, and Simeon who was called Niger, and Lucius the Cyrenean, and Manaen the foster-brother of Herod the tetrarch, and Saul.

2 And while they were ministering to the Lord, and fasting, the Holy Spirit said: Set apart for me Barnabas and Saul, unto the work to which I have called them. 3 Then, having fasted and prayed, and laid their hands on them, they sent them away.

4 They therefore, being sent forth by the Holy Spirit, came down to Seleucia; and from thence they sailed away to Cyprus. 5 And having come to Salamis, they preached the word of God in the synagogues of the Jews; and they had also John as an assistant.

6 And having gone through the island to Paphos, they found a certain Magian, a Jewish false prophet, whose name was Bar-jesus; 7 who was with the proconsul of the country, Sergius Paulus, an intelligent man. He, having called for Barnabas and Saul, desired to hear the word of God. 8 But Elymas the Magian (for so his name is interpreted), withstood them, seeking to turn away the proconsul from the faith.

9 Then Saul (who is also called Paul), filled with the Holy Spirit, fixed his eyes on him, 10 and said: O full of all deceit

and all wickedness, child of the Devil, enemy of all righteousness, wilt thou not cease to pervert the right ways of the Lord? ¹¹ And now, behold, the hand of the Lord is upon thee, and thou shalt be blind, not seeing the sun for a season. And immediately there fell on him a mist and darkness; and going about, he sought persons to lead him by the hand. ¹² Then the proconsul, seeing what was done, believed, being astonished at the teaching of the Lord.

¹³ And Paul and his companions, having put to sea from Paphos, came to Perga in Pamphylia; and John departing from them returned to Jerusalem. ¹⁴ But they, going on from Perga, came to Antioch in Pisidia; and entering into the synagogue on the sabbath day, they sat down. ¹⁵ And after the reading of the law and the prophets, the rulers of the synagogue sent to them, saying: Men, brethren, if ye have any word of exhortation for the people, speak.

¹⁶ And Paul arose, and beckoning with the hand, said: Men of Israel, and ye that fear God, hearken. ¹⁷ The God of this people of Israel chose our fathers; and he exalted the people in their sojourn in the land of Egypt, and with a high arm he brought them out of it. ¹⁸ And about the time of forty years he nourished them in the wilderness. ¹⁹ And having destroyed seven nations in the land of Canaan, he gave them their land as a possession, ²⁰ about four hundred and fifty years. And after that, he gave judges, until Samuel the prophet. ²¹ And afterward they desired a king; and God gave them Saul the Son of Kish, a man of the tribe of Benjamin, for forty years. ²² And having removed him, he raised up for them David to be their king; to whom also he gave testimony, saying: I found David the son of Jesse, a man after my own heart, who will do all my will. ²³ Of the seed of this man, God, according to promise, raised up to Israel a Savior, Jesus; ²⁴ John having first preached, before his entrance, the immersion of repentance to all the people of Israel. ²⁵ Now as John was finishing his course, he

---

V. 18. *In some ancient copies:* he bore with them

CHAPTER XIII.

said : Whom do ye suppose me to be? I am not he. But, behold, there comes one after me, the sandal of whose feet I am not worthy to loose.

²⁶ Men, brethren, children of the race of Abraham, and whoever among you fears God, to you the word of this salvation was sent forth. ²⁷ For they who dwell at Jerusalem, and their rulers, not knowing him, nor the voices of the prophets which are read every sabbath day, fulfilled them in condemning him. ²⁸ And though they found no cause of death, they demanded of Pilate that he should be slain. ²⁹ And when they had fulfilled all the things written of him, they took him down from the tree, and laid him in a tomb. ³⁰ But God raised him from the dead. ³¹ And he was seen for many days by those who came up with him from Galilee to Jerusalem, who are now his witnesses unto the people. ³² And we declare to you glad tidings of the promise made to the fathers, ³³ that God has fulfilled this to us their children, in raising Jesus; as also it is written in the second psalm :

Thou art my Son ;
I this day have begotten thee.

³⁴ And that he raised him up from the dead to return no more to corruption, he has thus spoken : I will give to you the holy, the sure promises of David. ³⁵ Wherefore also in another psalm he says: Thou wilt not suffer thy Holy One to see corruption. ³⁶ For David, having served his own generation according to the purpose of God, fell asleep, and was added to his fathers, and saw corruption. ³⁷ But he, whom God raised, saw not corruption.

³⁸ Be it known to you therefore, men, brethren, that remission of sins through this man is announced to you ; ³⁹ and by him all that believe are justified from all things, from which ye were not able to be justified by the law of Moses.

⁴⁰ Beware therefore, lest that come upon you, which is spoken in the prophets :

V. 33. *In the oldest copies :* in the first psalm

⁴¹ Behold, ye despisers, and wonder, and perish;
Because I work a work in your days,
A work which ye will not believe,
Though one should fully declare it to you.

⁴² And as they were going out, they besought that these words might be spoken to them on the next sabbath. ⁴³ And when the congregation was broken up, many of the Jews and of the proselyte worshipers followed Paul and Barnabas; who, speaking to them, persuaded them to continue in the grace of God.

⁴⁴ And on the next sabbath day, almost the whole city came together to hear the word of God. ⁴⁵ But the Jews, seeing the multitudes, were filled with indignation, and spoke against the things said by Paul, contradicting and blaspheming.

⁴⁶ Then Paul and Barnabas spoke boldly, and said: It was necessary that the word of God should first be spoken to you; but since ye thrust it from you, and judge yourselves not worthy of the eternal life, lo, we turn to the Gentiles. ⁴⁷ For so has the Lord commanded us:

I have set thee for a light of the Gentiles,
That thou shouldst be for salvation to the end of the earth.

⁴⁸ And the Gentiles hearing it rejoiced, and glorified the word of the Lord; and as many as were appointed unto eternal life believed. ⁴⁹ And the word of the Lord was spread abroad throughout all the region.

⁵⁰ But the Jews stirred up the devout and honorable women, and the chief men of the city, and raised persecution against Paul and Barnabas, and drove them out from their borders. ⁵¹ And they, having shaken off the dust of their feet against them, came to Iconium. ⁵² And the disciples were filled with joy, and with the Holy Spirit.

XIV. And it came to pass in Iconium, that they went together into the synagogue of the Jews, and so spoke, that a great multitude both of Jews and Greeks believed. ² But the Jews who disbelieved stirred up and embittered the minds of the Gentiles against the brethren. ³ They

CHAPTER XIV.

spent a long time, therefore, speaking boldly in the Lord, who gave testimony to the word of his grace, granting signs and wonders to be done by their hands.

⁴ But the multitude of the city was divided; and part held with the Jews, and part with the apostles. ⁵ And when a movement was made, both of the Gentiles and Jews with their rulers, to abuse and stone them, ⁶ they, being aware of it, fled to the cities of Lycaonia, Lystra and Derbe, and the region around; ⁷ and there they were publishing the good news.

⁸ And there sat a certain man at Lystra, impotent in his feet, being lame from his mother's womb, who never walked. ⁹ This man was listening to Paul as he spoke; who, fixing his eyes on him, and perceiving that he had faith to be healed, ¹⁰ said with a loud voice: Stand upright on thy feet. And he leaped up, and walked.

¹¹ And the multitudes, seeing what Paul did, lifted up their voices, saying in the speech of Lycaonia: The gods are come down to us in the likeness of men. ¹² And they called Barnabas, Jupiter; and Paul, Mercury, because he was the chief speaker. ¹³ And the priest of Jupiter, that was before the city, having brought oxen and garlands to the gates, would have offered sacrifice with the people. ¹⁴ But the apostles, Barnabas and Paul, hearing of it, rent their clothes, and rushed forth to the multitude; crying out, ¹⁵ and saying: Sirs, why do ye these things? We also are men of like nature with you, bringing you glad tidings, that ye should turn from these vanities to the living God, who made heaven, and earth, and the sea, and all things that are therein; ¹⁶ who, in the ages past, suffered all nations to walk in their own ways; ¹⁷ although he left not himself without witness, in that he did good, giving you rain from heaven, and fruitful seasons, filling your hearts with food and gladness.

¹⁸ And with these sayings they hardly restrained the people from sacrificing to them.

¹⁹ But there came thither Jews from Antioch and Iconium; and having persuaded the people, and stoned Paul, they drew him out of the city, supposing that he was dead. ²⁰ But the

disciples having gathered around him, he rose up, and came into the city; and on the morrow he departed with Barnabas to Derbe. ²¹ And having published the good news to that city, and made many disciples, they turned back to Lystra, and Iconium, and Antioch; ²² confirming the souls of the disciples, exhorting them to continue in the faith, and that we must through much affliction enter into the kingdom of God.

²³ And having appointed for them elders in every church, they commended them, with prayer and fasting, to the Lord, on whom they believed. ²⁴ And after passing through Pisidia, they came to Pamphylia. ²⁵ And having spoken the word in Perga, they went down to Attalia; ²⁶ and thence they sailed away to Antioch, from whence they had been commended to the grace of God for the work which they accomplished.

²⁷ And having come, and gathered the church together, they reported how great things God wrought with them, and that he opened to the Gentiles a door of faith. ²⁸ And they spent no little time with the disciples.

XV. And certain men, coming down from Judæa, taught the brethren: Except ye are circumcised after the custom of Moses, ye can not be saved. ² Paul and Barnabas having therefore had no little dissension and discussion with them, they determined that Paul and Barnabas, and certain others of them, should go up to Jerusalem to the apostles and elders, about this question.

³ They therefore, having been sent forward by the church, passed through Phœnicia and Samaria, declaring the conversion of the Gentiles; and they caused great joy to all the brethren. ⁴ And having come to Jerusalem, they were gladly received by the church, and the apostles and elders; and they reported how great things God wrought with them. ⁵ But there arose some of those from the sect of the Pharisees who believed, saying: It is necessary to circumcise them, and to command them to keep the law of Moses.

⁶ And the apostles and the elders came together to consider this matter. ⁷ And when there had been much discussion,

CHAPTER XV.

Peter arose, and said to them: Men, brethren, ye know that a long time ago God made choice among us, that by my mouth the Gentiles should hear the word of the glad tidings and believe. ⁸ And God who knows the heart bore them witness, giving to them the Holy Spirit, as also to us; ⁹ and made no difference between us and them, purifying their hearts by faith. ¹⁰ Now therefore why do ye tempt God, by putting a yoke upon the neck of the disciples, which neither our fathers nor we were able to bear? ¹¹ But, through the grace of the Lord Jesus, we believe that we shall be saved, in the same manner as they also.

¹² And all the multitude became silent, and listened to Barnabas and Paul, narrating how great signs and wonders God wrought among the Gentiles through them.

¹³ And after they were silent, James answered, saying: Men, brethren, hearken to me. ¹⁴ Simeon narrated how at first God visited the Gentiles, to take out of them a people for his name. ¹⁵ And with this agree the words of the prophets; as it is written:

¹⁶ After this I will return,
    And will rebuild the tabernacle of David, which is fallen down;
    And I will rebuild the ruins thereof, and will set it up again;
¹⁷ That the rest of men may seek after the Lord,
    And all the Gentiles, upon whom my name has been called,
    Saith the Lord, who does these things.
¹⁸ Known to God are all his works from the beginning of the world.

¹⁹ Wherefore my judgment is, that we trouble not those who from among the Gentiles are turning to God; ²⁰ but that we write to them, that they abstain from pollutions of idols, and from fornication, and from what is strangled, and from blood. ²¹ For Moses of old time has in every city those who preach him, being read in the synagogues every sabbath.

V. 17. *Or, who makes these things known of old (omitting v. 18, as in ancient copies).*

THE ACTS.

²² Then the apostles and the elders, with the whole church, resolved, having chosen men from themselves, to send them to Antioch with Paul and Barnabas; namely, Judas surnamed Barsabas, and Silas, leading men among the brethren. ²³ And they wrote by them thus:

The apostles and the elders and the brethren, to the brethren from the Gentiles throughout Antioch and Syria and Cilicia, greeting: ²⁴ Forasmuch as we heard, that some who went out from us troubled you with words, subverting your souls, saying that ye must be circumcised and keep the law, to whom we gave no commandment; ²⁵ it seemed good to us, having become of one mind, to choose men and send them to you, with our beloved Barnabas and Paul, ²⁶ men who have hazarded their lives for the name of our Lord Jesus Christ.

²⁷ We have sent therefore Judas and Silas, who will themselves also by word tell you the same things. ²⁸ For it seemed good to the Holy Spirit, and to us, to lay upon you no further burden except these necessary things; ²⁹ that ye abstain from things offered to idols, and from blood, and from what is strangled, and from fornication; from which if ye keep yourselves, ye will do well. Farewell.

³⁰ They therefore, being dismissed, came to Antioch; and assembling the multitude they delivered the letter. ³¹ And having read it, they rejoiced for the consolation. ³² And Judas and Silas, also themselves being prophets, exhorted the brethren with many words, and confirmed them.

³³ And having remained a while, they were dismissed with peace from the brethren to the apostles. ³⁴ But it pleased Silas to abide there still. ³⁵ Paul also and Barnabas continued in Antioch, teaching and publishing the glad tidings of the word of the Lord, with many others also.

³⁶ And some days after, Paul said to Barnabas: Let us return now, and visit the brethren in every city where we preached the word of the Lord, and see how they do. ³⁷ And

---

V. 24. *The oldest copies omit:* saying, that ye must be circumcised and keep the law

V. 34 *is omitted in the oldest copies.*

CHAPTER XVI.

Barnabas determined to take with them John, who was surnamed Mark. ³⁸ But Paul thought it proper not to take with them him who departed from them from Pamphylia, and went not with them to the work. ³⁹ And there arose a sharp contention, so that they parted one from the other, and Barnabas took Mark, and sailed to Cyprus. ⁴⁰ And Paul, having chosen Silas, went forth, being commended by the brethren to the grace of God. ⁴¹ And he went through Syria and Cilicia, confirming the churches.

XVI. And he came down to Derbe and Lystra. And, behold, a certain disciple was there, named Timothy, the son of a believing Jewish woman, but whose father was a Greek; ² who was well reported of by the brethren in Lystra and Iconium. ³ Him Paul wished to go forth with him, and took and circumcised him on account of the Jews who were in those places; for they all knew that his father was a Greek.

⁴ And as they journeyed through the cities, they delivered to them the decrees to keep, that were ordained by the apostles and elders who were in Jerusalem. ⁵ The churches, therefore, were established in the faith, and increased in number daily.

⁶ And having gone through the region of Phrygia and Galatia, and being forbidden by the Holy Spirit to speak the word in Asia, ⁷ they came to Mysia, and attempted to go into Bithynia; but the Spirit of Jesus did not permit them. ⁸ And passing by Mysia, they came down to Troas.

⁹ And a vision appeared to Paul in the night. There stood a man, a Macedonian, beseeching him, and saying: Come over into Macedonia and help us. ¹⁰ And when he had seen the vision, immediately we sought to go into Macedonia, concluding that the Lord had called us to publish the good news to them. ¹¹ Therefore setting sail from Troas, we ran with a straight course to Samothrace, and on the following day to Neapolis; ¹² and from thence to Philippi, which is a chief city of that part of Macedonia, a colony. And we continued in that city certain days.

¹³ And on the sabbath, we went forth out of the gate by a river side, where was wont to be a place of prayer; and we sat down, and spoke to the women who came together. ¹⁴ And a certain woman named Lydia, a seller of purple, of the city of Thyatira, who worshiped God, was listening; whose heart the Lord opened to attend to the things spoken by Paul. ¹⁵ And when she was immersed and her household, she besought us, saying: If ye have judged me to be a believer in the Lord, come into my house, and abide. And she constrained us.

¹⁶ And it came to pass, as we were going to the place of prayer, a certain bondmaid having a spirit of divination met us, who brought her masters much gain by soothsaying. ¹⁷ She, having followed Paul and us, cried, saying: These men are the servants of the most high God, who announce to us the way of salvation.

¹⁸ And this she did many days. But Paul, being indignant, turned and said to the spirit: I command thee in the name of Jesus Christ to come out from her. And he came out the same hour.

¹⁹ And her masters, seeing that the hope of their gain departed, laid hold of Paul and Silas, and drew them into the market-place before the rulers. ²⁰ And having brought them to the magistrates, they said: These men, being Jews, greatly disturb our city; ²¹ and teach customs, which it is not lawful for us to receive, or to observe, being Romans.

²² And the multitude rose up together against them; and the magistrates rent off their clothes, and commanded to beat them with rods. ²³ And having laid many stripes on them, they cast them into prison, charging the jailer to keep them safely; ²⁴ who, having received such a charge, thrust them into the inner prison, and made their feet fast in the stocks.

²⁵ And at midnight Paul and Silas prayed, and sang praises to God; and the prisoners listened to them. ²⁶ And suddenly there was a great earthquake, so that the foundations of the

---

V. 18. *Or,* being grieved

CHAPTER XVII.

prison were shaken; and immediately all the doors were opened, and the chains of all were loosed. ²⁷ And the jailer, awaking out of sleep, and seeing the prison doors open, drew his sword, and was about to kill himself, supposing that the prisoners had fled. ²⁸ But Paul cried with a loud voice, saying: Do thyself no harm; for we are all here. ²⁹ And calling for lights, he sprang in, and trembling fell down before Paul and Silas; ³⁰ and having brought them out, he said: Sirs, what must I do to be saved? ³¹ And they said: Believe on the Lord Jesus Christ, and thou shalt be saved, and thy house. ³² And they spoke to him the word of the Lord, and to all that were in his house.

³³ And taking them along, the same hour of the night, he washed their stripes; and was immersed, himself and all his, immediately. ³⁴ And having brought them up into his house, he set food before them, and rejoiced, with all his house, believing in God.

³⁵ And when it was day, the magistrates sent the sergeants, saying: Let those men go. ³⁶ And the keeper of the prison reported these words to Paul: The magistrates have sent to let you go; now therefore depart, and go in peace.

³⁷ But Paul said to them: They beat us openly, uncondemned, being Romans, and cast us into prison; and now do they send us forth secretly? Nay verily; but let them come themselves and bring us out.

³⁸ And the sergeants reported these words to the magistrates; and they were afraid, when they heard that they were Romans. ³⁹ And they came and besought them, and bringing them out, entreated them to depart out of the city.

⁴⁰ And they went out of the prison, and entered into the house of Lydia; and seeing the brethren they exhorted them, and departed.

XVII. AND passing through Amphipolis and Apollonia, they came to Thessalonica, where was the synagogue of the Jews. ² And Paul, as his custom was, went in to them, and for three sabbaths reasoned with them from the

Scriptures, ³ opening them, and setting forth that the Christ must suffer, and rise again from the dead; and that this is the Christ, Jesus whom I preach to you. ⁴ And some of them believed, and joined themselves to Paul and Silas; and of the devout Greeks a great multitude, and of the chief women not a few.

⁵ But the Jews, moved with envy, having taken to them, of the idlers in the market-place, certain vicious men, and having gathered a crowd, set the city in an uproar; and assaulting the house of Jason, they sought to bring them unto the people. ⁶ And not finding them, they dragged Jason and certain brethren before the rulers of the city, crying: These that have turned the world upside down are come hither also. ⁷ Whom Jason has received; and all these are acting contrary to the decrees of Cæsar, saying that there is another king, Jesus.

⁸ And they troubled the people and the rulers of the city, when they heard these things. ⁹ And having taken security of Jason, and of the others, they let them go.

¹⁰ And the brethren immediately sent away Paul and Silas by night to Berœa; who coming thither went into the synagogue of the Jews. ¹¹ These were more noble than those in Thessalonica, in that they received the word with all readiness, and searched the Scriptures daily whether these things were so.

¹² Many of them therefore believed; and of honorable Grecian women and men, not a few. ¹³ But when the Jews of Thessalonica knew that also at Berœa the word of God was preached by Paul, they came, stirring up the people there also. ¹⁴ And then immediately the brethren sent away Paul to journey as upon the sea; but Silas and Timothy abode there still. ¹⁵ And they who conducted Paul brought him to Athens; and having received a command to Silas and Timothy to come to him as soon as possible, they departed.

¹⁶ Now while Paul was waiting for them at Athens, his spirit was stirred in him, when he saw the city full of idols. ¹⁷There-

---

V. 4. *Or*, were allotted to
V. 5. *Some ancient copies omit:* moved with envy

CHAPTER XVII.

fore he reasoned in the synagogue with the Jews and the devout persons, and in the market daily with those who met with him. ¹⁸ And certain philosophers of the Epicureans, and of the Stoics, were disputing with him. And some said: What would this babbler say? and others: He seems to be a proclaimer of foreign gods; because he made known to them the good news of Jesus and the resurrection. ¹⁹ And taking hold of him, they brought him upon Mars' Hill, saying: May we know what this new doctrine is, of which thou speakest? ²⁰ For thou bringest certain strange things to our ears; we would know therefore what these things mean. ²¹ Now all Athenians, and the strangers residing there, spent their leisure for nothing else, but to tell or to hear something new.

²² And Paul, standing in the midst of Mars' Hill, said: Men of Athens, in all things I perceive that ye are very devout. ²³ For as I passed by, and observed your objects of worship, I found also an altar with this inscription: TO AN UNKNOWN GOD. Whom therefore, not knowing, ye worship, him I announce to you. ²⁴ The God who made the world and all things therein, he being Lord of heaven and earth, dwells not in temples made with hands; ²⁵ nor is ministered to by human hands, as if needing anything more, himself giving to all life, and breath, and all things. ²⁶ And he made of one blood every nation of men to dwell on all the face of the earth, having fixed the appointed seasons and bounds of their habitation; ²⁷ that they should seek the Lord, if haply they might feel after him, and find him, although he is not far from every one of us; ²⁸ for in him we live, and move, and have our being; as also some of your own poets have said: For his offspring also are we. ²⁹ Being therefore God's offspring, we ought not to think that the Godhead is like to gold, or silver, or stone, graven by art and man's device. ³⁰ The times of ignorance therefore God overlooked; but now, commands all men everywhere to repent. ³¹ Because he fixed a day, in which he will judge the world in righteousness, by the man whom he appointed, having given assurance to all by raising him from the dead.

THE ACTS.

⁸² And when they heard of a resurrection of the dead, some mocked; and others said: We will hear thee again of this matter. ⁸³ And thus Paul departed from among them.

³⁴ But certain ones, joining themselves to him, believed; among whom was also Dionysius the Areopagite, and a woman named Damaris, and others with them.

XVIII.

After these things Paul departed from Athens, and came to Corinth. ² And finding a certain Jew named Aquila, a native of Pontus, lately come from Italy, and Priscilla his wife (because Claudius had commanded all the Jews to depart from Rome), he came to them; ³ and because he was of the same trade, he abode with them, and labored; for by their occupation they were tentmakers. ⁴ And he reasoned in the synagogue every sabbath, and persuaded both Jews and Greeks.

⁵ And when Silas and Timothy came down from Macedonia, Paul was engrossed with the word, testifying to the Jews that Jesus is the Christ. ⁶ But they opposing themselves and blaspheming, he shook out his garments and said to them: Your blood be upon your own head; I am clean; from henceforth I will go to the Gentiles.

⁷ And departing thence he entered into a certain man's house, named Justus, one who worshiped God, whose house was adjoining the synagogue. ⁸ And Crispus, the ruler of the synagogue, believed on the Lord with all his house; and many of the Corinthians hearing believed, and were immersed.

⁹ And the Lord said to Paul, through a vision in the night: Be not afraid, but speak, and hold not thy peace; ¹⁰ for I am with thee, and no one shall assail thee to hurt thee; for I have much people in this city. ¹¹ And he continued there a year and six months, teaching the word of God among them.

¹² And when Gallio was proconsul of Achaia, the Jews rose up with one accord against Paul, and brought him before the judgment-seat, ¹³ saying: This man persuades men to worship God contrary to the law.

¹⁴ And as Paul was about to open his mouth, Gallio said to

CHAPTER XVIII.

the Jews: If it were some injustice, or wicked misdeed, O Jews, with reason I would have borne with you. ¹⁵ But if it is a question about a word, and names, and your own law, look to it yourselves; I will not be a judge of these things. ¹⁶ And he drove them away from the judgment-seat.

¹⁷ But having all seized upon Sosthenes, the ruler of the synagogue, they beat him before the judgment-seat. And Gallio cared for none of these things.

¹⁸ And Paul having remained yet many days, took leave of the brethren, and sailed thence to Syria, and with him Priscilla and Aquila; having shaven his head in Cenchrea, for he had a vow. ¹⁹ And they came to Ephesus, and he left them there; but entering himself into the synagogue, he reasoned with the Jews. ²⁰ And they desiring him to remain a longer time with them, he consented not; ²¹ but took leave of them, saying: [I must by all means keep the coming feast at Jerusalem; but] I will return again to you, if God will. And he sailed from Ephesus. ²² And having landed at Cæsarea, and gone up and saluted the church, he went down to Antioch. ²³ And after he had spent some time there, he departed, going through the country of Galatia and Phrygia in order, strengthening all the disciples.

²⁴ And a certain Jew named Apollos, a native of Alexandria, an eloquent man, and mighty in the Scriptures, came to Ephesus. ²⁵ This man was instructed in the way of the Lord; and being fervent in spirit, he spoke and taught correctly the things concerning Jesus, knowing only the immersion of John. ²⁶ And he began to speak boldly in the synagogue. But Aquila and Priscilla, having heard him, took him to them, and expounded to him the way of God more perfectly. ²⁷ And he wishing to pass through into Achaia, the brethren wrote, exhorting the disciples to receive him; who, when he was come, contributed much to those who had believed through grace. ²⁸ For he powerfully confuted the Jews in public, showing by the Scriptures that Jesus is the Christ.

V. 21. *The words in brackets are omitted in the oldest copies.*

THE ACTS.

XIX. And it came to pass, that, while Apollos was at Corinth, Paul having passed through the upper districts came to Ephesus. And finding certain disciples, ² he said to them: Did ye receive the Holy Spirit when ye believed? And they said to him: Nay, we did not even hear whether there is a Holy Spirit. ³ And he said to them: Unto what then were ye immersed? And they said: Unto John's immersion. ⁴ Then said Paul: John indeed immersed with the immersion of repentance; saying to the people, that they should believe on him who should come after him, that is, on Jesus. ⁵ And when they heard this, they were immersed in the name of the Lord Jesus. ⁶ And Paul having laid his hands upon them, the Holy Spirit came on them; and they spoke with tongues, and prophesied. ⁷ And all the men were about twelve.

⁸ And he went into the synagogue, and spoke boldly for three months, reasoning and persuading them of the things concerning the kingdom of God. ⁹ But when some were hardened, and believed not, speaking evil of the Way before the multitude, he departed from them, and separated the disciples, reasoning daily in the school of Tyrannus. ¹⁰ And this continued for two years; so that all who dwelt in Asia heard the word of the Lord, both Jews and Greeks. ¹¹ And God wrought special miracles by the hands of Paul; ¹² so that also there were carried from his body to the sick, handkerchiefs or aprons, and the diseases departed from them, and the evil spirits went out from them.

¹³ Then some of the wandering Jewish exorcists took upon them to name, over those who had the evil spirits, the name of the Lord Jesus, saying: I adjure you by the Jesus whom Paul preaches. ¹⁴ And there were seven sons of one Sceva, a Jewish chief priest, who did this. ¹⁵ And the evil spirit answering said: Jesus I know, and Paul I well know; but who are ye? ¹⁶ And the man in whom the evil spirit was leaped on them, and overcame them, and prevailed against both, so that they fled out of that house naked and wounded. ¹⁷ And this be-

CHAPTER XIX.

came known to all, both Jews and Greeks, who dwelt at Ephesus; and fear fell on them all, and the name of the Lord Jesus was magnified. ¹⁸ And many of the believers came, confessing, and declaring their deeds. ¹⁹ Many of those also who practiced curious arts brought together the books, and burned them before all; and they counted the price of them, and found it fifty thousand pieces of silver. ²⁰ So mightily grew the word of God and prevailed.

²¹ When these things were ended, Paul purposed to go to Jerusalem, passing through Macedonia and Achaia; saying: After I have been there, I must also see Rome. ²² And having sent into Macedonia two of those who ministered to him, Timothy and Erastus, he himself stayed in Asia for a season.

²³ And about that time, there arose no small tumult concerning the Way. ²⁴ For a certain man named Demetrius, a silversmith, who made silver shrines of Diana, brought no small gain to the craftsmen; ²⁵ whom he called together, with the workmen of like occupation, and said: Sirs, ye well know that by this craft we have our wealth. ²⁶ Moreover ye see and hear, that this Paul has persuaded and turned aside much people, not only of Ephesus, but of almost all Asia, saying that they are not gods, which are made with hands. ²⁷ And there is danger to us, not only that this branch of business will come into disrepute, but also that the temple of the great goddess Diana will be accounted nothing, and her magnificence will be destroyed, whom all Asia and the world worship.

²⁸ And hearing it, they became full of wrath, and continued crying out, saying: Great is Diana of the Ephesians. ²⁹ And the whole city was filled with confusion; and they rushed with one accord into the theatre, having seized Gaius and Aristarchus, men of Macedonia, Paul's companions in travel. ³⁰ And Paul wishing to enter in unto the people, the disciples suffered him not. ³¹ And some also of the chiefs of Asia, being his friends, sent to him, entreating him not to adventure himself into the theatre.

³² Some therefore were crying one thing, and some another; for the assembly was confused, and the greater part knew not wherefore they had come together. ³³ And they brought for-

ward Alexander out of the multitude, the Jews thrusting him forward. And Alexander beckoned with the hand, desiring to make his defense to the people. ³¹ But when they knew that he was a Jew, one voice arose from all, crying about two hours: Great is Diana of the Ephesians.

³⁵ And the town-clerk, having quieted the people, said: Men of Ephesus, what human being is there, who knows not that the city of the Ephesians is keeper of the great Diana, and of the image which fell down from Jupiter? ³⁶ These things being therefore undeniable, ye ought to be quiet, and to do nothing rashly. ³⁷ For ye brought hither these men, who are neither robbers of temples, nor blasphemers of your goddess. ³⁸ If therefore Demetrius, and the craftsmen with him, have a matter against any man, the law is open, and there are proconsuls; let them implead one another. ³⁹ But if ye make any demand concerning other matters, it shall be determined in the lawful assembly. ⁴⁰ For we are in danger of being called in question for this day's riot, there being no cause whereby we may give an account of this concourse. ⁴¹ And having thus spoken, he dismissed the assembly.

XX. And after the tumult ceased, Paul called to him the disciples, and having embraced them, departed to go into Macedonia. ² And having gone through those regions, and given them much exhortation, he came into Greece. ³ And after he had stayed three months, a plot being laid for him by the Jews, as he was about sailing to Syria, it was resolved that he should return through Macedonia. ⁴ And there accompanied him unto Asia, Sopater, son of Pyrrhus, a Berœan; and of the Thessalonians, Aristarchus and Secundus; and Gaius of Derbe, and Timothy; and of Asia, Tychicus and Trophimus. ⁵ These, having gone forward, were waiting for us at Troas. ⁶ But we sailed forth from Philippi, after the days of unleavened bread, and came to them to Troas in five days; where we abode seven days.

V. 38. The law is open: *Gr.* court-days are held

CHAPTER XX.

⁷ And on the first day of the week, we having come together to break bread, Paul discoursed to them (being about to depart on the morrow), and continued the discourse until midnight. ⁸ Now there were many lights in the upper room, where we were assembled. ⁹ And there sat on the window a certain young man named Eutychus, being fallen into a deep sleep; and as Paul was long discoursing, he sunk down with sleep, and fell down from the third loft, and was taken up dead. ¹⁰ And Paul went down, and fell on him, and embracing him said: Do not lament, for his life is in him. ¹¹ And having come up again, and broken the bread, and eaten, he talked a long while even till break of day, and so departed. ¹² And they brought the young man living, and were not a little comforted.

¹³ And we, going forward to the ship, embarked for Assos, intending there to take in Paul; for so he had appointed, intending himself to go on foot. ¹⁴ And when he met with us at Assos, we took him in, and came to Mitylene. ¹⁵ And sailing thence, we came the following day over against Chios; ‹ the next day we arrived at Samos; and having tarried at Trogyllium, we came the next day to Miletus. ¹⁶ For Paul had determined to sail past Ephesus, that he might not spend time in Asia; for he was hastening, if it were possible for him, to be at Jerusalem on the day of Pentecost.

¹⁷ And from Miletus he sent to Ephesus, and called the elders of the church. ¹⁸ And when they were come to him, he said to them: Ye know, from the first day that I came into Asia, after what manner I have been with you the whole time; ¹⁹ serving the Lord with all lowliness of mind, and with tears, and trials which befell me by the plottings of the Jews; ²⁰ how I kept back nothing that was profitable, that I should not announce it to you, and teach you, publicly and from house to house; ²¹ testifying, to both Jews and Greeks, repentance toward God, and faith toward our Lord Jesus Christ.

²² And now, behold, I go bound in the spirit to Jerusalem, not knowing the things that shall befall me there; ²³ save that the Holy Spirit witnesses to me in every city, saying that

THE ACTS.

bonds and afflictions await me. ²⁴ But none of these things move me, neither do I count my life dear to myself, so that I may finish my course with joy, and the ministry which I received from the Lord Jesus, to testify the good news of the grace of God.

²⁵ And now, behold, I know that all ye, among whom I went about preaching the kingdom of God, shall see my face no more. ²⁶ Wherefore I testify to you this day, that I am pure from the blood of all; ²⁷ for I shunned not to declare to you the whole counsel of God.

²⁸ Take heed therefore to yourselves, and to all the flock, in which the Holy Spirit made you overseers, to feed the church of the Lord, which he purchased with his own blood. ²⁹ For I know this, that after my departure grievous wolves will enter in among you, not sparing the flock. ³⁰ And from among yourselves will men arise, speaking perverse things, to draw away disciples after them. ³¹ Therefore watch, remembering that for the space of three years, night and day, I ceased not to warn every one with tears.

³² And now, brethren, I commend you to God, and to the word of his grace, who is able to build you up, and to give you an inheritance among all the sanctified. ³³ I coveted no one's silver, or gold, or apparel. ³⁴ Ye yourselves know, that these hands ministered to my necessities, and to those who were with me. ³⁵ In all ways I showed you that, so laboring, ye ought to assist the weak, and to remember the words of the Lord Jesus, that he himself said: It is more blessed to give than to receive.

³⁶ And having thus spoken, he kneeled down, and prayed with them all. ³⁷ And they all wept sorely, and fell on Paul's neck, and kissed him; ³⁸ sorrowing most of all for the word which he had spoken, that they should behold his face no more. And they accompanied him to the ship.

V. 24. *The oldest copies omit:* with joy

V. 28. *In some ancient copies:* church of God

CHAPTER XXI.

XXI. And it came to pass, that after we had torn ourselves from them, and had put to sea, we came with a straight course to Coos, and the day following to Rhodes, and from thence to Patara. ² And finding a ship crossing over to Phœnicia, we went aboard, and put to sea. ³ And bringing Cyprus in sight, and leaving it on the left hand, we sailed to Syria, and landed at Tyre; for there the ship was to unlade her burden. ⁴ And having found out the disciples, we remained there seven days; who said to Paul through the Spirit, that he should not go up to Jerusalem.

⁵ And when we had completed the days, we departed and went our way; they all accompanying us, with wives and children, till we were out of the city; and we kneeled down on the beach, and prayed. ⁶ And having embraced one another, we went on board the ship; and they returned to their homes.

⁷ And we, completing the voyage, came down from Tyre to Ptolemais; and having embraced the brethren, we remained with them one day. ⁸ And on the morrow we departed, and came to Cæsarea; and entering into the house of Philip the evangelist, being one of the Seven, we abode with him. ⁹ And this man had four daughters, virgins, who prophesied.

¹⁰ And while we were remaining several days, there came down from Judæa a certain prophet, named Agabus. ¹¹ And coming to us, he took off Paul's girdle, and bound his own hands and feet, and said: Thus 'says the Holy Spirit': So will the Jews at Jerusalem bind the man, whose this girdle is, and will deliver him into the hands of the Gentiles. ¹² And when we heard these things, both we, and they of that place, besought him not to go up to Jerusalem. ¹³ Then answered Paul: What mean ye, to weep and to break my heart? For I am ready not only to be bound, but also to die at Jerusalem, for the name of the Lord Jesus. ¹⁴ And when he would not be persuaded, we ceased, saying: The will of the Lord be done.

¹⁵ And after those days, having packed up our baggage, we went up to Jerusalem. ¹⁶ There went with us also some of the

disciples from Cæsarea, bringing us to Mnason of Cyprus, an old disciple, with whom we should lodge.

¹⁷ And when we were come to Jerusalem, the brethren received us gladly. ¹⁸ And on the following day, Paul went in with us to James; and all the elders were present. ¹⁹ And having embraced them, he recounted particularly what things God had wrought among the Gentiles through his ministry.

²⁰ And they, hearing it, glorified the Lord. And they said to him: Thou seest, brother, how many thousands of Jews there are who believe; and they are all zealots for the law. ²¹ And they were informed concerning thee, that thou teachest all the Jews who are among the Gentiles to forsake Moses, saying that they should not circumcise their children, nor walk after the customs. ²² What is it therefore? A multitude must surely come together; for they will hear that thou hast come. ²³ Do therefore this that we say to thee: We have four men who have a vow on them; ²⁴ these take with thee, and purify thyself with them, and bear the charges for them, that they may shave their heads; and all will know that those things, of which they have been informed concerning thee, are nothing, but that thou thyself also walkest orderly, keeping the law. ²⁵ But concerning the Gentiles who have believed, we wrote to them, deciding that they should observe no such thing, except that they keep themselves from things offered to idols, and from blood, and from what is strangled, and from fornication.

²⁶ Then Paul took the men, and the next day, having purified himself with them, entered into the temple, announcing the completion of the days of the purification, until the offering was brought for each one of them.

²⁷ And as the seven days were about to be completed, the Jews from Asia, having observed him in the temple, stirred up all the people, and laid hands on him, ²⁸ crying out: Men of Israel, help. This is the man who teaches all, everywhere, against the people, and the law, and this place; and further also, he brought Greeks into the temple, and has polluted this holy place. ²⁹ For they had before seen with him in the city

CHAPTER XXII.

Trophimus the Ephesian, whom they supposed that Paul brought into the temple. ³⁰ And all the city was moved, and the people ran together; and laying hold of Paul, they dragged him out of the temple; and forthwith the doors were shut. ³¹ And while they were seeking to kill him, a report came up to the chief captain of the band, that all Jerusalem was in an uproar; ³² who immediately took with him soldiers and centurions, and ran down to them; and they, seeing the chief captain and the soldiers, left off beating Paul. ³³ Then the chief captain came near, and took hold of him, and commanded him to be bound with two chains; and inquired who he was, and what he had done. ³⁴ And some cried one thing, some another, among the multitude; and not being able to know the certainty on account of the tumult, he commanded him to be led into the castle. ³⁵ And when he came upon the stairs, so it was, that he was borne by the soldiers on account of the violence of the people. ³⁶ For the multitude of the people followed after, crying: Away with him.

³⁷ And as he was about to be led into the castle, Paul says to the chief captain: May I speak to thee? And he said: Canst thou speak Greek? ³⁸ Art thou not then the Egyptian, who before these days made an uproar, and led out into the wilderness the four thousand men of the assassins? ³⁹ And Paul said: I am a Jew of Tarsus, a citizen of no obscure city of Cilicia; and I beseech thee, suffer me to speak to the people.

⁴⁰ And he having given him permission, Paul, standing on the stairs, beckoned with the hand to the people. And a great silence ensuing, he spoke to them in the Hebrew tongue, saying:

XXII. Brethren, and fathers, hear my defense, which I now make to you. ² And hearing that he spoke to them in the Hebrew tongue, they kept the more silence. ³ And he says: I am a Jew, born indeed in Tarsus of Cilicia, but brought up in this city, taught at the feet of Gamaliel, according to the strictness of the law of the fathers, being zealous for God, as ye all are this day. ⁴ And I persecuted this Way unto death, binding and delivering into prisons both men and women. ⁵ As also the high priest bears me witness, and all the eldership; from whom, moreover, I received letters to the brethren, and was journeying to Damascus, to bring also those who were there bound to Jerusalem, that they might be punished.

⁶ And it came to pass, that as I journeyed, and came near to Damascus, about midday, there suddenly flashed around me a great light out of heaven. ⁷ And I fell to the ground, and heard a voice saying to me: Saul, Saul, why persecutest thou me? ⁸ And I answered: Who art thou, Lord? And he said to me: I am Jesus the Nazarene, whom thou persecutest. ⁹ And they who were with me beheld indeed the light, and were afraid; but the voice of him who spoke to me they heard not. ¹⁰ And I said: What shall I do, Lord? And the Lord said to me: Arise, and go into Damascus; and there it shall be told thee concerning all things which it is appointed thee to do.

¹¹ And as I could not see, for the glory of that light, being led by the hand by those who were with me, I came into Damascus. ¹² And one Ananias, a devout man according to the law, having a good report from all the Jews who dwelt there, ¹³ came to me, and standing by me said to me: Brother Saul, receive sight. And I, in that very hour, looked up upon him. ¹⁴ And he said: The God of our fathers appointed thee to know his will, and to see the Just One, and to hear a voice out of his mouth. ¹⁵ For thou shalt be a witness for him to all men, of what thou hast seen, and didst hear. ¹⁶ And now why tarriest thou? Arise, be immersed and wash away thy sins, calling on his name.

¹⁷ And it came to pass, when I had returned to Jerusalem, and as I was praying in the temple, that I was in a trance, ¹⁸ and saw him saying to me: Make haste, and go forth quickly out of Jerusalem; for they will not receive thy testimony concerning me. ¹⁹ And I said: Lord, they well know that I imprisoned and beat in every synagogue those who believe on

---

V. 9. *Or*, they understood not

CHAPTER XXIII.

thee; ²⁰ and when the blood of thy witness Stephen was shed, then I myself was standing by, and consenting, and keeping the garments of those who slew him. ²¹ And he said to me: Depart; for I will send thee far hence to the Gentiles.

²² And they heard him unto this word, and then lifted up their voices, and said: Away with such a one from the earth; for it was not fit that he should live. ²³ And as they were crying out, and throwing up their garments, and casting dust into the air, ²⁴ the chief captain commanded him to be brought into the castle, and bade that he should be examined by scourging; that he might know for what charge they were thus crying out against him.

²⁵ And as they stretched him forth with the thongs, Paul said to the centurion who stood by: Is it lawful for you to scourge a man that is a Roman, and uncondemned? ²⁶ The centurion, hearing it, he went and told the chief captain, saying: What art thou about to do? For this man is a Roman. ²⁷ And the chief captain came, and said to him: Tell me, art thou a Roman? He said: Yes. ²⁸ And the chief captain answered: For a great sum I obtained this freedom. And Paul said: But I was born free.

²⁹ Immediately, therefore, they departed from him who were about to examine him; and the chief captain also was afraid, after he knew that he was a Roman, and because he had bound him.

³⁰ On the morrow, wishing to know the certainty, wherefore he was accused by the Jews, he released him, and commanded the chief priests and all the council to come together; and he brought Paul down, and set him before them.

XXIII. And Paul, earnestly beholding the council, said: Men, brethren, I have lived in all good conscience before God unto this day.

² And the high priest Ananias commanded those who stood by him to smite him on the mouth.

V. 25. Or, *for the thongs (namely, with which he was to be scourged).*

³ Then Paul said to him: God will smite thee, thou whited wall. And dost thou sit to judge me according to the law, and command me to be smitten contrary to law?

⁴ And they that stood by said: Revilest thou God's high priest?

⁵ And Paul said: I knew not, brethren, that he is high priest; for it is written: Thou shalt not speak evil of a ruler of thy people.

⁶ And Paul, knowing that the one part were Sadducees, and the other Pharisees, cried out in the council: Men, brethren, I am a Pharisee, the son of a Pharisee; for the hope of the resurrection of the dead I am now judged.

⁷ And when he had said this, there arose a dissension between the Pharisees and the Sadducees; and the multitude was divided. ⁸ For Sadducees say that there is no resurrection, nor angel, nor spirit; but Pharisees acknowledge both.

⁹ And there arose a great clamor; and the scribes of the party of the Pharisees arose, and contended, saying: We find no evil in this man; but if a spirit spoke to him, or an angel —?

¹⁰ And a great dissension arising, the chief captain, fearing lest Paul should be pulled in pieces by them, commanded the soldiery to go down, and to take him by force from among them, and to bring him into the castle.

¹¹ And the night following, the Lord stood by him, and said: Be of good courage; for as thou didst fully testify the things concerning me at Jerusalem, so must thou testify also at Rome.

¹² And when it was day, the Jews banded together, and bound themselves under a curse, saying that they would neither eat nor drink till they had killed Paul. ¹³ And they were more than forty who made this conspiracy. ¹⁴ And they came to the chief priests and the elders, and said: We bound ourselves under a great curse, to taste nothing until we have slain Paul.

¹⁵ Now therefore do ye, with the council, signify to the chief captain that he bring him down to you, as though ye would ascertain more exactly the matters concerning him; and we, before he comes near, are ready to kill him.

CHAPTER XXIII.

¹⁶ And the son of Paul's sister, hearing of their lying in wait, went and entered into the castle, and told Paul. ¹⁷ Then Paul called one of the centurions to him, and said: Bring this young man to the chief captain; for he has something to tell him. ¹⁸ So he took him, and brought him to the chief captain, and said: Paul, the prisoner, called me to him, and asked me to bring this young man to thee, as he has something to say to thee.
¹⁹ Then the chief captain took him by the hand, and went aside privately, and asked: What is that thou hast to tell me? ²⁰ And he said: The Jews agreed to desire thee, that thou wouldst bring down Paul to-morrow into the council, as though they would inquire somewhat more exactly concerning him. ²¹ But do not thou yield to them; for of them more than forty men are lying in wait for him, who bound themselves with an oath, neither to eat nor to drink till they have killed him; and now they are ready, looking for the promise from thee. ²² The chief captain therefore dismissed the young man, having charged him to say to no one, that thou didst show these things to me. ²³ And calling to him two or three of the centurions, he said: Make ready two hundred soldiers to go to Cæsarea, and seventy horsemen, two hundred spearmen, at the third hour of the night; ²⁴ and let them provide beasts, that they may set Paul thereon, and bring him safe to Felix the governor.

²⁵ And he wrote a letter after this manner: ²⁶ Claudius Lysias to the most excellent governor Felix, sends greeting. ²⁷ This man was taken by the Jews, and was about to be killed by them; but I came upon them with the soldiery, and rescued him, having learned that he is a Roman. ²⁸ And wishing to know the crime for which they were accusing him, I brought him down into their council; ²⁹ whom I found to be accused concerning questions of their law, but having nothing laid to his charge worthy of death or of bonds. ³⁰ And being informed that a plot was about to be laid against the man, I sent straightway to thee, having also commanded the accusers to say before thee what they had against him. Farewell.

³¹ The soldiers, therefore, as was commanded them, took up

Paul, and brought him by night to Antipatris. ³² But on the morrow, leaving the horsemen to go with him, they returned to the castle; ³³ who, when they had entered into Cæsarea, and delivered the letter to the governor, presented Paul also before him. ³⁴ And having read it, he asked of what province he was. And learning that he was from Cilicia, ³⁵ he said: I will hear thee fully, when thy accusers are also come. And he commanded him to be kept in the prætorium of Herod.

XXIV. And after five days, the high priest Ananias came down with the elders and a certain orator named Tertullus, who informed the governor against Paul; ² and he having been called, Tertullus began to accuse him, saying: Seeing that by thee we enjoy great quietness, and that very worthy deeds are done for this nation through thy providence, in every way and everywhere; ³ we accept it, most noble Felix, with all thankfulness.

⁴ But, not to hinder thee too long, I pray thee that thou wouldst hear us of thy clemency a few words. ⁵ For we have found this man to be a pest, and exciting disturbance among all the Jews throughout the world, and a ringleader of the sect of the Nazarenes; ⁶ who also attempted to profane the temple; whom we took, [and desired to judge according to our law. ⁷ But Lysias the chief captain came, and with great violence took him away out of our hands, ⁸ commanding his accusers to come before thee;] from whom thou canst thyself ascertain, by examination, concerning all these things whereof we accuse him.

⁹ And the Jews also joined in assailing him, saying that these things were so.

¹⁰ Then Paul, the governor having beckoned to him to speak, answered: Knowing that thou hast been for many years a judge for this nation, I do the more cheerfully answer for myself; ¹¹ inasmuch as thou mayest know, that there are not more than twelve days since I went up to Jerusalem to

---

VV. 6–8. *The words in brackets are wanting in the best ancient copies.*

CHAPTER XXIV.

worship; [12] and neither in the temple did they find me disputing with any one, or causing a tumult of the people, nor in the synagogues, nor in the city; [13] nor can they prove the things whereof they now accuse me.

[14] But this I acknowledge to thee, that according to the way which they call a sect, so I worship the God of our fathers, believing all things which are written in the law and the prophets; [15] having a hope toward God, which these themselves also look for, that there will be a resurrection both of the just and unjust. [16] Therefore do I also myself strive to have always a conscience void of offense toward God and men.

[17] And after many years I came to bring alms to my nation, and offerings. [18] Amidst which they found me purified in the temple, not with a crowd, nor with tumult; but certain Jews from Asia [caused it], [19] who ought to be here before thee, and make accusation, if they had aught against me. [20] Or let these themselves say what crime they found in me, while I stood before the council, [21] except for this one voice that I cried, standing among them: Concerning the resurrection of the dead I am judged by you this day.

[22] And Felix put them off, knowing the things concerning the Way more accurately, saying: When Lysias the chief captain shall come down, I will fully inquire into your matters. [23] And he commanded the centurion that he should be guarded, and should have indulgence; and to forbid none of his acquaintance to minister to him.

[24] And after certain days, Felix came with his wife Drusilla, who was a Jewess, and sent for Paul, and heard him concerning the faith in Christ. [25] And as he reasoned of righteousness, temperance, and the judgment to come, Felix trembled, and answered: Go thy way for this time; when I have a convenient season, I will call for thee. [26] He hoped also that money would be given him by Paul; wherefore he sent for him the oftener, and conversed with him.

[27] But after two years, Felix was succeeded by Porcius Festus; and Felix, wishing to gain favor with the Jews, left Paul bound.

XXV. ¹ Festus, therefore, having come into the province, after three days went up from Cæsarea to Jerusalem. ² And the high priest and the chief of the Jews informed him against Paul, and besought him, ³ asking for themselves a favor against him, that he would send for him to Jerusalem, preparing an ambush to slay him on the way. ⁴ But Festus answered, that Paul was to be kept a prisoner at Cæsarea, and that he himself should soon go thither. ⁵ Let them therefore, said he, who are powerful among you, go down with me, and accuse this man, if there is any wickedness in him.

⁶ And having tarried among them not more than eight or ten days, he went down to Cæsarea; and on the morrow, sitting on the judgment-seat, he commanded Paul to be brought. ⁷ And when he was come, the Jews who had come down from Jerusalem stood around, bringing many and grievous charges, which they could not prove; ⁸ while Paul said in defense: Neither against the law of the Jews, nor against the temple, nor against Cæsar, did I commit any offense.

⁹ But Festus, wishing to gain favor with the Jews, answered Paul, and said: Wilt thou go up to Jerusalem, and there be judged concerning these things, before me? ¹⁰ And Paul said: I stand at Cæsar's judgment-seat, where I ought to be judged. To Jews I did no wrong, as thou also very well knowest. ¹¹ If then I am an offender, and have done anything worthy of death, I refuse not to die; but if there be none of the things whereof these accuse me, no man can give me up to them. I appeal to Cæsar. ¹² Then Festus, having conferred with the council, answered: Thou hast appealed to Cæsar; to Cæsar thou shalt go.

¹³ And after certain days, Agrippa the king, and Bernice, came to Cæsarea to salute Festus. ¹⁴ And as they were spending some days there, Festus laid the case of Paul before the king, saying: There is a certain man left in bonds by

---

V. 10. *Or, also knowest too well (namely, to make such a proposal).*

CHAPTER XXV.

Felix ; [15] about whom, when I was at Jerusalem, the chief priests and the elders of the Jews made complaint, asking for judgment against him. [16] To whom I answered : It is not a custom for Romans to give up any man, before the accused has the accusers face to face, and has opportunity to answer for himself concerning the crime laid against him.
[17] When, therefore, they had come together here, without any delay on the morrow I sat on the judgment-seat, and commanded the man to be brought forth ; [18] and standing up around him, the accusers brought no accusation of such things as I supposed ; [19] but had certain controversies with him concerning their own religion, and concerning a certain Jesus who was dead, whom Paul affirmed to be alive. [20] And I, being perplexed in regard to the dispute about these things, asked whether he would go to Jerusalem, and there be judged concerning them. [21] But Paul having appealed, to be kept in custody for the decision of Augustus, I commanded him to be kept until I shall send him up to Cæsar.
[22] And Agrippa said to Festus : I would also hear the man myself. To-morrow, said he, thou shalt hear him.
[23] On the morrow, therefore, Agrippa and Bernice having come with great pomp, and entered into the place of hearing, with the chief captains and principal men of the city, at Festus' command Paul was brought forth. [24] And Festus said: King Agrippa, and all men who are here present with us, ye see this man, about whom all the multitude of the Jews interceded with me, both at Jerusalem and here, crying out that he ought not to live any longer. [25] But having found that he had committed nothing worthy of death, and he himself having appealed to Augustus, I determined to send him. [26] Of whom I have nothing certain to write to my lord. Wherefore I brought him forth before you, and specially before thee, king Agrippa, in order that, the examination having been made, I may have something to write. [27] For it seems to me unreasonable to send a prisoner, and not also signify the charges against him.

XXVI. And Agrippa said to Paul: Thou art permitted to speak for thyself. Then Paul stretched forth the hand, and answered for himself:

² I think myself happy, king Agrippa, because I shall answer for myself before thee this day, concerning all things whereof I am accused by Jews; ³ especially since thou art expert in all the customs and questions among Jews. Wherefore I beseech thee to hear me patiently.

⁴ My manner of life, therefore, from my youth, which was from the beginning among my own nation at Jerusalem, all Jews know; ⁵ having known me from the first, if they were willing to testify, that according to the strictest sect of our religion, I lived a Pharisee. ⁶ And now I stand and am judged for the hope of the promise made by God to the fathers; ⁷ unto which our twelve tribes, earnestly serving day and night, hope to attain; concerning which hope, O king, I am accused by Jews.

⁸ Why is it judged incredible with you, if God raises the dead?

⁹ I therefore thought to myself, that I ought to do many hostile things against the name of Jesus the Nazarene. ¹⁰ Which I also did in Jerusalem; and many of the saints did I myself shut up in prisons, having received authority from the chief priests; and when they were put to death, I gave my voice against them. ¹¹ And punishing them often, throughout all the synagogues, I constrained them to blaspheme; and being exceedingly mad against them, I persecuted them also unto foreign cities.

¹² Whereupon, as I went to Damascus with authority and a commission from the chief priests, ¹³ at midday, O king, I saw in the way a light from heaven, above the brightness of the sun, shining around me and those who journeyed with me. ¹⁴ And we all having fallen to the earth, I heard a voice speaking to me, and saying in the Hebrew tongue: Saul, Saul, why persecutest thou me? It is hard for thee to kick against the goads. ¹⁵ And I said: Who art thou, Lord? And he said: I

CHAPTER XXVI.

am Jesus, whom thou persecutest. ¹⁶ But arise, and stand upon thy feet; for I appeared to thee for this purpose, to appoint thee a minister and a witness both of the things which thou sawest, and of the things in which I will appear to thee; ¹⁷ delivering thee from the people, and the Gentiles, to whom I send thee, ¹⁸ to open their eyes, that they may turn from darkness to light, and from the power of Satan unto God, that they may obtain forgiveness of sins, and an inheritance among the sanctified, by faith in me.

¹⁹ Wherefore, O king Agrippa, I was not disobedient to the heavenly vision; ²⁰ but to those in Damascus first, and in Jerusalem, and unto all the region of Judæa, and to the Gentiles, I announced that they should repent and turn to God, doing works worthy of repentance.

²¹ For these causes the Jews, seizing me in the temple, attempted to kill me. ²² Having therefore obtained help from God, I continue unto this day, witnessing both to small and great, saying nothing except those things which the prophets and Moses said should come; ²³ whether the Christ should suffer, whether he, the first of the resurrection from the dead, shall show light to the people and to the Gentiles.

²⁴ And as he thus spoke for himself, Festus said with a loud voice: Paul, thou art mad; much learning makes thee mad. ²⁵ But he said: I am not mad, most noble Festus; but utter words of truth and soberness. ²⁶ For the king knows well concerning these things, to whom also I speak boldly; for I am persuaded that none of these things are hidden from him; for this has not been done in a corner. ²⁷ King Agrippa, believest thou the prophets? I know that thou believest.

²⁸ And Agrippa said to Paul: With little pains thou persuadest me to become a Christian. ²⁹ And Paul said: I could pray God, that with little or much, not only thou, but also all that hear me this day, may become such as I am, except these bonds.

V. 28. *Or*, In little time   V. 28. *Or*, dost thou persuade
V. 29. *Or*, that in little or much

³⁰ And the king rose up, and the governor, and Bernice, and they who sat with them. ³¹ And having withdrawn, they talked together, saying: This man does nothing worthy of death or of bonds. ³² And Agrippa said to Festus: This man could have been set at liberty, if he had not appealed to Cæsar.

XXVII. And when it was determined that we should sail to Italy, they delivered Paul and certain other prisoners to a centurion named Julius, of the Augustan band. ² And entering into a ship of Adramyttium, about to sail along the coasts of Asia, we put to sea, Aristarchus, a Macedonian of Thessalonica, being with us. ³ And on the second day we landed at Sidon. And Julius treated Paul humanely, and permitted him to go to his friends and receive their care. ⁴ And thence having put to sea, we sailed under Cyprus, because the winds were contrary ⁵ And having sailed over the sea along Cilicia and Pamphylia, we came to Myra, a city of Lycia. ⁶ And there the centurion found a ship of Alexandria sailing to Italy; and he put us on board of it. ⁷ And sailing slowly many days, and having come with difficulty over against Cnidus, the wind not suffering us to put in, we sailed under Crete, over against Salmone; ⁸ and coasting along it with difficulty, we came to a certain place called Fair Havens, near to which was the city Lasæa.

⁹ And much time having been spent, and the voyage being now dangerous, because also the fast had already passed by, Paul exhorted them, ¹⁰ saying: Sirs, I perceive that the voyage will be with violence and much loss, not only of the lading and the ship, but also of our lives. ¹¹ But the centurion believed the master and the owner of the ship, more than the things spoken by Paul. ¹² And as the haven was not well situated for wintering, the greater number advised to sail thence also, if by any means they might reach Phœnix, a haven of Crete, looking toward the southwest and northwest, and there winter.

¹³ And a south wind beginning to blow moderately, suppos-

V. 7. *Or*, not suffering us to go further

CHAPTER XXVII

ing that they had obtained their purpose, they weighed anchor, and coasted along close by Crete. ¹⁴ But not long after, there struck against it a tempestuous wind, called Euracylon. ¹⁵ And the ship being caught, and unable to face the wind, we yielded to it, and were driven along. ¹⁶ And running under a certain small island called Clauda, we were hardly able to come by the boat; ¹⁷ which when they had taken up, they used helps, undergirding the ship; and, fearing lest they should be cast away on the quicksand, they lowered the sail, and so were driven.

¹⁸ And we being violently tempest-tossed, the next day they lightened the ship; ¹⁹ and the third day we cast out with our own hands the tackling of the ship. ²⁰ And neither sun nor stars appearing for many days, and no small tempest lying on us, thenceforward all hope that we should be saved was utterly taken away. ²¹ But after much abstinence, then Paul, standing up in the midst of them, said: Sirs, ye should have hearkened to me and not put to sea from Crete, and so have escaped this violence and loss. ²² And now I exhort you to be of go cheer; for there shall be no loss of life among you, but only of the ship. ²³ For there stood by me this night an angel of God, whose I am, and whom I serve, ²⁴ saying: Fear not, Paul; thou must stand before Cæsar; and, lo, God has given thee all those who sail with thee. ²⁵ Wherefore, sirs, be of good cheer; for I believe God, that it will be even so, as it has been told me. ²⁶ But we must be cast away upon a certain island.

²⁷ And when the fourteenth night was come, as we were driven onward in the Adriatic sea, about midnight the seamen suspected that they were near to some country; ²⁸ and sounding, they found twenty fathoms; and having gone a little further, they sounded again, and found fifteen fathoms. ²⁹ Then fearing lest we should fall upon rocks, they cast four anchors out of the stern, and wished for day.

³⁰ And as the seamen were seeking to flee out of the ship, and had let down the boat into the sea, under color as if they were about to extend anchors out of the foreship, ³¹ Paul said to the centurion and to the soldiers: Except these abide in the

ship, ye can not be saved. ³² Then the soldiers cut off the ropes of the boat, and let it fall off.

³³ And while the day was coming on, Paul besought them all to take food, saying: This day is the fourteenth day that ye have waited, and continued fasting, having taken nothing. ³⁴ Wherefore I pray you to take food; for this is for your safety; for there shall not a hair fall from the head of one of you.

³⁵ And having thus spoken, he took bread, and gave thanks to God in presence of them all; and having broken it, he began to eat. ³⁶ Then were they all of good cheer, and they also took food. ³⁷ And we were in all in the ship two hundred and seventy-six souls. ³⁸ And when they had eaten enough, they lightened the ship, casting out the grain into the sea.

³⁹ And when it was day, they knew not the land; but they perceived a certain creek, having a beach, on which they determined, if they were able, to drive the ship ashore. ⁴⁰ And cutting the anchors entirely away, they abandoned them to the sea, at the same time unfastening the bands of the rudders; and hoisting the foresail to the wind, they made toward the beach. ⁴¹ And falling into a place where two seas met, they ran the ship aground; and the prow sticking fast remained immovable, but the stern was broken by the violence of the waves. ⁴² And it was the plan of the soldiers, that they should kill the prisoners, lest any one should swim out, and escape. ⁴³ But the centurion, wishing to save Paul, kept them from their purpose; and commanded that those who could swim should cast themselves first into the sea and get to land, ⁴⁴ and the rest, some on boards, and others on some of the pieces from the ship. And so it came to pass, that all escaped safe to land.

XXVIII.

And having escaped, they then learned that the island is called Melita. ² And the barbarians showed us no little kindness; for they kindled a fire, and received us all, because of the present rain, and because of the cold.

³ And Paul having gathered a bundle of sticks, and laid them

CHAPTER XXVIII.

on the fire, there came out a viper from the heat, and fastened on his hand. ⁴ And when the barbarians saw the animal hanging from his hand, they said among themselves: No doubt this man is a murderer, whom, though escaped from the sea, justice suffered not to live. ⁵ He, however, shaking off the animal into the fire, suffered no harm. ⁶ But they were expecting that he would become inflamed, or suddenly fall down dead; but after looking a great while, and seeing no harm befall him, they changed their minds, and said that he was a god.

⁷ In the region around that place, there were lands of the chief man of the island, whose name was Publius, who received and entertained us kindly three days. ⁸ Now it happened, that the father of Publius was lying sick with a fever and a bloody flux; to whom Paul entered in, and having prayed, laid his hands on him and healed him. ⁹ And this having been done, the others also, who had diseases in the island, came and were healed; ¹⁰ who also honored us with many honors; and when we put to sea, they loaded us with such things as were necessary.

¹¹ And after three months, we put to sea in a ship of Alexandria, which had wintered in the island, whose sign was Castor and Pollux. ¹² And landing at Syracuse, we remained three days. ¹³ And from thence, making a circuit, we came to Rhegium. And after one day, a south wind arose, and we came on the second day to Puteoli; ¹⁴ where we found brethren, and were entreated to remain with them seven days; and so we went toward Rome. ¹⁵ And from thence, the brethren, having heard of us, came to meet us as far as Appii Forum, and the Three Taverns; whom when Paul saw, he gave thanks to God, and took courage.

¹⁶ And when we came to Rome, the centurion delivered the prisoners to the commander of the camp; but Paul was suffered to dwell by himself, with the soldier who guarded him.

¹⁷ And it came to pass, that after three days Paul called together those who were the chief men of the Jews; and when they were come together, he said to them: Men, brethren,

---

V. 13. *Or*, coasting about

though I had done nothing against the people, or the customs of our fathers, yet I was delivered a prisoner from Jerusalem into the hands of the Romans; ¹⁸ who, when they had examined me, wished to release me, because there was no cause of death in me. ¹⁹ But as the Jews spoke against it, I was compelled to appeal to Cæsar; not that I have anything to charge against my nation. ²⁰ For this cause therefore I called for you, to see and to speak with you; for on account of the hope of Israel I am compassed with this chain.

²¹ And they said to him: We neither received letters from Judæa concerning thee, nor did any one of the brethren that came, report or speak any evil concerning thee. ²² But we desire to hear from thee what thou thinkest; for concerning this sect, we know that everywhere it is spoken against.

²³ And having appointed a day for him, they came to him in greater numbers to his lodging; to whom he expounded, testifying fully the kingdom of God, and persuading them of the things concerning Jesus, both from the law of Moses and the prophets, from morning till evening. ²⁴ And some believed the things spoken, and some believed not. ²⁵ And disagreeing among themselves, they departed, after Paul had spoken one word: Well did the Holy Spirit speak through Isaiah the prophet to our fathers, ²⁶ saying:

   Go to this people, and say;
   With the hearing ye will hear, and will not understand,
   And seeing ye will see, and will not perceive.
²⁷ For the heart of this people is become gross,
   And their ears are dull of hearing,
   And their eyes they have closed;
   Lest haply they see with their eyes,
   And hear with their ears,
   And understand with their heart,
   And turn, and I shall heal them.

²⁸ Be it known to you, therefore, that to the Gentiles the salvation of God was sent: they, moreover, will hear.

V. 29 *is wanting in the oldest and best copies.*

CHAPTER I.

³⁰ And Paul remained two whole years in his own hired house, and gladly received all that came in to him; ³¹ preaching the kingdom of God, and teaching the things concerning the Lord Jesus Christ, with all confidence, no one hindering him.

THE LETTER OF PAUL TO THE ROMANS.

I. Paul, a servant of Jesus Christ, a called apostle, set apart unto the gospel of God, ² which he before announced through his prophets in the Holy Scriptures, ³ concerning his Son, who was born of the seed of David according to the flesh, ⁴ who was declared to be the Son of God with power according to the spirit of holiness, by the resurrection from the dead, Jesus Christ our Lord; ⁵ through whom we received grace and apostleship, for obedience to the faith among all the nations, for his name's sake; ⁶ among whom are ye also, called of Jesus Christ; ⁷ to all the beloved of God that are in Rome, called to be saints: Grace to you, and peace, from God our Father and the Lord Jesus Christ.

⁸ First, I thank my God through Jesus Christ for you all, that your faith is spoken of in all the world. ⁹ For God is my witness, whom I serve in my spirit in the gospel of his Son, how without ceasing I make mention of you always in my prayers; ¹⁰ making request, if haply now at length I may be prospered by the will of God to come to you. ¹¹ For I long to see you, that I may impart to you some spiritual gift, to the end ye may be established; ¹² that is, to be comforted together among you, by each other's faith, both yours and mine.

¹³ Now I would not have you ignorant, brethren, that oftentimes I purposed to come to you (but was hindered hitherto), that I might have some fruit among you also, as among the rest of the Gentiles. ¹⁴ I am debtor both to Greeks and Barbarians; both to wise and unwise. ¹⁵ So, as far as lies in me, I am ready to preach the good news to you also who are at

Rome. ¹⁶ For I am not ashamed of the gospel; for it is the power of God unto salvation to every one that believes, to the Jew first, and also to the Greek. ¹⁷ For therein is revealed a righteousness of God, from faith to faith; as it is written: The just shall live by faith.

¹⁸ For the wrath of God is revealed from heaven against all ungodliness and unrighteousness of men, who hold the truth in unrighteousness; ¹⁹ because that which may be known of God is manifest in them; for God manifested it to them. ²⁰ For, from the creation of the world, his invisible things are clearly seen, being perceived by the things that are made, even his eternal power and Godhead; so that they are without excuse. ²¹ Because, knowing God, they glorified him not as God, nor gave thanks; but became vain in their reasonings, and their foolish heart was darkened. ²² Professing themselves to be wise, they became fools; ²³ and changed the glory of the incorruptible God into an image made like to corruptible man, and to birds, and fourfooted beasts, and creeping things.

²⁴ Wherefore God also gave them up in the lusts of their hearts to uncleanness, to dishonor their bodies among themselves; ²⁵ who changed the truth of God into a lie, and worshiped and served the creature more than the Creator, who is blessed forever. Amen.

²⁶ For this cause God gave them up to vile passions; for their women changed the natural use into that which is against nature; ²⁷ and in like manner the men also, leaving the natural use of the woman, burned in their lust one toward another; men with men working that which is unseemly, and receiving in themselves the recompense of their error which was meet.

²⁸ And as they did not choose to retain God in their knowledge, God gave them over to a reprobate mind, to do those things which are not becoming; ²⁹ being filled with all unrighteousness, wickedness, covetousness, maliciousness; full of envy, murder, strife, deceit, malignity; whisperers, ³⁰ slanderers,

---

V. 18. *Or*, who hinder the truth by unrighteousness
V. 20. *So that* they may be

CHAPTER II.

haters of God, overbearing, proud, boasters, devisers of evil things, disobedient to parents, ³¹ without understanding, covenant-breakers, without natural affection, implacable, unmerciful; ³² who, knowing the judgment of God, that they who commit such things are worthy of death, not only do them, but have pleasure in those who do them.

II. Wherefore thou art without excuse, O man, whosoever thou art that judgest; for wherein thou judgest another, thou condemnest thyself; for thou that judgest doest the same things. ² Now we know that the judgment of God is according to truth, upon those who commit such things. ³ And reckonest thou this, O man, that judgest those who do such things, and doest the same, that thou shalt escape the judgment of God? ⁴ Or despisest thou the riches of his goodness, and forbearance, and long-suffering, not knowing that the goodness of God is leading thee to repentance; ⁵ and after thy hardness and impenitent heart, art treasuring up for thyself wrath in the day of wrath and of the revelation of the righteous judgment of God; ⁶ who will render to every man according to his deeds; ⁷ to those who by patient continuance in well doing seek for glory and honor and immortality, eternal life; ⁸ but to those who are contentious, and do not obey the truth, but obey unrighteousness, indignation and wrath, ⁹ tribulation and distress, upon every soul of man that works evil, of the Jew first, and also of the Greek; ¹⁰ but glory, and honor, and peace, to every man that works good, to the Jew first, and also to the Greek.

¹¹ For there is no respect of persons with God. ¹² For as many as sinned without law shall also perish without law; and as many as sinned with law shall be judged by law; (¹³ for not the hearers of law are just before God, but the doers of law shall be justified: ¹⁴ for when Gentiles, who have no law, do by nature the things required by law, these, having no law, are a law to themselves; ¹⁵ who show the work of law written in

---

V. 15. *Or*, mutually accusing, or also excusing.

their hearts, their conscience witnessing therewith, and their thoughts alternately accusing, or also excusing;) ¹⁶ in the day when God will judge the secrets of men by Jesus Christ, according to my gospel.

¹⁷ But if thou art called a Jew, and restest upon law, and makest thy boast in God, ¹⁸ and knowest his will, and approvest the things that are more excellent, being instructed out of the law; ¹⁹ and art confident that thou thyself art a guide of the blind, a light of those who are in darkness, ²⁰ an instructor of the foolish, a teacher of babes, having the form of knowledge and of the truth in the law; ²¹ thou then, that teachest another, dost thou not teach thyself? Thou that preachest, a man should not steal, dost thou steal? ²² Thou that sayest, a man should not commit adultery, dost thou commit adultery? Thou that abhorrest idols, dost thou commit sacrilege? ²³ Thou that makest thy boast in law, through the transgression of the law dishonorest thou God? ²⁴ For, the name of God is blasphemed among the Gentiles because of you, as it is written.

²⁵ For circumcision indeed profits, if thou keep the law; but if thou art a transgressor of law, thy circumcision has become uncircumcision. ²⁶ If then the uncircumcision keep the requirements of the law, shall not his uncircumcision be counted for circumcision? ²⁷ And shall not the uncircumcision that is by nature, if it fulfill the law, judge thee, who with the letter and circumcision art a transgressor of law? ²⁸ For he is not a Jew, who is one outwardly; nor is that circumcision, which is outward in the flesh. ²⁹ But he is a Jew, who is one inwardly; and circumcision is that of the heart, in the spirit not in the letter; whose praise is not of men, but of God.

III. What then is the advantage of the Jew? Or what is the benefit of circumcision? ²Much every way; first, indeed, that they were intrusted with the oracles of God. ³For what if some did not believe? Shall their unbelief make void

---

V. 22. *Or*, dost thou rob the temple? *Or*, dost thou rob temples?

CHAPTER III.

the faithfulness of God? ⁴Far be it! Yea, let God be true, and every man a liar; as it is written:
That thou mayest be justified in thy words,
And mayest overcome when thou art judged.
⁵But if our unrighteousness commends the righteousness of God, what shall we say? Is God unrighteous who takes vengeance? (I speak as a man.) ⁶Far be it! For then how shall God judge the world? ⁷For if the truth of God, through my lie, abounded unto his glory, why am I also still judged as a sinner? ⁸And why not, as we are slanderously reported, and as some affirm that we say: Let us do evil, that good may come? Whose judgment is just.

⁹What then? Are we better? No, in no wise; for we before charged, that both Jews and Gentiles are all under sin. ¹⁰As it is written: There is none righteous, no, not one; ¹¹there is none that understands, there is none that seeks after God. ¹²They are all gone out of the way, they are together become unprofitable; there is none that does good, there is not so much as one. ¹³Their throat is an open sepulchre; with their tongues they have used deceit; the poison of asps is under their lips; ¹⁴whose mouth is full of cursing and bitterness. ¹⁵Their feet are swift to shed blood. ¹⁶Destruction and misery are in their ways; ¹⁷and the way of peace they have not known. ¹⁸There is no fear of God before their eyes.

¹⁹Now we know that whatever the law says, it says to those under the law; that every mouth may be stopped, and all the world may become guilty before God. ²⁰Because by works of law no flesh shall be justified in his sight; for by law is the knowledge of sin.

²¹But now, apart from law, a righteousness of God has been manifested, being witnessed by the law and the prophets: ²²a righteousness of God through faith in Jesus Christ, unto all and upon all that believe; (for there is no difference; ²³for all

sinned, and come short of the glory of God;) ²¹ being justified freely by his grace, through the redemption that is in Christ Jesus; ²⁵ whom God set forth as a propitiation through faith by his blood, for the exhibition of his righteousness, because of the passing over of the sins before committed in the forbearance of God; ²⁶ for the exhibition of his righteousness in this present time, that he may be just, and the justifier of him who believes in Jesus.

²⁷ Where then is the boasting? It is excluded. By what kind of law? Of works? Nay; but by the law of faith. ²⁸ Therefore we reckon that a man is justified by faith apart from works of law. Is he the God of Jews only? ²⁹ Is he not also of Gentiles? Yes, of Gentiles also; ³⁰ seeing that God is one, who will justify the circumcision by faith, and the uncircumcision through the faith. ³¹ Do we then make void law through the faith? Far be it! Yea, we establish law.

IV. What then shall we say that Abraham our father found, as pertaining to the flesh? ² For if Abraham was justified by works, he has ground of boasting; but not before God. ³ For what says the Scripture? And Abraham believed God, and it was reckoned to him for righteousness. ⁴ Now to him that works, the reward is not reckoned as of grace, but as a debt. ⁵ But to him that works not, but believes on him who justifies the ungodly, his faith is reckoned for righteousness. ⁶ As also David speaks of the happiness of the man, to whom God reckons righteousness, apart from works:

⁷ Happy they, whose iniquities were forgiven,
And whose sins were covered;
⁸ Happy the man to whom the Lord will not reckon sin!

⁹ Comes this happiness then on the circumcision, or also on the uncircumcision? For we say that faith was reckoned to Abraham for righteousness. ¹⁰ How then was it reckoned? When he was in circumcision, or in uncircumcision? Not in circumcision, but in uncircumcision. ¹¹ And he received the sign of circumcision, a seal of the righteousness of the faith

CHAPTER V.

which he had while in uncircumcision; that he might be father of all that believe while in uncircumcision, that the righteousness might be reckoned to them also, ¹² and father of circumcision to those who are not only of the circumcision, but who also walk in the steps of the faith of our father Abraham, which he had while in uncircumcision.

¹³ For not through law was the promise to Abraham, or to his seed, that he should be heir of the world, but through the righteousness of faith. ¹⁴ For if they that are of law are heirs, faith is made void, and the promise is made of no effect. ¹⁵ For the law works wrath; for where there is no law, neither is there transgression. ¹⁶ For this cause it is of faith, that it may be by grace; in order that the promise may be sure to all the seed; not to that only which is of the law, but to that also which is of the faith of Abraham; who is the father of us all, ¹⁷ (as it is written: A father of many nations have I made thee,) before God whom he believed, who quickens the dead, and calls the things that are not as though they were; ¹⁸ who against hope believed in hope, that he should become father of many nations, according to that which was spoken: So shall thy seed be. ¹⁹ And being not weak in faith, he considered not his own body already dead, being about a hundred years old, and the deadness of Sarah's womb. ²⁰ And in respect to the promise of God he wavered not through unbelief, but was strong in faith, giving glory to God, ²¹ and being fully persuaded, that what he has promised he is able also to perform. ²² Wherefore also it was reckoned to him for righteousness.

²³ And it was not written for his sake alone, that it was reckoned to him; ²⁴ but for ours also, to whom it shall be reckoned, if we believe on him who raised up Jesus our Lord from the dead; ²⁵ who was delivered up for our offenses, and was raised for our justification.

V. Being justified therefore by faith, we have peace with God through our Lord Jesus Christ; ² through whom also we obtained the access by faith into this grace wherein we stand, and rejoice in hope of the glory of God. ⁸ And not only so, but we rejoice in afflictions also; knowing that affliction works patience; ⁴ and patience approval; and approval hope; ⁵ and hope makes not ashamed; because the love of God has been poured forth in our hearts, by the Holy Spirit which was given to us.

⁶ For when we were yet without strength, in due season Christ died for the ungodly. ⁷ For scarcely for a righteous man will one die; though, for the good man, perhaps some one does even dare to die. ⁸ But God commends his love toward us, in that, while we were yet sinners, Christ died for us. ⁹ Much more therefore, being now justified by his blood, shall we be saved from the wrath through him. ¹⁰ For if, being enemies, we were reconciled to God through the death of his son; much more, being reconciled, shall we be saved by his life; ¹¹ and not only so, but also rejoicing in God through our Lord Jesus Christ, through whom we have now received the reconciliation.

¹² Wherefore, as by one man sin entered into the world, and death by sin; and so death passed upon all men, for that all sinned; (¹³ for until the law sin was in the world; but sin is not imputed when there is no law. ¹⁴ But yet death reigned from Adam to Moses, even over those who sinned not after the likeness of Adam's transgression, who is a type of him who was to come.

¹⁵ But not as the trespass, so also is the free gift; for if by the trespass of the one the many died, much more did the grace of God, and the gift by the grace of the one man, Jesus Christ, abound to the many.

¹⁶ And not as through one that sinned, is the gift; for the judgment came of one unto condemnation, but the free gift came of many trespasses unto justification. ¹⁷ For if by the trespass of the one, death reigned through the one; much more they who receive the abundance of the grace, and of the gift of righteousness, shall reign in life through the one, Jesus Christ.)

¹⁸ So then, as through one trespass it came upon all men

CHAPTER VI.

unto condemnation; so also through one righteous act it came upon all men unto justification of life. ¹⁹ For as through the disobedience of the one man the many were constituted sinners, so also through the obedience of the one will the many be constituted righteous.

²⁰ Moreover the law came in also, that the trespass might abound. But where sin abounded, grace did much more abound; ²¹ that as sin reigned in death, so also might grace reign through righteousness unto eternal life, through Jesus Christ our Lord.

VI. What then shall we say? Shall we continue in sin, that grace may abound? ² Far be it! How shall we, who died to sin, live any longer therein? ³ Know ye not, that all we who were immersed into Jesus Christ were immersed into his death? ⁴ We were buried therefore with him by the immersion into his death; that as Christ was raised from the dead by the glory of the Father, so we also should walk in newness of life. ⁵ For if we have become united with the likeness of his death, we shall be also with that of his resurrection; ⁶ knowing this, that our old man was crucified with him, that the body of sin might be destroyed, in order that we should no longer be in bondage to sin. ⁷ For he that died has been justified from sin. ⁸ And if we died with Christ, we believe that we shall also live with him; ⁹ knowing that Christ, being raised from the dead, dies no more; death has dominion over him no more. ¹⁰ For in that he died, he died to sin once; but in that he lives, he lives to God. ¹¹ So also reckon ye yourselves to be dead indeed to sin, but alive to God through Jesus Christ.

¹² Let not sin therefore reign in your mortal body, that ye should obey the lusts thereof; ¹³ nor yield your members to sin as instruments of unrighteousness; but yield yourselves to God, as being alive from the dead, and your members to God as instruments of righteousness. ¹⁴ For sin shall not have dominion over you; for ye are not under law, but under grace.

¹⁵ What then? Shall we sin, because we are not under law, but under grace? Far be it! ¹⁶ Know ye not, that to whom

ye yield yourselves servants to obey, his servants ye are whom ye obey; whether of sin unto death, or of obedience unto righteousness? [17] But thanks be to God, that ye were servants of sin, but obeyed from the heart that form of teaching which was delivered to you; [18] and being made free from sin, ye became servants of righteousness.

[19] I speak after the manner of men, because of the infirmity of your flesh. For as ye yielded your members servants to uncleanness, and to iniquity unto iniquity; so now yield your members servants to righteousness unto sanctification. [20] For when ye were servants of sin, ye were free as to righteousness. [21] What fruit therefore had ye then in those things whereof ye are now ashamed? For the end of those things is death. [22] But now, being made free from sin, and become servants to God, ye have your fruit unto sanctification, and the end everlasting life. [23] For the wages of sin is death; but the gift of God is eternal life, in Jesus Christ our Lord.

VII.

Know ye not, brethren (for I speak to those who know the law), that the law has dominion over a man for so long a time as he lives? [2] For the married woman is bound by law to her husband while he lives; but if the husband die, she is loosed from the law of the husband. [3] So then if, while the husband lives, she be married to another man, she shall be called an adulteress; but if the husband die, she is free from the law, so that she is not an adulteress, though she be married to another man.

[4] Wherefore, my brethren, ye also were made dead to the law through the body of Christ, in order that ye should be married to another, to him who was raised from the dead, that we might bring forth fruit to God. [5] For when we were in the flesh, the emotions of sins, which were by the law, wrought in our members to bring forth fruit unto death. [6] But now we are delivered from the law, having died to that wherein we were held; so that we serve in newness of spirit, and not in oldness of the letter.

V. 17, *Or*, unto which ye were delivered

CHAPTER VII.

⁷ What then shall we say? Is the law sin? Far be it! But I had not known sin, except through law; for I had not known coveting, if the law had not said: Thou shalt not covet. ⁸ But sin, taking occasion by the commandment, wrought in me all manner of coveting. For without law, sin is dead.

⁹ And I was alive without law once; but when the commandment came, sin revived, and I died. ¹⁰ And the commandment, which was for life, that I found to be for death. ¹¹ For sin, taking occasion by the commandment, deceived me, and by it slew me.

¹² So that the law is holy, and the commandment holy, and just, and good.

¹³ Has then that which is good become death to me? Far be it! But sin, that it might appear sin, working death to me by that which is good, that sin by the commandment might become exceedingly sinful.

¹⁴ For we know that the law is spiritual; but I am carnal, sold under sin. ¹⁵ For what I perform, I know not; for not what I desire, that do I; but what I hate, that I do. ¹⁶ But if what I desire not, that I do, I consent to the law that it is good.

¹⁷ Now then, it is no longer I that perform it, but the sin that dwells in me.

¹⁸ For I know that there dwells not in me, that is, in my flesh, any good; for to desire is present with me; but to perform that which is good I find not. ¹⁹ For the good that I desire, I do not; but the evil that I desire not, that I do. ²⁰ But if what I desire not, that I do, it is no more I that perform it, but the sin that dwells in me.

²¹ I find then the law, that, when I desire to do good, evil is present with me. ²² For I delight in the law of God after the inward man. ²³ But I see another law in my members, warring against the law of my mind, and bringing me into captivity to the law of sin which is in my members. ²⁴ Wretched man that I am! Who will deliver me from the body of this death? ²⁵ I thank God through Jesus Christ our Lord! So then I myself with the mind serve the law of God, but with the flesh the law of sin.

VIII. There is therefore now no condemnation to those who are in Christ Jesus. ² For the law of the Spirit of life in Christ Jesus set me free from the law of sin and death. ³ For what the law could not do, in that it was weak through the flesh, God sending his own Son in the likeness of sinful flesh, and for sin, condemned sin in the flesh; ⁴ that the requirement of the law might be fulfilled in us, who walk not according to the flesh, but according to the Spirit. ⁵ For they that are according to the flesh mind the things of the flesh; but they that are according to the Spirit, the things of the Spirit. ⁶ For to be carnally minded is death; but to be spiritually minded is life and peace. ⁷ Because the carnal mind is enmity against God; for it does not submit itself to the law of God, neither indeed can it; ⁸ and they that are in the flesh can not please God.

⁹ But ye are not in the flesh, but in the Spirit, if indeed the Spirit of God dwells in you. And if any man has not the Spirit of Christ, he is none of his. ¹⁰ And if Christ is in you, the body indeed is dead because of sin; but the Spirit is life because of righteousness. ¹¹ And if the Spirit of him who raised up Jesus from the dead dwells in you, he who raised up Christ from the dead will also quicken your mortal bodies, because of his Spirit that dwells in you.

¹² So that, brethren, we are debtors, not to the flesh, to live according to the flesh. ¹³ For if ye live according to the flesh, ye shall die; but if by the Spirit ye mortify the deeds of the body, ye shall live. ¹⁴ For as many as are led by the Spirit of God, they are sons of God. ¹⁵ For ye did not receive the spirit of bondage, again to fear; but ye received the Spirit of adoption, whereby we cry, Abba, Father. ¹⁶ The Spirit itself bears witness with our spirit, that we are children of God; ¹⁷ and if children, also heirs; heirs of God, and joint heirs with Christ; if indeed we suffer with him, that we may also be glorified with him.

¹⁸ For I reckon that the sufferings of this present time are of no account, in comparison with the glory which shall be revealed in us. ¹⁹ For the earnest longing of the creation is

CHAPTER VIII.

waiting for the revelation of the sons of God. ²⁰ For the creation was made subject to vanity, not willingly (but by reason of him who made it subject), in hope ²¹ that the creation itself also shall be delivered from the bondage of corruption into the glorious liberty of the children of God. ²² For we know that the whole creation groans and travails in pain together until now. ²³ And not only so, but ourselves also, though we have the first-fruits of the Spirit, even we ourselves groan within ourselves, waiting for the adoption, the redemption of our body.

²⁴ For we were saved in hope; but hope that is seen is not hope; for what a man sees, why does he also hope for? ²⁵ But if we hope for that we see not, we with patience wait for it. ²⁶ And in like manner does the Spirit also help our weakness; for we know not what we should pray for as we ought; but the Spirit itself makes intercession for us with groanings which can not be uttered. ²⁷ And he who searches the hearts knows what is the mind of the Spirit, because he makes intercession for the saints according to the will of God.

²⁸ And we know that all things work together for good to those who love God, to those who are called according to his purpose. ²⁹ Because whom he foreknew, he also predestined to be conformed to the image of his Son, that he might be the first-born among many brethren. ³⁰ And whom he predestined, them he also called; and whom he called, them he also justified; and whom he justified, them he also glorified.

³¹ What then shall we say to these things? If God is for us, who shall be against us? ³² He who spared not his own Son, but delivered him up for us all, how shall he not also with him freely give us all things? ³³ Who shall lay any thing to the charge of God's chosen? God is he that justifies; ³⁴ who is he that condemns? Christ is he that died, yea rather, that is risen again, who is also at the right hand of God, who also intercedes for us. ³⁵ Who shall separate us from the love of Christ? Shall tribulation, or distress, or persecution, or famine, or nakedness, or peril, or sword? ³⁶ As it is written:

For, for thy sake we are killed all the day long;
We were accounted as sheep for slaughter.

⁳⁷ Nay, in all these things we are more than conquerors through him who loved us. ³⁸ For I am persuaded, that neither death nor life, neither angels nor principalities nor powers, neither things present nor things to come, ³⁹ neither height nor depth, nor any other created thing, shall be able to separate us from the love of God, which is in Christ Jesus our Lord.

IX. I say the truth in Christ, I lie not, my conscience also bearing me witness in the Holy Spirit, ² that I have great grief and continual anguish in my heart. ³ For I myself could wish to be accursed from Christ for my brethren, my kinsmen according to the flesh ; ⁴ who are Israelites ; whose is the adoption, and the glory, and the covenants, and the giving of the law, and the service, and the promises ; ⁵ whose are the fathers, and of whom as to the flesh is Christ, who is over all, God blessed forever. Amen.

⁶ Not as though the word of God has failed. For not all they are Israel, who are of Israel ; ⁷ neither, because they are the seed of Abraham, are they all children ; but, In Isaac shall thy seed be called. ⁸ That is, not they who are the children of the flesh are children of God ; but the children of the promise are reckoned as seed. ⁹ For the word of promise is this: At this season I will come, and Sarah shall have a son. ¹⁰ And not only so ; but when Rebecca also had conceived by one, our father Isaac (¹¹ for they being not yet born, nor having done anything good or evil, that the purpose of God according to election might stand, not of works, but of him who calls), ¹² it was said to her: The elder shall serve the younger. ¹³ As it is written:

Jacob I loved,
But Esau I hated.

¹⁴ What then shall we say? Is there unrighteousness with God? Far be it! ¹⁵ For he says to Moses: I will have mercy on whomsoever I have mercy, and I will have compassion on whomsoever I have compassion. ¹⁶ So then it is not of him who wills, nor of him who runs, but of God who shows mercy. ¹⁷ For the

CHAPTER IX.

Scripture says to Pharaoh: Even for this very purpose did I raise thee up, that I might show forth my power in thee, and that my name might be declared in all the earth. [18] So that, on whom he will he has mercy, and whom he will he hardens.

[19] Thou wilt say then to me: Why then does he yet find fault? For who resists his will? [20] Nay but, O man, who art thou that repliest against God? Shall the thing formed say to him who formed it: Why didst thou make me thus? [21] Has not the potter power over the clay, of the same lump to make one vessel unto honor, and another unto dishonor? [22] And what if God, willing to show forth his wrath, and to make known his power, endured with much long-suffering vessels of wrath fitted for destruction; [23] and that he might make known the riches of his glory on vessels of mercy, which he had before prepared for glory; [24] whom he also called, even us, not from among the Jews only, but also from among the Gentiles? [25] As also he says in Hosea:

I will call them my people, who were not my people;
And her beloved, who was not beloved.

[26] And it shall be, that in the place where it was said to them, Ye are not my people, there shall they be called, Sons of the living God. [27] And Isaiah cries concerning Israel:

Though the number of the sons of Israel be as the sand
of the sea,
The remnant shall be saved;
[28] For he will finish the work,
And cut it short in righteousness;
Because a short work will the Lord make upon the earth.
And as Isaiah has said before:
Except the Lord of Sabaoth had left us a seed,
We had become as Sodom,
And been made like to Gomorrah.

V. 28. *Or*, the account   V. 28. *Or*, a short account

[30] What then shall we say? That Gentiles, who were not following after righteousness, obtained righteousness, the righteousness which is of faith; [31] but Israel, following after a law of righteousness, attained not to [such] a law. [32] Wherefore? Because [they sought it] not by faith, but as being by works of law. For they stumbled against the stone of stumbling; [33] as it is written: Behold, I lay in Zion a stone of stumbling, and a rock of offense; and he that believes on him shall not be put to shame.

X. Brethren, it is my heart's desire and prayer to God on their behalf, that they might be saved. [2] For I bear them witness, that they have a zeal for God, but not according to knowledge. [3] For not knowing the righteousness of God, and seeking to establish their own righteousness, they did not submit themselves to the righteousness of God. [4] For Christ is the end of the law for righteousness, to every one that believes.

[5] For Moses describes the righteousness which is of the law: The man that has done them, shall live by them. [6] But the righteousness which is of faith says thus: Say not in thy heart, Who shall ascend into heaven? (that is, to bring Christ down;) [7] or, Who shall descend into the abyss? (that is, to bring up Christ from the dead.) [8] But what says it? The word is nigh thee, in thy mouth, and in thy heart; that is, the word of faith, which we preach; [9] because, if thou shalt profess with thy mouth the Lord Jesus, and believe in thy heart that God raised him from the dead, thou shalt be saved. [10] For with the heart man believes unto righteousness; and with the mouth profession is made unto salvation. [11] For the Scripture says: Whoever believes on him shall not be put to shame. [12] For there is no difference between Jew and Greek; for the same is Lord of all, rich toward all that call upon him; [13] for every one who

---

V. 5. *Or*, shall live in them

CHAPTER XL

shall call upon the name of the Lord shall be saved.
¹⁴ How then shall they call on him on whom they believed not? And how shall they believe on him of whom they heard not? And how shall they hear without a preacher? ¹⁵ And how shall they preach, unless they are sent forth? As it is written :
How beautiful are the feet of those who bring glad
tidings of peace,
Who bring glad tidings of good things!
¹⁶ But they did not all hearken to the glad tidings. For Isaiah says: Lord, who believed our report? ¹⁷ So then faith comes of hearing, and hearing by the word of God.
¹⁸ But I say, did they not hear? Yes verily ;
Their sound went forth into all the earth,
And their words unto the ends of the world.
¹⁹ But I say, did Israel not know? First Moses says :
I will provoke you to jealousy by those who are no people,
By a foolish nation I will move you to anger.
²⁰ But Isaiah is very bold, and says :
I was found by those who sought me not ;
I became manifest to those who asked not after me.
²¹ But of Israel he says :
All the day long, I stretched forth my hands,
To a disobedient and gainsaying people.

XI. I say then, did God cast away his people? Far be it! For I also am an Israelite, of the seed of Abraham, of the tribe of Benjamin. ² God did not cast away his people whom he foreknew. Know ye not what the Scripture says in the story of Elijah ; how he pleads with God against Israel, saying: ³ Lord they killed thy prophets, and digged down thine altars; and I was left alone, and they seek my life. ⁴ But what says the answer of God to him? I reserved to myself seven thousand men, who bowed not the knee to Baal.

⁵ Even so then, at this present time also, there is a remnant according to the election of grace. ⁶ And if by grace, it is no longer of works; otherwise, grace becomes no longer grace. [But if of works, it is no longer grace; otherwise, work is no longer work.]

⁷ What then? What Israel seeks after, that he obtained not; but the election obtained it, and the rest were hardened. ⁸ According as it is written: God gave them a spirit of slumber, eyes that they should not see, and ears that they should not hear, unto this day. ⁹ And David says:

Let their table be made a snare, and a trap,
And a stumbling-block, and a recompense to them;
¹⁰ Let their eyes be darkened, that they may not see,
And bow down their back alway.

¹¹ I say then, did they stumble in order that they should fall? Far be it! But by their fall salvation is come to the Gentiles, to provoke them to jealousy. ¹² But if their fall is the riches of the world, and their diminution the riches of the Gentiles, how much more their fullness?

¹³ For I am speaking to you Gentiles; inasmuch as I am the apostle of the Gentiles, I magnify my office; ¹⁴ if by any means I may provoke to emulation those who are my flesh, and may save some of them. ¹⁵ For if the casting away of them is the reconciling of the world, what shall the receiving of them be, but life from the dead? ¹⁶ And if the first-fruit is holy, so also is the lump; and if the root is holy, so also are the branches. ¹⁷ And if some of the branches were broken off, and thou, being a wild olive-tree, wert grafted in among them, and became a partaker with them of the root and the fatness of the olive-tree; ¹⁸ boast not over the branches. But if thou boast, it is not thou that bearest the root, but the root thee.

¹⁹ Thou wilt say then: The branches were broken off, that I might be grafted in. ²⁰ Well; because of their want of faith they were broken off, and thou standest by thy faith. Be not

---

. V. 6. *Ancient copies omit the words in brackets.*

CHAPTER XI.

high-minded, but fear; ²¹ for if God spared not the natural branches, take heed lest he also spare not thee.

²² Behold then the goodness and severity of God; toward those who fell, severity; but toward thee, goodness, if thou continue in his goodness ; otherwise, thou also shalt be cut off. ²³ And they also, if they continue not in their unbelief, shall be grafted in; for God is able again to graft them in. ²⁴ For if thou wast cut out of the olive-tree which is wild by nature and wast grafted contrary to nature into a good olive-tree : how much more shall these, who are the natural branches, be grafted into their own olive-tree ?

²⁵ For I would not, brethren, that ye should be ignorant of this mystery, lest ye should be wise in your own conceits, that hardness has come upon Israel in part, until the fullness of the Gentiles come in. ²⁶ And so all Israel shall be saved; as it is written : There shall come out of Zion the Deliverer; he will turn away ungodliness from Jacob; ²⁷ and this is the covenant from me to them, when I shall take away their sins. ²⁸ As concerning the gospel, they are enemies for your sakes ; but as concerning the election, they are beloved for the fathers' sakes. ²⁹ For unrepented are the gifts and the calling of God. ³⁰ For as ye in times past disobeyed God, but now obtained mercy through their disobedience ; ³¹ so also they now disobeyed through the mercy shown to you, that they also might obtain mercy. ³² For God included all in disobedience, that he might have mercy upon all.

³³ Oh, the depth of the riches, and wisdom, and knowledge of God ! How unsearchable are his judgments, and his ways past finding out ! ³⁴ For,

Who knew the mind of the Lord?
Or who became his counselor ?

³⁵ Or who first gave to him, and it shall be given back to him again ? ³⁶ For of him, and through him, and unto him, are all things : to him be the glory forever. Amen.

V. 32. *Or*, shut up all to unbelief

XII. I beseech you, therefore, brethren, by the mercies of God, to present your bodies a living sacrifice, holy, well pleasing to God, which is your rational service. ² And be not conformed to this world ; but be transformed by the renewing of your mind, that ye may discern what is the will of God, the good, and well pleasing, and perfect.

³ For I say, through the grace given to me, to every one that is among you, not to think of himself more highly than he ought to think ; but to think soberly, according as God imparted to each one the measure of faith. ⁴ For as we have many members in one body, and all the members have not the same office ; ⁵ so we, the many, are one body in Christ, and severally members one of another. ⁶ And having gifts differing according to the grace that is given to us, whether prophecy, [let us prophesy] according to the proportion of our faith ; ⁷ or ministry, [let us wait] on the ministry ; or he that teaches, on the teaching ; ⁸ or he that exhorts, on the exhortation ; he that gives, [let him do it] with simplicity ; he that presides, with diligence ; he that shows mercy, with cheerfulness.

⁹ Let love be unfeigned. Abhor that which is evil ; cleave to that which is good. In brotherly love, ¹⁰ be kindly affectioned one to another ; in honor, preferring one another ; ¹¹ in diligence, not slothful ; in spirit, fervent, serving the Lord ; ¹² in hope, rejoicing ; in affliction, patient ; in prayer, persevering ; ¹³ communicating to the necessities of the saints ; given to hospitality. ¹⁴ Bless those who persecute you ; bless, and curse not. ¹⁵ Rejoice with those who rejoice ; weep with those who weep. ¹⁶ Be of the same mind one toward another. Aspire not to things that are high, but condescend to the lowly. Be not wise in your own conceits. ¹⁷ Recompense to no one evil for evil. Provide things honorable in the sight of all men. ¹⁸ If it be possible, as far as depends on you, be at peace with all men. ¹⁹ Avenge not yourselves, beloved, but give place to the wrath [of God]. For it is written : To me belongs vengeance ; I

V. 13. *Or*, sharing in the necessities of the saints

CHAPTER XIII.

will recompense, saith the Lord. [20] Therefore,
If thy enemy hungers, feed him ;
If he thirsts, give him drink.
For, in doing this,
Thou wilt heap coals of fire on his head.
[21] Be not overcome by evil, but overcome evil with good.

XIII. Let every soul submit himself to the higher powers. For there is no power but from God ; the powers that be have been ordained by God. [2] So that he who resists the power, resists the ordinance of God; and they that resist will receive to themselves condemnation. [3] For rulers are not a terror to good works, but to the evil. And dost thou wish not to be afraid of the power? Do that which is good, and thou wilt have praise from it ; [4] for he is God's minister to thee for good. But if thou do that which is evil, be afraid: for he bears not the sword in vain ; for he is God's minister, an avenger for wrath to him that does evil. [5] Wherefore it is necessary to submit yourselves, not only because of the wrath, but also for conscience' sake.

[6] For, for this cause ye pay tribute also ; for they are God's ministers, attending continually to this very thing. [7] Render therefore to all their dues ; tribute to whom tribute is due ; custom to whom custom ; fear to whom fear ; honor to whom honor. [8] Owe no one anything, but to love one another ; for he that loves another has fulfilled the law. [9] For this : Thou shalt not commit adultery, Thou shalt not kill, Thou shalt not steal, Thou shalt not covet; and if there is any other commandment, it is briefly comprehended in this saying, namely: Thou shalt love thy neighbor as thyself. [10] Love works no ill to one's neighbor ; therefore love is the fulfillment of the law. [11] And that, knowing the time, that it is high time that we already were awaked out of sleep ; for now is our salvation nearer than when we believed. [12] The night is far advanced, the day is at hand. Let us therefore cast off the works of darkness,

and let us put on the armor of light. ¹³ Let us walk becomingly, as in the day; not in reveling and drunkenness, not in lewdness and wantonness, not in strife and envying; ¹⁴ but put on the Lord Jesus Christ, and make not provision for the flesh, to fulfill its lusts.

XIV. Him that is weak in faith receive; not for the decision of disputes. ² For one believes, that he may eat all things; but he that is weak eats herbs. ³ Let not him that eats despise him that eats not; and let not him that eats not judge him that eats; for God received him. ⁴ Who art thou that judgest another's servant? To his own master he stands or falls. But he shall be made to stand; for God is able to make him stand.

⁵ One man esteems one day above another; another esteems every day alike. Let each one be fully persuaded in his own mind. ⁶ He that regards the day, regards it to the Lord; and he that eats, eats to the Lord, for he gives thanks to God; and he that eats not, to the Lord he eats not, and gives thanks to God.

⁷ For none of us lives to himself, and none dies to himself. ⁸ For if we live, we live to the Lord; and if we die, we die to the Lord; whether we live therefore, or die, we are the Lord's. ⁹ For to this end Christ died, and lived, that he might be Lord of both the dead and living.

¹⁰ But why dost thou judge thy brother? Or why dost thou despise thy brother? For we shall all stand before the judgment-seat of God. ¹¹ For it is written: As I live, saith the Lord, to me every knee shall bow, and every tongue shall confess to God. ¹² So then, each one of us shall give account of himself to God.

¹³ Let us therefore no longer judge one another; but judge this rather, not to put a stumbling-block, or an occasion to fall, in a brother's way. ¹⁴ I know, and am persuaded in the Lord Jesus, that nothing is unclean of itself; but to him that ac-

---

V. 11. Or, shall give praise to God.

CHAPTER XV.

counts anything to be unclean, to him it is unclean. [15] But if because of food thy brother is grieved, thou no longer walkest in accordance with love. Destroy not him by thy food, for whom Christ died. [16] Let not then your good be evil spoken of. [17] For the kingdom of God is not food and drink ; but righteousness, and peace, and joy in the Holy Spirit. [18] For he that in these things serves Christ, is well pleasing to God, and approved by men.

[19] So then, let us follow after the things which make for peace, and things by which one may edify another. [20] For the sake of food destroy not the work of God. All things indeed are pure ; but it is evil for that man who eats with offense. [21] It is good neither to eat flesh, nor to drink wine, nor anything whereby thy brother stumbles, or is made to offend, or is weak. [22] Hast thou faith ? Have it to thyself before God. Happy is he that judges not himself in that which he allows. [23] And he that doubts is condemned if he eat, because it is not of faith ; and all that is not of faith is sin.

XV. Now we that are strong ought to bear the infirmities of the weak, and not to please ourselves. [2] Let each one of us please his neighbor, for his good, to edification. [3] For also Christ pleased not himself ; but, as it is written : T h e r e p r o a c h e s   o f   t h o s e   w h o   r e p r o a c h e d   t h e e, f e l l   o n   m e. [4] For whatever things were written aforetime were for our instruction, that we through patience and consolation of the Scriptures may have hope. [5] And the God of patience and consolation grant you to be of the same mind one with another, according to Christ Jesus ; [6] that with one accord ye may with one mouth glorify God, the Father of our Lord Jesus Christ.

[7] Wherefore receive ye one another, as Christ also received us, to the glory of God. [8] For I say that Jesus Christ has been made a minister of the circumcision, for the sake of God's truth, in order to confirm the promises made to the fathers ; [9] and that the Gentiles should glorify God for his mercy ; as it is written:

For this cause I will give thee praise among Gentiles,
And to thy name will sing.
¹⁰ And again he says:
Rejoice, ye Gentiles, with his people.
¹¹ And again:
Praise the Lord, all ye Gentiles;
And extol him, all ye peoples.
¹² And again, Isaiah says:
There shall be the root of Jesse,
And he who rises up to rule the Gentiles;
On him will Gentiles hope.
¹³ And the God of hope fill you with all joy and peace in believing, that ye may abound in hope, by the power of the Holy Spirit.
¹⁴ And I myself also am persuaded of you, my brethren, that ye also yourselves are full of goodness, filled with all knowledge, able also to admonish one another. ¹⁵ But I wrote the more boldly to you, brethren, in part as putting you in mind, because of the grace that is given to me by God; ¹⁶ that I should be a minister of Christ Jesus to the Gentiles, ministering as a priest in the gospel of God, that the offering up of the Gentiles may be acceptable, being sanctified by the Holy Spirit. ¹⁷ I have therefore my glorying in Christ Jesus, as to things pertaining to God. ¹⁸ For I will not dare to speak of any of the things which Christ wrought not through me, to bring the Gentiles to obedience, by word and deed, ¹⁹ in the power of signs and wonders, in the power of the Holy Spirit; so that from Jerusalem, and around as far as to Illyricum, I have fully preached the good news of Christ; ²⁰ being emulous so to preach the good news, not where Christ was named, lest I should build upon another's foundation; ²¹ but as it is written:
They to whom it was not announced concerning him shall see,
And they that have not heard shall understand.
²² For which cause also, for the most part, I was hindered from coming to you. ²³ But now having no longer place in these regions, and having a great desire these many years to

CHAPTER XVI.

come to you, ²⁴ whenever I go into Spain, I hope to see you in my journey, and to be sent forward thither by you, if first I shall be satisfied in a measure with your company.
²⁵ But now I am going to Jerusalem to minister to the saints. ²⁶ For Macedonia and Achaia thought it good, to make a certain contribution for the poor among the saints who were at Jerusalem. ²⁷ For they thought it good; and their debtors are they. For if the Gentiles shared in their spiritual things, they ought also to minister to them in carnal things. ²⁸ When therefore I have performed this, and have sealed to them this fruit, I will go by you into Spain. ²⁹ And I know that, when I come to you, I shall come in the fullness of the blessing of Christ.
³⁰ And I beseech you, brethren, by our Lord Jesus Christ, and by the love of the Spirit, to strive together with me in your prayers to God for me ; ³¹ that I may be delivered from the unbelieving in Judæa, and that my service which is for Jerusalem may prove acceptable to the saints ; ³² that with joy I may come to you by the will of God, and may with you be refreshed. ³³ And the God of peace be with you all. Amen.

XVI. I COMMEND to you Phœbe our sister, who is a deaconess of the church which is at Cenchræa; ²that ye receive her in the Lord as becomes saints, and assist her in whatever business she may have need of you; for she has been a helper of many, and of myself.
³ Salute Prisca and Aquila, my fellow-laborers in Christ Jesus (⁴ who for my life laid down their own necks ; to whom not only I give thanks, but also all the churches of the Gentiles), ⁵ and salute the church that is in their house.

Salute Epenetus, my beloved, who is the first-fruits of Asia unto Christ.

⁶ Salute Mary, who bestowed much labor on us.

⁷ Salute Andronicus and Junia, my kinsmen, and my fellow-prisoners, who are of note among the apostles, who also were in Christ before me.

V. 6. *In some ancient copies :* on you

⁸ Salute Amplias, my beloved in the Lord.

⁹ Salute Urbanus, our fellow-laborer in Christ, and Stachys my beloved.

¹⁰ Salute Apelles, the approved in Christ.

Salute those of the household of Aristobulus.

¹¹ Salute Herodion my kinsman.

Salute those of the household of Narcissus, who are in the Lord.

¹² Salute Tryphæna and Tryphosa, who labor in the Lord.

Salute Persis the beloved, who labored much in the Lord.

¹³ Salute Rufus, the chosen in the Lord, and his mother and mine.

¹⁴ Salute Asyncritus, Phlegon, Hermes, Patrobas, Hermas, and the brethren who are with them.

¹⁵ Salute Philologus, and Julia, Nereus and his sister, and Olympas, and all the saints who are with them.

¹⁶ Salute one another with a holy kiss. All the churches of Christ salute you.

¹⁷ Now I beseech you, brethren, to mark those who cause divisions and offenses, contrary to the teaching which ye learned, and avoid them. ¹⁸ For they that are such serve not our Lord Christ, but their own belly; and by their good words and fair speeches deceive the hearts of the simple. ¹⁹ For your obedience is come abroad unto all men. I rejoice therefore over you; but I would have you wise as to that which is good, and simple as to that which is evil. And the God of peace will shortly bruise Satan under your feet. The grace of our Lord Jesus Christ be with you. Amen.

²¹ Timothy, my fellow-laborer, salutes you, and Lucius, and Jason, and Sosipater, my kinsmen.

²² I, Tertius, who wrote the letter, salute you in the Lord.

²³ Gaius my host, and of the whole church, salutes you.

Erastus the chamberlain of the city salutes you, and Quartus the brother.

²⁴ The grace of our Lord Jesus Christ be with you all. Amen.

CHAPTER I.

²⁵ Now to him who is able to establish you, according to my gospel and the preaching of Jesus Christ, according to the revelation of the mystery kept in silence during eternal ages ²⁶ but now made manifest, and through the scriptures of the prophets, according to the commandment of the eternal God, made known to all nations for obedience to the faith, ²⁷ to God only wise, through Jesus Christ, be the glory forever. Amen.

THE FIRST LETTER OF PAUL TO THE CORINTHIANS.

I. Paul, a called apostle of Christ Jesus through the will of God, and Sosthenes the brother, ² to the church of God which is at Corinth, those sanctified in Christ Jesus, called to be saints, with all that in every place call upon the name of Jesus Christ our Lord, both theirs and ours : ³ Grace to you, and peace, from God our Father, and the Lord Jesus Christ.

⁴ I thank my God always on your behalf, for the grace of God which was given you in Christ Jesus ; ⁵ that in everything ye were made rich in him, in all utterance and all knowledge ; ⁶ according as the testimony of Christ was confirmed in you ; ⁷ so that ye are behind in no gift, waiting for the revelation of our Lord Jesus Christ ; ⁸ who will also confirm you unto the end, unaccused in the day of our Lord Jesus Christ. ⁹ God is faithful, by whom ye were called into the fellowship of his Son, Jesus Christ our Lord.

¹⁰ But I beseech you, brethren, by the name of our Lord Jesus Christ, that ye all speak the same thing, and that there be no divisions among you ; but that ye be made complete in the same mind, and in the same judgment. ¹¹ For it was made known to me concerning you, my brethren, by those of the house of Chloe, that there are contentions among you. ¹² And I mean this, that each of you says, I am of Paul ; and I of Apollos ; and I of Cephas ; and I of Christ. ¹³ Is Christ divided ? Was Paul crucified for you ? Or were ye immersed

I. CORINTHIANS.

in the name of Paul? ¹⁴ I thank God that I immersed none of you, but Crispus and Gaius; ¹⁵ that no one may say that I immersed in my own name. ¹⁶ And I immersed also the household of Stephanas; besides, I know not whether I immersed any other.

¹⁷ For Christ did not send me to immerse, but to preach the glad tidings; not with wisdom of speech, lest the cross of Christ should be made of no effect. ¹⁸ For the preaching of the cross is to those who perish, foolishness; but to us who are saved, it is the power of God. ¹⁹ For it is written:

I will destroy the wisdom of the wise,
And will bring to nothing the prudence of the prudent.

²⁰ Where is the wise? Where is the scribe? Where is the disputer of this world? Did not God make foolish the wisdom of the world? ²¹ For since, in the wisdom of God, the world through its wisdom knew not God, God was pleased through the foolishness of preaching to save those who believe; ²² since Jews require signs, and Greeks seek after wisdom, ²³ but we preach Christ crucified, to Jews a stumbling-block, and to Gentiles foolishness, ²⁴ but to those who are the called, both Jews and Greeks, Christ the power of God, and the wisdom of God. ²⁵ Because the foolishness of God is wiser than men: and the weakness of God is stronger than men.

²⁶ For see your calling, brethren, that not many are wise after the flesh, not many mighty, not many noble: ²⁷ but God chose the foolish things of the world, that he might put to shame the wise; and God chose the weak things of the world, that he might put to shame the things which are strong; ²⁸ and the base things of the world, and the things which are despised, did God choose, and the things which are not, that he might bring to naught things that are; ²⁹ that no flesh should glory before God. ³⁰ But of him are ye in Christ Jesus, who from God was made wisdom to us, both righteousness and sanctification, and redemption: ³¹ that, according as it is written: He that glories, let him glory in the Lord.

CHAPTER II.

II. ¹ ALSO, when I came to you, brethren, came not with excellency of speech or of wisdom, declaring to you the testimony of God. ² For I determined not to know anything among you, save Jesus Christ, and him crucified. ³ And I was with you in weakness, and in fear, and in much trembling. ⁴ And my speech and my preaching were not with persuasive words of man's wisdom, but with demonstration of the Spirit and of power; ⁵ that your faith might not stand in the wisdom of men, but in the power of God.

⁶ But we speak wisdom among those who are perfect; but a wisdom not of this world, nor of the rulers of this world, who come to naught. ⁷ But we speak God's wisdom in a mystery, the hidden wisdom which God predestined before the worlds unto our glory; ⁸ which no one of the rulers of this world has known; for had they known it, they would not have crucified the Lord of glory; ⁹ but (as it is written) t h i n g s w h i c h e y e s a w n o t, n o r e a r h e a r d, a n d w h i c h e n- t e r e d n o t i n t o t h e h e a r t o f m a n, w h i c h G o d p r e p a r e d f o r t h o s e w h o l o v e h i m ; ⁰ but to us God revealed them by his Spirit, for the Spirit searches all things, even the deep things of God. ¹¹ For who among men knows the things of a man, save the spirit of the man, which is in him? So also the things of God no one knows, but the Spirit of God. ¹² And we received, not the spirit of the world, but the spirit which is of God; that we might know the things that were freely given to us by God. ¹³ Which things also we speak, not in words taught by man's wisdom, but in those taught by the Spirit; comparing spiritual things with spiritual.

¹⁴ But the natural man receives not the things of the Spirit of God, for they are foolishness to him; and he can not know them, because they are spiritually judged. ¹⁵ But he that is spiritual judges all things; but he himself is judged by no one. ¹⁶ For who knew the mind of the Lord, that he m a y i n s t r u c t h i m ? But we have the mind of Christ.

V. 13. *Or*, interpreting spiritual things to the spiritual. *Or*, combining spiritual things with spiritual.

I. CORINTHIANS.

III. ¹ I ALSO, brethren, was not able to speak to you as spiritual, but as carnal, as babes in Christ. ² I fed you with milk, and not with meat; for ye were not yet able to bear it; nay, nor even now are ye able. ³ For ye are yet carnal; for whereas there is among you envying, and strife, and divisions, are ye not carnal, and do ye not walk as men? ⁴ For when one says, I am of Paul; and another, I am of Apollos; are ye not carnal? ⁵ Who then is Paul, and who is Apollos, but ministers through whom ye believed, even as the Lord gave to each one? ⁶ I planted, Apollos watered; but God gave the increase. ⁷ So then neither is he that plants anything, nor he that waters; but God that gives the increase. ⁸ And he that plants and he that waters are one: and each will receive his own reward according to his own labor.

⁹ For we are God's fellow-laborers; ye are God's field, God's building. ¹⁰ According to the grace of God which was given to me, as a wise master-builder I laid a foundation, and another builds thereon. But let each one take heed how he builds thereon. ¹¹ For other foundation can no one lay than that which is laid, which is Jesus Christ. ¹² And if any one builds on this foundation gold, silver, precious stones, wood, hay, stubble; ¹³ the work of each one will be made manifest; for the day will show it, because it is revealed in fire, and the fire itself will prove of what sort is each one's work. ¹⁴ If any one's work which he built thereon remains, he will receive reward. ¹⁵ If any one's work shall be burned up, he will suffer loss; but he himself will be saved; yet so as through fire.

¹⁶ Know ye not that ye are God's temple, and that the Spirit of God dwells in you? ¹⁷ If any one defiles the temple of God, him will God destroy; for the temple of God is holy, the which are ye.

¹⁸ Let no one deceive himself. If any one seems to be wise among you in this world, let him become a fool, that he may become wise. ¹⁹ For the wisdom of this world is foolishness

---

V. 17. *Or,* If any one destroys

CHAPTER IV.

with God. For it is written: He that takes the wise in their craftiness. [20] And again:

The Lord knows the thoughts of the wise,
That they are vain.

[21] So then, let no one glory in men. For all things are yours; [22] whether Paul, or Apollos, or Cephas, or the world, or life, or death, or things present, or things to come, all are yours; [23] and ye are Christ's, and Christ is God's.

IV. So let a man account us, as ministers of Christ, and stewards of the mysteries of God. [2] Moreover, it is required in stewards, that a man be found faithful. [3] But with me it is a very small thing that I should be judged by you, or by man's day; nay, neither do I judge myself. [4] For I am conscious to myself of nothing; yet am I not hereby justified, but he that judges me is the Lord. [5] So then judge not anything before the time, until the Lord come, who will both bring to light the hidden things of darkness, and make manifest the counsels of the hearts; and then shall each one have his praise of God.

[6] And these things, brethren, I have in a figure transferred to myself and Apollos for your sakes; that in us ye may learn not to go beyond that which is written, that ye be not puffed up each for one against another. [7] For who makes thee to differ? And what hast thou, that thou didst not receive? But if thou didst receive it, why dost thou glory, as if thou hadst not received it? [8] Already ye are filled full, already ye became rich, without us ye reigned as kings; and I would ye did reign, that we also might reign with you.

[9] For I think that God set forth us the apostles last, as condemned to death; for we have become a spectacle to the world, both to angels and to men. [10] We are fools for Christ's sake, but ye are wise in Christ; we are weak, but ye are strong; ye

---

V. 3. Man's day: *namely, the present, in contrast with the coming* Day of the Lord, *when he, and not man, will judge. (Acts* xvii., 31; *Rom.* ii., 16; 1 *Cor.* i., 8, *etc.)*

are honorable, but we are despised. ¹¹ Even unto this present hour we both hunger, and thirst, and are naked, and are buffeted, and have no certain dwelling-place; ¹² and labor, working with our own hands; being reviled, we bless; being persecuted, we suffer it; ¹³ being defamed, we entreat; we have become as the filth of the world, the offscouring of all things unto this day.

¹⁴ I write not these things to shame you, but as my beloved sons I admonish you. ¹⁵ For though ye have ten thousand instructors in Christ, yet have ye not many fathers; for in Christ Jesus I begot you through the gospel. ¹⁶ I beseech you therefore, be followers of me.

¹⁷ For this cause I sent to you Timothy, who is my child, beloved and faithful in the Lord, who will bring to your remembrance my ways in Christ, as I teach everywhere in every church.

¹⁸ Now some were puffed up, as though I were not coming to you. ¹⁹ But I will come to you shortly, if the Lord will, and will know, not the word of those who are puffed up, but the power. ²⁰ For the kingdom of God is not in word, but in power. ²¹ What will ye? Shall I come to you with a rod, or in love, and the spirit of meekness?

V. It is commonly reported that there is fornication among you, and such fornication as is not even among the Gentiles, that one should have his father's wife. ² And ye are puffed up, and did not rather mourn, that he who did this deed might be taken away from among you. ³ For I verily, as absent in body but present in spirit, have already judged, as though I were present, concerning him who has so done this; ⁴ in the name of our Lord Jesus Christ, ye being gathered together, and my spirit, with the power of our Lord Jesus Christ, ⁵ to deliver such a one to Satan for the destruction of the flesh, that the spirit may be saved in the day of the Lord Jesus.

⁶ Your glorying is not good. Know ye not that a little leaven leavens the whole lump? ⁷ Cleanse out therefore the old leaven, that ye may be a new lump, according as ye are

---

V. 16 *Gr* become imitators of me

CHAPTER VI.

unleavened. For our passover, Christ, was sacrificed for us; ⁸ therefore let us keep the feast, not with old leaven, nor with the leaven of malice and wickedness, but with the unleavened bread of sincerity and truth.

⁹ I wrote to you, in my letter, not to keep company with fornicators; ¹⁰ yet not, altogether, with the fornicators of this world, or with the covetous, or extortioners, or idolaters; for then ye must needs go out of the world. ¹¹ But as it is, I wrote to you not to keep company, if any one called a brother be a fornicator, or covetous, or an idolater, or a railer, or a drunkard, or an extortioner, with such a one not even to eat.

¹² For what have I to do with judging those also who are without? Do not ye judge those who are within? ¹³ But those who are without God judges. Therefore put away that wicked man from among yourselves.

VI. Dare any one of you, having a matter against another, go to law before the unjust, and not before the saints? ² Do ye not know that the saints shall judge the world? And if the world shall be judged by you, are ye unworthy to judge the smallest matters? ³ Know ye not that we shall judge angels? How much more the things of this life? ⁴ If then ye have judgments about things of this life, set those to judge who are of no esteem in the church.

⁵ I speak to your shame. Is it so, that there is not a wise man among you, not even one that shall be able to judge between his brethren; ⁶ but brother goes to law with brother, and that before unbelievers? ⁷ Now therefore, it is altogether a fault among you, because ye go to law one with another. Why do ye not rather take wrong? Why do ye not rather suffer yourselves to be defrauded? ⁸ Nay, ye do wrong, and defraud, and that your brethren. ⁹ Know ye not that the unrighteous shall not inherit the kingdom of God? Be not deceived; neither fornicators, nor idolaters, nor adulterers, nor the effeminate, nor abusers of themselves with mankind, ¹⁰ nor thieves, nor the covetous, nor drunkards, nor revilers, nor extortioners, shall inherit the kingdom of God. ¹¹ And such were some of

you; but ye were washed, but ye were sanctified, but ye were justified in the name of the Lord Jesus, and by the Spirit of our God.

[12] All things are lawful for me, but not all things are expedient; all things are lawful for me, but I will not be brought under the power of anything. [13] Meats for the belly, and the belly for meats; but God will destroy both it and them. But the body is not for fornication, but for the Lord; and the Lord for the body. [14] And God both raised the Lord, and will also raise up us by his power.

[15] Know ye not that your bodies are members of Christ? Shall I then take the members of Christ, and make them members of a harlot? Far be it! [16] Know ye not that he who is joined to a harlot is one body? For the two, says he, shall be one flesh. [17] But he that is joined to the Lord is one spirit. [18] Flee fornication. Every sin that a man commits is without the body; but he that commits fornication, sins against his own body. [19] Know ye not that your body is the temple of the Holy Spirit, who is in you, whom ye have from God, and ye are not your own? [20] For ye are bought with a price; therefore glorify God in your body.

VII. Now concerning the things whereof ye wrote to me: It is good for a man not to touch a woman; [2] but because of fornication, let each man have his own wife, and let each woman have her own husband. [3] Let the husband render to the wife her due; and in like manner the wife also to the husband. [4] The wife has not power over her own body, but the husband; and in like manner the husband also has not power over his own body, but the wife. [5] Defraud not one the other, except it be with consent for a time, that ye may give yourselves to fasting and prayer, and come again together, that Satan may not tempt you on account of your incontinency.

[6] But this I say by way of permission, not of command. [7] But I would that all men were as myself. But each one has his own gift from God, one after this manner, and another after that.

CHAPTER VII.

⁸ And I say to the unmarried and the widows, it is good for them if they remain as I also am. ⁹ But if they have not self-control, let them marry; for it is better to marry than to burn.

¹⁰ And the married not I command, but the Lord, that the wife depart not from the husband. ¹¹ But if she have departed, let her remain unmarried, or let her be reconciled to her husband; and let the husband not put away his wife.

¹² But to the rest say I, not the Lord: If any brother has a wife that believes not, and she is pleased to dwell with him, let him not put her away. ¹³ And a woman who has a husband that believes not, and he is pleased to dwell with her, let her not leave her husband. ¹⁴ For the unbelieving husband is sanctified in the wife, and the unbelieving wife is sanctified in the husband; else your children are unclean; but now they are holy.

¹⁵ But if the unbelieving departs, let him depart. The brother or the sister is not under bondage in such cases; but God has called us to peace. ¹⁶ For what knowest thou, O wife, whether thou shalt save thy husband? Or what knowest thou, O man, whether thou shalt save thy wife? ¹⁷ Only, as the Lord apportioned to each one, as God has called each one, so let him walk. And so I ordain in all the churches.

¹⁸ Was any one called being circumcised? Let him not become uncircumcised. Has any one been called in uncircumcision? Let him not be circumcised. ¹⁹ Circumcision is nothing, and uncircumcision is nothing; but the keeping of the commandments of God.

²⁰ Let each one abide in the same calling wherein he was called. ²¹ Wast thou called being a servant? Care not for it; but if thou canst become free, use it rather. ²² For he that was called in the Lord, being a servant, is the Lord's freedman; in like manner also the freeman, being called, is Christ's servant. ²³ Ye were bought with a price; become not servants of men. ²⁴ Brethren, let every man, wherein he was called, therein abide with God.

²⁵ Now concerning virgins I have no commandment of the

Lord; but I give my judgment, as one that has obtained mercy of the Lord to be faithful. ²⁶ I consider therefore that this is good on account of the present necessity, that it is good for a man so to be. ²⁷ Art thou bound to a wife? Seek not to be loosed. Art thou loosed from a wife? Seek not a wife. ²⁸ But if also thou marry, thou sinnedst not; and if a virgin marry, she sinned not. But such shall have affliction in the flesh; but I spare you.

²⁹ But this I say, brethren, the time that remains is short; that both they who have wives may be as though they had none; ³⁰ and they that weep, as though they wept not; and they that rejoice, as though they rejoiced not; and they that buy, as though they possessed not; ³¹ and they that use this world, as not abusing it; for the fashion of this world is passing away.

³² But I would have you without cares. He that is unmarried cares for the things of the Lord, how he shall please the Lord; ³³ but he that is married cares for the things of the world, how he shall please his wife. ³⁴ There is a difference also between the wife and the virgin. The unmarried woman cares for the things of the Lord, that she may be holy both in body and spirit; but she that is married cares for the things of the world, how she shall please her husband.

³⁵ And this I say for your own profit; not that I may cast a snare upon you, but for that which is seemly, and that ye may attend upon the Lord without distraction. ³⁶ But if any one thinks that he behaves himself unseemly toward his virgin, if she be past the flower of her age, and need so require, let him do what he will, he sins not; let them marry. ³⁷ But he that stands steadfast in his heart, having no necessity, but has power over his own will, and has determined this in his heart that he will keep his virgin, does well. ³⁸ So that both he that gives her in marriage does well, and he that gives her not in marriage does better.

³⁹ A wife is bound as long as her husband lives; but if her

V. 28. *Or*, and I desire to spare you

CHAPTER IX.

husband be dead, she is at liberty to be married to whom she will; only in the Lord. ⁴⁰ But she is happier if she so abide, after my judgment; and I too think that I have the Spirit of God.

VIII. Now concerning the things offered to idols, we know that we all have knowledge. Knowledge puffs up, but love edifies. ² If any one thinks that he knows anything, he has known nothing yet as he ought to know. ³ But if any one loves God, the same is known by him.

⁴ As concerning then the eating of the things offered to idols, we know that an idol is nothing in the world, and that there is no other God but one. ⁵ For though there are gods so-called, whether in heaven or on earth (as there are gods many, and lords many), ⁶ yet to us there is but one God, the Father, of whom are all things, and we unto him; and one Lord Jesus Christ, by whom are all things, and we by him.

⁷ But there is not in all men this knowledge; for some, with a consciousness till now of the idol, eat it as a thing offered to an idol; and their conscience being weak is defiled. ⁸ But food commends us not to God; for neither, if we eat, are we the better; nor, if we eat not, are we the worse. ⁹ But take heed, lest haply this liberty of yours become a stumbling-block to the weak. ¹⁰ For if any one sees thee, who hast knowledge, reclining at table in an idol's temple, will not the conscience of him who is weak be emboldened to eat the things offered to idols? ¹¹ And through thy knowledge he that is weak perishes, the brother for whom Christ died! ¹² But when ye so sin against the brethren, and wound their weak conscience, ye sin against Christ. ¹³ Wherefore, if food cause my brother to offend, I will eat no flesh for ever more, that I may not cause my brother to offend.

IX. Am I not an apostle? Am I not free? Have I not seen Jesus Christ our Lord? Are not ye my work in the Lord? ² If I am not an apostle to others, yet at least I am to you; for the seal of my apostleship are ye in the Lord

³ This is my answer to those who examine me. ⁴ Have we not power to eat and to drink? ⁵ Have we not power to lead about a sister as a wife, as well as the other apostles, and the brothers of the Lord, and Cephas? ⁶ Or have only I and Barnabas not power to forbear working? ⁷ Who ever goes to war at his own charges? Who plants a vineyard, and eats not of the fruit thereof? Or who tends a flock, and eats not of the milk of the flock?

⁸ Say I these things as a man? Or does not the law also say these things? ⁹ For it is written in the law of Moses: Thou shalt not muzzle an ox while treading out the grain. Is it for the oxen that God cares? ¹⁰ Or does he say it altogether for our sakes? For, for our sakes it was written; that he who plows ought to plow in hope; and he who threshes, in hope of partaking. ¹¹ If we sowed for you the things that are spiritual, is it a great thing if we shall reap your carnal things? ¹² If others partake of this power over you, do not we still more? But we used not this power; but we bear all things, that we may not cause any hindrance to the gospel of Christ.

¹³ Do ye not know that they who minister about the holy things eat of the temple, and they who wait at the altar partake with the altar? ¹⁴ So also did the Lord appoint to those who preach the gospel, to live by the gospel. ¹⁵ But I have used none of these things; and I wrote not these things, that it should be so done to me; for it were better for me to die, than that any one should make my glorying void. ¹⁶ For if I preach the gospel, I have nothing to glory of; for a necessity is laid upon me; for, woe is to me, if I preach not the gospel! ¹⁷ For if I do this willingly, I have a reward; but if unwillingly, I have a stewardship intrusted to me.

¹⁸ What then is my reward? That, in preaching the gospel, I may make the gospel without charge, that I use not to the full my power in the gospel. ¹⁹ For being free from all men, I made myself servant to all, that I might gain the more. ²⁰ And to the Jews I became as a Jew, that I might gain Jews; to those under law, as under law, not being myself under law,

CHAPTER X.

that I might gain those under law ; ²¹ to those without law, as without law (not being without law to God, but under law to Christ), that I might gain those without law. ²² To the weak I became as weak, that I might gain the weak. I have become all things to all, that I may by all means save some. ²³ And all things I do for the gospel's sake, that I may become a partaker thereof with others.

²⁴ Know ye not that they who run in a race, all indeed run, but one receives the prize ? So run, that ye may obtain. ²⁵ And every one who contends for the prize is temperate in all things ; they indeed to obtain a corruptible crown, but we an incorruptible. ²⁶ I therefore so run, as not uncertainly ; I so fight, as not beating the air. ²⁷ But I keep under my body, and bring it into subjection ; lest haply, having preached to others, I myself should be rejected.

X. For I would not have you ignorant, brethren, that our fathers were all under the cloud, and all passed through the sea ; ² and were all immersed unto Moses in the cloud and in the sea ; ³ and all ate the same spiritual food, ⁴ and all drank the same spiritual drink ; for they drank of the spiritual rock that followed them, and the rock was Christ. ⁵ But in the most of them God had no pleasure ; for they were overthrown in the wilderness.

⁶ Now these things were examples to us, in order that we should not lust after evil things, as they also lusted. ⁷ Nor be ye idolaters, as were some of them ; as it is written : T h e p e o p l e   s a t   d o w n   t o   e a t   a n d   d r i n k,   a n d   r o s e   u p   t o   p l a y. ⁸ Nor let us commit fornication, as some of them did, and fell in one day three and twenty thousand. ⁹ Nor let us tempt Christ, as some of them tempted, and perished by the serpents. ¹⁰ Nor murmur ye, as some of them murmured, and perished by the destroyer.

¹¹ Now all these things happened to them as examples, and they were written for our admonition, upon whom the ends of

---

V. 23. *Or*, may become a partaker with it

the ages are come. ¹² Wherefore let him that thinks he stands, take heed lest he fall. ¹³ There has no temptation taken you but such as belongs to man; and God is faithful, who will not suffer you to be tempted beyond what ye are able, but will with the temptation make also the way of escape, that ye may be able to bear it.

¹⁴ Wherefore, my beloved, flee from idolatry. ¹⁵ I speak as to wise men; judge ye what I say. ¹⁶ The cup of blessing which we bless, is it not a partaking of the blood of Christ? The loaf which we break, is it not a partaking of the body of Christ? ¹⁷ Because we, the many, are one loaf, one body; for we all share in that one loaf.

¹⁸ Behold Israel according to the flesh. Are not they who eat of the sacrifices partakers of the altar?

¹⁹ What then do I say? That an idol is anything, or that what is offered to idols is anything? ²⁰ Nay; but that what they sacrifice, they sacrifice to demons, and not to God; and I would not that ye should be partakers of the demons. ²¹ Ye can not drink the cup of the Lord, and the cup of demons; ye can not share in the table of the Lord, and the table of demons.

²² Do we provoke the Lord to jealousy? Are we stronger than he? ²³ All things are lawful, but not all things are expedient; all things are lawful, but not all things edify. ²⁴ Let no one seek his own, but his neighbor's good.

²⁵ Whatever is sold in the market eat, asking no question for conscience' sake; ²⁶ for the earth is the Lord's, and the fullness thereof.

²⁷ If any of the unbelieving bids you to a feast, and ye choose to go, whatever is set before you eat, asking no question for conscience' sake. ²⁸ But if any one say to you: This is a thing sacrificed to a god, eat it not, for his sake that showed it, and for conscience' sake. ²⁹ Conscience, I say, not thine own, but that of the other; for why is my liberty judged by another's conscience? ³⁰ If I partake with thanks, why am I evil spoken of, for that for which I give thanks?

³¹ Whether therefore ye eat, or drink, or whatever ye do, do

CHAPTER XI.

all to the glory of God. ²²Give no occasion of stumbling, either to Jews or Greeks, or to the church of God; ³³as I also please all in all things, not seeking my own profit, but that of the many, that they may be saved. ¹Be ye followers of me, as I also am of Christ.

²Now I praise you, brethren, that ye remember me in all things, and hold fast the traditions, as I delivered them to you. ³And I would have you know, that the head of every man is Christ; and the head of the woman is the man; and the head of Christ is God. ⁴Every man praying or prophesying, having his head covered, dishonors his head. ⁵But every woman praying or prophesying with the head uncovered, dishonors her head; for it is one and the same as if she were shaven. ⁶For if a woman is not covered, let her also be shorn; but if it is a shame for a woman to be shorn or shaven, let her be covered. ⁷For a man indeed ought not to cover his head, being the image and glory of God; but the woman is the glory of the man. ⁸For the man is not of the woman; but the woman of the man. ⁹And the man was not created for the woman, but the woman for the man. ¹⁰For this cause ought the woman to have [the token of] authority on her head, because of the angels.

¹¹Nevertheless, neither is the woman without the man, nor the man without the woman, in the Lord. ¹²For as the woman is of the man, so also is the man by the woman; but all things of God.

¹³Judge in your own selves; is it seemly that a woman pray to God uncovered? ¹⁴Does not even nature itself teach you, that, if a man have long hair, it is a shame to him? ¹⁵But if a woman have long hair, it is a glory to her; for her hair is given her for a covering.

¹ But if any man seems to be contentious, we have no such custom, nor the churches of God.

¹⁷And while I enjoin this, I praise you not, that ye come

V. 2. Traditions: *things delivered from one to another; received from the Lord, and delivered to them (v. 23, and ch. xv., 3.)*

I. CORINTHIANS.

together not for the better, but for the worse. [18] For first of all, when ye come together in the church, I hear that there are divisions among you; and I partly believe it. [19] For there must be also sects among you, that they who are appre may be made manifest among you.

[20] When therefore ye come together into one place, there i. no eating of a supper of the Lord. [21] For in eating, each takes without waiting his own supper; and one is hungry, and another is drunken. [22] What! have ye not houses to eat and to drink in? Or despise ye the church of God, and shame those who have not? What shall I say to you? Shall I praise you in this? I praise you not.

[23] For I received from the Lord, what I also delivered to you, that the Lord Jesus, in the night in which he was betrayed, took a loaf; [24] and having given thanks, he broke it, and said: This is my body, which is for you; this do in remembrance of me. [25] In like manner also the cup, after they had supped, saying: This cup is the new covenant in my blood; this do, as often as ye drink it, in remembrance of me. [26] For as often as ye eat this bread, and drink this cup, ye show the Lord's death till he come.

[27] So that whoever eats the bread or drinks the cup of the Lord unworthily, shall be guilty of the body and the blood of the Lord. [28] But let a man examine himself, and so let him eat of the bread, and drink of the cup. [29] For he that eats and drinks, eats and drinks condemnation to himself, if he discern not the body.

[30] For this cause many are weak and sickly among you, and many sleep. [31] For if we judged ourselves; we should not be judged. [32] But being judged, we are chastened by the Lord, that we may not be condemned with the world.

[33] Wherefore, my brethren, when coming together to eat, wait for one another. [34] If any one is hungry, let him eat at home; that ye come not together unto condemnation. And the rest I will set in order when I come.

V. 20. *Or,* it is not to eat the Supper of the Lord

CHAPTER XII.

XII. Now concerning the spiritual gifts, brethren, I would not have you ignorant. ² Ye know that ye were Gentiles carried away to the dumb idols, as ye were led. ³ Wherefore I give you to understand, that no one speaking by the Spirit of God calls Jesus accursed; and no one can say, Jesus is Lord, but by the Holy Spirit.

⁴ Now there are diversities of gifts, but the same Spirit. ⁵ And there are diversities of ministrations, and the same L. ⁶ And there are diversities of operations, but the same God wh. works all in all. ⁷ But to each is given the manifestation of the Spirit, for profiting. ⁸ For to one is given through the Spirit the word of wisdom; to another the word of knowledge according to the same Spirit; ⁹ to another faith, by the same Spirit; to another gifts of healings by the one Spirit; ¹⁰ to another the working of miracles; to another prophecy; to another discerning of spirits; to another diversities of tongues; to another the interpretation of tongues. ¹¹ But all these works the one and self-same Spirit, dividing to each one severally as he will.

¹² For as the body is one and has many members, and all the members of the body, being many, are one body, so also is Christ. ¹³ For by one Spirit we were all immersed into one body, whether Jews or Greeks, whether bond or free; and were all made to drink of one Spirit.

¹⁴ For the body is not one member, but many. ¹⁵ If the foot say: Because I am not a hand, I am not of the body; it is not therefore not of the body. ¹⁶ And if the ear say: Because I am not an eye, I am not of the body; it is not therefore not of the body. ¹⁷ If the whole body were an eye, where were the hearing? If the whole were hearing, where were the smelling?

¹⁸ But now, God set the members each one of them in the body, as it pleased him. ¹⁹ And if they were all one member, where were the body? ²⁰ But now there are many members, but one body. ²¹ And the eye can not say to the hand, I have no need of thee; nor again the head to the feet, I have no

need of you. ²²Nay, much more those members of the body, which seem to be more feeble, are necessary; ²³and those which we think to be less honorable parts of the body, on these we bestow more abundant honor; and our uncomely parts have more abundant comeliness. ²⁴And our comely parts have no need; but God attempered the body together, giving more abundant honor to that which lacked; ²⁵that there may be no division in the body, but that the members should have the same care one for another. ²⁶And whether one member suffers, all the members suffer with it; or one member is honored, all the members rejoice with it.

²⁷Now ye are the body of Christ, and members each one. ²⁸And God set some in the church, apostles first, secondly prophets, thirdly teachers, after that miracles, then gifts of healings, helps, governings, diversities of tongues. ²⁹Are all apostles? Are all prophets? Are all teachers? Are all workers of miracles? ³⁰Have all gifts of healings? Do all speak with tongues? Do all interpret? ³¹But desire earnestly the greater gifts; and moreover, I show to you a more excellent way.

¹Though I speak with the tongues of men and of angels, and have not love, I am become as sounding brass, or a tinkling cymbal. ²And though I have the gift of prophecy, and understand all mysteries, and all knowledge; and though I have all faith, so as to remove mountains, and have not love, I am nothing. ³And though I bestow all my goods in food, and though I give up my body that I may be burned, and have not love, it profits me nothing.

⁴Love suffers long, is kind; love envies not; love vaunts not itself, is not puffed up, ⁵does not behave itself unseemly, seeks not its own, is not easily provoked, imputes no evil; ⁶rejoices not at unrighteousness, but rejoices with the truth; ⁷bears all things, believes all things, hopes all things, endures all things. ⁸Love never fails; but whether there are prophesyings, they will be done away; whether tongues, they will cease; whether knowledge, it will be done away. ⁹For we know in part, and

---

V. 27. *Or,* each in his place.

CHAPTER XIV.

we prophesy in part. ¹⁰ But when that which is perfect is come, then that which is in part will be done away.
¹¹ When I was a child, I spoke as a child, I thought as a child, I reasoned as a child; but now that I am become a man, I have done away the things of the child. ¹² For we see now in a mirror, obscurely; but then face to face. Now I know in part; but then I shall know fully, even as I also am fully known.
¹³ And now remain faith, hope, love, these three; and the greatest of these is love.

¹ Pursue after love; and desire earnestly the spiritual gifts, but rather that ye may prophesy. ² For he that speaks in an unknown tongue speaks not to men, but to God; for no one understands; but with the spirit he speaks mysteries. ³ But he that prophesies, to men he speaks edification, and exhortation, and comfort. ⁴ He that speaks in an unknown tongue edifies himself; but he that prophesies edifies the church.
⁵ I would that ye should all speak with tongues, but rather that ye should prophesy; for greater is he that prophesies than he that speaks with tongues, except he interpret, that the church may receive edification.
⁶ And now, brethren, if I come to you speaking with tongues, what shall I profit you, except I shall speak to you either in revelation, or in knowledge, or in prophesying, or in teaching? ⁷ And things without life giving sound, whether pipe or harp, yet if they give no distinction in the sounds, how shall that be known which is piped or harped? ⁸ For if a trumpet give an uncertain sound, who shall prepare himself for battle? ⁹ So also ye, if ye utter not by the tongue words easily understood, how shall that be known which is spoken? For ye will be speaking into the air.
¹⁰ So many, it may be, are the kinds of speaking sounds in the world, and none is without significance. ¹¹ If then I know not the meaning of the sound, I shall be to him that speaks a barbarian, and he that speaks a barbarian to me. ¹² So also ye, since ye are zealous of spiritual gifts, seek that ye may abound in them to the edification of the church.
¹³ Wherefore let him that speaks in an unknown tongue pray

that he may interpret. ¹⁴ For if I pray in an unknown tongue, my spirit prays, but my understanding is unfruitful. ¹⁵ What then? I will pray with the spirit, and I will pray with the understanding also; I will sing with the spirit, and I will sing with the understanding also. ¹⁶ Else, if thou shalt bless with the spirit, how shall he that occupies the place of the unlearned say the Amen at thy giving of thanks, since he knows not what thou sayest? ¹⁷ For thou indeed givest thanks well, but the other is not edified.

¹⁸ I thank God, I speak with tongues more than ye all. ¹⁹ Yet in the church I would rather speak five words with my understanding, that I may also instruct others, than ten thousand words in an unknown tongue.

²⁰ Brethren, be not children in your understandings; but in malice be as children, but in your understandings be men.

²¹ In the law it is written:

For with men of other tongues, and with strange lips,
I will speak to this people;
And not even so will they hearken to me, saith the Lord.

²² So that the tongues are for a sign, not to those who believe, but to the unbelieving; but prophesying is not for the unbelieving, but for those who believe.

²³ If therefore the whole church is come together into one place, and all speak with tongues, and there come in those who are unlearned, or unbelievers, will they not say that ye are mad? ²⁴ But if all prophesy, and there come in one that is an unbeliever, or unlearned, he is convicted by all, he is judged by all. ²⁵ The secrets of his heart are made manifest; and so falling on his face he will worship God, reporting that God is in truth among you.

²⁶ How is it then, brethren? When ye come together, each of you has a psalm, has an instruction, has a tongue, has a revelation, has an interpretation. Let all things be done to edification. ²⁷ If any one speaks in an unknown tongue, let it be by two, or at the most by three, and in turn; and let one interpret. ²⁸ But if there be no interpreter, let him keep silence in the church; and let him speak to himself, and to God.

CHAPTER XV.

²⁹ And of prophets, let two or three speak, and the others judge. ³⁰ But if a revelation be made to another sitting by, let the first be silent. ³¹ For ye can all prophesy one by one, that all may learn, and all be comforted. ³² And the spirits of the prophets are subject to the prophets. ³³ For God is not a God of confusion, but of peace, as in all churches of the saints.

³⁴ Let your women keep silence in the churches; for it is not permitted to them to speak, but they are to be in subjection, as the law also says. ³⁵ And if they wish to learn anything, let them ask their husbands at home; for it is a shame for a woman to speak in the church.

³⁶ Did the word of God come forth from you? Or came it unto you alone? ³⁷ If any one thinks himself to be a prophet, or spiritual, let him acknowledge that the things which I write to you are the Lord's commandments. ³⁸ But if any one is ignorant, let him be ignorant. ³⁹ Wherefore, brethren, desire earnestly the gift of prophecy, and forbid not to speak with tongues. ⁴⁰ But let all things be done decently and in order.

XV. And I make known to you, brethren, the gospel which I preached to you, which also ye received, in which also ye stand; ² through which also ye are saved, if ye hold fast the word with which I preached to you, unless ye believed in vain.

³ For I delivered to you first of all what I also received, that Christ died for our sins according to the Scriptures; ⁴ and that he was buried, and that he has risen on the third day according to the Scriptures; ⁵ and that he appeared to Cephas, then to the twelve; ⁶ after that, he appeared to above five hundred brethren at once; of whom the greater part remain until now, but some are fallen asleep. ⁷ After that, he appeared to James; then to all the apostles. ⁸ And last of all he appeared to me also, as the one born out of due time. ⁹ For I am the least of the apostles, who am not worthy to be called an apostle, because I persecuted the church of God. ¹⁰ But by the grace of God I am what I am; and his grace which was be-

stowed upon me was not in vain; but I labored more abundantly than they all; yet not I, but the grace of God which was with me. ¹¹Therefore whether it were I or they, so we preach, and so ye believed.

¹²Now if Christ is preached that he has risen from the dead, how say some among you that there is no resurrection of the dead? ¹³But if there is no resurrection of the dead, then neither has Christ risen; ¹⁴and if Christ has not risen, then is our preaching vain, and vain also your faith. ¹⁵And we are also found false witnesses of God: because we testified of God, that he raised up Christ; whom he raised not, if it be so that the dead rise not. ¹⁶For if the dead rise not, neither has Christ risen; ¹⁷and if Christ has not risen, your faith is vain; ye are yet in your sins. ¹⁸Then also they who have fallen asleep in Christ have perished. ¹⁹If in this life only we have hope in Christ, we are of all men most miserable.

²⁰But now Christ has risen from the dead, the first-fruits of those who sleep. ²¹For since by man came death, by man came also the resurrection of the dead. ²²For as in Adam all die, so also in Christ will all be made alive. ²³But each in his own order; Christ the first-fruits; afterward they who are Christ's at his coming. ²⁴Then comes the end, when he delivers up the kingdom to God, the Father; when he shall have done away all rule, and all authority and power. ²⁵For he must reign, till he has put all enemies under his feet. ²⁶As the last enemy, Death shall be done away. For he subjected all things under his feet. ²⁷But when he says, All things are subjected, it is manifest that he is excepted, who subjected all things to him. ²⁸And when all things shall be subjected to him, then will also the Son himself be subject to him who subjected all things to him, that God may be all in all.

²⁹Else what shall they do who are immersed for the dead? If the dead rise not at all, why are they then immersed for them? ³⁰Why also are we in peril every hour? ³¹I protest by my glorying in you, which I have in Christ Jesus our Lord, I die daily. ³²If after the manner of men I fought with wild

CHAPTER XV.

beasts at Ephesus, what is the profit to me, if the dead rise not?
Let us eat and drink;
For to-morrow we die.
³³ Be not deceived; evil communications corrupt good manners. ³⁴ Awake to righteousness, and sin not; for some have not the knowledge of God. I say it to your shame.

³⁵ But some one will say: How do the dead rise? And with what kind of body do they come? ³⁶ Thou fool, that which thou sowest is not quickened, except it die; ³⁷ and what thou sowest, not the body that shall be sowest thou, but bare grain, perchance of wheat, or of some other grain. ³⁸ But God gives it a body as it pleased him, and to each of the seeds its own body.

³⁹ All flesh is not the same flesh; but there is one flesh of men, another flesh of beasts, another of fishes, another of birds. ⁴⁰ There are also heavenly bodies, and earthly bodies; but the glory of the heavenly is one, and that of the earthly is another. ⁴¹ There is one glory of the sun, and another glory of the moon, and another glory of the stars; for star differs from star in glory.

⁴² So also is the resurrection of the dead. It is sown in corruption, it rises in incorruption. ⁴³ It is sown in dishonor, it rises in glory. It is sown in weakness, it rises in power. ⁴⁴ It is sown a natural body, it rises a spiritual body.

If there is a natural body, there is also a spiritual. ⁴⁵ So also it is written: The first man Adam was made a living soul; the last Adam a life-giving spirit. ⁴⁶ But the spiritual is not first, but the natural; and afterward the spiritual. ⁴⁷ The first man was of the earth, earthy; the second man is from heaven. ⁴⁸ As was the earthy, such are they also that are earthy; and as is the heavenly, such are they also that are heavenly. ⁴⁹ And as we bore the image of the earthy, we shall also bear the image of the heavenly.

⁵⁰ And this I say, brethren, that flesh and blood can not inherit the kingdom of God; nor does corruption inherit incorruption. ⁵¹ Behold, I tell you a mystery. We shall not all

sleep, but we shall all be changed, ⁵² in a moment, in the twinkling of an eye, at the last trump; for the trumpet will sound, and the dead will be raised incorruptible, and we shall be changed. . ⁵³ For this corruptible must put on incorruption, and this mortal must put on immortality. ⁵⁴ And when this corruptible shall have put on incorruption, and this mortal shall have put on immortality, then will be brought to pass the saying, that is written: D e a t h   i s   s w a l l o w e d   u p   i n   v i c t o r y. ⁵⁵ Where, O death, is thy sting? Where, O death, is thy victory? ⁵⁶ The sting of death is sin; and the strength of sin is the law. ⁵⁷ But thanks be to God, who gives us the victory, through our Lord Jesus Christ.

⁵⁸ Therefore, my beloved brethren, be steadfast, immovable, always abounding in the work of the Lord, knowing that your labor is not in vain in the Lord.

XVI. Now concerning the collection for the saints, as I gave order to the churches of Galatia, so also do ye. ² On each first day of the week, let every one of you lay by him in store, according as he is prospered, that there may be no collections when I come. ³ And when I come, whomsoever ye shall approve, them I will send with letters to carry your benefaction to Jerusalem. ⁴ And if it be worthy of my going also, they shall go with me.

⁵ And I will come to you, when I shall pass through Macedonia. For I pass through Macedonia; ⁶ and it may be that I will remain, or even pass the winter with you, that ye may bring me on my journey whithersoever I go. ⁷ For I wish not to see you now, in passing; for I hope to remain some time with you, if the Lord permit. ⁸ But I shall remain at Ephesus until the Pentecost. ⁹ For a great and effectual door is open to me, and there are many adversaries.

¹⁰ Now if Timothy come, see that he may be with you without fear; for he works the work of the Lord, as I also do. ¹¹ Let no one therefore despise him; but send him forward in peace, that he may come to me; for I look for him with the brethren.

CHAPTER I.

¹² And concerning Apollos the brother, I besought him much to come to you with the brethren; and it was not at all his will to come at this time, but he will come when he shall have a convenient time.
¹³ Watch, stand fast in the faith, acquit you like men, be strong. ¹⁴ Let all your acts be done in love.
¹⁵ And I beseech you, brethren, (ye know the house of Stephanas, that it is the first-fruits of Achaia, and that they devoted themselves to the service of the saints,) ¹⁶ that ye also submit yourselves to such, and to every one that works with us, and labors.
¹⁷ I am glad of the coming of Stephanas and Fortunatus and Achaicus; for what was lacking on your part they supplied. ¹⁸ For they refreshed my spirit and yours; therefore acknowledge those who are such.
¹⁹ The churches of Asia salute you.
Aquila and Priscilla salute you much in the Lord, with the church that is in their house. ²⁰ All the brethren salute you. Salute one another with a holy kiss.
²¹ The salutation of me, Paul, with my own hand.
²² If any one loves not the Lord Jesus Christ, let him be accursed. Maran atha!
²³ The grace of our Lord Jesus Christ be with you. ²⁴ My love be with you all in Christ Jesus. Amen.

THE SECOND LETTER OF PAUL TO THE CORINTHIANS.

I. Paul, an apostle of Jesus Christ by the will of God, and Timothy the brother, to the church of God which is at Corinth, with all the saints who are in all Achaia: ² Grace to you and peace from God our Father and the Lord Jesus Christ.
³ Blessed be God, the Father of our Lord Jesus Christ, the

V. 22. Maran atha: *that is*, The Lord comes! (*Compare Philipp.* iv., 5.)

II. CORINTHIANS.

Father of mercies, and the God of all consolation ; ⁴ who consoles us in all our affliction, that we may be able to console those who are in any affliction, by the consolation wherewith we ourselves are consoled by God. ⁵ Because, as the sufferings of Christ abound toward us, so through Christ abounds also our consolation.

⁶ But whether we are afflicted, it is for your consolation and salvation, which is effective in the endurance of the same sufferings which we also suffer ; or whether we are consoled, it is for your consolation and salvation. ⁷ And our hope of you is steadfast, knowing, that as ye are partakers of the sufferings, so are ye also of the consolation.

⁸ For we would not, brethren, that ye should be ignorant of our affliction which befell us in Asia, that we were exceedingly oppressed, above our strength, so that we despaired even of life. ⁹ Yea, we ourselves had in ourselves the sentence of death, that we should not trust in ourselves, but in God who raises the dead ; ¹⁰ who delivered us from so great a death, and does deliver ; in whom is our hope that he will still deliver ; ¹¹ ye also helping together on our behalf by your supplication, that for the mercy bestowed on us through many persons, thanks may be given by many on our behalf.

¹² For our glorying is this, the testimony of our conscience, that in simplicity and godly sincerity, not in fleshly wisdom, but in the grace of God, did we deport ourselves in the world, and more abundantly toward you. ¹³ For we write no other things to you, than what ye read or even acknowledge, and I trust ye will acknowledge even to the end ; ¹⁴ as also ye did acknowledge us in part, that we are your glorying, even as ye also are ours in the day of the Lord Jesus.

¹⁵ And in this confidence I was desirous to come to you before, that ye might have a second benefit ; ¹⁶ and to pass by you into Macedonia, and from Macedonia to come again to you, and by you to be brought on my way to Judæa. ¹⁷ When therefore I purposed this, did I act with levity ? Or the things that I purpose, do I purpose according to the flesh, that with me there should be the yea, yea, and the nay, nay ? ¹⁸ But God is faith-

CHAPTER II.

ful, our word to you is not yea and nay. ¹⁹ For the Son of God, Jesus Christ, who was preached among you by us, by me and Silvanus and Timothy, was not made yea and nay, but has been made yea in him. ²⁰ For however many are the promises of God, in him is the yea, and in him the Amen, to the glory of God through us. ²¹ Now he who establishes us with you in Christ, and anointed us, is God; ²² he who also sealed us, and gave the earnest of the Spirit in our hearts.

²³ But I invoke God for a witness upon my soul, that to spare you I came not yet to Corinth. ²⁴ Not that we have dominion over your faith, but are helpers of your joy; for in faith ye stand fast.

II. And I determined this with myself, that I would not come again to you in sorrow. ² For if I make you sorry, who then is he that makes me glad, but the same who is made sorry by me? ³ And I wrote this very thing to you, that I might not, when I came, have sorrow from those of whom I ought to have joy; having confidence in you·all, that my joy is the joy of you all. ⁴ For out of much affliction and anguish of heart I wrote to you, with many tears; not that ye might have sorrow, but that ye might know the love which I have more abundantly toward you.

⁵ But if any has caused sorrow, he has not caused sorrow to me, but in part (that I be not too severe on him) to you all. ⁶ Sufficient for such a one is this punishment, which was inflicted by the many. ⁷ So that, on the contrary, ye ought rather to forgive and console him, lest perhaps such a one should be swallowed up with overmuch sorrow. ⁸ Wherefore I beseech you to confirm your love toward him.

⁹ For to this end also I wrote, that I might know the proof of you, whether ye are obedient in all things. ¹⁰ To whom ye forgive anything, I forgive also; for what I have forgiven, if I have forgiven anything, for your sakes I forgave it in the person of Christ, ¹¹ that no advantage might be gained over us by Satan; for we are not ignorant of his devices.

¹² And when I came to Troas to preach the good news of

II. CORINTHIANS.

Christ, and a door was opened to me in the Lord, ¹³I had no rest in my spirit, because I found not Titus my brother; but taking leave of them, I went forth into Macedonia. ¹⁴But thanks be to God, who always causes us to triumph in Christ, and makes manifest by us in every place the savor of the knowledge of him. ¹⁵Because we are to God a sweet savor of Christ, in those who are saved, and in those who perish; ¹⁶to the one a savor of death unto death, to the other a savor of life unto life. And who is sufficient for these things? ¹⁷For we are not as the many, corrupting the word of God; but as of sincerity, but as of God, in the sight of God we speak in Christ.

III. Do we again begin to commend ourselves? Or need we, as some, letters of commendation to you, or of commendation from you? ²Ye are our letter, written in our hearts, known and read by all men; ³being made manifest that ye are a letter of Christ ministered by us, written not with ink, but with the Spirit of the living God; not in tablets of stone, but in fleshly tablets of the heart.

⁴And such confidence have we through Christ, toward God. ⁵Not that we are sufficient of ourselves to think anything as of ourselves; but our sufficiency is of God; ⁶who also made us sufficient as ministers of a new covenant; not of the letter, but of the spirit; for the letter kills, but the spirit makes alive.

⁷But if the ministration of death, engraven with letters in stones, was made glorious, so that the sons of Israel could not look steadfastly on the face of Moses for the glory of his countenance, which glory was to be done away; ⁸how shall not the ministration of the spirit be more glorious? ⁹For if the ministration of condemnation is glory, much more does the ministration of righteousness abound in glory. ¹⁰For even that which was made glorious has no glory in this respect, on account of the glory that excels. ¹¹For if that which is done away was glorious, much more that which abides is glorious.

¹²Having therefore such hope, we use great plainness of speech; ¹³and not as Moses put a vail over his face, that the children of Israel might not steadfastly look on the end of that

CHAPTER IV.

which was to be done away. ¹⁴ But their understandings were hardened; for until this day the same vail on the reading of the old covenant remains, not being taken away; which vail is done away in Christ. ¹⁵ But even unto this day, when Moses is read, a vail lies upon their heart. ¹⁶ But whenever it turns to the Lord, the vail is taken away.

¹⁷ Now the Lord is the Spirit; and where the Spirit of the Lord is, there is liberty. ¹⁸ But we all, with unvailed face beholding in a mirror the glory of the Lord, are transformed into the same image from glory to glory, as, by the Spirit of the Lord.

IV. Therefore, having this ministry, as we received mercy, we faint not. ² But we renounced the hidden things of shame, not walking in craftiness, nor falsifying the word of God; but, by the manifestation of the truth, commending ourselves to every man's conscience in the sight of God. ³ But if our gospel is vailed, it is vailed in those who perish; ⁴ in whom the god of this world blinded the understandings of the unbelieving, that they should not discern the light of the gospel of the glory of Christ, who is the image of God. ⁵ For we preach not ourselves, but Christ Jesus as Lord; and ourselves as your servants for Jesus' sake. ⁶ Because it is God, who commands light to shine out of darkness; who shined in our hearts, to give the light of the knowledge of the glory of God in the face of Christ.

⁷ But we have this treasure in earthen vessels, that the exceeding greatness of the power may be God's, and not of us; ⁸ being pressed in every way, yet not straitened; perplexed, yet not despairing; ⁹ persecuted, yet not forsaken; cast down, yet not destroyed; ¹⁰ always bearing about in the body the dying of Jesus, that also the life of Jesus might be made manifest in our body. ¹¹ For we who live are always delivered to death for Jesus' sake, that the life also of Jesus might be

---

V 14. *Or*, because it is done away in Christ
V. 4. *Or*, that the light of the gospel of the glory of Christ, who is God's image, should not shine.

II. CORINTHIANS.

made manifest in our mortal flesh. ¹² So that death works in us, but life in you.

¹³ But having the same spirit of faith, according to what is written, I believed, therefore did I speak, we also believe, therefore also speak; ¹⁴ knowing that he who raised up the Lord Jesus will raise up us also with Jesus, and will present us with you. ¹⁵ For all things are for your sakes; that the grace, abounding through the greater number, might make the thanksgiving more abundant, to the glory of God.

¹⁶ For which cause we faint not; but though our outward man perishes, yet the inward man is renewed day by day. ¹⁷ For our light affliction, which is but for a moment, works out for us a far more exceeding, an eternal weight of glory; ¹⁸ while we look not at the things which are seen, but at the things which are not seen; for the things which are seen are temporal, but the things which are not seen are eternal.

V. For we know that, if our earthly house of the tabernacle were dissolved, we have a building of God, a house not made with hands, eternal in the heavens. ² For in this we groan, longing to be clothed upon with our house which is from heaven; ³ seeing that we shall be found clothed, not naked. ⁴ For we who are in the tabernacle groan, being burdened; in that we do not desire to be unclothed, but to be clothed upon, that what is mortal might be swallowed up by life.

⁵ Now he who wrought us out for this very thing is God, who also gave to us the earnest of the Spirit. ⁶ Being therefore always confident, and knowing that while at home in the body we are absent from the Lord (⁷ for we walk by faith, not by sight), ⁸ we are confident, and are well pleased rather to be absent from the body, and to be at home with the Lord.

⁹ Wherefore we also strive, that, whether at home or absent, we may be well pleasing to him. ¹⁰ For we must all be made

---

V. 1 Of the tabernacle; *that is, of the body.*
V. 3 *Or,* if indeed we shall be found clothed, not naked.

CHAPTER VI.

manifest before the judgment-seat of Christ; that each one may receive the things done in the body, according to the things which he did, whether good or bad. ¹¹ Knowing therefore the fear of the Lord, we persuade men; but to God we have been made manifest, and I hope that we have been made manifest also in your consciences. ¹² For we are not again commending ourselves to you, but giving you occasion of glorying on our behalf, that ye may have somewhat to answer those who glory in appearance and not in heart. ¹³ For whether we were beside ourselves, it was for God; or whether we are of sound mind, it is for you. ¹⁴ For the love of Christ constrains us; because we thus judged, that if one died for all, then they all died. ¹⁵ And he died for all, that they who live should live no longer to themselves, but to him who for them died and rose again. ¹⁶ So that we henceforth know no one according to the flesh; and if also we have known Christ according to the flesh, yet now we no longer know him. ¹⁷ So that if any one is in Christ, he is a new creature; the old things passed away; behold, all things have become new. ¹⁸ And all things are of God, who reconciled us to himself through Christ, and gave to us the ministry of reconciliation; ¹⁹ as that God was in Christ reconciling a world to himself, not reckoning to them their trespasses, and having committed to us the word of reconciliation.
²⁰ We are then ambassadors on behalf of Christ, as though God were beseeching by us; on behalf of Christ we pray: Be reconciled to God! ²¹ Him who knew not sin he made to be sin for us, that we might become God's righteousness in him.

VI. And, as workers together with him, we also beseech you that ye receive not the grace of God in vain; (² for he says:

In an accepted time I heard thee,
And in the day of salvation I helped thee;
behold, now is the well accepted time, behold, now is the day

---

V 20 *Or*, in Christ's stead

of salvation;) ³ giving no cause of offense in anything, that the ministry be not blamed; ⁴ but as God's ministers, commending ourselves in everything, in much patience, in afflictions, in necessities, in distresses, ⁵ in stripes, in imprisonments, in tumult, in labors, in watchings, in fastings; ⁶ in pureness, in knowledge, in long-suffering, in kindness, in the Holy Spirit, in love unfeigned, ⁷ in the word of truth, in the power of God, by the armor of righteousness on the right hand and on the left, ⁸ through glory and dishonor, through evil report and good report; as deceivers, and true; ⁹ as unknown, and well known; as dying, and, behold, we live; as chastened, and not killed; ¹⁰ as sorrowful, yet always rejoicing; as poor, yet making many rich; as having nothing, and possessing all things.

¹¹ O Corinthians, our mouth is open to you, our heart is enlarged. ¹² Ye are not straitened in us, but ye are straitened in your own bowels. ¹³ Now as a recompense in the same kind (I speak as to my children), be ye also enlarged.

¹⁴ Be not yoked unequally with unbelievers; for what fellowship has righteousness with lawlessness? And what communion has light with darkness? ¹⁵ And what concord has Christ with Belial? Or what part has a believer with an unbeliever? ¹⁶ And what agreement has the temple of God with idols? For ye are a temple of the living God; as God said: I will dwell in them, and walk among them; and I will be their God, and they shall be to me a people.

¹⁷ Wherefore, come out from among them, and be separated, saith the Lord, and touch not anything unclean; and I will receive you, ¹⁸ and will be to you a Father, and ye shall be to me sons and daughters, saith the Lord Almighty.

VII. Having therefore these promises, dearly beloved, let us cleanse ourselves from every pollution of flesh and spirit, perfecting holiness in the fear of God.

² Receive us; we wronged no one, we corrupted no one, we

CHAPTER VII.

defrauded no one. ³ I say it not for condemnation; for I have before said, that ye are in our hearts, to die together and to live together. ⁴ Great is my confidence toward you, great is my glorying on account of you; I am filled with the consolation, I am made to abound with the joy, in all our affliction.

⁵ For indeed, when we were come into Macedonia, our flesh had no rest, but we were afflicted in every way; without were fightings, within were fears. ⁶ But God, who consoles those who are cast down, consoled us by the coming of Titus; ⁷ and not by his coming only, but also by the consolation with which he was consoled in you, when he told us your earnest desire, your mourning, your zeal for me; so that I rejoiced the more. ⁸ Because, though I made you sorry with the letter, I do not regret it, though I did regret it; for I perceive that that letter made you sorry, though but for a season. ⁹ Now I rejoice, not that ye were made sorry, but that ye were made sorry unto repentance; for ye were made sorry after a godly manner, that ye might in nothing receive harm from us. ¹⁰ For godly sorrow works repentance unto salvation, not to be regretted; but the sorrow of the world works out death.

¹¹ For behold this very thing, that ye were made sorry after a godly manner, what earnestness it wrought in you; yea, what clearing of yourselves; yea, what indignation; yea, what fear; yea, what longing desire; yea, what zeal; yea, what avenging! In every thing ye commended yourselves as pure in the matter. ¹² So then, though I wrote to you, it was not on account of him who did the wrong, nor of him who suffered wrong, but that your care for us might be made manifest to you in the sight of God.

¹³ For this cause we were consoled; but in our consolation, we rejoiced abundantly more at the joy of Titus, because his spirit has been refreshed by you all. ¹⁴ For if in any thing I have boasted to him of you, I was not made ashamed; but as we spoke all things to you in truth, so also our boasting before Titus was found to be truth. ¹⁵ And his tender affection is

---

V. 13. *Or,* but besides our consolation

more abundantly toward you, while he remembers the obedience of you all, how with fear and trembling ye received him. ¹⁶ I rejoice, that in every thing I have confidence in you.

VIII.
And we made known to you, brethren, the grace of God which has been bestowed on the churches of Macedonia; ² that in much trial of affliction was the abundance of their joy, and their deep poverty abounded to the riches of their liberality. ³ For according to their power, I bear witness, and beyond their power, they were willing of themselves; ⁴ with much entreaty beseeching of us the grace, and the participation in the ministering to the saints; ⁵ and not as we expected, but themselves they gave first to the Lord, and to us by the will of God. ⁶ So that we exhorted Titus, that as he had before begun, so he would also finish among you this grace also.

⁷ But, as in everything ye abound, in faith, and utterance, and knowledge, and all diligence, and your love to us, see that ye abound in this grace also. ⁸ I say it not by way of command, but through the forwardness of others proving also the sincerity of your love. ⁹ For ye know the grace of our Lord Jesus Christ, that, though he was rich, yet for your sakes he became poor, that ye through his poverty might be rich. ¹⁰ And I give an opinion in this matter; for this is expedient for you, who began before others, not only to do, but also to will, a year ago. ¹¹ And now perform the doing of it also; that as there was the readiness to will, so there may be the performance according to what ye have.

¹² For if there be first the willing mind, it is accepted according to what a man has, not according to what he has not. ¹³ For it is not that others may be eased, and ye burdened; ¹⁴ but, by the rule of equality, at this present time your abundance being a supply for their want, that also their abundance may be a supply for your want, that there may be equality; as it is written: ¹⁵ He that gathered much had nothing over, and he that gathered little did not lack.

CHAPTER IX.

¹⁶ But thanks be to God, who put the same earnest care for you into the heart of Titus. ¹⁷ For he accepted indeed the exhortation; but being very zealous, he went to you of his own accord. ¹⁸ And together with him we sent the brother, whose praise in the gospel is throughout all the churches; ¹⁹ and not that only, but who was also appointed by the churches, as our fellow-traveler with this gift which is administered by us, to further the glory of the Lord, and our zeal: ²⁰ being careful of this, that no one should blame us in this abundance which is administered by us; ²¹ for we provide for what is honorable, not only in the sight of the Lord, but also in the sight of men.

²² And we sent with them our brother, whom we have often in many things proved to be diligent, but now much more diligent, through the great confidence which he has toward you. ²³ As to Titus, he is my partner, and in regard to you a fellow-laborer; as to our brethren, they are messengers of the churches, the glory of Christ. ²⁴ Therefore show toward them, and before the churches, the proof of your love, and of our boasting on your behalf.

IX. For concerning the ministering to the saints, it is superfluous for me to write to you. ² For I know your readiness of mind, of which I boast for you to the Macedonians, that Achaia has been prepared since a year ago; and your zeal stirred up the greater part of them. ³ But I sent the brethren, that our boasting of you might not be made in vain in this respect; that, as I said, ye may be prepared; ⁴ lest haply, if Macedonians come with me, and find you unprepared, we (that we say not, ye) should be put to shame in respect to this confidence.

⁵ I thought it necessary, therefore, to exhort the brethren, that they should go before to you, and make up beforehand your bounty before promised, that this may be ready, in manner as a bounty and not as covetousness. ⁶ But as to this,

---

V. 19. *Or*, in this charity

he that sows sparingly shall also reap sparingly; and he that sows with blessings shall also reap with blessings; ⁷but each as he purposes in his heart, not grudgingly or of necessity, for God loves a cheerful giver.

⁸And God is able to make every grace abound toward you: that ye, always having all sufficiency in everything, may abound toward every good work; (⁹as it is written:

He dispersed abroad, he gave to the poor;

His righteousness abides forever;)

¹⁰and he who supplies seed to the sower and bread for food, will supply and multiply your seed sown, and increase the fruits of your righteousness; ¹¹being enriched in everything to all liberality, which works through us thanksgiving to God. ¹²Because the ministration of this service not only supplies the wants of the saints, but also abounds through many thanksgivings to God; ¹³while by the proof of this ministration they glorify God for the obedience to your profession of the gospel of Christ, and for the liberality of the contribution to them, and to all; ¹⁴they also, with supplication for you, longing after you on account of the exceeding grace of God in you. ¹⁵Thanks be to God for his unspeakable gift!

X. Now I, Paul, myself beseech you by the meekness and gentleness of Christ, who in presence indeed am lowly among you, but being absent am bold toward you; ²but I entreat, that I may not when I am present be bold with that confidence, wherewith I think to be bold against some, who think of us as walking according to the flesh. ³For though walking in the flesh, we do not war after the flesh; (⁴for the weapons of our warfare are not fleshly, but mighty before God to the pulling down of strongholds;) ⁵casting down imaginations, and every high thing that exalts itself against the knowledge of God, and bringing every thought into captivity to the obedience of Christ; ⁶and being in readiness to punish every disobedience, when your obedience is made perfect.

⁷Do ye look on things after the outward appearance? If any man trusts to himself that he is Christ's, let him of himself

CHAPTER XI.

consider this again, that, as he is Christ's, so also are we. ⁸ For even if I should boast somewhat more abundantly of our authority, which the Lord gave us for edification, and not for your destruction, I shall not be put to shame ; ⁹ that I may not seem as if I would terrify you by my letters. ¹⁰ For his letters, says one, are weighty and strong; but his bodily presence is weak, and his speech contemptible. ¹¹ Let such a one consider this, that such as we are in word by letters when absent, such will we be also in deed when present.

¹² For we venture not to reckon ourselves among, or to compare ourselves with, some of those who commend themselves ; but they, measuring themselves among themselves, and comparing themselves with themselves, are not wise. ¹³ But we will not boast of things without measure, but according to the measure of the line which God apportioned to us, a measure to reach even to you. ¹⁴ For we do not stretch ourselves beyond our measure, as though we reached not to you ; for as far as to you also did we come, in the gospel of Christ ; ¹⁵ not boasting of things without measure in other men's labors ; but having hope, when your faith increases, that we shall be enlarged among you according to our line abundantly, ¹⁶ to preach the gospel in the regions beyond you, not to make our boast, in another's line, of things made ready to our hand. ¹⁷ But he that boasts, let him boast in the Lord. ¹⁸ For not he that commends himself is approved, but he whom the Lord commends.

XI. Would that ye could bear with me in a little folly! Nay, ye do bear with me. ² For I am jealous over you with a godly jealousy ; for I espoused you to one husband, that I may present a chaste virgin to Christ. ³ But I fear, lest by any means, as the serpent beguiled Eve by his subtlety, so your minds should be corrupted from your simplicity toward Christ. ⁴ For if indeed he that comes preaches another Jesus, whom we preached not, or if ye receive a different spirit,

---

v. 8. *Or*, for building up, and not for casting you down

which ye received not, or a different gospel, which ye accepted not, ye might well bear with it. ⁵ For I reckon that I am in no respect behind these overmuch apostles. ⁶ And though I be rude in speech, yet not in knowledge; but in everything we have been made manifest among all, in respect to you.

⁷ Did I commit an offense in abasing myself that ye might be exalted, because I preached to you the gospel of God without charge. ⁸ I robbed other churches, taking wages of them, in order to do you service. ⁹ And when I was present with you, and in want, I was a charge to no one; for what was lacking to me the brethren who came from Macedonia supplied; and in every thing I kept myself from being burdensome to you, and so will keep myself.

¹⁰ As the truth of Christ is in me, this boasting shall not be shut up against me in the regions of Achaia. ¹¹ Wherefore? Because I love you not? God knows. ¹² But what I do, and will do, is that I may cut off the occasion of those who desire an occasion, that wherein they boast they may be found even as we. ¹³ For such are false apostles, deceitful workers, transforming themselves into apostles of Christ. ¹⁴ And no wonder; for Satan himself transforms himself into an angel of light. ¹⁵ It is no great thing then, if also his ministers transform themselves as ministers of righteousness; whose end shall be according to their works.

¹⁶ I say again, let no one think me foolish; but if it can not be so, yet receive me even if as foolish, that I too may boast myself a little. ¹⁷ What I speak, I speak not after the Lord, but as in foolishness, in this confidence of boasting. ¹⁸ Seeing that many boast after the flesh, I also will boast. ¹⁹ For ye gladly bear with the foolish, being yourselves wise. ²⁰ For ye bear with it, if one brings you into bondage, if one devours you, if one takes you, if one exalts himself, if one smites you on the face.

²¹ I say it as a reproach, that we were weak. But in whatever any one is bold (I say it in foolishness), I also am bold. ²² Are they Hebrews? So am I. Are they Israelites? So am I. Are they Abraham's seed? So am I. ²³ Are they min-

CHAPTER XII.

isters of Christ? (I speak as beside myself,) I am more; in labors more abundantly, in stripes above measure, in prisons more abundantly, in deaths often; ²⁴ of the Jews five times I received forty stripes save one; ²⁵ thrice I was beaten with rods; once I was stoned; thrice I suffered shipwreck; a night and a day I have spent in the deep; ²⁶ by journeyings often, by perils of rivers, by perils of robbers, by perils from my countrymen, by perils from the heathen, by perils in the city, by perils in the wilderness, by perils in the sea, by perils among false brethren; ²⁷ by weariness and painfulness, in watchings often, in hunger and thirst, in fastings often, in cold and nakedness. ²⁸ Beside those things that are without, there is that which comes upon me daily, the care of all the churches. ²⁹ Who is weak, and I am not weak? Who is offended, and I do not burn? ³⁰ If I must needs boast, I will boast of things which belong to my infirmity. ³¹ God, the Father of our Lord Jesus Christ, who is blessed forevermore, knows that I lie not. ³² In Damascus, the governor under Aretas the king kept guard over the city of the Damascenes, wishing to apprehend me; ³³ and through a window I was let down in a basket through the wall, and escaped his hands.

XII. To boast is surely not expedient for me; for I will come to visions and revelations of the Lord.

² I know a man in Christ, above fourteen years ago (whether in the body I know not, or whether out of the body I know not, God knows) such a one caught up even to the third heaven. ³ And I know such a man (whether in the body or without the body I know not, God knows), ⁴ that he was caught up into paradise, and heard unspeakable words, which it is not lawful for a man to utter.

⁵ Of such a one I will boast; but of myself I will not boast, save in my infirmities. ⁶ For if I should desire to boast, I shall not be foolish, for I shall speak truth; but I forbear, lest any one should reckon of me above what he sees me to be, or hears from me.

⁷ And that I might not be exalted overmuch through the

II. CORINTHIANS.

abundance of the revelations, there was given to me a thorn in the flesh, a messenger of Satan to buffet me, that I might not be exalted overmuch. ⁸ Concerning this I besought the Lord thrice, that it might depart from me. ⁹ And he said to me: My grace is sufficient for thee; for my power is made perfect in weakness. Most gladly therefore will I rather boast in my infirmities, that the power of Christ may abide upon me.

¹⁰ Wherefore I take pleasure in infirmities, in reproaches, in necessities, in persecutions, in distresses for Christ's sake: for when I am weak, then I am powerful.

¹¹ I have become foolish; ye compelled me. For I ought to have been commended by you; for in nothing was I behind these overmuch apostles, though I am nothing. ¹² Truly the signs of an apostle were wrought among you in all patience, by signs, and wonders, and miracles. ¹³ For what is there, wherein ye were inferior to the rest of the churches, except that I myself was not a charge to you? Forgive me this wrong.

¹⁴ Behold, I am ready to come to you the third time; and I will not be a charge to you; for I seek not yours, but you; for the children ought not to lay up for the parents, but the parents for the children. ¹⁵ And I will most gladly spend and be spent for your souls; though the more abundantly I love you, the less I am loved. ¹⁶ But be it so, I was not myself a charge to you; but yet, being crafty, I caught you with guile. ¹⁷ Did I make gain of you, by any of those whom I have sent to you? ¹⁸ I exhorted Titus [to go], and sent with him the brother. Did Titus make gain of you? Did we not walk in the same spirit; did we not in the same steps?

¹⁹ Do ye again suppose that we are excusing ourselves to you? Before God in Christ we speak; and all, beloved, for your edification. ²⁰ For I fear, lest haply, when I come, I shall find you not such as I would, and I too shall be found by you such as ye would not; lest there be wranglings, envyings,

---

V. 16. *The accusation of his opposers, which he answers in verses* 17 *and* 18.
V. 19. *In ancient copies:* Ye are supposing, this long while, that we excuse ourselves to you.

CHAPTER XIII.

wraths, rivalries, backbitings, whisperings, swellings, tumults; [21] lest, when I come again, my God shall humble me among you, and I shall bewail many of those who have sinned before, and repented not of the uncleanness, and fornication, and wantonness, which they committed.

XIII. This third time I am coming to you. In the mouth of two witnesses, and of three, shall every word be established. [2] I have before said, and now say beforehand, as when present the second time, so also now when absent, to those who heretofore have sinned, and to all the rest, that if I come again I will not spare; [3] since ye seek a proof of Christ speaking in me, who toward you is not weak, but is mighty in you. [4] For even if he was crucified through weakness, yet he lives by the power of God. For we also are weak in him, but we shall live with him by the power of God toward you.

[5] Try your own selves, whether ye are in the faith; prove your own selves. Know ye not your own selves, that Jesus Christ is in you, except ye are reprobate? [6] But I trust that ye shall know, that we are not reprobate.

[7] Now I pray to God that ye do no evil; not that we should appear approved, but that ye may do what is good, though we be as reprobate. [8] For we have no power against the truth, but for the truth. [9] For we are glad, when we are weak, and ye are powerful; this also we pray for, even your perfection.

[10] For this cause I write these things being absent, that when present I may not use sharpness, according to the power which the Lord gave me for edification, and not for destruction.

[11] Finally, brethren, farewell. Be perfect, be of good comfort, be of the same mind, be at peace; and the God of love and peace will be with you.

Salute one another with a holy kiss. [13] All the saints salute you.

[14] The grace of the Lord Jesus Christ, and the love of God, and the communion of the Holy Spirit, be with you all.

THE LETTER OF PAUL TO THE GALATIANS.

I. Paul, an apostle, not from men, neither through man, but through Jesus Christ, and God the Father who raised him from the dead, ² and all the brethren who are with me, to the churches of Galatia: ³ Grace to you, and peace, from God the Father, and our Lord Jesus Christ; ⁴ who gave himself for our sins, that he might deliver us out of the present evil world, according to the will of God and our Father; ⁵ to whom be the glory forever and ever. Amen.

⁶ I marvel that ye are so soon removing from him who called you in the grace of Christ, to a different gospel; ⁷ which is not another, except that there are some who trouble you, and wish to pervert the gospel of Christ. ⁸ But even if we, or an angel from heaven, should preach a gospel to you contrary to that which we preached to you, let him be accursed. ⁹ As we have said before, so I now say again, if any one preaches a gospel to you contrary to that which ye received, let him be accursed. ¹⁰ For do I now seek the favor of men or of God? Or am I seeking to please men? If I were still pleasing men, I should not be Christ's servant.

¹¹ Now I make known to you, brethren, that the gospel which was preached by me is not according to man; ¹² for I also did not receive it from man, nor was I taught it, but through the revelation of Jesus Christ. ¹³ For ye heard of my conduct formerly in Judaism; that beyond measure I persecuted the church of God, and was destroying it, ¹⁴ and pressed forward in Judaism beyond many companions of the same age in my nation, being more exceedingly a zealot for the traditions of my fathers.

¹⁵ But when it pleased God, who set me apart from my mother's womb, and called me through his grace, ¹⁶ to reveal his Son in me, that I should make known the glad news of him among the Gentiles; immediately I conferred not with flesh and blood; ¹⁷ neither went up to Jerusalem to those who were

---

V. 17. *In some ancient copies:* neither went away

CHAPTER II.

apostles before me, but went away into Arabia, and returned again to Damascus. ¹⁸ Then, after three years, I went up to Jerusalem to become acquainted with Cephas, and remained with him fifteen days. ¹⁹ But no other of the apostles did I see, save James, the brother of the Lord. ²⁰ Now as to the things which I write to you, behold before God, I lie not.

²¹ Afterward, I came into the regions of Syria and Cilicia; ²² and was unknown by face to the churches of Judæa which were in Christ; ²³ but they were only hearing, that he who was once our persecutor now preaches the faith which once he was destroying; ²⁴ and they glorified God in me.

II. Then, after fourteen years, I went up again to Jerusalem with Barnabas, taking also Titus with me. ² And I went up by revelation, and communicated to them the gospel which I preach among the Gentiles; but privately, to those of reputation, lest by any means I should run, or had run in vain. ³ But not even Titus, who was with me, being a Greek, was compelled to be circumcised; ⁴ and that because of the false brethren stealthily brought in, who crept in to spy out our liberty which we have in Christ Jesus, that they might bring us into bondage; ⁵ to whom not even for an hour did we yield by the [required] submission, that the truth of the gospel might continue with you. ⁶ But from those reputed to be something,—whatever they were, it matters not to me, God accepts not man's person,—for to me those of reputation communicated nothing in addition. ⁷ But, on the contrary, seeing that I have been entrusted with the gospel of the uncircumcision, as Peter was with that of the circumcision; (⁸ for he who wrought for Peter in behalf of the apostleship of the circumcision, wrought also for me in behalf of the Gentiles;) ⁹ and having learned the grace that was given to me, James and Cephas and John, who were reputed to be pillars, gave to me and Barnabas right hands of fellowship, that we should go to the

---

. V. 6. *Or*, whatever they once were

Gentiles, and they to the circumcision; ¹⁰ only, that we should remember the poor, which very thing also I was forward to do.

¹¹ But when Cephas came to Antioch, I withstood him to the face, because he was blamed. ¹² For before certain ones came from James, he ate with the Gentiles; but when they came, he withdrew and separated himself, fearing those who were of the circumcision. ¹³ And the other Jews also dissembled with him, so that Barnabas also was carried away with their dissimulation. ¹⁴ But when I saw that they walk not uprightly according to the truth of the gospel, I said to Peter in the presence of all: If thou, being a Jew, livest after the manner of Gentiles and not that of Jews, how dost thou compel the Gentiles to become as Jews? ¹⁵ We are Jews by nature, and not sinners from among the Gentiles; ¹⁶ but knowing that a man is not justified by works of law, but through faith in Jesus Christ, we also believed on Christ Jesus, that we might be justified by faith in Christ, and not by works of law; because by works of law no flesh shall be justified. ¹⁷ But if, while seeking to be justified in Christ, we ourselves also were found sinners, is then Christ a minister of sin? Far be it! ¹⁸ For if the things which I pulled down these I build up again, I make myself a transgressor. ¹⁹ For I through law died to law, that I might live to God. ²⁰ I have been crucified with Christ; and no longer do I live, but Christ lives in me; and the life which I now live in the flesh I live in the faith of the Son of God, who loved me, and gave himself for me. ²¹ I do not set aside the grace of God; for if there be righteousness through law, then Christ died without cause.

III. O FOOLISH Galatians, who bewitched you, before whose eyes Jesus Christ was evidently set forth, crucified among you? ² This only I desire to learn from you: Was it from works of law that ye received the Spirit, or from the hearing of faith? ³ Are ye so foolish? Having begun with the Spirit, are ye now being made perfect with the flesh? ⁴ Did ye

---

V. 1. *Or*, was formerly set forth   V. 3. *Or*, are ye now ending

CHAPTER III.

suffer so many things in vain? If indeed it be in vain. ⁵Does he, therefore, who supplies to you the Spirit, and works miracles among you, do it from works of law, or from the hearing of faith? ⁶As Abraham believed God, and it was reckoned to him for righteousness. ⁷Know then that they who are of faith, these are sons of Abraham. ⁸And the Scripture, foreseeing that God justifies the Gentiles by faith, announced beforehand the glad tidings to Abraham, saying: In thee shall all the nations be blessed. ⁹So that they who are of faith are blessed with the faithful Abraham.

¹⁰ For as many as are of works of law are under a curse; for it is written: Cursed is every one that continues not in all the things written in the book of the law, to do them. ¹¹And that in the law no one is justified with God, is evident; because, the just shall live by faith. ¹²Now the law is not of faith; but, he that has done them shall live in them. ¹³ Christ redeemed us from the curse of the law, having become a curse for us; because it is written: Cursed is every one that is hanged on a tree; ¹⁴that unto the Gentiles the blessing of Abraham might come in Christ Jesus, that we might receive the promise of the Spirit through faith.

¹⁵ Brethren, I speak after the manner of men. If a covenant has been confirmed, though it be a man's, no one sets it aside, or adds thereto. ¹⁶ Now to Abraham were the promises spoken, and to his seed. He says not, and to seeds, as concerning many; but as concerning one, and to thy seed, which is Christ. ¹⁷ But this I say, that a covenant before confirmed by God, the law, which came four hundred and thirty years after, does not annul, to make the promise of no effect. ¹⁸ For if the inheritance is of law, it is no more of promise; but God has freely given it to Abraham by promise.

¹⁹ What then is the law? It was added because of the transgressions, until the seed should come to whom the promise has

---

V. 5. *Or,* works miracles in you

been made; having been ordained through angels, by the hand of a mediator. ²⁰ Now the mediator is not of one; but God is one. ²¹ Is then the law against the promises of God? Far be it! For if a law had been given which is able to make alive, truly righteousness would have been of law. ²² But the Scripture shut up all under sin, that the promise by faith in Jesus Christ might be given to those who believe. ²³ But before faith came, we were guarded under law, shut up unto the faith which was to be revealed. ²⁴ So that the law has become our schoolmaster, unto Christ, that we might be justified by faith. ²⁵ But faith having come, we are no longer under a schoolmaster. ²⁶ For ye are all sons of God by faith in Christ Jesus. ²⁷ For all ye who were immersed unto Christ, did put on Christ. ²⁸ There is neither Jew nor Greek, there is neither bond nor free, there is no male and female; for ye are all one in Christ Jesus. ²⁹ And if ye are Christ's, then are ye Abraham's seed, heirs according to the promise.

IV. Now I say, as long as the heir is a child, he differs in nothing from a servant though he is lord of all; ² but is under guardians and stewards, until the time appointed by the father. ³ So also we, when we were children, were held in bondage under the elements of the world. ⁴ But when the fullness of the time came, God sent forth his son, born of a woman, born under law, ⁵ that he might redeem those under law, that we might receive the adoption of sons. ⁶ And because ye are sons, God sent forth the Spirit of his Son into our hearts, crying, Abba, Father. ⁷ So that thou art no longer a servant, but a son; and if a son, also an heir through God. ⁸ But at that time indeed, when ye knew not God, ye served those which are not in their nature gods. ⁹ But now, after having known God, or rather having been known by God, how is it that ye turn back again to the weak and poor elements, to which ye desire to be in bondage again anew? ¹⁰ Do ye carefully observe

---

V. 27. *Or*, into Christ V. 3. *Or*, under the rudiments
V. 9. *Or*, weak and poor rudiments

CHAPTER IV.

days, and months, and seasons, and years? ¹¹ I am afraid of you, lest by any means I have bestowed labor upon you in vain. ¹² Become as I am, for I also became as ye are, brethren, I beseech you. Ye injured me in nothing. ¹³ Nay, ye know that by reason of weakness of the flesh I preached the glad tidings to you the former time; ¹⁴ and my trial, which was in my flesh, ye despised not nor spurned, but received me as an angel of God, as Christ Jesus. ¹⁵ Where is then the happiness of which ye spoke? For I bear you witness, that if possible, ye would have plucked out your eyes, and given them to me. ¹⁶ So then, have I become your enemy, because I tell you the truth? ¹⁷ They zealously seek you, not well; but they wish to exclude you, that ye may zealously seek them. ¹⁸ But it is good to be zealously sought in a good cause always, and not only when I am present with you. ¹⁹ My little children, of whom I travail again in birth, until Christ be formed in you! ²⁰ And I could wish to be present with you now, and to change my voice; for I am perplexed on account of you.

²¹ Tell me, ye who desire to be under law, do ye not hear the law? ²² For it is written, that Abraham had two sons, one by the bondwoman, and one by the freewoman. ²³ But the one by the bondwoman was born after the flesh, and the one by the freewoman through the promise. ²⁴ Which things are an allegory. For these women are two covenants, one from mount Sinai, bearing children into bondage, ²⁵ which is Hagar (for the word Hagar is mount Sinai in Arabia), and answers to the Jerusalem that now is, for she is in bondage with her children. ²⁶ But the Jerusalem that is above is free, which is the mother of us all. ²⁷ For it is written:

Rejoice, thou barren that bearest not;
Break forth and cry, thou that travailest not;
Because many are the children of the desolate, rather
    than of her who has the husband.

²⁸ But ye, brethren, after the manner of Isaac, are children of

---

V. 14. *In some copies:* your trial   V. 15. *In some copies:* What was
V. 24. *Or,* are allegorized
V. 26. *In some ancient copies:* which is our mother

promise. ²⁹ But as then, the one born after the flesh persecuted the one born after the spirit, so also is it now. ³⁰ But what says the Scripture? Cast out the bondwoman and her son; for the son of the bondwoman shall not be heir with the son of the freewoman. ³¹ So then, brethren, we are not children of a bondwoman, but of the freewoman.

V. Stand fast, therefore, in the liberty with which Christ made us free, and be not again entangled with the yoke of bondage. ² Behold, I, Paul, say to you, that if ye be circumcised, Christ shall profit you nothing. ³ Now I testify again to every man who becomes circumcised, that he is a debtor to keep the whole law. ⁴ Ye are separated from Christ, whoever of you are justified in the law; ye are fallen away from grace. ⁵ For we through the Spirit wait for the hope of righteousness by faith. ⁶ For in Christ Jesus neither circumcision avails any thing, nor uncircumcision, but faith working by love.

⁷ Ye were running well; who hindered you, that ye should not obey the truth? ⁸ The persuasion is not from him who calls you. ⁹ A little leaven leavens the whole lump. ¹⁰ I have confidence toward you in the Lord, that ye will be no otherwise minded; but he that troubles you shall bear his judgment, whoever he may be. ¹¹ But as for me, brethren, if I still preach circumcision, why am I still persecuted? Then has the offense of the cross ceased. ¹² I would that they were even cut off who unsettle you.

¹³ For ye were called unto liberty, brethren; only use not the liberty for an occasion to the flesh, but by love serve one another. ¹⁴ For all the law is fulfilled in one word, in this: Thou shalt love thy neighbor as thyself. ¹⁵ But if ye bite and devour one another, beware lest ye be consumed by one another.

¹⁶ But I say, walk by the Spirit, and ye will not fulfill the desire of the flesh. ¹⁷ For the flesh has desires against the Spirit, and the Spirit against the flesh; and these are contrary the one to the other, that ye may not do those things that ye

CHAPTER VI.

would. [18] But if ye are led by the Spirit, ye are not under law.

[19] Now the works of the flesh are manifest; which are, fornication, uncleanness, wantonness, [20] idolatry, sorcery, hatreds, strife, emulation, wraths, contentions, divisions, factions, [21] envyings, murders, drunkenness, revelings, and things like these; of which I tell you beforehand, as I also said before, that they who do such things shall not inherit the kingdom of God.

[22] But the fruit of the Spirit is love, joy, peace, long-suffering, kindness, goodness, faith, [23] meekness, temperance; against such things there is no law. [24] And they that are Christ's crucified the flesh with its passions and desires. [25] If we live by the Spirit, let us also walk by the Spirit. [26] Let us not become vainglorious, provoking one another, envying one another.

VI. Brethren, even if a man be overtaken in a fault, ye who are spiritual restore such a one in the spirit of meekness; considering thyself, lest thou also be tempted. [2] Bear one another's burdens, and so fulfill the law of Christ. [3] For if a man thinks himself to be something, when he is nothing, he deceives himself. [4] But let each one prove his own work, and then shall he have ground of glorying in reference to himself alone, and not to another. [5] For each one shall bear his own load.

[6] But let him that is taught in the word share with him that teaches, in all good things. [7] Be not deceived; God is not mocked; for whatever a man sows, that shall he also reap. [8] Because he that sows to his flesh shall of the flesh reap corruption; but he that sows to the Spirit shall of the Spirit reap life everlasting. [9] And let us not be weary in well doing; for in due season we shall reap, if we faint not. [10] So then, as we have opportunity, let us do good to all, especially to those who are of the household of faith.

---

[11] See with what large letters I wrote to you with my own hand.

V. 2. *In many ancient copies:* and so shall ye fulfill

¹² As many as desire to make a fair show in the flesh, these constrain you to be circumcised; only that they may not suffer persecution for the cross of Christ. ¹³ For neither do they themselves who are circumcised keep the law; but they desire that ye should be circumcised, that they may glory in your flesh. ¹⁴ But far be it from me to glory, save in the cross of our Lord Jesus Christ, through whom the world is crucified to me, and I to the world. ¹⁵ For in Christ Jesus neither circumcision avails anything, nor uncircumcision, but a new creation. ¹⁶ And as many as walk by this rule, peace be on them, and mercy, and on the Israel of God.

¹⁷ Henceforth let no one trouble me; for I bear the marks of Jesus in my body.

¹⁸ The grace of our Lord Jesus Christ be with your spirit, brethren. Amen.

THE LETTER OF PAUL TO THE EPHESIANS.

I. Paul, an apostle of Jesus Christ by the will of God, to the saints who are in Ephesus, and believers in Christ Jesus: ² Grace to you, and peace, from God our Father and the Lord Jesus Christ.

³ Blessed be the God and Father of our Lord Jesus Christ, who has blessed us with every spiritual blessing in the heavenly places in Christ; ⁴ as he chose us in him before the foundation of the world, that we should be holy and blameless before him in love; ⁵ having predestined us unto the adoption of sons by Jesus Christ to himself, according to the good pleasure of his will, ⁶ to the praise of the glory of his grace, which he freely bestowed on us in the beloved; ⁷ in whom we have the redemption through his blood, the remission of our trespasses, according to the riches of his grace, ⁸ which he made to abound toward

---

V. 14. *Or*, through which   V. 8. *Or*, with which he abounded

CHAPTER I.

us in all wisdom and understanding; ⁹making known to us the mystery of his will, according to his good pleasure which he purposed in himself, ¹⁰in reference to the dispensation of the fullness of times, to gather for himself into one all things in the Christ, the things which are in the heavens, and the things on the earth; ¹¹in him, in whom we obtained also the inheritance, being predestinated according to the purpose of him who works all things after the counsel of his own will, ¹²that we should be to the praise of his glory who before have hoped in the Christ; ¹³in whom ye also, after having heard the word of truth, the good news of your salvation, in whom [I say] having also believed, ye were sealed with the Holy Spirit of promise; ¹⁴which is an earnest of our inheritance until the redemption of the purchased possession, to the praise of his glory.

¹⁵For this cause I also, having heard of your faith in the Lord Jesus, and love to all the saints, ¹⁶cease not to give thanks for you, making mention of you in my prayers; ¹⁷that the God of our Lord Jesus Christ, the Father of glory, would give to you the spirit of wisdom and of revelation in the full knowledge of him; ¹⁸the eyes of your heart being enlightened; that ye may know what is the hope of his calling, and what the riches of the glory of his inheritance in the saints, ¹⁹and what the exceeding greatness of his power toward us who believe, according to the working of his mighty power, ²⁰which he wrought in Christ when he raised him from the dead and seated him at his own right hand in the heavenly places, ²¹far above all principality, and power, and might, and dominion, and every name that is named, not only in this world, but also in that which is to come; ²²and subjected all things under his feet, and gave him to be head over all things to the church, ²³which is his body, the fullness of him who fills all in all.

V. 11. *Or*, in whom we were also chosen as the inheritance
V. 13. *Or*, in whom are ye also, ... in which having also believed
V. 14. *Or*, for the redemption   V 23. *Or*, fills all with all

II. ¹ You also, being dead in trespasses and sins;—² in which ye once walked according to the course of this world, according to the prince of the power of the air, the spirit that is now working in the sons of disobedience; ³ among whom we also all walked in time past in the desires of our flesh, doing the will of the flesh and of the mind, and were by nature children of wrath, even as others;—⁴ but God, being rich in mercy, on account of his great love wherewith he loved us, made us, ⁵ even when we were dead in sins, alive with Christ, (by grace ye are saved,) ⁶ and raised us with him, and made us sit with him in the heavenly places in Christ Jesus; ⁷ that he might show, in the ages to come, the exceeding richness of his grace, in his kindness toward us in Christ Jesus.

⁸ For by grace ye are saved through faith; and that not of yourselves, it is the gift of God; ⁹ not of works, lest any one should boast. ¹⁰ For we are his workmanship, created in Christ Jesus unto good works, which God before prepared that we should walk in them.

¹¹ Wherefore remember, that in time past ye, the Gentiles in the flesh, who are called Uncircumcision by that which is called Circumcision, in the flesh, made by hand,—¹² that at that time ye were without Christ, being aliens from the commonwealth of Israel, and strangers from the covenants of the promise, having no hope, and without God in the world. ¹³ But now, in Christ Jesus, ye, who in time past were afar off, were made near by the blood of Christ. ¹⁴ For he is our peace, who made both one, and broke down the middle wall of partition; ¹⁵ having abolished in his flesh the enmity, the law of commandments contained in ordinances, that he might make the two one new man in himself, making peace; ¹⁶ and might reconcile both to God in one body by the cross, having slain the enmity thereby. ¹⁷ And he came and brought the good news of peace to you who were afar off, and to those who were near. ¹⁸ Because through him we both have the access in one Spirit to the Father.

¹⁹ So then ye are no longer strangers and sojourners, but ye

CHAPTER III.

are fellow-citizens with the saints, and of the household of God; ²⁰ having been built upon the foundation of the apostles and prophets, Christ Jesus himself being the chief corner-stone; ²¹ in whom all the building, fitly framed together, grows unto a holy temple in the Lord; ²² in whom ye also are builded together for a habitation of God in the Spirit.

III. For this cause I, Paul, the prisoner of Jesus Christ for you Gentiles,—² if indeed ye heard of the dispensation of the grace of God which was given me toward you, ³ that by revelation the mystery was made known to me, as I wrote before in few words; ⁴ whereby, when ye read, ye can perceive my understanding in the mystery of Christ, ⁵ which in other generations was not made known to the sons of men, as it has now been revealed to his holy apostles and prophets in the Spirit; ⁶ that the Gentiles are fellow-heirs, and of the same body, and partakers with us of the promise, in Christ Jesus, through the gospel; ⁷ whereof I was made a minister, according to the gift of the grace of God, which was given to me according to the working of his power. ⁸ To me, who am less than the least of all the saints, was this grace given, to preach among the Gentiles the unsearchable riches of Christ; ⁹ and to make all see what is the dispensation of the mystery, which from ages has been hidden in God, who created all things; ¹⁰ that now, to the principalities and powers in the heavenly places might be made known through the church the manifold wisdom of God, ¹¹ according to the eternal purpose which he made in Christ Jesus our Lord, ¹² in whom we have boldness and access with confidence through faith in him.

¹³ Wherefore I entreat that ye faint not at my afflictions for you, which is your glory. ¹⁴ For this cause I bow my knees to the Father of our Lord Jesus Christ, ¹⁵ from whom the whole family in heaven and on earth is named, ¹⁶ that he would grant to you, according to the riches of his glory, to be strengthened

---
V. 11. *Or*, which he wrought
V. 12. *Or*, our boldness and our access
V. 14. *Ancient copies omit:* of our Lord Jesus Christ

with might through his Spirit as to the inner man, ¹⁷ that Christ may dwell in your hearts by faith; having been rooted and grounded in love, ¹⁸ that ye may be able to comprehend, with all the saints, what is the breadth, and length, and depth, and height, ¹⁹ and to know the love of Christ, which passes knowledge, that ye may be filled unto all the fullness of God.

²⁰ Now to him who is able to do exceeding abundantly above all that we ask or think, according to the power that works in us, ²¹ to him be the glory in the church, in Christ Jesus, throughout all ages, world without end. Amen.

IV. I, THE prisoner in the Lord, exhort you, therefore, to walk worthy of the calling with which ye were called, ² with all lowliness and meekness, with long-suffering, bearing with one another in love; ³ endeavoring to keep the unity of the Spirit in the bond of peace. ⁴ There is one body, and one Spirit, as also ye were called in one hope of your calling; ⁵ one Lord, one faith, one immersion, ⁶ one God and Father of all, who is over all, and through all, and in all. ⁷ But to each one of us the grace was given according to the measure of the gift of Christ. ⁸ Wherefore he says:

> When he ascended on high,
> He led captivity captive,
> And gave gifts to men.

⁹ Now this, h e a s c e n d e d, what is it but that he also descended into the lower parts of the earth? ¹⁰ The one who descended, he is also the one who ascended above all the heavens, that he may fill all things. ¹¹ And he gave some as apostles, some as prophets, some as evangelists, some as pastors and teachers; ¹² for the perfecting of the saints, for the work of the ministry, for the building up of the body of Christ; ¹³ till we all attain to the unity of the faith and of the knowledge of the Son of God, to a perfect man, to the measure of the stature of the fullness of Christ; ¹⁴ that we may no longer be children, tossed to and fro, and carried about with every wind of doctrine, by the sleight of men, by cunning craftiness after the wily manner of error; ¹⁵ but holding the truth, may in

CHAPTER V.

love grow up into him in all things, who is the head, Christ; [16] from whom all the body, fitly framed together and compacted by means of every joint of the supply, according to the working in the measure of each single part, effects the increase of the body to the upbuilding of itself in love.

[17] This therefore I say, and testify in the Lord, that ye no longer walk as the rest of the Gentiles walk, in the vanity of their mind, [18] having the understanding darkened, being alienated from the life of God because of the ignorance that is in them, because of the hardness of their heart; [19] who, as being past feeling, gave themselves up to wantonness, to work all uncleanness in greediness. [20] But ye did not so learn Christ, [21] if indeed ye heard him, and were taught in him, as the truth is in Jesus; [22] that ye put off, as concerns your former deportment, the old man who is corrupted according to the lusts of deceit, [23] and be renewed in the spirit of your mind, [24] and put on the new man, who was created after God in the righteousness and holiness of the truth.

[25] Wherefore, having put away falsehood, speak truth each one with his neighbor; because we are members one of another. [26] Be angry and sin not; let not the sun go down upon your wrath, [27] neither give place to the Devil.

[28] Let him that stole steal no more; but rather let him labor, working with his hands that which is good, that he may have to impart to him that has need. [29] Let no corrupt discourse proceed out of your mouth, but whatever is good for needful edification, that it may impart grace to the hearers. [30] And grieve not the Holy Spirit of God, in whom ye were sealed unto the day of redemption. [31] Let all bitterness, and wrath, and anger, and clamor, and evil speaking, be put away from you, with all malice; [32] and be kind to one another, tender-hearted, forgiving one another, as also God in Christ forgave you.

V. Become therefore followers of God, as beloved children; [2] and walk in love, as also Christ loved us, and gave him-

---

V. 17. *In ancient copies:* as the Gentiles walk
V. 19. *Or,* in covetousness

self up for us, an offering and a sacrifice to God for an odor of sweet smell.

³ But fornication, and all uncleanness, or covetousness, let it not even be named among you, as becomes saints, ⁴ and filthiness, and foolish talking, and jesting, which are not becoming, but rather giving of thanks. ⁵ For this ye know, being aware that no fornicator, nor unclean person, nor covetous man, who is an idolater, has an inheritance in the kingdom of Christ and God. ⁶ Let no one deceive you with vain words; for because of these things comes the wrath of God upon the sons of disobedience.

⁷ Become not therefore partakers with them. ⁸ For ye were once darkness, but now light in the Lord. Walk as children of light,—⁹ for the fruit of the light is in all goodness and righteousness and truth,—¹⁰ proving what is acceptable to the Lord; ¹¹ and have no fellowship with the unfruitful works of darkness, but rather also reprove them. ¹² For it is a shame even to speak of the things done by them in secret. ¹³ But all things, when reproved, are by the light made manifest; for whatever makes manifest is light. ¹⁴ Wherefore he says: Awake, thou that sleepest, and arise from the dead, and Christ will give thee light.

¹⁵ See to it then, how ye walk with exactness, not as unwise, but as wise, ¹⁶ redeeming the time, because the days are evil. ¹⁷ Therefore be not foolish, but understanding what is the will of the Lord.

¹⁸ And be not drunk with wine, wherein is excess, but be filled with the Spirit; ¹⁹ speaking to one another in psalms and hymns and spiritual songs, singing and making melody in your heart to the Lord; ²⁰ giving thanks always for all things, to God and the Father, in the name of our Lord Jesus Christ; ²¹ submitting yourselves to one another in the fear of Christ; ²² wives to their own husbands, as to the Lord. ²³ Because a husband is the head of the wife, as also Christ is the head of the church; himself the Savior of the body. ²⁴ But as the church is subjected to Christ, so also are the wives to their own husbands in everything.

CHAPTER VI.

²⁵ Husbands, love your wives, as also Christ loved the church, and gave himself up for it; ²⁶ that he might sanctify it, having cleansed it by the bathing of water in the word, ²⁷ that he might himself present to himself the church, glorious, having no spot, or wrinkle, or any such thing, but that it may be holy and blameless. ²⁸ So husbands ought to love their wives as their own bodies. He that loves his wife loves himself. ²⁹ For no one ever hated his own flesh; but nourishes and cherishes it, as also Christ the church; ³⁰ because we are members of his body, [being] of his flesh, and of his bones. ³¹ For this cause shall a man leave father and mother, and shall cleave to his wife, and the two shall be one flesh.

³² This mystery is great; but I am speaking of Christ and of the church. ³³ Nevertheless, do ye also, severally, each so love his wife even as himself; and let the wife see that she reverence her husband.

VI. Children, obey your parents, in the Lord; for this is right. ² Honor thy father and mother, which is the first commandment with promise, ³ that it may be well with thee, and thou mayest live long on the earth.

⁴ And fathers, do not provoke your children to anger, but bring them up in the nurture and admonition of the Lord.

⁵ Servants, obey your masters according to the flesh, with fear and trembling, in singleness of your heart, as to Christ; ⁶ not with eye-service, as men-pleasers; but as servants of Christ, doing the will of God from the heart; ⁷ with good will doing service, as to the Lord, and not to men; ⁸ knowing that whatever good thing each may have done, that shall he receive from the Lord, whether bond or free.

⁹ And masters, do the same things to them, forbearing threatening; knowing that both their Master and yours is in heaven, and there is no respect of persons with him.

¹⁰ Finally, be strong in the Lord, and in the power of his might. ¹¹ Put on the whole armor of God, that ye may be able

to stand against the wiles of the Devil. [12] For to us, the contest is not against flesh and blood, but against principalities, against powers, against the rulers of the darkness of this world, against the spiritual powers of evil in the heavenly places. [13] Therefore take on the whole armor of God, that ye may be able to withstand in the evil day, and having fully done all, to stand. [14] Stand therefore, having girded your loins about with truth, and having put on the breastplate of righteousness; [15] and having shod your feet with the preparation of the gospel of peace; [16] in addition to all, having taken on the shield of faith, in which ye will be able to quench all the fiery darts of the wicked one. [17] And receive the helmet of salvation, and the sword of the Spirit, which is the word of God; [18] praying at every fitting season in the Spirit, with all prayer and supplication, and watching thereunto with all perseverance and supplication for all the saints; [19] and for me, that utterance may be given to me, in the opening of my mouth with boldness, to make known the mystery of the gospel, [20] for which I am an ambassador in bonds; that therein I may speak boldly, as I ought to speak.

[21] But that ye also may know my affairs, how I do, Tychicus, the beloved brother and a faithful minister in the Lord, will make all known to you; [22] whom I sent to you for this very thing, that ye might know our affairs, and that he might encourage your hearts.

[23] Peace be to the brethren, and love with faith, from God the Father, and the Lord Jesus Christ.

[24] Grace be with all who love our Lord Jesus Christ in sincerity.

V. 12. The heavenly places *(the material heavens, the air; see ch. ii., 2).*

THE LETTER OF PAUL TO THE PHILIPPIANS.

I. Paul and Timothy, servants of Jesus Christ, to all the saints in Christ Jesus who are at Philippi, with the overseers and deacons: ² Grace to you, and peace, from God our Father and the Lord Jesus Christ.

³ I thank my God on every remembrance of you,—⁴ always, in every supplication of mine, making the supplication for you all with joy,—⁵ for your fellowship in respect to the gospel from the first day until now; ⁶ being confident of this very thing, that he who began a good work in you will complete it until the day of Jesus Christ. ⁷ As it is just for me to think this of you all, because I have you in my heart; being all of you, both in my bonds, and in the defense and confirmation of the gospel, partakers of the grace with me. ⁸ For God is my witness, how greatly I long for you all, with the tender affection of Jesus Christ.

⁹ And this I pray, that your love may abound yet more and more, in knowledge and all discernment; ¹⁰ in order that ye may approve the things that are most excellent, that ye may be pure and without offense unto the day of Christ; ¹¹ being filled with the fruit of righteousness, which is by Jesus Christ, to the glory and praise of God.

¹² But I desire that ye should know, brethren, that the things which befell me have resulted rather in the furtherance of the gospel; ¹³ so that my bonds have become manifest in Christ in all the Prætorium, and to all the rest; ¹⁴ and that the greater part of the brethren, made confident in the Lord by my bonds, are much more bold to speak the word without fear.

¹⁵ Some indeed preach Christ also from envy and strife, but some also from good will; ¹⁶ the one, out of love, knowing that

---

V. 1. Overseers: *as the word is properly translated in Acts* xx., 28.
V. 5. *Or,* for your participation in the gospel. *Or,* for your contribution to the gospel
V. 7. *Or,* because you have me in your heart
V. 10. *Or,* may prove things that differ

I am set for the defense of the gospel; ¹⁷ the other, out of contentiousness, proclaim Christ not with pure intent, supposing that they shall add affliction to my bonds. ¹⁸ What then? Notwithstanding, in every way, whether in pretense or in truth, Christ is proclaimed; and therein I rejoice, yea, and shall rejoice. ¹⁹ For I know that this will turn out for my salvation, through your supplication, and the supply of the Spirit of Jesus Christ; ²⁰ according to my earnest expectation and hope, that I shall in nothing be put to shame, but that with all boldness, as always, so also now Christ shall be magnified in my body, whether by life, or by death.

²¹ For to me to live is Christ, and to die is gain. ²² But if it be to live in the flesh, this to me is fruit of labor; and which I shall choose I know not; ²³ but am constrained by the two, having the desire to depart, and to be with Christ, for it is far better; ²⁴ but to remain in the flesh is more needful for your sakes. ²⁵ And being persuaded of this, I know that I shall remain, and shall continue with you all for your furtherance and joy in the faith; ²⁶ that your glorying may be more abundant in Jesus Christ for me, through my coming to you again.

²⁷ Only let your deportment be as becomes the gospel of Christ; that whether I come and see you, or remain absent, I may hear of your affairs, that ye stand fast in one spirit, with one mind striving together for the faith of the gospel; ²⁸ and in nothing terrified by the adversaries; which is to them an evident token of perdition, but to you of salvation, and that from God. ²⁹ Because to you it was granted in behalf of Christ,—not only to believe on him,—but in his behalf to suffer also; ³⁰ having the same conflict as ye saw in me, and now hear of in me.

II. If then there is any consolation in Christ, if any comfort from love, if any communion of the Spirit, if any tender affection and compassion, ² make my joy complete, that ye be

---

V. 17. *In ancient copies:* shall raise up affliction
V. 28. *In many ancient copies:* but of your salvation
V. 1. *Or,* there is any exhortation

CHAPTER II.

of the same mind, having the same love, being of one accord, of the one mind; ³ doing nothing through contentiousness or vainglory, but in lowliness of mind each esteeming others better than himself; ⁴ regarding not each one his own, but each one also the things of others. ⁵ Let this mind be in you, which was also in Christ Jesus; ⁶ who, being in the form of God, did not account it robbery to be equal with God; ⁷ but emptied himself, taking the form of a servant, being made in the likeness of men. ⁸ And being found in fashion as a man, he humbled himself, becoming obedient unto death, even the death of the cross. ⁹ Wherefore also God highly exalted him, and gave him a name which is above every name; ¹⁰ that at the name of Jesus every knee should bow, of beings in heaven, and of beings on earth, and of beings under the earth, ¹¹ and every tongue confess that Jesus Christ is Lord, to the glory of God the Father.

¹² Wherefore, my beloved, as ye always obeyed, not as in my presence only, but now much more in my absence, work out your own salvation with fear and trembling; ¹³ for it is God who works in you both to will and to perform, of his good pleasure.

¹⁴ Do all without murmurings and disputings; ¹⁵ that ye may become blameless and simple, children of God, unreproachable, in the midst of a crooked and perverse generation, among whom ye appear as do the heavenly lights in the world; ¹⁶ holding forth the word of life; for a ground of glorying to me at the day of Christ, that I did not run in vain, or labor in vain.

¹⁷ But even if I am poured out on the sacrifice and ministration of your faith, I rejoice, and I rejoice with you all. ¹⁸ For the same cause, do ye also rejoice, and rejoice with me.

¹⁹ But I hope in the Lord Jesus to send Timothy shortly to you, that I also may be cheered, when I know your state. ²⁰ For I have no one like-minded, who will sincerely care for your state. ²¹ For all seek their own, not the things of Jesus

---

V. 16. *Or*, holding fast . V. 18. *Or*, In like manner

Christ. ²²But ye know the proof of him, that, as a child with a father, he served with me for the gospel. ²³Him therefore I hope to send without delay, so soon as I shall see how it will go with me; ²⁴but I trust in the Lord that I also myself shall come shortly. ²⁵Yet I supposed it necessary to send to you Epaphroditus, my brother, and companion in labor, and fellow-soldier, but your messenger and minister to my wants. ²⁶For he was longing after you all, and was much distressed, because ye heard that he was sick. ²⁷For indeed he was sick near to death; but God had mercy on him, and not on him only, but on me also, that I might not have sorrow upon sorrow. ²⁸I sent him therefore with the more haste, that seeing him again ye might rejoice, and that I may be less sorrowful. ²⁹Receive him therefore in the Lord with all gladness, and hold such in honor; ³⁰because for the work of Christ he came near to death, hazarding his life, that he might supply what things were lacking on your part, of the ministration to me.

III. Finally, my brethren, rejoice in the Lord. To write the same things to you, to me is not burdensome, and for you it is safe.

²Beware of the dogs, beware of the evil workers, beware of the concision. ³For we are the circumcision, who worship by the Spirit of God, and glory in Christ Jesus, and have no confidence in the flesh. ⁴Though I have confidence also in the flesh. If any other thinks that he has confidence in the flesh, I more; ⁵circumcised the eighth day, of the stock of Israel, of the tribe of Benjamin, a Hebrew of Hebrews; as to the law, a Pharisee; ⁶as to zeal, persecuting the church; as to the righteousness which is in the law, blameless.

⁷But what things were gain to me, these I have accounted loss for Christ. ⁸Nay more, and I account all things to be loss for the excellency of the knowledge of Christ Jesus my Lord; for whom I suffered the loss of all things, and account them refuse, that I may gain Christ, ⁹and be found in him, not having my own righteousness, which is of law, but that which is through faith in Christ, the righteousness which is of God,

CHAPTER IV.

upon faith; [10] that I may know him, and the power of his resurrection, and the fellowship of his sufferings, being conformed to his death; [11] if by any means I may attain to the resurrection from the dead.

[12] Not that I already·obtained [the prize], or have already been perfected; but I pursue onward, if I may lay hold of that for which I was laid hold of by Christ Jesus. [13] Brethren, I do not count myself to have laid hold of it; but one thing I do, forgetting the things behind, and reaching forth to the things before, [14] I pursue on toward the mark, for the prize of the heavenly calling of God in Christ Jesus.

[15] Let us therefore, as many as are perfect, be of this mind; and if in any thing ye are otherwise minded, this also God will reveal to you. [16] Nevertheless, whereto we have attained, in the same let us walk.

[17] Brethren, be followers together of me, and mark those who so walk, as ye have us for an example. [18] For many walk, of whom I told you often, and now tell you even weeping, that they are the enemies of the cross of Christ; [19] whose end is destruction, whose God is their belly, and whose glory is in their shame, who mind earthly things. [20] For our citizenship is in heaven; from whence we also look for a Savior, the Lord Jesus Christ; [21] who will transform the body of our humiliation, that it may be conformed to the body of his glory, according to the working with which he is able also to subject all things to himself.

[1] Therefore, my brethren beloved and longed for, my joy and crown, so stand fast in the Lord, beloved.

[2] I beseech Euodia, and I beseech Syntyche, to be of the same mind in the Lord. [3] Yea, I entreat thee also, true yokefellow, help these women, who labored with me in the gospel, with Clement also, and the rest of my fellow-laborers, whose names are in the book of life.

V. 10. *Or*, participation of his sufferings
V. 12. *Or*, have already finished [the course]
V. 20. *Or*, our country

PHILIPPIANS.

⁴ Rejoice in the Lord always; again I will say, rejoice. ⁵ Let your forbearance be known to all men. The Lord is at hand. ⁶ Be anxious for nothing; but in every thing, by prayer and supplication with thanksgiving, let your requests be made known to God. ⁷ And the peace of God, which passes all understanding, will keep your hearts and your minds in Christ Jesus.

⁸ Finally, brethren, whatever things are true, whatever things are honorable, whatever things are just, whatever things are pure, whatever things are lovely, whatever things are of good report, if there be any virtue, and if there be any praise, think on these things. ⁹ The things also, which ye learned, and received, and heard, and saw in me, these do; and the God of peace will be with you.

¹⁰ But I rejoiced in the Lord greatly, that now at length ye revived again in your care for my welfare; for which ye were also careful, but lacked opportunity. ¹¹ Not that I speak in respect of want; for I learned, in whatever state I am, to be content. ¹² I both know how to be abased, and I know how to abound; in every thing, and in all things, I am instructed, both to be full and to be hungry, both to abound and to be in want. ¹³ I can do all things, in him who strengthens me.

¹⁴ Notwithstanding, ye did well to share with me in my affliction. ¹⁵ And ye also know, Philippians, that in the beginning of the gospel, when I went forth from Macedonia, no church communicated with me in an account of giving and receiving, but ye only; ¹⁶ that also in Thessalonica, ye sent once and again to my necessity. ¹⁷ Not that I seek for the gift; but I seek for the fruit that abounds to your account.

¹⁸ But I have all, and abound; I am full, having received of Epaphroditus the things sent from you, an odor of sweet smell, a sacrifice acceptable, well pleasing to God. ¹⁹ But my God will supply all your need, according to his riches in glory, in Christ Jesus.

²⁰ Now to God and our Father be the glory forever and ever. Amen.

V 15. *Or,* in an account of debt and credit

CHAPTER I.

²¹ Salute every saint in Christ Jesus. The brethren who are with me salute you.
²² All the saints salute you, but especially they that are of Cæsar's household.
²³ The grace of the Lord Jesus Christ be with your spirits.

THE LETTER OF PAUL TO THE COLOSSIANS.

I. Paul, an apostle of Christ Jesus by the will of God, and Timothy the brother, ² to the saints in Colosse, and faithful brethren in Christ: Grace to you, and peace, from God our Father and the Lord Jesus Christ.
³ We give thanks to God the Father of our Lord Jesus Christ, praying always for you, ⁴ having heard of your faith in Christ Jesus, and of the love which ye have toward all the saints, ⁵ because of the hope which is laid up for you in heaven, of which ye heard before in the word of the truth of the gospel; ⁶ which is come to you, as also in all the world, and is bringing forth fruit and increasing also in you, since the day ye heard it, and knew the grace of God in truth; ⁷ as ye learned from Epaphras our beloved fellow-servant, who is for you a faithful minister of Christ, ⁸ who also made known to us your love in the Spirit.
⁹ For this cause we also, since the day we heard it, do not cease to pray for you, and to ask that ye may be filled with the knowledge of his will, in all wisdom and spiritual understanding; ¹⁰ that ye may walk worthy of the Lord unto all pleasing, bringing forth fruit in every good work, and increasing in the knowledge of God; ¹¹ being strengthened with all strength, according to his glorious power, unto all patience and long-suffering with joy; ¹² giving thanks to the Father, who made us meet for the portion of the inheritance of the saints in light; ¹³ who delivered us out of the power of darkness, and translated us into the kingdom of the Son of his love; ¹⁴ in whom we have the redemption, the remission of our sins; ¹⁵ who is the image

of the invisible God, the first-born of every creature; ¹⁶because in him were all things created, the things in the heavens, and the things on the earth, the visible and the invisible, whether thrones, or dominions, or principalities, or powers; all things have been created by him, and for him; ¹⁷and he is before all things, and in him all things subsist. ¹⁸And he is the head of the body, the church; who is the beginning, the first-born from the dead; that he may become in all things pre-eminent. ¹⁹For He was pleased, that in him should all the fullness dwell; ²⁰and through him to reconcile all things to himself, having made peace through the blood of his cross; through him, whether the things on the earth, or the things in the heavens.

²¹And you also, being in time past alienated, and enemies in your mind in wicked works, yet now has he reconciled ²²in the body of his flesh through death, to present you holy and blameless and unaccused before him; ²³if indeed ye continue in the faith grounded and settled, and not moved away from the hope of the gospel, which ye heard, which was preached in the whole creation which is under heaven; of which I Paul was made a minister.

²⁴Now I rejoice in my sufferings for you, and fill up that which is behind of the afflictions of Christ in my flesh for his body, which is the church; ²⁵of which I was made a minister, according to the dispensation of God which was given to me for you, to fulfill the word of God, ²⁶the mystery which has been hidden from ages and from generations, but now has been manifested to his saints; ²⁷to whom God willed to make known what is the riches of the glory of this mystery among the Gentiles, which is Christ in you, the hope of glory; ²⁸whom we announce, warning every man, and teaching every man in all wisdom, that we may present every man perfect in Christ; ²⁹to which end I also labor, striving according to his working, which works in me with power.

II. For I would have you know how great a conflict I have for you, and for those in Laodicea, and for as many as have not seen my face in the flesh; ²that their hearts might be

CHAPTER II.

encouraged, they being knit together in love, and unto all the riches of the full assurance of the understanding, unto the full knowledge of the mystery of God, even Christ; ³in whom are all the treasures of wisdom and knowledge hidden.

⁴And this I say, that no one may beguile you with enticing words. ⁵For though I am absent in the flesh, yet in the spirit I am with you, rejoicing and beholding your order, and the steadfastness of your faith toward Christ.

⁶As therefore ye received Christ Jesus the Lord, so walk in him; ⁷having been rooted and being built up in him, and being established in the faith as ye were taught, abounding therein with thanksgiving.

⁸Beware lest there shall be any one that despoils you through philosophy and vain deceit, after the tradition of men, after the rudiments of the world, and not after Christ. ⁹Because in him dwells all the fullness of the Godhead bodily. ¹⁰And ye are made complete in him, who is the head of all principality and power; ¹¹in whom ye were also circumcised with a circumcision not made with hands, in the putting off of the body of the flesh, in the circumcision of Christ; ¹²being buried with him in the immersion, wherein ye were also raised with him through faith in the working of God, who raised him from the dead. ¹³And you also, being dead in your trespasses and the uncircumcision of your flesh, he made alive together with him, graciously forgiving us all our trespasses; ¹⁴blotting out the handwriting in ordinances that was against us, which was opposed to us, and he has taken it out of the way, nailing it to the cross; ¹⁵despoiling principalities and powers, he made a show of them openly, triumphing over them in it.

¹⁶Let not any one therefore judge you in food, or in drink, or in respect of a feast-day, or of a new-moon, or of a sabbath; ¹⁷which are a shadow of the things to come, but the body is of Christ. ¹⁸Let no one defraud you of the prize, seeking it in humiliation and worship of the angels, intruding into things

---

V. 10. *Or,* are in him made full
V. 15. *Or,* putting off principalities and powers   V. 15. *Or,* in him
V. 18   *Or,* willing it *(namely, to defraud).*

which he has not seen, vainly puffed up by his fleshly mind, ¹⁹ and not holding fast the head, from whom all the body, by means of the joints and bands having nourishment ministered, and being knit together, increases with the increase of God.

²⁰ If ye died with Christ from the rudiments of the world, why, as though living in the world, are ye subject to ordinances, ²¹ "Handle not, nor taste, nor touch," ²² (which are all to perish with the using,) after the commandments and teachings of men? ²³ Which things have indeed a show of wisdom in self-chosen worship, and humiliation, and neglecting of the body, not in any honor, for the satisfying of the flesh.

III. If then ye were raised together with Christ, seek the things above, where Christ is, sitting on the right hand of God. ² Set your mind on the things above, not on the things upon the earth. ³ For ye died, and your life is hid with Christ in God. ⁴ When Christ, our life, shall be manifested, then will ye also with him be manifested in glory.

⁵ Mortify therefore your members which are upon the earth: fornication, uncleanness, passion, evil desire, and covetousness, which is idolatry; ⁶ on account of which things the wrath of God comes on the sons of disobedience; ⁷ in which ye also once walked, when ye lived in these things. ⁸ But now, do ye also put all away, anger, wrath, malice, reviling, filthy communication out of your mouth. ⁹ Lie not one to another, seeing that ye have put off the old man with his deeds, ¹⁰ and have put on the new man, who is being renewed unto knowledge after the image of him who created him; ¹¹ where there is no Greek and Jew, circumcision and uncircumcision, Barbarian, Scythian, bondman, freeman; but Christ is all, and in all.

¹² Put on therefore, as God's chosen, holy and beloved, bowels of compassion, kindness, lowliness of mind, meekness, long-suffering, ¹³ forbearing one another, and freely forgiving each other, if any one have a complaint against any, even as Christ freely forgave you, so also do ye; ¹⁴ and over all these, love, which is the bond of perfectness. ¹⁵ And let the peace of Christ rule in your hearts, to which ye were also called in one body; and be thankful.

CHAPTER IV.

¹⁶ Let the word of Christ dwell in you richly; in all wisdom teaching and admonishing one another, with psalms, hymns, spiritual songs, in grace singing in your hearts to God. ¹⁷ And whatever ye do, in word or deed, do all in the name of the Lord Jesus, giving thanks to God the Father through him.

¹⁸ Wives, submit yourselves to your own husbands, as is fitting in the Lord.

¹⁹ Husbands, love your wives, and be not bitter toward them.

²⁰ Children, obey your parents in all things; for this is well pleasing, in the Lord.

²¹ Fathers, provoke not your children, that they be not discouraged.

²² Servants, obey in all things your masters according to the flesh; not with eye-service, as men-pleasers, but in singleness of heart, fearing the Lord. ²³ Whatever ye do, do it heartily, as to the Lord, and not to men; ²⁴ knowing that from the Lord ye will receive the recompense of the inheritance. Serve the Lord Christ. ²⁵ For he that does wrong will receive that which he did wrongfully; and there is no respect of persons.

¹ Masters, render to your servants that which is just and equal; knowing that ye also have a Master in heaven.

² Persevere in prayer, being watchful therein with thanksgiving; ³ at the same time praying also for us, that God would open to us a door for the word, to speak the mystery of Christ, for the sake of which I am also in bonds, ⁴ that I may make it manifest, as I ought to speak.

⁵ Walk in wisdom toward those without, redeeming the time. ⁶ Let your speech be always with grace, seasoned with salt, that ye may know how ye ought to answer every man.

⁷ **All my affairs will Tychicus** make known to you, the beloved brother, and a faithful minister and fellow-servant in the Lord; ⁸ whom I sent to you for this very purpose, that he may know your condition, and may comfort your hearts; ⁹ together with Onesimus, the faithful and beloved brother, who is one of you. They will make known to you all the things here.

¹⁰ Aristarchus my fellow-prisoner salutes you, and **Mark** the

cousin of Barnabas, concerning whom ye received commands (if he come to you, receive him), ¹¹ and Jesus, who is called Justus, who are of the circumcision. These only are my fellow-workers, for the kingdom of God, who have been a comfort to me.

¹² Epaphras, who is one of you, a servant of Christ Jesus, salutes you, always striving for you in his prayers, that ye may stand perfect and fully assured in all the will of God. ¹³ For I bear him witness, that he has much concern for you, and those in Laodicea, and those in Hierapolis.

¹⁴ Luke, the beloved physician, and Demas, salute you.

¹⁵ Salute the brethren in Laodicea, and Nymphas, and the church in his house. ¹⁶ And when the letter has been read among you, cause that it be read also in the church of the Laodiceans, and that ye also read that from Laodicea. ¹⁷ And say to Archippus: Take heed to the ministry which thou didst receive in the Lord, that thou fulfill it.

¹⁸ The salutation by the hand of me, Paul. Remember my bonds. Grace be with you.

THE FIRST LETTER OF PAUL TO THE THESSALONIANS.

I. Paul, and Silvanus, and Timothy, to the church of the Thessalonians in God the Father and the Lord Jesus Christ: Grace to you, and peace.

² We give thanks to God always for you all, making mention of you in our prayers; ³ remembering without ceasing your work of faith, and labor of love, and patience of the hope of our Lord Jesus Christ, before God and our Father; ⁴ knowing, brethren beloved of God, your election; ⁵ because our gospel came not to you in word only, but also in power, and in the Holy Spirit, and in much assurance; as ye know what manner

---

V. 13. *Or,* much labor

CHAPTER II.

of men were we among you, for your sake. ⁶ And ye became followers of us, and of the Lord, having received the word in much affliction, with joy of the Holy Spirit; ⁷ so that ye became an example to all that believe in Macedonia and Achaia. ⁸ For from you has sounded forth the word of the Lord, not only in Macedonia and Achaia, but also in every place your faith toward God has gone forth; so that we have no need to speak anything. ⁹ For they themselves report concerning us, what manner of entrance we had to you, and how ye turned to God from idols, to serve the living and true God, ¹⁰ and to wait for his Son from heaven, whom he raised from the dead, Jesus, who delivers us from the wrath to come.

II. For yourselves, brethren, know our entrance to you, that it has not become vain. ² But having before suffered, and been shamefully treated, as ye know, at Philippi, we were bold in our God to speak to you the gospel of God in much conflict. ³ For our exhortation is not of error, nor of uncleanness, nor in guile; ⁴ but as we have been approved by God to be entrusted with the gospel, so we speak; not as pleasing men, but God, who proves our hearts. ⁵ For neither at any time used we flattering words, as ye know, nor a cloak of covetousness; God is witness; ⁶ nor of men sought we glory, neither from you, nor from others, though able to use authority, as Christ's apostles. ⁷ But we were gentle among you, as a nurse cherishes her children; ⁸ so, being affectionately desirous of you, we were willing to impart to you, not only the gospel of God, but also our own souls, because ye were dear to us. ⁹ For ye remember, brethren, our labor and toil; night and day working, in order not to burden any of you, we preached to you the gospel of God.

¹⁰ Ye are witnesses, and God, how holily and justly and unblamably we behaved ourselves to you that believe; ¹¹ as ye know how we exhorted, and encouraged, and charged every one of you, as a father his children, ¹² that ye should walk worthy of God, who is calling you into his kingdom and glory.

¹³ For this cause we also thank God without ceasing, that

when ye received the word of God heard from us, ye received not the word of men, but, as it is in truth, the word of God, which also works in you that believe. [14] For ye, brethren, became followers of the churches of God which are in Judæa in Christ Jesus; for ye also suffered the same things of your own countrymen, as they have of the Jews; [15] who both killed the Lord Jesus and the prophets, and drove us forth, and please not God, and are contrary to all men; [16] hindering us from speaking to the Gentiles that they might be saved, to fill up their sins always; and the wrath came upon them to the utmost.

[17] But we, brethren, having been severed from you for a short time, in presence, not in heart, endeavored the more abundantly to see your face, with great desire. [18] Wherefore we would fain have come to you, even I, Paul, once and again; and Satan hindered us. [19] For what is our hope, or joy, or crown of glorying? Are not also ye, in the presence of our Lord Jesus Christ at his coming? [20] For ye are our glory and joy.

III. Wherefore, when we could no longer forbear, we thought it good to be left behind at Athens alone; [2] and sent Timothy, our brother, and a fellow-worker with God in the gospel of Christ, to establish you, and to exhort you concerning your faith; [3] that no one should be shaken by these afflictions, for yourselves know that unto this we are appointed. [4] For even when we were with you, we told you before that we are to suffer affliction; as also it came to pass, and ye know. [5] For this cause, when I too could no longer forbear, I sent to know your faith, lest by some means the tempter tempted you, and our labor should be in vain.

[6] But now, when Timothy came to us from you, and brought us good tidings of your faith and love, and that ye have good remembrance of us always, desiring greatly to see us, as we also to see you; [7] for this cause we were consoled, brethren, over you in all our affliction and distress, through your faith; [8] because now we live, if ye stand fast in the Lord. [9] For what

CHAPTER IV.

thanks can we render to God for you, for all the joy wherewith we rejoice for your sakes before our God; ¹⁰ night and day praying exceedingly that we may see your face, and may perfect that which is lacking in your faith? ¹¹ Now God and our Father himself, and our Lord Jesus Christ, direct our way to you. ¹² And the Lord make you increase and abound in love toward one another, and toward all, as we also do toward you; ¹³ to the end he may establish your hearts unblamable in holiness before God and our Father, at the coming of our Lord Jesus Christ with all his saints.

IV. Furthermore then, brethren, we beseech you, and exhort you in the Lord Jesus, that as ye received from us how ye ought to walk and to please God, as also ye are walking, ye would abound yet more. ² For ye know what commands we gave you, through the Lord Jesus. ³ For this is the will of God, your sanctification, that ye abstain from fornication; ⁴ that each one of you know how to possess his vessel in sanctification and honor; ⁵ not in lustful passion, as also the Gentiles who know not God. ⁶ That no one go beyond and defraud his brother in any matter; because the Lord is the avenger for all these things, as we also told you before, and testified. ⁷ For God did not call us to uncleanness, but in sanctification. ⁸ Therefore he that rejects, rejects not man, but God, who also gave to you his Holy Spirit.

⁹ But concerning brotherly love ye need not that I write to you; for ye yourselves are taught of God to love one another. ¹⁰ For indeed ye do it, toward all the brethren who are in all Macedonia. But we beseech you, brethren, to abound yet more; ¹¹ and to study to be quiet, and to do your own business, and to work with your own hands, as we commanded you; ¹² that ye may walk becomingly toward those without, and may have need of nothing.

¹³ But we desire that you should not be ignorant, brethren, concerning those who are sleeping, that ye sorrow not, as

---

V. 4. *Or*, know how to obtain   V. 6. *Or*, in the matter

others who have no hope. ¹⁴ For if we believe that Jesus died and rose again, so also those who fell asleep through Jesus will God bring with him.

¹⁵ For this we say to you, in the word of the Lord, that we the living, who remain unto the coming of the Lord, shall not precede those who fell asleep. ¹⁶ Because the Lord himself will descend from heaven with a shout, with the voice of the archangel, and with the trump of God; and the dead in Christ will first rise. ¹⁷ Then we the living, who remain, will be caught up together with them in clouds, to meet the Lord in the air; and so shall we ever be with the Lord.

¹⁸ Wherefore, encourage one another with these words.

V. But of the times and the seasons, brethren, ye have no need that I write to you. ² For yourselves know perfectly that the day of the Lord so comes as a thief in the night. ³ For when they shall say, Peace and safety, then sudden destruction comes upon them, as travail upon a woman with child; and they shall not escape.

⁴ But ye, brethren, are not in darkness, that the day should overtake you as a thief. ⁵ For all ye are sons of light, and sons of day; we are not of night, nor of darkness. ⁶ So then let us not sleep, as others; but let us watch and be sober. ⁷ For they that sleep, sleep in the night; and they that are drunken, are drunken in the night. ⁸ But let us, being of the day, be sober, putting on the breastplate of faith and love, and for a helmet, the hope of salvation; ⁹ because God did not appoint us to wrath, but to obtain salvation through our Lord Jesus Christ; ¹⁰ who died for us, that, whether we wake or sleep, we should live together with him. ¹¹ Wherefore encourage each other, and edify one the other, as also ye do.

¹² And we beseech you, brethren, to know those who labor among you, and preside over you in the Lord, and admonish you; ¹³ and to esteem them very highly in love for their work's sake. Be at peace among yourselves.

¹⁴ Now we exhort you, brethren, admonish the unruly, comfort the feeble-minded, support the weak, be long-suffering

CHAPTER I.

toward all. ¹⁵ See that none render evil for evil to any one; but ever follow that which is good, both toward one another, and toward all.

¹⁶ Rejoice always. ¹⁷ Pray without ceasing. ¹⁸ In everything give thanks; for this is the will of God in Christ Jesus, toward you.

¹⁹ Quench not the Spirit. ²⁰ Despise not prophesyings; ²¹ but prove all things, hold fast that which is good. ²² Abstain from every form of evil. ²³ And the God of peace himself sanctify you wholly; and may your spirit and soul and body be preserved whole without blame at the coming of our Lord Jesus Christ. ²⁴ Faithful is he who calls you, who also will do it.

²⁵ Brethren, pray for us.

²⁶ Salute all the brethren with a holy kiss.

²⁷ I adjure you by the Lord, that this letter be read to all the holy brethren.

²⁸ The grace of our Lord Jesus' Christ be with you.

THE SECOND LETTER OF PAUL TO THE THESSALONIANS.

I. Paul, and Silvanus, and Timothy, to the church of the Thessalonians, in God our Father, and the Lord Jesus Christ: ² Grace to you, and peace, from God the Father and the Lord Jesus Christ.

³ We are bound to thank God always for you, brethren, as it is meet, because your faith grows exceedingly, and the love of each one of you all toward one another abounds; ⁴ so that we ourselves glory in you in the churches of God, for your patience and faith in all your persecutions and the afflictions which ye endure; ⁵ a token of the righteous judgment of God, that ye may be counted worthy of the kingdom of God, for which ye also suffer; ⁶ since it is a righteous thing with God to recompense affliction to those who afflict you, ⁷ and to you who are afflicted rest with us, at the revelation of the Lord

II. THESSALONIANS.

Jesus from heaven with the angels of his power, ⁸ in flaming fire, taking vengeance on those who know not God, and those who obey not the gospel of our Lord Jesus Christ ; ⁹ who shall suffer justice, eternal destruction, from the presence of the Lord and from the glory of his power ; ¹⁰ when he shall come to be glorified in his saints, and to be admired in all who believed (because our testimony to you was believed), in that day.

¹¹ To which end we also pray for you always, that our God may count you worthy of the calling, and accomplish all the good pleasure of goodness and the work of faith, with power ; ¹² that the name of our Lord Jesus Christ may be glorified in you, and ye in him, according to the grace of our God and the Lord Jesus Christ.

II. Now we beseech you, brethren, concerning the coming of our Lord Jesus Christ, and our gathering together to him, ² that ye be not hastily shaken in mind, or be troubled, neither by spirit, nor by word, nor by letter, as through us, as that the day of the Lord is at hand. ³ Let not any one deceive you in any manner; because [that day will not come], except there come first the falling away, and the man of sin be revealed, the son of perdition ; ⁴ he that opposes and exalts himself against all that is called God, or that is worshiped ; so that he sits in the temple of God, showing himself that he is God.

⁵ Remember ye not, that, when I was yet with you, I told you these things ? ⁶ And now ye know what withholds, in order that he may be revealed in his own time. ⁷ For the mystery of iniquity is already working ; only until he who now withholds shall be out of the way. ⁸ And then will the Lawless One be revealed, whom the Lord Jesus will consume with the breath of his mouth, and will destroy with the manifestation of his coming ; ⁹ [him,] whose coming is after the working of Satan, in all power and signs and lying wonders, ¹⁰ and in all deceit of

---

V. 2. *Gr.* shaken from your mind   V. 2. *Or,* is come

CHAPTER III.

unrighteousness for those who perish; because they received not the love of the truth, that they might be saved. [11] And for this cause God sends them a working of delusion, in order that they may believe the lie; [12] that they may all be judged, who believed not the truth, but had pleasure in unrighteousness.

[13] But we are bound to give thanks to God always for you, brethren beloved of the Lord, because God from the beginning chose you to salvation, in sanctification of the Spirit and belief of the truth; [14] whereunto he called you by our gospel, to the obtaining of the glory of our Lord Jesus Christ. [15] So then, brethren, stand fast, and hold the traditions which ye were taught, whether by word, or by our letter.

[16] Now our Lord Jesus Christ himself, and God and our Father, who loved us, and gave us everlasting consolation and good hope through grace, [17] encourage your hearts, and establish you in every good work and word.

III. Finally, brethren, pray for us, that the word of the Lord may run, and be glorified, as also with you; [2] and that we may be delivered from perverse and evil men; for all have not the faith. [3] But faithful is the Lord, who will establish you, and guard you from evil. [4] And we have confidence in the Lord concerning you, that ye both do, and will do, the things which we command you. [5] And the Lord direct your hearts into the love of God, and into the patience of Christ.

[6] Now we command you, brethren, in the name of our Lord Jesus Christ, that ye withdraw yourselves from every brother walking disorderly, and not after the tradition which they received from us. [7] For yourselves know how ye ought to follow us; that we were not disorderly among you, [8] nor did we eat bread of any one for naught, but with labor and toil, working night and day that we might not be burdensome to any of you; [9] not because we have not power, but to make ourselves an example to you, that ye should follow us. [10] For also when we were with you, this we commanded you: If

---

VV. 15 and 6. Traditions: *See note on* 1 *Cor.* xi., 2.   V. 3. *Or*, from the Evil One

any will not work, neither let him eat. ¹¹ For we hear of some who walk among you disorderly, working not at all, but are busy-bodies. ¹² Now such we command, and exhort, in the Lord Jesus Christ, that with quietness working, they eat their own bread.

¹³ But ye, brethren, be not weary in well doing. ¹⁴ And if any one obeys not our word by this letter, mark that man, and keep not company with him, that he may be shamed. ¹⁵ And count him not as an enemy, but admonish him as a brother.

¹⁶ Now the Lord of peace himself give you peace always, in every way. The Lord be with you all.

¹⁷ The salutation of Paul with my own hand, which is a token in every letter; so I write.

¹⁸ The grace of our Lord Jesus Christ be with you all.

THE FIRST LETTER OF PAUL TO TIMOTHY.

I. Paul, an apostle of Christ Jesus, according to the commandment of God our Savior and Christ Jesus our hope, ² to Timothy, a true child in the faith: Grace, mercy, peace, from God the Father and Christ Jesus our Lord.

³ As I besought thee to remain still in Ephesus, when I was going into Macedonia, that thou mightest charge certain ones not to teach other doctrine, ⁴ nor to give heed to fables and endless genealogies, which further disputes rather than God's dispensation, which is in faith, [so do.]

⁵ Now the end of the commandment is love, out of a pure heart and a good conscience and faith unfeigned; ⁶ from which some swerving turned aside to idle prattling; ⁷ desiring to be teachers of the law, understanding neither what they say, nor whereof they affirm. ⁸ But we know that the law is good, if a man use it lawfully; ⁹ knowing this, that the law is not made for a righteous man, but for the lawless and unruly, for the ungodly and sinful, for the unholy and profane, for mur-

CHAPTER II.

derers of fathers and murderers of mothers; for man-slayers, [10] for fornicators, for those who defile themselves with mankind, for slave-dealers, for liars, for false swearers, and whatever else is contrary to the sound teaching; [11] according to the glorious gospel of the blissful God, with which I was entrusted.

[12] And I thank him who gave me strength, Christ Jesus our Lord, that he accounted me faithful, putting me into the ministry, [13] who was formerly a blasphemer, and a persecutor, and overbearing. But I obtained mercy, because I did it ignorantly, in unbelief; [14] and the grace of our Lord abounded exceedingly, with faith and love which is in Christ Jesus.

[15] Faithful is the saying, and worthy of all acceptance, that Christ Jesus came into the world to save sinners; of whom I am chief. [16] But for this cause I obtained mercy, that in me first Christ Jesus might show forth all his long-suffering, for a pattern to those who should hereafter believe on him to life everlasting.

[17] Now to the King eternal, the imperishable, invisible, only God, be honor and glory forever and ever. Amen.

[18] This charge I commit to thee, my child Timothy, according to the prophecies which went before concerning thee, that thou mayest wage in them the good warfare; [19] having faith, and a good conscience, which some thrusting away made shipwreck concerning the faith. [20] Of whom is Hymenæus and Alexander; whom I delivered over to Satan, that they might be taught not to blaspheme.

II. I EXHORT then, first of all, that supplications, prayers, intercessions, thanksgivings, be made for all men; [2] for kings, and all that are in authority; that we may lead a quiet and peaceful life in all godliness and decorum. [3] For this is good and acceptable in the sight of our Savior God; [4] who desires that all should be saved, and come to the knowledge of the truth.

[5] For there is one God, one mediator also between God and

V. 9. *Or*, for smiters of fathers and smiters of mothers
V. 16. *Or*, in me as chief   V. 16. *Or*, all that long-suffering

men, the man Christ Jesus; ⁶ who gave himself a ransom for all, to be testified in due time; ⁷ whereunto I was appointed a preacher, and an apostle (I speak truth, I lie not), a teacher of the Gentiles in faith and truth.

⁸ I desire, therefore, that the men pray in every place, lifting up holy hands, without wrath and disputing; ⁹ in like manner also that women, in becoming apparel, adorn themselves with modesty and sobriety; not in braided hair, or gold, or pearls, or costly raiment; ¹⁰ but, which becomes women professing godliness, by means of good works.

¹¹ Let the woman learn in silence, with all subjection. ¹² But I permit not the woman to teach, nor to have authority over the man, but to be in silence. ¹³ For Adam was first formed, then Eve. ¹⁴ And Adam was not deceived; but the woman, being deceived, has fallen into transgression. ¹⁵ But she shall be saved through child-bearing, if they continue in faith, and love, and holiness, with sobriety.

III. Faithful is the saying, if any one desires the office of overseer, he desires a good work. ² The overseer then must be blameless, the husband of one wife, sober, discreet, orderly, hospitable, apt in teaching; ³ not given to wine, not a striker, but forbearing, averse to strife, not a lover of money; ⁴ presiding well over his own house, having his children in subjection with all decorum; (⁵ but if one knows not how to preside over his own house, how shall he take care of the church of God?) ⁶ not a novice, lest being lifted up with pride he fall into the condemnation of the Devil. ⁷ But he must also have a good testimony from those without, lest he fall into reproach and the snare of the Devil.

⁸ Deacons in like manner must be grave, not double-tongued, not given to much wine, not greedy of gain; ⁹ holding the mystery of the faith in a pure conscience. ¹⁰ And let these also first be proved; then let them serve as deacons, being without

---

V. 1. Overseer: *as properly translated in Acts* xx., 28.
V. 6. *Or*, not a new convert

CHAPTER IV.

reproach. [11] [Their] wives in like manner must be grave, not slanderers, sober, faithful in all things.
[12] Let the deacons be husbands of one wife, presiding well over their children and their own houses. [13] For they that have served well as deacons obtain for themselves a good degree, and great boldness in the faith which is in Christ Jesus.
[14] These things I write to thee, hoping to come to thee shortly; [15] but if I tarry long, that thou mayest know how thou oughtest to conduct thyself in the house of God, which is the church of the living God, the pillar and ground of the truth. [16] And confessedly, great is the mystery of godliness; God was manifested in the flesh, was justified in the Spirit, was seen by angels, was preached among the Gentiles, was believed on in the world, was received up in glory.

IV. Now the Spirit says expressly, that in after-times some will depart from the faith, giving heed to seducing spirits, and teachings of demons; [2] of those who speak lies in hypocrisy, having their conscience seared with a hot iron; [3] forbidding to marry, commanding to abstain from food, which God created to be received with thanksgiving, for those who believe and know the truth. [4] For every creature of God is good, and nothing to be refused, if it be received with thanksgiving; [5] for it is sanctified by the word of God and prayer.
[6] If thou put the brethren in mind of these things, thou shalt be a good minister of Christ Jesus, nurtured in the words of the faith and of the good teaching, which thou hast strictly followed. [7] But the profane and silly fables avoid, and exercise thyself unto godliness. [8] For bodily exercise is profitable for little; but godliness is profitable for all things, having promise of the life that now is, and of that which is to come. [9] Faithful is the saying, and worthy of all acceptance. [10] For to this end we both labor and suffer reproach, because we have hoped in the living God, who is the Savior of all men, especially of believers.

V. 13. *Or*, a good rank
V. 16. *In ancient copies:* who was manifested. *Or*, which was manifested.
V. 3. *Or*, by those   V. 7. *Gr.* old women's fables

I. TIMOTHY.

¹¹ These things command and teach. ¹² Let no one despise thy youth; but become an example of the believers, in word, in deportment, in love, in faith, in purity. ¹³ Till I come, give attention to reading, to exhortation, to teaching. ¹⁴ Neglect not the gift that is in thee, which was given thee through prophecy, with the laying on of the hands of the eldership. ¹⁵ Meditate on these things; give thyself wholly to them; that thy progress may be manifest to all. ¹⁶ Give heed to thyself, and to the teaching; continue in them; for in doing this thou wilt save both thyself, and those who hear thee.

V. Rebuke not an elder, but entreat him as a father; younger men as brethren; ² elder women as mothers, the younger as sisters, with all purity. ³ Honor as widows those who are widows indeed. ⁴ But if any widow has children or grand-children, let these learn first to show piety to their own household, and to requite their parents, for this is acceptable before God. ⁵ Now she that is a widow indeed, and left alone, has set her hope on God, and continues in supplications and prayers, night and day. ⁶ But she that lives in pleasure is dead while she lives. ⁷ And these things command, that they may be blameless. ⁸ But if any one provides not for his own, and especially for those of his own house, he has denied the faith, and is worse than an unbeliever.

⁹ Let not one be enrolled as a widow under threescore years old, having been the wife of one husband; ¹⁰ well reported of for good works; if she brought up children, if she lodged strangers, if she washed the feet of the saints, if she relieved the afflicted, if she diligently followed every good work. ¹¹ But younger widows refuse; for when they have become wanton against Christ, they desire to marry; ¹² having condemnation, because they broke their first faith. ¹³ And at the same time they also learn to be idle, going about from house to house; and not only idle, but tattlers also and busy-bodies, speaking things which they ought not.

V. 15. *Or,* Practice these things

CHAPTER VI.

¹⁴ I desire therefore that younger widows marry, bear children, guide the house, give no occasion to the adversary to speak reproachfully. ¹⁵ For already, some turned aside after Satan.

¹⁶ If any believing man or woman has widows, let them relieve them, and let not the church be burdened; that it may relieve those who are widows indeed.

¹⁷ Let elders who preside well be counted worthy of double honor, especially they who labor in the word and teaching. ¹⁸ For the Scripture says: Thou shalt not muzzle an ox while treading out the grain; and, The laborer is worthy of his hire.

¹⁹ Against an elder receive not an accusation, except before two or three witnesses.

²⁰ Those who sin rebuke before all, that the rest also may fear.

²¹ I charge thee before God, and Christ Jesus, and the elect angels, that thou observe these things without prejudging, doing nothing with partiality.

²² Lay hands hastily on no one, neither share in other men's sins. Keep thyself pure.

²³ No longer drink water only, but use a little wine for thy stomach's sake, and for thy frequent infirmities.

²⁴ The sins of some men are openly manifest, going before to judgment; and some men they follow after. ²⁵ In like manner also the good works are openly manifest; and those that are otherwise can not be hidden.

VI. LET as many as are servants under the yoke count their own masters worthy of all honor, that the name of God and the teaching be not blasphemed. ² And they that have believing masters, let them not despise them because they are brethren; but the rather do them service, because they who receive the benefit are faithful and beloved. These things teach and exhort.

V. 19. *Or*, except on the authority of two or three witnesses

I. TIMOTHY.

³ If any one teaches otherwise, and assents not to sound words, the words of our Lord Jesus Christ, and to the teaching which is according to godliness, ⁴ he is puffed up with pride, knowing nothing, but doting about questions and strifes of words, whereof comes envy, strife, railings, evil surmisings, ⁵ vain disputings of men corrupted in mind, and robbed of the truth, supposing that godliness is a means of gain. ⁶ But godliness with contentment is a great means of gain. ⁷ For we brought nothing into the world; it is certain we can also carry nothing out; ⁸ and having food and raiment, let us be therewith content. ⁹ But they who desire to be rich fall into temptation and a snare, and many foolish and hurtful lusts, which sink men into destruction and perdition. ¹⁰ For the love of money is a root of all evils; which some coveting after wandered away from the faith, and pierced themselves through with many sorrows.

¹¹ But thou, O man of God, flee these things; and follow after righteousness, godliness, faith, love, patience, meekness of spirit. ¹² Fight the good fight of the faith, lay hold on the eternal life, unto which thou wast called, and didst make the good profession before many witnesses.

¹³ I charge thee in the sight of God, who preserves all alive, and of Jesus Christ, who before Pontius Pilate witnessed the good profession, ¹⁴ that thou keep the commandment without spot, blameless, until the appearing of our Lord Jesus Christ; ¹⁵ which in his own times he will show, who is the blissful and only Potentate, the King of kings, and Lord of lords; ¹⁶ who only has immortality, dwelling in light unapproachable; whom no man has seen, or can see; to whom be honor and power everlasting. Amen.

¹⁷ Charge those who are rich in this world, that they be not high-minded, nor place their hope on the uncertainty of riches, but in God, who gives us all things richly for enjoyment; ¹⁸ that they do good, be rich in good works, be free in imparting, willing to communicate; ¹⁹ laying up in store for themselves a

---

V. 15. *Or*, in its own times

CHAPTER I.

good foundation against the time to come, that they may lay hold on the true life.

²⁰ O Timothy, keep that which is committed to thy trust, avoiding the profane babblings, and oppositions of that which is falsely called knowledge; ²¹ which some professing erred concerning the faith. Grace be with thee.

THE SECOND LETTER OF PAUL TO TIMOTHY.

I. Paul, an apostle of Jesus Christ by the will of God, according to the promise of life which is in Christ Jesus, ²to Timothy, a beloved child : Grace, mercy, peace, from God the Father and Christ Jesus our Lord.

³ I thank God, whom I serve from my forefathers with pure conscience, that without ceasing I have remembrance of thee in my prayers night and day ; ⁴ longing to see thee, remembering thy tears, that I may be filled with joy ; ⁵ calling to remembrance the unfeigned faith that is in thee, which dwelt first in thy grandmother Lois, and thy mother Eunice ; and I am persuaded that it dwells in thee also. ⁶ For which cause I put thee in remembrance, that thou stir up the gift of God, which is in thee by the laying on of my hands. ⁷ For God did not give us a spirit of fear ; but of power, and of love, and of chastisement.

⁸ Be not then ashamed of the testimony of our Lord, nor of me his prisoner ; but endure hardship with me for the gospel, according to the power of God ; ⁹ who saved us, and called us with a holy calling, not according to our works, but according to his own purpose, and the grace which was given us in Christ Jesus before eternal ages, ¹⁰ but now made manifest by the appearing of our Savior Jesus Christ ; who abolished death, and brought life and incorruption to light through the gospel ; ¹¹ for which I was appointed a preacher, and an apostle, and a teacher ? the Gentiles. ¹² For which cause I suffer also these things.

II. TIMOTHY.

But I am not ashamed; for I know whom I have believed, and am persuaded that he is able to keep that which I have committed to him, unto that day. ¹³ Hold fast the form of sound words, which thou heardest from me, in faith and love which is in Christ Jesus. ¹⁴ The good thing committed to thee keep, through the Holy Spirit who dwells in us.

¹⁵ Thou knowest this, that all those in Asia turned away from me; of whom are Phygellus and Hermogenes. ¹⁶ The Lord give mercy to the house of Onesiphorus: because he often refreshed me, and was not ashamed of my chain; ¹⁷ but when he was in Rome, he sought me out very diligently, and found me. ¹⁸ The Lord grant to him, that he may find mercy of the Lord in that day! And in how many things he ministered to me at Ephesus, thou knowest very well.

II. Thou therefore, my child, be strong in the grace that is in Christ Jesus. ² And the things that thou heardest from me by many witnesses, the same commit thou to faithful men, who will be able to teach others also. ³ Endure hardship with me, as a good soldier of Jesus Christ. ⁴ No one serving as a soldier entangles himself with the affairs of life, that he may please him who chose him to be a soldier. ⁵ And if a man also contends in the games, he is not crowned, unless he contends lawfully. ⁶ The husbandman that labors must first partake of the fruits. ⁷ Consider what I say; for the Lord will give thee understanding in all things.

⁸ Remember Jesus Christ, raised from the dead, of the seed of David, according to my gospel; ⁹ in which I endure hardship, even unto bonds, as an evil-doer; but the word of God is not bound. ¹⁰ For this cause, I endure all things for the sake of the chosen, that they also may obtain the salvation which is in Christ Jesus, with eternal glory. ¹¹ Faithful is the saying: For if we died with him, we shall also live with him; ¹² if we endure, we shall also reign with him; if we shall deny him, he

---

V. 2. *Or, among many witnesses*

CHAPTER III.

also will deny us; [13] if we are faithless, he remains faithful, for he can not deny himself.

[14] Of these things put them in remembrance, charging them before the Lord not to strive about words to no profit, to the subverting of the hearers.

[15] Endeavor to present thyself approved to God, a workman not made ashamed, rightly dividing the word of truth. [16] But shun the profane babblings; for they will go on to more ungodliness. [17] And their word will eat as does a canker; of whom is Hymenæus and Philetus; [18] who erred concerning the truth, saying that the resurrection has already taken place, and overturn the faith of some.

[19] Nevertheless, God's firm foundation stands, having this seal: The Lord knew those who are, his; and, Let every one that names the name of the Lord depart from iniquity. [20] But in a great house there are not only vessels of gold and of silver, but also of wood and of earth; and some for honor and some for dishonor. [21] If a man therefore cleanse himself from these, he shall be a vessel for honor, sanctified, useful for the master, prepared for every good work.

[22] But flee youthful lusts; and follow righteousness, faith, love, peace, with those who call on the Lord out of a pure heart. [23] But the foolish and ignorant questionings avoid, knowing that they beget strifes. [24] And a servant of the Lord must not strive, but be gentle toward all, apt in teaching, patient of evil; [25] in meekness admonishing those who oppose themselves; if haply God may give them repentance unto the full knowledge of the truth; [26] and that they may awake to soberness out of the snare of the Devil, being taken captive by him, to do his will.

III. But know this, that in the last days perilous times will come. [2] For men will be lovers of themselves, lovers of money, boasters, proud, blasphemers, disobedient to parents, unthankful, unholy, [3] without natural affection, implacable, false

---

V. 15. *Or*, rightly handling V. 26. *Or*, to do His will

II. TIMOTHY.

accusers, incontinent, fierce, without love to the good, ⁴ betrayers, headlong, puffed up, lovers of pleasure rather than lovers of God; ⁵ having a form of godliness, but denying the power thereof; and from these turn away. ⁶ For of these are they who creep into houses, and lead captive silly women laden with sins, led away with divers lusts, ⁷ ever learning, and never able to come to the full knowledge of the truth.

⁸ Now as Jannes and Jambres withstood Moses, so also do these withstand the truth; men corrupted in mind, reprobate concerning the faith. ⁹ But they shall proceed no further; for their folly shall be fully manifest to all, as was also theirs.

¹⁰ But thou didst strictly follow my teaching, manner of life, purpose, faith, long-suffering, love, patience, ¹¹ persecutions, afflictions; what things came upon me at Antioch, at Iconium, at Lystra; what persecutions I endured, and out of all the Lord delivered me. ¹² Yea, and all who desire to live godly in Christ Jesus will suffer persecution. ¹³ But evil men and seducers will grow worse and worse, deceiving, and being deceived. ¹⁴ But do thou continue in the things which thou learnedst and wast assured of, knowing of whom thou didst learn; ¹⁵ and that from a child thou didst know the Holy Scriptures, which are able to make thee wise unto salvation, through faith which is in Christ Jesus.

¹⁶ All Scripture is inspired by God, and is profitable for teaching, for reproof, for correction, for instruction in righteousness; ¹⁷ that the man of God may be perfect, thoroughly furnished unto all good works.

IV. I charge thee before God, and Christ Jesus who will judge the living and the dead, and by his appearing and his kingdom, ² preach the word; apply thyself in season, out of season; reprove, rebuke, exhort, with all long-suffering and teaching. ³ For the time will come when they will not endure the sound teaching, but according to their own desires will to themselves heap up teachers, having itching ears; ⁴ and they

---

V. 16. *Or*, Every Scripture, inspired by God, is also profitable

CHAPTER IV.

will turn away their ears from the truth, and will turn aside to fables.

⁵ But be thou watchful in all things, endure hardship, do the work of an evangelist, fully accomplish thy ministry. ⁶ For I am now about to be offered, and the time of my departure is at hand. ⁷ I have fought the good fight, I have finished my course, I have kept the faith; ⁸ henceforth there is laid up for me the crown of righteousness, which the Lord, the righteous judge, will give me in that day; and not to me only, but also to all those who have loved his appearing.

⁹ Endeavor to come to me shortly. ¹⁰ For Demas forsook me, having loved the present world, and departed to Thessalonica; Crescens to Galatia, Titus to Dalmatia. ¹¹ Luke alone is with me. Take Mark and bring him with thee; for he is useful to me for the ministry. ¹² But Tychicus I sent to Ephesus.

¹³ The cloak, which I left at Troas with Carpus, when thou comest bring, and the books, especially the parchments.

¹⁴ Alexander the coppersmith did me much evil; the Lord reward him according to his works. ¹⁵ Of whom do thou also beware; for he has greatly withstood our words.

¹⁶ At my first answer no one came forward with me, but all forsook me. May it not be laid to their charge! ¹⁷ But the Lord stood by me, and strengthened me; that through me the preaching might be fully accomplished, and all the Gentiles might hear; and I was delivered out of the mouth of the lion. ¹⁸ The Lord will deliver me from every evil work, and will bring me safe to his heavenly kingdom; to whom be the glory, forever and ever. Amen.

¹⁹ Salute Prisca and Aquila, and the household of Onesiphorus.

²⁰ Erastus remained in Corinth, but Trophimus I left at Miletus sick.

²¹ Endeavor to come before winter. Eubulus salutes thee, and Pudens, and Linus, and Claudia, and all the brethren.

²² The Lord Jesus Christ be with thy spirit. Grace be with you.

THE LETTER OF PAUL TO TITUS.

I. Paul, a servant of God, and an apostle of Jesus Christ, for the faith of God's chosen, and the knowledge of the truth which is according to godliness; ² upon hope of eternal life, which God, who can not lie, promised before eternal ages, ³ but in its own times manifested his word in the preaching, with which I was entrusted according to the commandment of our Savior God; ⁴ to Titus, a true child according to the common faith: Grace, mercy, peace, from God the Father and Christ Jesus our Savior.

⁵ For this cause I left thee behind in Crete, that thou shouldest set in order the things that are wanting, and appoint elders in each city, as I directed thee; ⁶ if any one is without reproach, the husband of one wife, having believing children not accused of rioting or unruly. ⁷ For the overseer must be without reproach, as God's steward; not self-willed, not soon angry, not given to wine, not a striker, not greedy of gain; ⁸ but hospitable, a lover of the good, discreet, just, holy, temperate; ⁹ holding fast the faithful word according to the teaching, that he may be able with the sound teaching both to exhort, and to refute the gainsayers. ¹⁰ For there are many unruly vain talkers and deceivers, chiefly they of the circumcision; ¹¹ whose mouths must be stopped, who overturn whole houses, teaching things which they ought not, for the sake of base gain. ¹² One of themselves, a prophet of their own, said: Cretans are always liars, evil beasts, lazy gluttons. ¹³ This testimony is true. For which cause reprove them sharply, that they may be sound in the faith; ¹⁴ not giving heed to Jewish fables, and commandments of men, who turn away from the truth.

¹⁵ To the pure all things are pure; but to the defiled and unbelieving nothing is pure; but both their mind and con-

---

V. 3. *Or,* in his own
V. 7. Overseer: *as properly translated in Acts* xx., 28.

CHAPTER III.

science are defiled. ¹⁶ They profess that they know God; but by their works they deny him, being abominable, and disobedient, and for every good work reprobate.

II. But do thou speak the things which become the sound teaching; ² that aged men be sober, grave, discreet, sound in the faith, in love, in patience; ³ that aged women likewise be in behavior as becomes holiness, not false accusers, not enslaved to much wine, teachers of that which is good; ⁴ that they may teach the young women to love their husbands, to love their children, ⁵ to be discreet, chaste, keepers at home, good, obedient to their own husbands, that the word of God be not blasphemed.

⁶ The younger men likewise exhort to be sober-minded. ⁷ In all things showing thyself a pattern of good works; in teaching, showing uncorruptness, gravity, ⁸ sound speech, that can not be condemned; that he that is of the contrary part may be put to shame, having no evil thing to say of us.

⁹ Exhort servants to submit themselves to their own masters, to be well-pleasing in all things; not contradicting, ¹⁰ not purloining, but showing all good faith; that they may adorn the teaching of our Savior God in all things,

¹¹ For the saving grace of God appeared to all men, ¹² teaching us that, having denied ungodliness and worldly lusts, we should live soberly, righteously, and godly, in this present world; ¹³ looking for the blissful hope and appearing of the glory of the great God and our Savior Jesus Christ; ¹⁴ who gave himself for us, that he might redeem us from all iniquity, and cleanse for himself a people to be his own, zealous of good works.

¹⁵ These things speak, and exhort, and reprove with all authority. Let no one despise thee.

III. Put them in mind to submit themselves to governments, to authorities, to obey magistrates, to be ready to every good work, ² to speak evil of no one, to be averse to strife, forbearing, showing all meekness to all men.

TITUS.

³ For we ourselves also were once foolish, disobedient, going astray, serving divers lusts and pleasures, living in malice and envy, hateful, hating one another. ⁴ But when the kindness and the love toward man of our Savior God appeared, ⁵ not by works of righteousness which we did, but according to his mercy he saved us, through the bathing of regeneration, and renewing of the Holy Spirit; ⁶ which he poured out on us richly through Jesus Christ our Savior; ⁷ that, having been justified by his grace, we should be made heirs according to the hope of eternal life.

⁸ Faithful is the saying; and concerning these things I will that thou affirm constantly, that they who have believed God may be careful to take the lead in good works. These things are good and profitable to men. ⁹ But avoid foolish questionings, and genealogies, and strifes, and contentions about the law; for they are unprofitable and vain.

¹⁰ A man that causes divisions, after a first and second admonition, avoid; ¹¹ knowing that he that is such is perverted, and sins, being self-condemned.

¹² When I shall send Artemas to thee, or Tychicus, endeavor to come to me to Nicopolis; for I have determined there to winter.

¹³ Zenas the lawyer, and Apollos, send forward on their journey zealously, that nothing may be wanting to them. ¹⁴ And let ours also learn to take the lead in good works for necessary wants, that they may not be unfruitful.

¹⁵ All that are with me salute thee. Salute those who love us in the faith. Grace be with you all.

V. 10. *Or,* reject

THE LETTER OF PAUL TO PHILEMON.

PAUL, a prisoner of Christ Jesus, and Timothy the brother, to Philemon the beloved and our fellow-laborer, ²and to Apphia the beloved, and Archippus our fellow-soldier, and to the church in thy house : ³Grace to you, and peace, from God our Father and the Lord Jesus Christ.

⁴I thank my God always, making mention of thee in my prayers, ⁵hearing of thy love and faith, which thou hast toward the Lord Jesus, and unto all the saints ; ⁶that the fellowship of thy faith may become effectual in the knowledge of every good thing which is in us, unto Christ Jesus. ⁷For I had much joy and consolation in thy love, because the hearts of the saints have been refreshed by thee, brother. ⁸Wherefore, though having much boldness in Christ to enjoin upon thee that which is becoming, ⁹yet for love's sake I beseech rather ; being such a one, as Paul an old man, and now also a prisoner of Jesus Christ, ¹⁰I beseech thee for my child, whom I begot in my bonds, Onesimus ; ¹¹who in time past was unprofitable to thee, but is now profitable to thee and to me ; ¹²whom I sent back to thee. But do thou receive him, that is, my own flesh ; ¹³whom I would have retained with myself, that in thy stead he might minister to me in the bonds of the gospel. ¹⁴But without thy consent I desired to do nothing ; that thy benefit may not be as it were of necessity, but willingly. ¹⁵For perhaps he departed for a season to this end, that thou shouldest receive him as thine forever ; ¹⁶no longer as a servant, but above a servant, a brother beloved, specially to me, but how much more to thee, both in the flesh, and in the Lord !

¹⁷If thou countest me therefore a partner, receive him as myself.

¹⁸But if he wronged thee in any thing, or owes aught, put

V. 2. *In many ancient copies :* Apphia the sister
V. 6. *Or,* the communion of thy faith
V. 7. *In many copies :* we have   *Or,* we had

that to my account. ¹⁹ I, Paul, wrote it with my own hand, I will repay. Not to say to thee, that to me thou owest also thine own self besides. ²⁰ Yea, brother, let me have joy of thee in the Lord. Refresh my heart in Christ. ²¹ Having confidence in thy obedience I wrote to thee, knowing that thou wilt also do more than I say.

²² But at the same time be preparing for me also a lodging; for I hope that through your prayers I shall be given to you.

²³ There salute thee Epaphras, my fellow-captive in Christ Jesus; ²⁴ Mark, Aristarchus, Demas, Luke, my fellow-laborers.

²⁵ The grace of our Lord Jesus Christ be with your spirit.

LETTER TO THE HEBREWS.

I. God, who in many parts and in many ways spoke of old to the fathers by the prophets, ² in these last days spoke to us by his Son, whom he appointed heir of all things, by whom he also made the worlds; ³ who, being the brightness of his glory and the impress of his substance, and upholding all things by the word of his power, when he had by himself made a cleansing of sins, sat down on the right hand of the Majesty on high; ⁴ having become so much superior to the angels, as he has inherited a more excellent name than they.

⁵ For to whom of the angels said he ever:
    Thou art my Son,
    I this day have begotten thee;
and again: I will be to him a Father, and he shall be to me a Son. ⁶ But when he has again brought in the first-begotten into the world, he says:

V. 3. *Some ancient copies omit:* by himself
V. 6. *Or,* shall again have brought in

CHAPTER II.

And let all the angels of God worship him. ⁷And of the angels he says:
Who makes his angels winds,
And his ministers a flame of fire;
⁸but of the Son:
Thy throne, O God, is forever and ever;
A sceptre of righteousness is the sceptre of thy
    kingdom;
⁹Thou lovedst righteousness, and hatedst iniquity;
Therefore God, thy God, anointed thee,
With the oil of gladness, above thy fellows;
¹⁰ and:
Thou, Lord, in the beginning, didst found the earth,
And the heavens are the works of thy hands;
¹¹They will perish, but thou remainest;
And they all will become old, as does a garment,
¹²And as a vesture thou wilt fold them up, and they
    will be changed;
But thou art the same,
And thy years will not fail.
¹³But to whom of the angels has he ever said:
Sit on my right hand,
Until I make thine enemies thy footstool.
¹⁴Are they not all ministering spirits, sent forth for ministration, for the sake of those who are to inherit salvation?

II. On this account, we ought to give the more earnest heed to the things heard, lest haply we should let them slip. ²For if the word spoken through angels proved steadfast, and every transgression and disobedience received just retribution, ³how shall we escape, having neglected so great a salvation; which began to be spoken by the Lord, and was confirmed to us by those who heard, ⁴God also bearing witness, with signs and wonders, and divers miracles, and distributions of the Holy Spirit, according to his own will?

V. 1. *Or*, we should be diverted from them.

⁵ For not to the angels did he put in subjection the world to come, of which we are speaking. ⁶ But one in a certain place testified, saying:

⁵ What is man, that thou art mindful of him,
Or the son of man, that thou visitest him?
⁷ Thou madest him a little lower than the angels;
Thou crownedst him with glory and honor;
⁸ Thou didst put all things in subjection under his feet.

For in that he put all in subjection under him, he left nothing that is not put under him.

But now we do not yet see all things put under him. ⁹ But we behold him, who was made a little lower than the angels, Jesus, on account of the suffering of death, crowned with glory and honor, in order that he by the grace of God might taste death for every one. ¹⁰ For it became him, for whom are all things, and by whom are all things, in bringing many sons to glory, to make the captain of their salvation perfect through sufferings.

¹¹ For both he that sanctifies and they who are sanctified are all of one; for which cause he is not ashamed to call them brethren, ¹² saying:

I will declare thy name to my brethren;
In the midst of the congregation I will sing praise
to thee.

¹³ And again: I will put my trust in him. And again: Behold, I and the children whom God gave me. ¹⁴ Forasmuch then as the children are partakers of flesh and blood, he also himself in like manner took part in the same; that through death he might destroy him who had the power of death, that is, the Devil; ¹⁵ and might deliver those who, through fear of death, were all their lifetime subject to bondage.

¹⁶ For surely he does not succor angels; but he succors the seed of Abraham. ¹⁷ Wherefore, in all things it became him to be made like to his brethren, that he might become a merciful and faithful high priest in things pertaining to God, to make propitiation for the sins of the people. ¹⁸ For in that he him-

CHAPTER III.

self has suffered being tempted, he is able to help those who are tempted.

III. WHEREFORE, holy brethren, partakers of the heavenly calling, consider the Apostle and High Priest of our profession, Jesus, ² who was faithful to him who appointed him, as also was Moses in all His house. ³ For he has been accounted worthy of more glory than Moses, inasmuch as he who has built the house has more honor than the house. ⁴ For every house is builded by some one; but he who built all things is God. ⁵ And Moses indeed was faithful in all His house as a servant, as a testimony of the things which were to be afterward spoken; ⁶ but Christ as son over His house; whose house are we, if we hold fast the boldness and the joyousness of the hope firm unto the end.

⁷ Wherefore, as the Holy Spirit says:
To-day, if ye will hear his voice,
⁸ Harden not your hearts, as in the provocation,
In the day of the temptation in the wilderness;
⁹ Where your fathers tempted me,
Proved me, and saw my works, forty years.
¹⁰ Wherefore, I was offended with that generation;
And I said: They always go astray in their heart,
And they knew not my ways;
¹¹ As I swore in my wrath,
They shall not enter into my rest.

¹² Take heed, brethren, lest there shall be in any one of you an evil heart of unbelief, in departing from the living God. ¹³ But exhort one another daily, as long as it is called To-day, that no one of you may be hardened through the deceitfulness of sin. ¹⁴ For we have become partakers of Christ, if we hold fast the beginning of our confidence firm unto the end. ¹⁵ When it is said: To-day, if ye will hear his voice, harden not your hearts as in the provocation; ¹⁶ who then, when they had heard, provoked?

• V. 6. *Some ancient copies omit:* firm unto the end

Nay, was it not all who came forth out of Egypt by Moses? ¹⁷ But with whom was he offended forty years? Was it not with those who sinned? whose carcasses fell in the wilderness. ¹⁸ And to whom did he swear, that they should not enter into his rest, but to those who believed not? ¹⁹ And we see that they were not able to enter in, because of unbelief.

IV. Let us fear therefore, lest, a promise being still left us of entering into his rest, any one of you should seem to have come short of it. ² For to us were the glad tidings preached, as also to them; but the word which they heard did not profit them, not being mingled with faith in those who heard. ³ For we who believed enter into the rest, as he said: As I swore in my wrath, they shall not enter into my rest, although the works were finished from the foundation of the world. ⁴ For he has spoken in a certain place of the seventh day thus: And God rested on the seventh day from all his works; ⁵ and in this again: They shall not enter into my rest.

⁶ Since then it remains that some do enter into it, and they to whom the glad tidings were first preached entered not in because of unbelief, again ⁷ he limits a certain day, To-day, (saying in David, after so long a time, as has before been said,)

To-day, if ye will hear his voice,
Harden not your hearts.

⁸ For if Joshua had given them rest, he would not, after this, have spoken of another day.

⁹ So then, there remains a Sabbath-rest to the people of God. ¹⁰ For he that entered into his rest, himself rested from his works, as God did from his own. ¹¹ Let us therefore endeavor to enter into that rest, that no one may fall into the same example of unbelief.

¹² For the word of God is living, and powerful, and sharper than any two-edged sword, piercing even to the dividing of soul and spirit, of joints and marrow, and is a discerner of the thoughts and intents of the heart. ¹³ And there is no creature

CHAPTER V.

that is not manifest in his sight; but all things are naked and opened to the eyes of him with whom we have to do.

¹⁴ Having therefore a great high priest, who has passed through the heavens, Jesus the Son of God, let us hold fast our profession. ¹⁵ For we have not a high priest who can not be touched with the feeling of our infirmities, but who has in all points been tempted in like manner, without sin. ¹⁶ Let us therefore come boldly to the throne of grace, that we may obtain mercy, and find grace to help in time of need.

V. For every high priest, being taken from among men, is appointed for men in things pertaining to God, that he may offer both gifts and sacrifices for sins; ² being able to bear with the ignorant and erring, since he himself also is encompassed with infirmity; ³ and on account of it he ought, as for the people, so also for himself, to make offering for sins. ⁴ And no one takes to himself the honor, but being called by God, as was also Aaron. ⁵ So also Christ did not glorify himself to be made high priest, but he who spoke to him:

Thou art my Son,
I this day have begotten thee;

⁶ as also in another place, he says:

Thou art a priest forever,
After the order of Melchizedek;

⁷ who, in the days of his flesh offering up prayers and supplications, with strong crying and tears, to him who was able to save him from death, and being heard on account of his godly fear, ⁸ though a Son yet learned from what he suffered the [required] obedience, ⁹ and being perfected became the author of eternal salvation to all who obey him; ¹⁰ called by God, High Priest, after the order of Melchizedek.

¹¹ Of whom we have much to say, and hard to be explained, since ye have become dull of hearing. ¹² For though ye ought, on account of the time, to be teachers, ye again have need that some one teach you the first principles of the oracles of God,

---

V. 10. *Or,* addressed by God, as High Priest

and are become such as have need of milk, and not of solid food. ¹³ For every one who partakes of milk is inexperienced in the word of righteousness; for he is a child. ¹⁴ But solid food belongs to those who are of full age, who by use have their senses exercised to discern good and evil.

VI. Wherefore, leaving the first principles of the doctrine of Christ, let us go on to perfection; not laying again the foundation of repentance from dead works, and of faith toward God, ²of the doctrine of immersions, and of the laying on of hands, and of the resurrection of the dead, and of eternal judgment. ³And this we will do, if God permit. ⁴ For it is impossible that they who have once been enlightened, and have tasted of the heavenly gift, and been made partakers of the Holy Spirit, ⁵and have tasted the good word of God, and the powers of the world to come, ⁶and have fallen away, should again be renewed to repentance; seeing they crucify to themselves the Son of God afresh, and put him to open shame. ⁷ For the earth which has drunk in the rain oft coming upon it, and brings forth herbs fit for those for whose sake it is tilled, receives blessing from God; ⁸ but if it bears thorns and briers it is rejected, and is near to cursing; whose end is to be burned.

⁹ But, beloved, we are persuaded of better things concerning you, and things that accompany salvation, though we thus speak. ¹⁰ For God is not unrighteous to forget your work, and the love which ye showed toward his name, in that ye ministered and still do minister to the saints.

¹¹ But we desire that each one of you show the same diligence, for the full assurance of the hope unto the end; ¹² that ye may not become slothful, but followers of those who through faith and patience inherit the promises. ¹³ For when God made the promise to Abraham, because he could swear by none greater, he swore by himself, ¹⁴saying: S u r e l y, b l e s s - i n g   I   w i l l   b l e s s   t h e e,   a n d   m u l t i p l y i n g   I w i l l   m u l t i p l y   t h e e.   ¹⁵And so, having patiently

---

V. 3. *In some ancient copies:* And this let us do

CHAPTER VII.

endured, he obtained the promise. [16] For men indeed swear by the greater; and the oath is to them an end of all gainsaying, for a confirmation. [17] Wherein God, wishing more abundantly to show to the heirs of the promise the immutability of his counsel, interposed with an oath; [18] that by two immutable things, in which it is impossible that God should lie, we may have strong encouragement, who fled for refuge to lay hold on the hope set before us, [19] which we have as an anchor of the soul, sure and steadfast, and entering within the vail; [20] where as forerunner for us Jesus entered, having become a high priest forever, after the order of Melchizedek.

VII. For this Melchizedek, king of Salem, priest of the most high God, who met Abraham returning from the slaughter of the kings, and blessed him; [2] to whom also Abraham apportioned a tenth of all; first indeed being interpreted King of righteousness, and then also King of Salem, which is, King of peace; [3] without father, without mother, without table of descent, having neither beginning of days, nor end of life, but likened to the Son of God, remains a priest continually.

[4] Now consider how great this man was, to whom Abraham the patriarch also gave a tenth of the spoils. [5] And they indeed that are of the sons of Levi, who receive the office of the priesthood, have a commandment to take tithes of the people according to the law, that is, of their brethren, though they have come out of the loins of Abraham; [6] but he whose descent is not reckoned from them has taken tithes of Abraham, and has blessed him who had the promises. [7] And without any contradiction, the less is blessed by the better. [8] And here indeed men who die receive tithes; but there, one of whom it is testified that he lives. [9] And so to speak, Levi also, who receives tithes, has paid tithes in Abraham; [10] for he was yet in the loins of his father, when Melchizedek met him.

[11] If therefore perfection were by the Levitical priesthood (for under it the people have received the law), what further

---

V. 3. *That is, as to any record of it.*

need was there that a different priest should arise, after the order of Melchizedek, and not be called after the order of Aaron? ¹² For the priesthood being changed, of necessity there comes also a change of law. ¹³ For he of whom these things are spoken pertains to a different tribe, of which no one has given attendance at the altar. ¹⁴ For it is evident that our Lord has arisen out of Judah; of which tribe Moses spoke nothing concerning priests. ¹⁵ And it is yet more abundantly manifest, if after the similitude of Melchizedek there arises a different priest, ¹⁶ who has been made, not after the law of a carnal commandment, but after the power of an indissoluble life. ¹⁷ For it is testified of him:

Thou art a priest forever,
After the order of Melchizedek.

¹⁸ For on the one hand, there is an annulling of the commandment that went before, on account of its weakness and unprofitableness,—¹⁹ for the law perfected nothing,—and on the other the bringing in of a better hope, by which we draw near to God.

²⁰ And inasmuch as it was not without an oath,—²¹ for they indeed were made priests without an oath, but he with an oath by him who said to him: T h e   L o r d   s w o r e   a n d   w i l l   n o t   r e p e n t, t h o u   a r t   a   p r i e s t   f o r e v e r   a f t- e r   t h e   o r d e r   o f   M e l c h i z e d e k,—²² by so much has Jesus become a surety of a better covenant. ²³ And they indeed have been many priests, because they were hindered by death from continuing; ²⁴ but he, because he remains forever, has an unchangeable priesthood. ²⁵ Whence also he is able to save to the utmost those who come to God through him, since he ever lives to intercede for them.

²⁶ For such a high priest became us, holy, harmless, undefiled, separated from sinners, and made higher than the heavens; ²⁷ who has not necessity daily, as the high priests, to offer up sacrifices, first for his own sins, and then for those of the people; for this he did once for all, in offering up himself.

V. 21 *Some ancient copies omit:* after the order of Melchizedek.

CHAPTER VIII.

²⁸ For the law makes men high priests who have infirmity; but the word of the oath, which was since the law, makes the Son, who is perfected forever.

VIII. Now of the things which we are saying, this is the chief: We have such a high priest, who sat down on the right hand of the throne of the Majesty of the heavens; ² a minister of the holy places, and of the true tabernacle, which the Lord pitched, and not man.

³ For every high priest is appointed to offer gifts and sacrifices; wherefore it is necessary, that this one have something which he may offer. ⁴ For if he were on earth, he would not be a priest, since there are those who offer gifts according to the law, ⁵ who minister after an outline and a shadow of the heavenly things, as Moses was admonished by God, when he was about to make the tabernacle; for, See, says he, that thou make all things according to the pattern which was showed thee in the mount. ⁶ But now he has obtained a more excellent ministry, by so much as he is also mediator of a better covenant, which has been established upon better promises.

⁷ For if that first had been faultless, a place would not have been sought for the second. ⁸ For finding fault with them, he says:

> Behold the days are coming, saith the Lord,
> When I will make with the house of Israel,
> And with the house of Judah, a new covenant;
> ⁹ Not-according to the covenant that I made for their
>   fathers,
> In the day when I took hold of their hand,
> To bring them out of the land of Egypt;
> Because they continued not in my covenant,
> And I regarded them not, saith the Lord.
> ¹⁰ For this is the covenant that I will establish for the
>   house of Israel,

V. 8. *Or*, finding fault, he says to them:

After those days, saith the Lord,
Putting my laws into their mind,
And on their hearts I will write them;
And I will be to them a God,
And they shall be to me a people;
¹¹ And they shall not teach,
Each one his neighbor, and each one his brother,
Saying: Know the Lord;
Because all shall know me, from the least to the greatest;
¹² Because I will be merciful to their unrighteousness,
And their sins and their iniquities I will remember no more.

¹³ In that he says, A n e w, he has made the first old. Now that which is grown old, and worn out with age, is ready to vanish away.

IX. Now the first had indeed also ordinances of service, and the worldly sanctuary. ² For a tabernacle was prepared; the first, wherein is the lamp-stand, and the table, and the show-bread; which is called holy. ³ And after the second vail, the tabernacle which is called most holy, ⁴ having a golden altar of incense, and the ark of the covenant overlaid on every side with gold, wherein was the golden pot containing the manna, and the rod of Aaron which budded, and the tables of the covenant; ⁵ and above it the cherubim of glory overshadowing the mercy-seat; of which we can not now speak particularly.

⁶ Now these things being thus prepared, into the first tabernacle the priests enter at all times, performing the services; ⁷ but into the second, the high priest alone, once every year, not without blood, which he offers for himself, and for the errors of the people; ⁸ the Holy Spirit signifying this, that the way into the holy places has not yet been made manifest, while the first tabernacle is yet standing; ⁹ which is a figure for the time present, under which are offered both gifts and sacrifices. unable as to the conscience to perfect the worshiper; ¹⁰ only

CHAPTER IX.

with meats and drinks, and divers immersions, ordinances of the flesh, imposed until the time of reformation. [11] But Christ, having come as a high priest of the good things to come, through the greater and more perfect tabernacle, not made with hands (that is, not of this creation), [12] and not through the blood of goats and calves but through his own blood, entered once for all into the holy places, obtaining eternal redemption. [13] For if the blood of goats and bulls, and ashes of a heifer sprinkling those who have been defiled, sanctifies to the purity of the flesh; [14] how much more shall the blood of Christ, who through the eternal Spirit offered himself without spot to God, cleanse your conscience from dead works to serve the living God? [15] And for this cause he is mediator of a new covenant, in order that, death having taken place, for the redemption of the transgressions under the first covenant, they who have been called may receive the promise of the eternal inheritance.

[16] For where there is a testament, there must also of necessity be brought in the death of the testator. [17] For a testament is of force after men are dead; since it is of no strength at all while the testator lives.

[18] Wherefore, neither has the first been dedicated without blood. [19] For, when Moses had spoken every precept to all the people according to the law, he took the blood of the calves and of the goats, with water, and scarlet wool, and hyssop, and sprinkled both the book itself and all the people, saying: [20] This is the blood of the covenant, which God enjoined in respect to you. [21] And moreover, the tabernacle, and all the vessels of the service, he in like manner sprinkled with blood. [22] And nearly all things are cleansed according to the law with blood; and without shedding of blood there is no remission.

[23] It was therefore necessary, that the outlines of things in the heavens should be cleansed with these; but the heavenly things themselves, with better sacrifices than these. [24] For Christ entered not into holy places made with hands, figures of

---

V. 10. *Or, only with conditions of meats and drinks*
V. 16. *The same Greek word means covenant, and also testament.*

the true ; but into heaven itself, now to appear in the presence of God for us; ²⁵nor yet that he should many times offer himself, as the high priest enters into the holy places every year with blood of others ; ²⁶for then must he many times have suffered since the foundation of the world ; but now once, in the end of the ages, he has been manifested for the putting away of sin by the sacrifice of himself. ²⁷And inasmuch as it is appointed to men once to die, but after this the judgment ; ²⁸so also the Christ, having been once offered to bear the sins of many, will to those who look for him appear a second time without sin, unto salvation.

X. For the law having a shadow of the good things to come, not the very image of the things, can never, with the same sacrifices which they offer year by year continually, make those who come to them perfect. ²For then would they not have ceased to be offered, because the worshipers would have had no more consciousness of sins, having once been cleansed ? ³But in them there is a remembrance of sins year by year. ⁴For it is impossible that the blood of bulls and of goats should take away sins. ⁵Wherefore, when he comes into the world, he says :

    Sacrifice and offering thou wouldest not,
    But a body didst thou prepare for me ;
  ⁶In whole burnt-offerings, and sacrifices for sin, thou
    hadst no pleasure.
  ⁷Then said I : Lo, I come,
    In the volume of the book it is written of me,
    To do thy will, O God.

⁸Saying above, Sacrifices and offerings and whole burnt-offerings and sacrifices for sin thou wouldest not, nor hadst pleasure therein, which are offered by the law, ⁹then has he said : Lo, I come to do thy will, O God. He takes away the first, that he may establish the second. ¹⁰In which will we have been sanctified, through the offering of the body of Jesus Christ once for all.

    V. 26 *Or,* by his sacrifice
    V. 1. *Or,* those who draw near [to God]

CHAPTER X.

¹¹ And every priest indeed stands daily ministering, and offering oftentimes the same sacrifices, which can never take away sins; ¹² but he, having offered one sacrifice for sins, for ever sat down on the right hand of God; ¹³ from henceforth expecting until his enemies be made his footstool. ¹⁴ For by one offering he has perfected forever those who are sanctified. ¹⁵ Moreover, the Holy Spirit also is a witness to us; for after he had said, ¹⁶ This is the covenant that I will make with them after those days, saith the Lord, putting my laws upon their hearts, and on their minds I will write them, [he further says,] ¹⁷ and their sins and iniquities I will remember no more. ¹⁸ But where there is remission of these, there is no longer offering for sin.

¹⁹ Having therefore, brethren, boldness as to the entrance into the holy places by the blood of Jesus, which [entrance] he instituted for us, ²⁰ a new and living way, through the vail, that is to say, his flesh; ²¹ and having a great priest over the house of God; ²² let us draw near with a true heart in full assurance of faith, having had our hearts sprinkled from an evil conscience; and having had our body washed with pure water, ²³ let us hold fast the profession of the hope without wavering, for he is faithful who promised; ²⁴ and let us consider one another, to incite to love and to good works; ²⁵ not forsaking the assembling of ourselves together, as is the custom of some, but exhorting, and so much the more as ye see the day approaching.

²⁶ For if we willingly sin, after having received the knowledge of the truth, there no longer remains a sacrifice for sins, ²⁷ but a certain fearful looking for of judgment, and a fiery indignation, which will devour the adversaries. ²⁸ He that despised Moses' law died without mercy, under two or three witnesses. ²⁹ Of how much worse punishment, suppose ye, will he be thought worthy, who has trodden under foot the Son of God, and has accounted the blood of the covenant, wherewith

---

V. 11. *In the oldest copies:* every high priest

he was sanctified, an unholy thing, and has done despite to the Spirit of grace? ³⁰ For we know him who said: To me belongs vengeance; I will recompense, saith the Lord; and again: The Lord will judge his people. ³¹ It is a fearful thing to fall into the hands of the living God.

³² But call to remembrance the former days, in which, after ye were enlightened, ye endured a great contest of sufferings; ³³ partly, whilst ye were made a spectacle both by reproaches and afflictions; and partly, whilst ye became partakers with those who were so used. ³⁴ For ye sympathized with those in bonds, and ye took joyfully the plundering of your goods, knowing that ye have for yourselves a better and an enduring substance.

³⁵ Cast not away therefore your confidence, which has great recompense of reward. ³⁶ For ye have need of patience, that having done the will of God ye may receive the promise. ³⁷ For yet a little while, he that is to come will come, and will not delay. ³⁸ Now, the just shall live by faith; but if he draw back, my soul has no pleasure in him. ³⁹ But we are not of those who draw back unto perdition; but of those who believe to the saving of the soul.

XI. Now faith is the assurance of things hoped for, the conviction of things not seen. ² For in this the elders obtained a good report.

³ Through faith we perceive that the worlds were framed by the word of God, so that what is seen has not arisen out of things which appear.

⁴ By faith Abel offered to God a more excellent sacrifice than Cain, by which he received testimony that he was righteous, God testifying of his gifts; and through it, being dead, he yet speaks.

⁵ By faith Enoch was translated, that he should not see

V. 1. *Or*, is the substance of things hoped for
V. 3. *Or*, in order that what is seen should not have arisen

CHAPTER XI.

death; and he was not found, because God translated him; for before his translation, he has had the testimony that he pleased God. ⁶ But without faith it is impossible to please him; for he who comes to God must believe that he is, and that he is a rewarder to those who seek after him.

⁷ By faith Noah, being warned by God concerning things not yet seen, moved with fear, prepared an ark for the saving of his house; by which he condemned the world, and became heir of the righteousness which is according to faith.

⁸ By faith Abraham when called obeyed, to go **forth** into a place which he should afterward receive for an inheritance, and went forth, not knowing whither he went. ⁹ By faith **he** sojourned in the land of promise, as a foreign land, dwelling in tents with Isaac and Jacob, heirs with him of the same promise; ¹⁰ for he looked for the city which has the foundations, whose builder and maker is God.

¹¹ By faith Sarah herself also received power to conceive seed, even when she was past age, because she accounted him faithful who had promised. ¹² Wherefore also there sprang from one, and him become as dead, even as the stars of heaven in multitude, and as the sand which is by the sea shore innumerable.

¹³ These all died in faith, not having received the promises, but having seen them from afar, and greeted them, and professed that they were strangers and sojourners on the earth. ¹⁴ For they that say such things declare plainly, that they are seeking a country. . ¹⁵ And if indeed, they had in mind that from which they came out, they would have had opportunity to return. ¹⁶ But now they desire a better, that is, a heavenly; wherefore God is not ashamed to be called their God; for he prepared for them a city.

¹⁷ By faith Abraham, when tried, has offered up Isaac; and he who had accepted the promises offered up his only begotten, ¹⁸ of whom it was said: In Isaac shall thy seed be called; ¹⁹ accounting that God is able even to raise from the dead; whence he also received him back in a figure.

V 16. *Or,* But as it is

²⁰ By faith Isaac blessed Jacob and Esau, concerning things to come.

²¹ By faith Jacob, when dying, blessed each of the sons of Joseph; and he worshiped, [leaning] on the top of his staff.

²² By faith Joseph, when dying, made mention of the departure of the sons of Israel, and gave commandment concerning his bones.

²³ By faith Moses, when born, was hidden three months by his parents, because they saw that the child was fair; and they feared not the king's commandment.

²⁴ By faith Moses, when grown up, refused to be called son of a daughter of Pharaoh; ²⁵ choosing rather to suffer affliction with the people of God, than to enjoy the pleasures of sin for a season; ²⁶ esteeming the reproach of Christ greater riches than the treasures of Egypt; for he looked for the reward.

²⁷ By faith he forsook Egypt, not fearing the wrath of the king; for he endured, as seeing him who is invisible.

²⁸ Through faith he has kept the passover, and the affusion of the blood, that he who destroyed the first-born might not touch them.

²⁹ By faith they passed through the Red sea as by dry land; which the Egyptians attempting were swallowed up.

³⁰ By faith the walls of Jericho fell, after they had been encompassed during seven days.

³¹ By faith Rahab the harlot did not perish with those who believed not, after having received the spies with peace.

³² And why say I more? For the time would fail me to tell of Gideon, of Barak and Samson and Jephthah, of David and Samuel and the prophets; ³³ who through faith subdued kingdoms, wrought righteousness, obtained promises, stopped the mouths of lions, ³⁴ quenched the power of fire, escaped the edge of the sword, from weakness were made strong, became mighty in war, turned to flight the armies of the aliens.

V. 31. *Or*, that were disobedient

CHAPTER XII.

³⁵ Women received their dead, by resurrection to life; and others were tortured, not accepting deliverance, that they might obtain a better resurrection. ³⁶ And others had trial of mockings, and scourgings, and, moreover, of bonds and imprisonment. ³⁷ They were stoned, they were sawn asunder, they were tempted, they were slain with the sword; they went about in sheep-skins and goats' skins, being destitute, afflicted, tormented; ³⁸ of whom the world was not worthy; wandering in deserts and mountains and caves, and the clefts of the earth.

³⁹ And all these, having obtained a good report through faith, did not receive the promise; ⁴⁰ God having provided something better concerning us, that they should not without us be made perfect.

XII. Therefore, let us also, having so great a cloud of witnesses surrounding us, lay aside every weight, and the easily besetting sin, and with patience run the race that is set before us, ² looking away to the author and finisher of the faith, Jesus; who for the joy set before him endured the cross, despising the shame, and has sat down on the right hand of the throne of God. ³ For consider him who has endured such contradiction by sinners against him, that ye become not weary, fainting in your souls.

⁴ Not yet did ye resist unto blood, contending against sin; ⁵ and ye have forgotten the exhortation, which discourses with you as with sons:

My son, despise not the chastening of the Lord,
Nor faint when reproved by him;
⁶ For whom the Lord loves he chastens,
And scourges every son whom he receives.

⁷ If ye endure chastening, God deals with you as with sons; for what son is there whom his father chastens not? ⁸ But if ye are without chastening, of which all have been made partakers, then are ye bastards, and not sons.

⁹ Furthermore, we had fathers of our flesh, who chastened us, and we gave them reverence; shall we not much rather be in

subjection to the Father of spirits, and live? ¹³ For they indeed for a few days chastened us as seemed good to them; but he for our profit, that we might be partakers of his holiness.

¹¹ Now all chastening for the present indeed seems not joyous, but grievous; but afterward, it yields the peaceable fruit of righteousness, to those who have been exercised thereby.

¹² Wherefore lift up the hands which hang down, and the feeble knees; ¹³ and make straight paths for your feet, that the lame be not turned out of the way, but rather be healed.

¹⁴ Follow peace with all, and holiness, without which no one shall see the Lord; ¹⁵ looking diligently, lest any one come short of the grace of God; lest any root of bitterness springing up trouble you, and the many be thereby defiled; ¹⁶ lest there be any fornicator, or profane person, as Esau, who for one meal sold his birthright. ¹⁷ For ye know that he also afterward, when he wished to inherit the blessing, was rejected; for he found no place of repentance, though he sought after it with tears.

¹⁸ For ye have not come to a mount that is touched, and burning with fire, nor to blackness, and darkness, and tempest, ¹⁹ and the sound of a trumpet, and the voice of words; which voice they who heard refused that more should be spoken to them; ²⁰ for they could not bear that which was commanded, Even if a beast touch the mountain, it shall be stoned; ²¹ and so terrible was the sight, that Moses said: I fear, and tremble. ²² But ye have come to mount Zion, and to the city of the living God, the heavenly Jerusalem, and to myriads of angels, ²³ to the general assembly and church of the first-born, who are enrolled in heaven, and to God the Judge of all, and to the spirits of just ones made perfect; ²⁴ and to Jesus the mediator of the new covenant, and to the blood of sprinkling, that speaks better than Abel.

²⁵ See that ye refuse not him who speaks; for if they did not escape, refusing him who declared the divine will on earth, much more shall not we, who turn away from him who speaks from heaven; ²⁶ whose voice then shook the earth; but now he

CHAPTER XIII.

has promised, saying: Yet once more I shake, not the earth only, but also heaven. ²⁷And this, Yet once more, signifies the removing of the things shaken, as of things that have been made, that the things which are not shaken may remain.

²⁸ Wherefore, receiving a kingdom which can not be shaken, let us have grace whereby we may serve God acceptably, with reverence and godly fear; ²⁹ for our God is a consuming fire.

XIII. Let brotherly love continue.
² Be not forgetful to entertain strangers; for thereby some entertained angels unawares.

³ Remember those in bonds, as bound with them; those in adversity, as being yourselves also in the body.

⁴ Marriage is honorable in all, and the bed undefiled; but fornicators and adulterers God will judge.

⁵ Let your disposition be without covetousness, and be content with what ye have; for he has said: I will never leave thee, nor forsake thee. ⁶ So that we boldly say:

The Lord is my helper, and I will not fear;
What shall man do to me?

⁷ Remember those who were your leaders, who spoke to you the word of God; considering the end of whose manner of life, imitate their faith.

⁸ Jesus Christ is yesterday and to-day the same, and forever. ⁹ Be not carried away with various and strange teachings; for it is good that the heart be established with grace, not with meats, which did not profit those who walked therein.

¹⁰ We have an altar, whereof they have no right to eat who serve the tabernacle. ¹¹ For the bodies of those beasts, whose blood is brought into the holy places by the high priest for sin, are burned without the camp. ¹² Wherefore Jesus also, that he might sanctify the people through his own blood, suffered without the gate. ¹³ So then, let us go forth to him without

---

V. 4. *Or*, Let marriage be honorable in all, and the bed be undefiled

the camp, bearing his reproach. ¹⁴ For here we have not an abiding city, but are seeking for that which is to come. ¹⁵ Through him, therefore, let us offer up the sacrifice of praise to God continually, that is, the fruit of lips giving thanks to his name. ¹⁶ But to do good and to communicate forget not; for with such sacrifices God is well pleased.

¹⁷ Obey those who are your leaders, and submit; for they watch for your souls, as those who shall give account; that they may do this with joy, and not with sighing, for that is unprofitable for you.

¹⁸ Pray for us; for we are persuaded that we have a good conscience, in all things desiring to deport ourselves well. ¹⁹ But I the more earnestly beseech you to do this, that I may the sooner be restored to you.

²⁰ Now the God of peace, who brought up from the dead our Lord Jesus, the great Shepherd of the sheep in virtue of the blood of an eternal covenant, ²¹ make you perfect in every good work to do his will, doing in you that which is well pleasing in his sight, through Jesus Christ; to whom be the glory, forever and ever. Amen.

²² But I beseech you, brethren, bear with the word of exhortation; for I wrote to you in few words.

²³ Know that the brother, Timothy, has been set at liberty; with whom, if he come shortly, I will see you.

²⁴ Salute all that are your leaders, and all the saints. Those of Italy salute you.

²⁵ Grace be with you all. Amen.

THE GENERAL LETTER OF JAMES.

I. James, a servant of God and of the Lord Jesus Christ, to the twelve tribes which are scattered abroad, greeting.
² Count it all joy, my brethren, when ye fall into various temptations; ³ knowing that the proving of your faith works patience. ⁴ But let patience have a perfect work, that ye may be perfect and entire, lacking in nothing.

⁵ But if any one of you is lacking in wisdom, let him ask of God, who gives to all liberally, and upbraids not, and it will be given him. ⁶ But let him ask in faith, nothing wavering; for he that wavers is like a wave of the sea driven by the wind and tossed. ⁷ For let not that man suppose that he shall receive anything from the Lord; ⁸ a double-minded man, unstable in all his ways.

⁹ Let the brother of low degree glory in that he is exalted; ¹⁰ but the rich, in that he is made low; because as the flower of the grass he will pass away. ¹¹ For the sun rose with the burning heat, and withered the grass, and its flower fell off, and the grace of its fashion perished; so also will the rich man fade away in his ways.

¹² Happy is the man that endures temptation; because, when he is approved, he will receive the crown of life, which He promised to those who love him.

¹³ Let no one say when he is tempted, I am tempted by God; for God can not be tempted with evil, and himself tempts no one. ¹⁴ But each one is tempted, when by his own lust he is drawn away and enticed. ¹⁵ Then lust, having conceived, brings forth sin; and sin, when completed, brings forth death.

¹⁶ Do not err, my beloved brethren. ¹⁷ Every good gift and every perfect gift is from above, coming down from the Father of the lights, with whom there is no variableness, or shadow of turning. ¹⁸ Of his own will he begot us with the word of truth, that we should be a kind of first-fruits of his creatures.

V. 1. *Gr.* which are in the dispersion

¹⁹ So that, my beloved brethren, let every man be swift to hear, slow to speak, slow to wrath; ²⁰ for the wrath of man works not the righteousness of God.

²¹ Wherefore, putting off all filthiness and excess of wickedness, receive with meekness the implanted word, which is able to save your souls.

²² But be doers of the word, and not hearers only, deceiving yourselves. ²³ For if any one is a hearer of the word, and not a doer, he is like to a man beholding his natural face in a mirror. ²⁴ For he beheld himself, and has gone away; and immediately he forgot what manner of man he was. ²⁵ But he who looked into the perfect law, the law of liberty, and remained thereby, being not a forgetful hearer, but a doer of work, this man shall be happy in his doing.

²⁶ If any one thinks that he is religious, and bridles not his tongue, but deceives his own heart, this man's religion is vain.

²⁷ Religion, pure and undefiled before God and the Father, is this: To visit the orphans and widows in their affliction; to keep himself unspotted from the world.

II. My brethren, hold not the faith of our Lord Jesus Christ, [the Lord] of glory, with respect of persons. ² For if there have come into your assembly a man with a gold ring, in gay clothing, and there have come in also a poor man in mean clothing; ³ and ye have respect to him that wears the gay clothing, and say: Sit thou here in a good place, and say to the poor man: Stand thou there, or, Sit under my footstool; ⁴ were ye not partial in yourselves, and become judges with evil thoughts?

⁵ Hearken, my beloved brethren. Did not God choose the poor as to this world to be rich in faith, and heirs of the kingdom which he promised to those who love him? ⁶ But ye dishonored the poor man. Do not the rich oppress you, and do not they drag you before the judgment-seats? ⁷ Do not they blaspheme the worthy name by which ye are called?

V. 5. *Or,* the poor in view of the world

CHAPTER II.

⁸ If indeed ye fulfill the royal law, according to the scripture, Thou shalt love thy neighbor as thyself, ye do well. ⁹ But if ye have respect to persons, ye commit sin, being convicted by the law as transgressors. ¹⁰ For whoever shall keep the whole law, and yet offend in one point, he is guilty of all. ¹¹ For he who said: Do not commit adultery, said also: Do not kill. Now if thou commit not adultery, yet if thou kill, thou art become a transgressor of the law. ¹² So speak, and so do, as they that shall be judged by the law of liberty. ¹³ For the judgment shall be without mercy, to him that showed no mercy. Mercy glories over judgment.

¹⁴ What does it profit, my brethren, if any one say that he has faith, and have not works? Can the faith save him? ¹⁵ But if a brother or a sister be naked, and destitute of daily food, ¹⁶ and one of you say to them: Depart in peace, be warmed, and be filled, but ye give them not the things needful for the body, what does it profit? ¹⁷ So also faith, if it has not works, is dead in itself. ¹⁸ But some will say: Thou hast faith, and I have works; show me thy faith without the works, and I will show thee the faith by my works. ¹⁹ Thou believest that God is one. Thou doest well; the demons also believe, and tremble. ²⁰ But wilt thou know, O vain man, that faith without works is dead?

²¹ Was not Abraham our father justified by works, when he offered Isaac his son upon the altar? ²² Thou seest that faith wrought with his works, and by works was faith made complete. ²³ And the scripture was fulfilled which says: Abraham believed God, and it was reckoned to him for righteousness; and he was called, Friend of God.

²⁴ Ye see that by works a man is justified, and not by faith only. ²⁵ And in like manner, was not also Rahab the harlot justified by works, when she received the messengers, and sent them out by another way? ²⁶ For as the body without the spirit is dead, so also faith without works is dead.

III. My brethren, be not many teachers, knowing that we shall receive greater condemnation. ² For in many things we all offend. If any one offends not in word, the same is a perfect man, able to bridle also the whole body.

³ Now if we put the bits into the horses' mouths, that they may obey us, we turn about also their whole body. ⁴ Behold also the ships, though they are so great, and driven by fierce winds, are turned about by a very small helm, whithersoever the steersman may desire. ⁵ So also the tongue is a little member, and boasts great things. Behold, how great a forest a little fire kindles! ⁶ And the tongue is a fire, that world of iniquity! The tongue among our members is that which defiles the whole body, and sets on fire the course of life, and is set on fire by hell. ⁷ For every nature of beasts and birds, of reptiles and things in the sea, is tamed, and has been tamed, by the nature of man. ⁸ But the tongue no man can tame; a restless evil, full of deadly poison. ⁹ Therewith we bless the Lord and Father; and therewith we curse men, who have been made after the likeness of God. ¹⁰ Out of the same mouth comes forth blessing and cursing. My brethren, these things ought not so to be. ¹¹ Does the fountain, out of the same opening, send forth the sweet and the bitter? ¹² Can a fig-tree, my brethren, bear olives, or a vine figs? Neither can salt water yield fresh.

¹³ Who is wise and endued with knowledge among you? Let him show, out of his good deportment, his works in meekness of wisdom. ¹⁴ But if ye have bitter envying and strife in your hearts, do not glory, and lie against the truth. ¹⁵ This wisdom is not one that comes down from above, but earthly, sensual, devilish. ¹⁶ For where there is emulation and strife, there is confusion and every evil work. ¹⁷ But the wisdom from above is first pure, then peaceable, forbearing, easily persuaded, full of mercy and good fruits, without partiality, and

V. 3. *Or, Now if we put the horses' bits into their mouths*

V. 15. Sensual: *more correctly*, natural; *compare*, the natural man, 1 **Cor.** ii., 14.

CHAPTER IV.

without hypocrisy. ¹⁸ And the fruit of righteousness is sown in peace, by those who work peace.

IV. From whence are wars, and from whence are fightings among you? Are they not from hence, from your lusts that war in your members? ² Ye desire, and have not; ye kill, and envy, and can not obtain; ye fight and war. Ye have not, because ye ask not; ³ ye ask, and receive not, because ye ask amiss, that ye may consume it upon your lusts.

⁴ Ye adulteresses, know ye not that the friendship of the world is enmity with God? Whoever therefore desires to be a friend of the world makes himself an enemy of God. ⁵ Do ye think that the Scripture says in vain, the spirit he made to dwell in us has jealous longings? ⁶ But he gives the more grace. Wherefore he says:

God resists the proud,
But gives grace to the humble.

⁷ Submit yourselves therefore to God. Resist the Devil, and he will flee from you. ⁸ Draw nigh to God, and he will draw nigh to you. Cleanse your hands, ye sinners; and purify your hearts, ye double-minded. ⁹ Be afflicted, and mourn, and weep; let your laughter be turned into mourning, and your joy into heaviness. ¹⁰ Humble yourselves in the sight of the Lord, and he will exalt you.

¹¹ Do not speak against one another, brethren. He that speaks against his brother, or judges his brother, speaks against the law, and judges the law. But if thou judge the law, thou art not a doer of the law, but a judge. ¹² One is the lawgiver and judge, he who is able to save and to destroy. Who art thou that judgest thy neighbor?

¹³ Come now, ye that say: To-day and to-morrow we will go into this city, and spend one year there, and buy and sell, and get gain; (¹⁴ whereas ye know not what belongs to the morrow; for what is your life? for ye are a vapor, that appears for a little time, and then vanishes away;) ¹⁵ instead of saying: If the Lord will, we shall both live, and do this or that. ¹⁶ But now ye glory in your boastings. All such glorying is evil. ¹⁷ There-

fore to him that knows to do good, and does it not, to him it is sin.

V. Come now, ye rich, weep, wailing for your miseries that are coming upon you. ² Your riches are corrupted, and your garments are become moth-eaten. ³ Your gold and silver is rusted; and the rust of them will be a witness against you, and will eat your flesh as fire. Ye heaped up treasure, in the last days.

⁴ Behold, the hire of the laborers who reaped your fields, which is fraudulently kept back by you, cries out; and the cries of those who reaped have entered into the ears of the Lord of Sabaoth. ⁵ Ye have been luxurious on the earth, and lived in pleasure; ye have nourished your hearts, in the day of slaughter. ⁶ Ye have condemned, ye have killed the just; he does not resist you.

⁷ Be patient therefore, brethren, until the coming of the Lord. Behold, the husbandman waits for the precious fruit of the earth, being patient over it, till it shall have received the early and latter rain. ⁸ Be ye also patient; establish your hearts, because the coming of the Lord draws nigh. ⁹ Murmur not against one another, brethren, that ye be not judged. Behold, the judge stands before the door. ¹⁰ Take, my brethren, the prophets, who spoke in the name of the Lord, for an example of affliction, and of patience. ¹¹ Behold, we count those happy who endure. Ye heard of the patience of Job, and saw the end of the Lord; that the Lord is very pitiful, and of tender mercy.

¹² But above all things, my brethren, swear not; neither by heaven, nor by the earth, nor by any other oath; but let your yea be yea, and your nay, nay; that ye fall not under condemnation.

¹³ Is any afflicted among you, let him pray. Is any cheerful, let him sing praise. ¹⁴ Is any sick among you, let him call for the elders of the church; and let them pray over him,

V. 4. Sabaoth: *that is*, hosts.
V. 11. *In some ancient copies:* See also the end of the Lord.

CHAPTER I.

anointing him with oil in the name of the Lord. ¹⁵And the prayer of faith will save the sick, and the Lord will raise him up; and even if he have committed sins, it will be forgiven him.

¹⁶ Confess therefore your trespasses to one another, and pray for one another, that ye may be healed. The earnest prayer of a righteous man avails much. ¹⁷ Elijah was a man of like nature with us; and he prayed earnestly that it might not rain, and it rained not on the earth for three years and six months. ¹⁸And again he prayed, and the heaven gave rain, and the earth brought forth her fruit.

¹⁹Brethren, if any one among you be led astray from the truth, and one convert him; ²⁰ let him know, that he who converts a sinner from the error of his way will save a soul from death, and will hide a multitude of sins.

THE FIRST GENERAL LETTER OF PETER.

I. Peter, an apostle of Jesus Christ, to the strangers scattered through Pontus, Galatia, Cappadocia, Asia, and Bithynia; ² chosen according to the foreknowledge of God the Father, in sanctification of the Spirit, unto obedience and sprinkling of the blood of Jesus Christ: Grace and peace be multiplied to you.

³ Blessed be the God and Father of our Lord Jesus Christ, who according to his abundant mercy begot us again unto a living hope through the resurrection of Jesus Christ from the dead; ⁴ unto an inheritance imperishable, and undefiled, and unfading, reserved in heaven for you, ⁵ who by the power of God are kept through faith, unto a salvation ready to be revealed in the last time. ⁶ Wherein ye greatly rejoice, though now for a little time, if need be, made sorrowful by manifold

---

V. 1. *Or*, the strangers of the dispersion
V. 3. *Or*, into a living hope

I. PETER.

trials; ⁷ that the proof of your faith, much more precious than gold that perishes, but is proved by fire, may be found unto praise and glory and honor at the revelation of Jesus Christ; ⁸ whom having not seen ye love; in whom, though now ye see him not, yet believing, ye rejoice with joy unspeakable and full of glory; ⁹ receiving the end of your faith, the salvation of your souls.

¹⁰ Concerning which salvation the prophets diligently sought and searched, who prophesied of the grace toward you; ¹¹ searching as to what or what manner of time the Spirit of Christ which was in them signified, when it testified beforehand the sufferings destined for Christ, and the glories that should follow; ¹² to whom it was revealed, that not to themselves, but to you they were ministering them, which now have been announced to you, through those who brought you the good news by the Holy Spirit sent from heaven; which things angels desire to look into.

¹³ Wherefore, girding up the loins of your mind, be sober, and hope perfectly for the grace that is to be brought to you at the revelation of Jesus Christ; ¹⁴ as children of obedience, not conforming yourselves to the former lusts in your ignorance; ¹⁵ but as he who called you is holy, be ye yourselves holy in all your deportment; ¹⁶ because it is written: Y e s h a l l b e h o l y, f o r I a m h o l y.

¹⁷ And if ye call him Father, who without respect of persons judges according to each one's work, pass the time of your sojourning in fear; ¹⁸ knowing that not with perishable things, silver and gold, ye were redeemed from your vain course of life received by tradition from your fathers, ¹⁹ but with the precious blood of Christ, as of a lamb without blemish and without spot; ²⁰ who was foreknown indeed before the foundation of the world, but manifested in these last times for you, ²¹ who through him believe on God, who raised him from the dead, and gave him glory; so that your faith and hope are on God.

V. 17. *Or*, if ye call upon him as Father

CHAPTER II.

²² Having purified your souls in obeying the truth unto unfeigned brotherly love, love one another from the heart fervently ; ²³ being born again, not of perishable seed, but of imperishable, through the word of God, which lives and abides forever. ²⁴ Because,
All flesh is as grass,
And all its glory as the flower of grass.
The grass withered, and its flower fell off ;
²⁵ But the word of the Lord abides forever.
And this is the word which was preached to you.

II. Laying aside therefore all malice, and all guile, and hypocrisies, and envyings, and all backbitings, ² as newborn babes, long for the spiritual, unadulterated milk, that ye thereby may grow unto salvation ; ³ if indeed ye tasted that the Lord is gracious ; ⁴ to whom coming, a living stone, disallowed indeed by men, but with God chosen, honored, ⁵ ye yourselves also, as living stones, are built up a spiritual house, a holy priesthood, to offer up spiritual sacrifices, acceptable to God through Jesus Christ. ⁶ Because it is contained in the Scripture : Behold, I lay in Zion a chief corner-stone, chosen, honored ; and he that believes on him shall not be put to shame.

⁷ To you therefore who believe is the honor ; but to the disobedient, the stone which the builders disallowed, the same is become the head of the corner, ⁸ and a stone of stumbling, and a rock of offense, who stumble, being disobedient to the word ; to which they were also appointed.

⁹ But ye are a chosen generation, a royal priesthood, a holy nation, a people for a possession ; that ye should show forth the excellencies of him who called you out of darkness into his marvelous light ; ¹⁰ who once were not a people, but are now the people of God ; who had not obtained mercy, but now have obtained mercy.

V. 5. *Or,* be ye yourselves also . . . built up

¹¹ Beloved, I exhort you as sojourners and strangers, to abstain from fleshly lusts, which war against the soul ; ¹² having your deportment honorable among the Gentiles ; that, wherein they speak against you as evil-doers, they may from your good works, beholding them, glorify God in the day of visitation.

¹³ Submit yourselves to every human institution, for the Lord's sake ; whether to the king, as pre-eminent, ¹⁴ or to governors as being sent by him for the punishment of evil-doers, and the praise of those who do well. ¹⁵ For so is the will of God, that with well-doing ye may put to silence the ignorance of the foolish men ; ¹⁶ as free, and as not having your freedom for a vail of wickedness, but as God's servants.

¹⁷ Honor all men ; love the brotherhood ; fear God ; honor the king ; ¹⁸ ye servants, being in subjection to your masters with all fear, not only to the good and reasonable, but also to the perverse. ¹⁹ For this is acceptable, if a man for conscience toward God endures griefs, suffering wrongfully. ²⁰ For what glory is it, if when ye are beaten for your faults, ye shall take it patiently? But if when ye do well, and suffer for it, ye take it patiently, this is acceptable with God. ²¹ For to this ye were called ; because Christ also suffered for you, leaving you an example, that ye should follow his steps ; ²² who committed no sin, neither was guile found in his mouth ; ²³ who, when he was reviled, reviled not again ; when he suffered, threatened not ; but committed it to him who judges righteously ; ²⁴ who himself bore our sins in his own body on the tree, that we, having died to our sins, should live to righteousness ; by whose stripes ye were healed. ²⁵ For ye were going astray like sheep ; but have returned now unto the Shepherd and Overseer of your souls.

III. In like manner, ye wives, being in subjection to your own husbands ; that even if any obey not the word, they may without the word be won by the deportment of their

---

V. 19. *Or*, from a consciousness of God

CHAPTER III.

wives, ² when they behold your chaste deportment coupled with fear. ³ Whose adorning, let it not be the outward one of braiding the hair, and of wearing golden ornaments, or of putting on apparel; ⁴ but the hidden man of the heart, in that which is imperishable of the meek and quiet spirit, which in the sight of God is of great price. ⁵ For so in the old time the holy women also, who hoped in God, adorned themselves, being in subjection to their own husbands, ⁶ (as Sarah obeyed Abraham, calling him lord; of whom ye became children,) doing good, and fearing no alarm.

⁷ Ye husbands, in like manner, dwelling with them according to knowledge, giving honor to the female, as the weaker vessel, as also heirs together of the grace of life; that your prayers be not hindered.

⁸ Finally, all being of one mind, sympathizing, loving the brethren, tender-hearted, humble-minded; ⁹ not rendering evil for evil, or railing for railing; but on the contrary blessing, because to this end ye were called, that ye might inherit blessing.

¹⁰ For he who desires to love life, and to see good days, let him refrain his tongue from evil, and his lips from speaking guile; ¹¹ let him turn away from evil, and do good; let him seek peace, and pursue it. ¹² Because the eyes of the Lord are upon the righteous, and his ears are toward their supplications; but the face of the Lord is against those who do evil. ¹³ And who is he that shall harm you, if ye are followers of that which is good? ¹⁴ But if ye even suffer for righteousness' sake, happy are ye; but fear not with their fear, nor be troubled; ¹⁵ but sanctify Christ as Lord in your hearts; ready always to give an answer to every one that asks you a reason of the hope that is in you, with meekness and fear; ¹⁶ having a good conscience, that wherein they speak against you as evil-doers, they may be ashamed that falsely accuse your good deportment in Christ. ¹⁷ For it is better, if

it be the will of God, that ye suffer for well-doing, than for evil-doing. ¹⁸ Because Christ also suffered once for sins, the just for the unjust, that he might bring us to God, being put to death in the flesh, but made alive by the Spirit; ¹⁹ in which also he went and preached to the spirits in prison, ²⁰ who were disobedient in times past, when the long-suffering of God waited in the days of Noah, while the ark was preparing, wherein a few, that is, eight souls, were saved through water; ²¹ which in an antitype, immersion, now saves us also (not the putting away of the filth of the flesh, but the requirement of a good conscience toward God), by the resurrection of Jesus Christ; ²² who is on the right hand of God, having gone into heaven, angels and authorities and powers being made subject to him.

IV. Christ then having suffered for us in the flesh, do ye also arm yourselves with the same mind; because he who suffered in the flesh has ceased from sin; ²that ye no longer may live the remaining time in the flesh by the lusts of men, but by the will of God. ³For the time past suffices us to have wrought the will of the Gentiles, when we walked in wantonness, lusts, excess of wine, revelings, carousings, and unhallowed idolatries; ⁴ at which thing they are astonished, as ye run not with them to the same excess of riot, speaking evil of you; ⁵ who shall give account to him who is ready to judge the living and the dead. ⁶ For to this end was the good news preached also to those who are dead, that they might indeed be judged according to men in the flesh, but may live according to God in the spirit.

⁷ But the end of all things is at hand. Be therefore sober, and watch unto prayer; ⁸but above all things having your love toward one another fervent, because l o v e c o v e r s a m u l t i t u d e of s i n s; ⁹hospitable to one another, without grudging; ¹⁰according as each received a gift, ministering the same to one another, as good stewards of the manifold grace of God; ¹¹if any one speaks, as [uttering] God's oracles; if any one ministers, as of the ability which God bestows; that

CHAPTER V.

God in all things may be glorified, through Jesus Christ, to whom is the glory and the dominion, forever and ever. Amen.

¹² Beloved, be not astonished at the fiery test taking place among you to prove you, as though a strange thing were befalling you; ¹³ but, in so far as ye share in Christ's sufferings, rejoice; that also, at the revelation of his glory, ye may rejoice with exceeding joy. ¹⁴ If ye are reproached for the name of Christ, happy are ye; because the spirit of glory and of God rests upon you; [on their part he is evil spoken of, but on your part he is glorified.]

¹⁵ For let none of you suffer as a murderer, or a thief, or an evil-doer, or as a busy-body in other men's matters; ¹⁶ but if as a Christian, let him not be ashamed, but let him glorify God in this name. ¹⁷ Because the time is come that judgment should begin from the house of God; but if it begin first from us, what shall be the end of those who obey not the gospel of God? ¹⁸ And if the righteous is with difficulty saved, where shall the ungodly and the sinner appear?

¹⁹ Wherefore let those also, who suffer according to the will of God, commit the keeping of their souls to him in well-doing, as to a faithful Creator.

V. The elders among you I exhort, who am a fellow-elder, and a witness of the sufferings of Christ, who am also a partaker of the glory that shall be revealed; ² tend the flock of God which is among you, overseeing it not by constraint but willingly, not for base gain but with good will; ³ neither as being lords over the heritage, but being examples to the flock. ⁴ And when the chief Shepherd is manifested, ye shall receive the unfading crown of glory.

⁵ In like manner, ye younger, submit yourselves to the elder. Yea, all of you submitting to one another, gird yourselves with humility; because, God resists the proud, but gives grace to the humble. ⁶ Humble yourselves therefore under the mighty hand of God, that he may

---

V. 14. *The words in brackets are omitted in the best copies.*

exalt you in due time; casting all your care upon him, because he cares for you.

⁸ Be sober, be watchful. Your adversary the Devil, as a roaring lion, walks about, seeking whom he may devour; ⁹ whom resist, steadfast in the faith, knowing that the same sufferings are being accomplished in your brethren that are in the world.

¹⁰ But the God of all grace, who called you to his eternal glory in Christ Jesus, after ye have suffered a little while, make you perfect, establish, strengthen, settle you. ¹¹ To him be the glory, and the dominion, forever and ever. Amen.

¹² By Silvanus, the faithful brother, as I consider, I wrote to you in few words, exhorting, and testifying that this is the true grace of God, wherein ye stand.

¹³ The [church that is] in Babylon, chosen with you, salutes you; and Mark, my son.

¹⁴ Salute one another with a kiss of love. Peace to you all, that are in Christ.

THE SECOND GENERAL LETTER OF PETER.

I. Simon Peter, a servant and apostle of Jesus Christ, to those who have obtained like precious faith with us in the righteousness of our God and Savior Jesus Christ: ² Grace and peace be multiplied to you, in the knowledge of God, and of Jesus our Lord.

³ Seeing that his divine power has given us all things that pertain to life and godliness, through the knowledge of him who called us by his own glory and might; ⁴ through which he has given us exceeding great and precious promises, that by these ye may become partakers of the divine nature, having escaped from the corruption that is in the world through lust;

V. 13. *Or*, The sister chosen with you, in Babylon, salutes you

CHAPTER I.

⁵ yea for this very reason, giving all diligence, add to your faith fortitude ; and to fortitude, knowledge ; ⁶ and to knowledge, self-control ; and to self-control, patience ; and to patience, godliness ; ⁷ and to godliness, brotherly kindness ; and to brotherly kindness, love. ⁸ For if these things are in you, and abound, they cause that ye shall not be inactive nor unfruitful in attaining to the full knowledge of our Lord Jesus Christ. ⁹ But he that lacks these things is blind, not seeing afar off, having forgotten the cleansing away of his old sins.

¹⁰ Wherefore the rather, brethren, give diligence to make your calling and election sure ; for if ye do these things, ye shall never fall. ¹¹ For so shall be richly ministered to you the entrance into the everlasting kingdom of our Lord and Savior Jesus Christ.

¹² Wherefore, I will not neglect to put you always in remembrance of these things, though ye know them, and are established in the truth that is with you. ¹³ But I think it right, so long as I am in this tabernacle, to stir you up by putting you in remembrance ; ¹⁴ knowing that I must soon put off my tabernacle, as also our Lord Jesus Christ showed me. ¹⁵ Moreover I will endeavor that at all times ye may be able after my departure to call these things to mind.

¹⁶ For we did not follow cunningly devised fables, when we made known to you the power and coming of our Lord Jesus Christ, but had been eye-witnesses of his majesty. ¹⁷ For he received from God the Father honor and glory, when such a voice was borne to him from the excellent glory : This is my beloved Son, in whom I am well pleased ; ¹⁸ and this voice we heard borne from heaven, being with him in the holy mount. ¹⁹ And we have more sure the prophetic word ; to which ye do well that ye take heed, as to a lamp shining in a dark place, until the day dawn, and the day-star arise in your hearts ; ²⁰ knowing this first, that no prophecy of the Scripture comes of private interpretation ; ²¹ for prophecy was never brought

---

V. 5. *Or*, furnish in your faith fortitude, and in your fortitude knowledge, *etc.*

V. 14. *Or*, that the putting off of my tabernacle is speedy

II. PETER.

by the will of man; but moved by the Holy Spirit, men spoke from God.

II. But there were false prophets also among the people, as there will be false teachers among you also, who stealthily will bring in destructive factions, even denying as Master him who bought them, bringing upon themselves swift destruction. ² And many will follow their dissolute ways; by reason of whom the way of truth will be evil spoken of. ³ And in covetousness will they with feigned words make merchandise of you; for whom the judgment from of old lingers not, and their destruction slumbers not.

⁴ For if God spared not angels, having sinned, but casting them down to hell delivered them over to chains of darkness, reserved unto judgment; ⁵ and spared not the old world, but kept Noah the eighth person, a preacher of righteousness, bringing the flood on the world of ungodly men, ⁶ and turning to ashes the cities of Sodom and Gomorrah condemned them to overthrow, having made them an example of those who should afterward live ungodly; ⁷ and delivered righteous Lot, wearied out with the lewd conduct of the lawless; (⁸ for that righteous man, dwelling among them, with seeing and hearing vexed his righteous soul from day to day with their unlawful deeds;) ⁹ the Lord knows how to deliver the godly out of temptation, and to reserve the unjust under punishment to the day of judgment; ¹⁰ but chiefly those who walk after the flesh in the lust of uncleanness, and despise dominion. Presumptuous, self-willed, they are not afraid to rail at dignities; ¹¹ whereas angels, being greater in strength and power, bring not a railing judgment against them before the Lord.

¹² But these, as natural brute beasts born to be taken and destroyed, railing at things that they understand not, shall utterly perish in their own corruption, ¹³ receiving the wages of unrighteousness, as they who account reveling for a day pleas-

---

V. 4. *In some ancient copies:* pits of darkness

V. 12. *In some ancient copies:* as brute beasts, born naturally to be taken

CHAPTER III.

ure; spots, and blemishes, reveling in their own deceits while feasting with you; ¹⁴ having eyes full of the adulteress, and that cease not from sin; alluring unstable souls; having a heart exercised in covetousness; children of a curse; ¹⁵ forsaking the right way, they went astray, following the way of Balaam the son of Bosor, who loved the wages of unrighteousness, ¹⁶ but was rebuked for his iniquity; the dumb ass, speaking with man's voice, forbade the madness of the prophet.

¹⁷ These are wells without water, mists driven by a tempest, to whom the blackness of darkness is reserved forever. ¹⁸ For, speaking swelling words of vanity, in lusts of the flesh they allure, by wanton ways, such as partly escape those who live in error; ¹⁹ promising them liberty, while they themselves are servants of corruption; for by what a man is overcome, by the same he is also brought into bondage. ²⁰ For if, having escaped the pollutions of the world through the knowledge of the Lord and Savior Jesus Christ, but having again become entangled therein they are overcome, the last state is become worse with them than the first. ²¹ For it were better for them not to have known the way of righteousness, than, having known it, to turn back from the holy commandment delivered to them. ²² But it has happened to them according to the true proverb: A d o g, r e t u r n e d to h i s o w n v o m i t; and, A s o w t h a t w a s w a s h e d, to t h e w a l l o w i n g i n t h e m i r e.

III. This second letter, beloved, I now write to you; in both which I stir up your pure mind by putting you in remembrance; ² that ye may be mindful of the words spoken before by the holy prophets, and of the commandment of the Lord and Savior by your apostles; ³ knowing this first, that there shall come in the last of the days scoffers, in their scoffings, walking after their own lusts, ⁴ and saying: Where is the promise of his coming? for from the day the fathers fell asleep, all things so continue, from the beginning of the creation. ⁵ For of this they willingly are ignorant, that by the word of God there were heavens of old, and earth framed out of water and by means of water, ⁶ whereby the world that then was, being overflowed with water, perished; ⁷ but the heavens that now are, and the earth, by his word are kept in store, being reserved for fire unto the day of judgment and of perdition of ungodly men.

⁸ But, beloved, be not ignorant of this one thing, that one day is with the Lord as a thousand years, and a thousand years as one day. ⁹ The Lord is not tardy in respect to the promise, as some account tardiness; but is long-suffering toward us, not wishing that any should perish, but that all should come to repentance. ¹⁰ But the day of the Lord will come as a thief; in which the heavens will pass away with a rushing noise, and the elements will be dissolved with burning heat, and the earth and the works therein will be burned up.

¹¹ Seeing then that all these things are dissolving, what manner of men ought ye to be, in all holy deportment and godliness; ¹² looking for and hastening the coming of the day of God, because of which the heavens being on fire will be dissolved, and the elements will melt with burning heat? ¹³ But, according to his promise, we look for new heavens and a new earth, wherein dwells righteousness.

¹⁴ Wherefore, beloved, seeing that ye look for these things, be diligent that ye may be found without spot and blameless in his sight, in peace. ¹⁵ And the long-suffering of our Lord account salvation; as also our beloved brother Paul, according to the wisdom given him, wrote to you; ¹⁶ as also in all his letters, speaking in them of these things; in which things are some that are hard to be understood, which they that are unlearned and unstable wrest, as also the other Scriptures, unto their own destruction.

¹⁷ Ye therefore, beloved, seeing ye know beforehand, beware lest, being carried away with the error of the lawless, ye fall from your own steadfastness. ¹⁸ But grow in the grace and knowledge of our Lord and Savior Jesus Christ. To him be the glory, both now and forever. Amen.

V. 9. *In some ancient copies:* toward you

THE FIRST GENERAL LETTER OF JOHN.

I. That which was from the beginning, that which we have heard, that which we have seen with our eyes, that which we looked upon, and our hands handled, concerning the Word of life; (² and the life was manifested, and we have seen, and bear witness, and report to you the eternal life, which was with the Father, and was manifested to us;) ³ that which we have seen and have heard we report to you also, that ye also may have fellowship with us; and indeed our fellowship is with the Father, and with his Son Jesus Christ. ⁴ And these things we write to you, that your joy may be full.

⁵ And this is the message which we have heard from him, and announce to you, That God is light, and in him there is no darkness.

⁶ If we say that we have fellowship with him, and walk in the darkness, we lie, and do not the truth; ⁷ but if we walk in the light, as he is in the light, we have fellowship with one another, and the blood of Jesus Christ his Son cleanses us from all sin.

⁸ If we say that we have not sin, we deceive ourselves, and the truth is not in us. ⁹ If we confess our sins, he is faithful and righteous, that he may forgive us our sins, and cleanse us from all unrighteousness. ¹⁰ If we say that we have not sinned, we make him a liar, and his word is not in us.

II. My little children, these things I write to you, that ye may not sin. And if any one have sinned, we have an advocate with the Father, Jesus Christ the righteous. ² And he is a propitiation for our sins; and not for ours only, but also for the whole world.

³ And in this we know that we know him, if we keep his commandments. ⁴ He that says, I know him, and keeps not his commandments, is a liar, and the truth is not in him. ⁵ But

---

V. 7. *Some ancient copies omit :* Christ

whoever keeps his word, of a truth in him the love of God is perfected. In this we know that we are in him. ⁶ He that says he abides in him ought, as he walked, himself also so to walk.

⁷ Beloved, I write not to you a new commandment, but an old commandment which ye had from the beginning. The old commandment is the word which ye heard from the beginning. ⁸ Again, a new commandment I write to you, which thing is true in him and in you; because the darkness is passing away, and the true light now shines. ⁹ He that says he is in the light, and hates his brother, is in the darkness until now. ¹⁰ He that loves his brother abides in the light, and there is no occasion of stumbling in him. ¹¹ But he that hates his brother is in the darkness, and walks in the darkness, and knows not where he goes, because the darkness blinded his eyes.

¹² I write to you, little children, because your sins have been forgiven you for his name's sake. ¹³ I write to you, fathers, because ye know him that was from the beginning. I write to you, young men, because ye have overcome the evil one.

I wrote to you, little children, because ye know the Father. ¹⁴ I wrote to you, fathers, because ye know him that was from the beginning. I wrote to you, young men, because ye are strong, and the word of God abides in you, and ye have overcome the evil one.

¹⁵ Love not the world, neither the things in the world. If any one loves the world, the love of the Father is not in him. ¹⁶ Because all that is in the world, the lust of the flesh, and the lust of the eyes, and the empty pomp of life, is not of the Father, but is of the world. ¹⁷ And the world is passing away, and the lust thereof; but he that does the will of God abides forever.

¹⁸ Little children, it is the last time; and as ye heard that antichrist should come, even now many antichrists have arisen; from whence we know that it is the last time. ¹⁹ They went out from among us, but they were not of us; for if they had been of us, they would have remained with us; but it was in order that they might be made manifest, that all are not of us.

V. 7 *(second sentence); ancient copies omit:* from the beginning

CHAPTER III.

²⁰ And ye have an anointing from the Holy One, and know all things. ²¹ I wrote not to you because ye do not know the truth, but because ye know it, and because no lie is of the truth. ²² Who is the liar, but he that denies that Jesus is the Christ? This is the antichrist, who denies the Father and the Son. ²³ Every one that denies the Son, the same has not the Father; he that acknowledges the Son has also the Father.

²⁴ What ye heard from the beginning, let it abide in you. If what ye heard from the beginning shall abide in you, ye also will abide in the Son, and in the Father. ²⁵ And this is the promise which he himself promised to us, the life eternal.

²⁶ These things I wrote to you concerning those who seduce you. ²⁷ And the anointing which ye received from him abides in you, and ye have no need that any one teach you; but as the same anointing teaches you concerning all things, and is truth, and is not a lie, and even as it taught you, abide in him.

²⁸ And now, little children, abide in him; that, if he should be manifested, we may have confidence, and not turn away from him with shame at his coming. ²⁹ If ye know that he is righteous, ye know that every one that does righteousness has been begotten of him.

III. Behold what manner of love the Father has given to us, that we should be called children of God. For this cause the world knows not us, because it knew not him. ² Beloved, now are we the children of God, and it was never yet manifested what we shall be. We know that if it shall be manifested, we shall be like him, because we shall see him as he is. ³ And every one, that has this hope on him, purifies himself even as he is pure. ⁴ Every one that commits sin also commits transgression of law; and sin is transgression of law. ⁵ And ye know that he was manifested that he might take away our sins; and in him is no sin. ⁶ Every one that abides in him sins not; whoever sins has not seen him, neither has known him.

V. 5. Our *is omitted in some ancient copies.*

⁷ Little children, let no one deceive you. He that does righteousness is righteous, even as he is righteous. ⁸ He that commits sin is of the Devil; because the Devil sins from the beginning. To this end the Son of God was manifested, that he might destroy the works of the Devil. ⁹ Whoever has been begotten of God does not commit sin; because his seed abides in him; and he can not sin, because he has been begotten of God. ¹⁰ In this are manifest the children of God, and the children of the Devil. Every one that does not righteousness is not of God, neither he that loves not his brother; ¹¹ because this is the message that ye heard from the beginning, that we should love one another · ¹² Not as Cain was of the evil one, and slew his brother. And wherefore did he slay him? Because his own works were evil, and his brother's righteous. ¹³ Wonder not, brethren, if the world hates you.

¹⁴ We know that we have passed out of death into life, because we love the brethren. He that loves not his brother abides in death. ¹⁵ Every one that hates his brother is a murderer; and ye know that no murderer has eternal life abiding in him. ¹⁶ In this we know love, that he laid down his life for us; and we ought to lay down our lives for the brethren. ¹⁷ But whoever has the world's sustenance, and sees his brother having need, and shuts up his pity from him, how abides the love of God in him?

¹⁸ Little children, let us not love in word, neither in tongue; but in deed and in truth. ¹⁹ And in this we shall know that we are of the truth, and shall assure our hearts before him. ²⁰ Because if our heart accuse us, God is greater than our heart, and knows all things. ²¹ Beloved, if our heart accuse us not, we have confidence toward God. ²² And whatever we ask, we receive of him, because we keep his commandments, and do the things that are pleasing in his sight. ²³ And this is his

---

V. 14. *Ancient copies omit:* his brother

V. 15. *Or,* is a man-killer

VV. 19, 20. *Or,* and we shall assure our hearts before him, whatever our heart may accuse us of, because God is greater than our heart and knows all things.

CHAPTER IV.

commandment, that we should believe on the name of his Son Jesus Christ, and should love one another, as he gave us commandment. ²¹ And he that keeps his commandments abides in him, and he in him. And in this we know that he abides in us, from the Spirit which he gave us.

IV. Beloved, believe not every spirit, but try the spirits whether they are of God; because many false prophets have gone forth into the world. ² In this ye know the Spirit of God: ³ Every spirit that acknowledges that Jesus Christ is come in the flesh, is of God; and every spirit that does not acknowledge Jesus, is not of God; and this is that of the antichrist, of which ye have heard that it should come; and now, it is already in the world.

⁴ Ye are of God, little children, and have overcome them; because greater is he who is in you, than he who is in the world. ⁵ They are of the world; for this cause they speak of the world, and the world hears them. ⁶ We are of God; he that knows God, hears us; he that is not of God, hears us not. From this we know the spirit of truth, and the spirit of error.

⁷ Beloved, let us love one another; because love is of God, and every one that loves has been begotten of God, and knows God. ⁸ He that loves not, knew not God; because God is love. ⁹ In this was manifested the love of God in respect to us, that God has sent his only begotten Son into the world, that we might live through him. ¹⁰ Herein is love, not that we loved God, but that he loved us, and sent his Son, a propitiation for our sins.

¹¹ Beloved, if God so loved us, we also ought to love one another. ¹² No man has ever seen God. If we love one another, God abides in us, and the love of him is perfected in us. ¹³ In this we know that we abide in him, and he in us, because he has given us of his Spirit. ¹⁴ And we have seen, and bear witness, that the Father has sent forth the Son, a Savior of the world. ¹⁵ Whoever acknowledges that Jesus is the Son of God, God abides in him, and he in God. ¹⁶ And we have known, and have believed, the love that God has in

I. JOHN.

respect to us. God is love; and he that abides in love abides in God, and God in him.

[17] In this has love been perfected with us, that we have confidence in the day of judgment; because as he is, we also are in this world. [18] There is no fear in love; but perfect love casts out fear, because fear has torment; and he that fears is not made perfect in love. [19] We love, because he first loved us. [20] If any one say, I love God, and hates his brother, he is a liar; for he that loves not his brother whom he has seen, how can he love God whom he has not seen? [21] And this commandment we have from him, that he who loves God love also his brother.

V. Every one who believes that Jesus is the Christ has been begotten of God; and every one that loves him who begot, loves also him that has been begotten of him. [2] In this we know that we love the children of God, when we love God, and do his commandments. [3] For this is the love of God, that we keep his commandments. And his commandments are not burdensome; [4] because all that is begotten of God overcomes the world; and this is the victory that overcomes the world, our faith. [5] Who is he that overcomes the world, but he that believes that Jesus is the Son of God?

[6] This is he who came by water and blood, Jesus the Christ; not in the water only, but in the water and in the blood. And the Spirit is that which bears witness, because the Spirit is the truth. [7] For there are three who bear witness; the Spirit, and the water, and the blood; [8] and the three agree in the one. [9] If we receive the witness of men, the witness of God is greater; for this is the witness of God, that he has borne witness concerning his Son. [10] He that believes on the Son of God has the witness in himself; he that believes not God has made him a liar; because he has not believed in the witness which God has borne concerning his Son. [11] And this

---

V. 17. *Or*, toward us V. 18. *Or*, has punishment
V. 8. *Or*, in the one thing. (*The words omitted are wanting in all ancient copies.*)

CHAPTER 1.

is the witness, that God gave to us eternal life, and this life is in his Son. ¹² He that has the Son has the life ; he that has not the Son of God has not the life.

¹³ These things I wrote to you, that ye may know that ye have eternal life, who believe on the name of the Son of God.

¹⁴ And this is the confidence that we have toward him, that, if we ask anything according to his will, he hears us. ¹⁵ And if we know that he hears us, whatever we ask, we know that we have the petitions which we have asked of him.

¹⁶ If any one see his brother sin a sin not unto death, he shall ask, and he will give him life,—to those who sin not unto death. There is a sin unto death ; for that I do not say that he shall pray.

¹⁷ All unrighteousness is sin ; and there is a sin not unto death.

¹⁸ We know that every one who has been begotten of God sins not ; but he that was begotten of God keeps himself, and the evil one touches him not.

¹⁹ We know that we are of God, and the whole world is lying in the evil one. ²⁰ And we know that the Son of God is come, and has given us understanding, that we may know the True One ; and we are in the True One, in his Son Jesus Christ. This is the true God, and eternal life.

²¹ Little children, keep yourselves from the idols.

THE SECOND LETTER OF JOHN.

THE elder to the elect lady, and to her children, whom I love in truth,—and not I alone but also all that know the truth,— ² for the sake of the truth, which abides in us, and will be with us forever : ³ Grace, mercy, peace, shall be with you, from God the Father, and from Jesus Christ, the Son of the Father, in truth and love.

⁴ I rejoiced greatly, that I have found of thy children walking

in truth, as we received commandment from the Father. ⁵ And now I beseech thee, lady, not as writing to thee a new commandment, but that which we had from the beginning, that we love one another. ⁶ And this is love, that we walk according to his commandment; and this is the commandment, as ye heard from the beginning, that ye should walk in it. ⁷ Because many deceivers went out into the world, who acknowledge not that Jesus Christ comes in the flesh. This is the deceiver, and the antichrist.

⁸ Look to yourselves, that ye lose not the things which we wrought, but receive a full reward. ⁹ Every one who transgresses, and abides not in the teaching of Christ, has not God. He that abides in the teaching, he has both the Father and the Son.

¹⁰ If any one comes to you, and brings not this teaching, receive him not into your house, and do not bid him good speed; ¹¹ for he that bids him good speed shares in his evil deeds.

¹² Having many things to write to you, I would not [write] with paper and ink; but I hope to come to you, and to speak face to face, that our joy may be full. ¹³ The children of thy elect sister salute thee.

THE THIRD LETTER OF JOHN.

The elder to Gaius the beloved, whom I love in truth.

² Beloved, concerning all things I pray that thou mayest prosper and be in health, as thy soul prospers. ³ For I rejoiced greatly, when brethren came and bore witness to thy truth, as thou walkest in the truth. ⁴ I have no greater joy than this, to hear of my children walking in the truth.

⁵ Beloved, thou doest a faithful thing, in whatever thou doest

---

V. 9. *In ancient copies:* Every one who goes onward, and abides not

CHAPTER I.

to the brethren, and that to strangers, ⁶who bore witness to thy love before the church; whom if thou send forward on their journey worthily of God, thou wilt do well; ⁷for on behalf of the NAME they went forth, taking nothing of the Gentiles. ⁸We therefore ought to sustain such persons, that we may become fellow-workers for the truth.

⁹I wrote somewhat to the church; but Diotrephes, who loves to have the pre-eminence among them, receives us not. ¹⁰Therefore, if I come, I will bring to remembrance his deeds which he does, prating against us with evil words. And not content therewith, neither does he himself receive the brethren, and those who are willing he forbids, and casts them out of the church.

¹¹Beloved, do not imitate what is evil, but what is good. He that does good, is of God; he that does evil, has not seen God.

¹²To Demetrius, testimony has been borne by all, and by the truth itself; yea, we also bear witness, and thou knowest that our witness is true.

¹³I had many things to write to thee, but I wish not to write to thee with ink and pen; ¹⁴but I hope immediately to see thee, and we shall speak face to face.

Peace be to thee. The friends salute thee. Salute the friends, by name.

THE GENERAL LETTER OF JUDE.

JUDE, a servant of Jesus Christ, and brother of James, to the called, beloved in God the Father, and kept by Jesus Christ: ²Mercy, and peace, and love, be multiplied to you.

³Beloved, while giving all diligence to write to you concerning the common salvation, I found it needful for me to write to

---

V. 1. *Or*, kept for Jesus Christ

you exhorting to contend earnestly for the faith, delivered once for all to the saints. ⁴ For there crept in stealthily certain men, who of old were appointed beforehand to this condemnation, ungodly men, turning the grace of our God into wantonness, and denying the only Master, and our Lord Jesus Christ.

⁵ But I wish to remind you, as once knowing all, that Jesus, having saved the people out of the land of Egypt, afterward destroyed those who believed not. ⁶ And angels who kept not their principality, but left their own habitation, he has kept in everlasting chains under darkness, unto the judgment of the great day. ⁷ As Sodom and Gomorrah, and the cities about them, in like manner with them giving themselves over to fornication, and going away after other flesh, are set forth for an example, suffering the vengeance of eternal fire.

⁸ Yet, in like manner, these also in their dreamings defile the flesh, despise dominion, and rail at dignities. ⁹ But Michael the archangel, when, contending with the Devil, he disputed concerning the body of Moses, dared not bring against him a railing judgment, but said: The Lord rebuke thee. ¹⁰ But these rail at the things which they know not; but what things naturally, as the brute beasts, they understand, in these they corrupt themselves.

¹¹ Woe to them! For they went in the way of Cain, and rushed on in the error of Balaam for reward, and perished in the gainsaying of Korah.

¹² These are rocks in your feasts of love, feasting with you fearlessly, feeding their own selves; clouds without water, carried away by winds; autumnal trees, without fruit, twice dead, plucked up by the roots; ¹³ raging waves of the sea, foaming out their own shame; wandering stars, for whom the blackness of darkness is reserved forever.

¹⁴ Yea, and of these Enoch the seventh from Adam prophesied, saying: Behold, the Lord came, with his holy myriads, ¹⁵ to execute judgment upon all, and to convict all the ungodly among them of all their acts of ungodliness which they committed, and of all the hard things which ungodly sinners spoke against him.

CHAPTER I.

¹⁶ These are murmurers, complaining of their lot, walking according to their lusts; and their mouth speaks swelling words; having respect to persons, for the sake of profit.
¹⁷ But ye, beloved, remember the words which were before spoken by the apostles of our Lord Jesus Christ; ¹⁸ that they told you, that at the last of the time there will be scoffers, walking after their own lusts of ungodliness. ¹⁹ These are they who separate; sensual, having not the Spirit. ²⁰ But ye, beloved, building up yourselves on your most holy faith, praying in the Holy Spirit, ²¹ keep yourselves in the love of God, looking for the mercy of our Lord Jesus Christ, unto eternal life.
²² And some refute when they are contending; but others save, snatching them out of the fire; ²³ and others compassionate with fear, hating even the garment spotted by the flesh.
²⁴ Now to him who is able to keep you from falling, and to present you faultless before the presence of his glory with exceeding joy; ²⁵ to the only God our Savior, through Jesus Christ our Lord, be glory, majesty, dominion, and power, before all time, and now, and forever. Amen.

THE REVELATION.

I. The Revelation of Jesus Christ, which God gave to him, to show to his servants what things must shortly come to pass; and he sent and signified it by his angel to his servant John; ² who testified of the word of God and the testimony of Jesus Christ, of whatever things he saw. ³ Happy he that reads, and they that hear the words of this prophecy, and keep the things written therein; for the time is at hand.
⁴ John to the seven churches which are in Asia: Grace to you, and peace, from him who is, and who was, and who is to come; and from the seven spirits that are before his throne; ⁵ and from Jesus Christ, the faithful witness, the first-born of

the dead, and the Ruler of the kings of the earth. To him who loves us, and washed us from our sins in his own blood, ⁶ and made us a kingdom, priests to God and his Father, to him be the glory, and the dominion, forever and ever. Amen.

⁷ Behold, he comes amidst the clouds; and every eye shall see him, and they who pierced him; and all the tribes of the earth shall wail because of him. Even so, Amen.

⁸ I am the Alpha and the Omega, saith the Lord God, he who is, and who was, and who is to come, the Almighty.

⁹ I, John, your brother, and partner with you in the affliction, and kingdom, and patient endurance in Jesus, was in the island called Patmos, on account of the word of God and the testimony of Jesus.

¹⁰ I was in the Spirit on the Lord's day; and I heard behind me a loud voice, as of a trumpet, ¹¹ saying: What thou seest, write in a book, and send to the seven churches; to Ephesus, and to Smyrna, and to Pergamus, and to Thyatira, and to Sardis, and to Philadelphia, and to Laodicea.

¹² And I turned to see the voice that was speaking with me. And having turned, I saw seven golden lamp-stands; ¹³ and in the midst of the lamp-stands one like to the Son of Man, clothed with a garment falling down to the feet, and girded round at the breasts with a golden girdle. ¹⁴ But his head and his hairs were white, as white wool, as snow; and his eyes were as a flame of fire; ¹⁵ and his feet were like to burnished brass, as if burning in a furnace; and his voice was as the sound of many waters. ¹⁶ And he had in his hand seven stars; and out of his mouth went a sharp two-edged sword; and his countenance was as the sun shining in his strength.

¹⁷ And when I saw him, I fell at his feet as dead. And he laid his right hand on me, saying: Fear not: I am the first and the last, ¹⁸ and the living one; and I became dead, and behold I am alive forevermore; and I have the keys of death and of the underworld. ¹⁹ Write therefore the things which thou sawest, and the things which are, and the things which

---

V. 15. *Or (according to some ancient authorities),* as if in a fiery furnace

CHAPTER II.

shall be after these ; [20] the mystery of the seven stars which thou sawest on my right hand, and the seven golden lamp-stands. The seven stars are the angels of the seven churches; and the seven lamp-stands are the seven churches.

II. To the angel of the church in Ephesus write: These things says he who holds the seven stars in his right hand, who walks in the midst of the seven golden lamp-stands. [2] I know thy works, and thy labor and patience, and how thou canst not bear evil men ; and thou didst try those who say they are apostles, and are not, and didst find them liars ; [3] and thou hast patience, and didst bear for my name's sake, and hast not been weary.

[4] But I have this against thee, that thou hast left thy first love. [5] Remember therefore from whence thou hast fallen, and repent, and do the first works ; but if not, I am coming to thee, and will remove thy lamp-stand out of its place, if thou repent not.

[6] But this thou hast, that thou hatest the works of the Nicolaitans, which I also hate.

[7] He that has an ear, let him hear what the Spirit says to the churches. To him that overcomes, to him I will give to eat of the tree of life, which is in the paradise of God.

[8] And to the angel of the church in Smyrna write: These things says the first and the last, who became dead, and lived again. [9] I know thy affliction, and poverty (but thou art rich), and the blasphemy of those who say they are Jews, and are not, but are the synagogue of Satan. [10] Fear not the things which thou art about to suffer. Behold, the Devil is about to cast some of you into prison, that ye may be tried ; and ye will have affliction ten days. Be thou faithful unto death, and I will give thee the crown of life.

[11] He that has an ear, let him hear what the Spirit says to the churches. He that overcomes shall not be hurt by the second death.

[12] And to the angel of the church in Pergamus write: These things says he who has the sharp two-edged sword. [13] I know

THE REVELATION.

where thou dwellest, where the throne of Satan is; and thou holdest fast my name, and didst not deny the faith in me, even in the days in which Antipas was my faithful witness, who was slain among you, where Satan dwells. ¹⁴ But I have a few things against thee. Thou hast there men holding the teaching of Balaam, who taught Balak to cast a stumbling-block before the sons of Israel, to eat things offered to idols, and to commit fornication. ¹⁵ Thus thou also hast men holding the teaching of the Nicolaitans, in like manner. ¹⁶ Repent therefore; but if not, I come to thee quickly, and will make war with them, with the sword of my mouth.

¹⁷ He that has an ear, let him hear what the Spirit says to the churches. To him that overcomes, to him I will give of the hidden manna; and I will give to him a white stone, and on the stone a new name written, which no one knows but he that receives it.

¹⁸ And to the angel of the church in Thyatira write: These things says the Son of God, who has his eyes as a flame of fire, and his feet are like to burnished brass. ¹⁹ I know thy works, and thy love, and faith, and service, and patience; and thy last works are more than the first.

²⁰ But I have against thee, that thou sufferest the woman Jezebel, who calls herself a prophetess; and she teaches and seduces my servants to commit fornication, and to eat things offered to idols. ²¹ And I gave her time that she might repent; and she will not repent of her fornication. ²² Behold, I cast her into a bed, and those who together with her commit adultery, into great affliction, if they repent not of their works. ²³ And her children I will slay with death; and all the churches shall know that I am he who searches the reins and hearts; and I will give to you every one according to your works.

²⁴ But to you I say, the rest who are in Thyatira, as many as have not this teaching, who knew not the depths of Satan, as they speak: I put upon you no other burden; ²⁵ but that which

---

V. 20. *In some ancient copies:* sufferest thy wife Jezebel
V. 22. *In some ancient copies:* of her works

CHAPTER III.

ye have, hold fast till I come. ²⁶And he that overcomes, and he that keeps my works until the end, to him I will give authority over the nations; ²⁷and he shall rule them with a rod of iron, as the vessels of a potter are they dashed in pieces, as I also have received from my Father; ²⁸and I will give him the morning star.

²⁹ He that has an ear, let him hear what the Spirit says to the churches.

III. AND to the angel of the church in Sardis write: These things says he who has the seven spirits of God, and the seven stars. I know thy works, that thou hast a name that thou livest, and art dead. ² Be watchful, and strengthen the remaining things, that were ready to die; for I have not found thy works complete before my God. ³ Remember therefore how thou hast received, and didst hear, and keep, and repent. If therefore thou shalt not watch, I will come as a thief, and thou shalt not know at what hour I will come upon thee.

⁴ But thou hast a few names in Sardis, which did not defile their garments; and they shall walk with me in white, for they are worthy.

⁵ He that overcomes, the same shall be clothed in white garments; and I will not blot out his name out of the book of life, and I will acknowledge his name before my Father, and before his angels.

⁶ He that has an ear, let him hear what the Spirit says to the churches.

⁷ And to the angel of the church in Philadelphia write: These things says the Holy, the True, he who has the key of David, he who opens, and no one shall shut, and shuts, and no one opens. ⁸ I know thy works. Behold, I have set before thee a door opened, which no one can shut; because thou hast little power and didst keep my word, and didst not deny my name.

⁹ Behold, I make those of the synagogue of Satan, who say they are Jews, and they are not, but do lie,—behold, I will

---

V. 5. *In many ancient copies:* He that overcomes shall be so clothed

make them to come and bow down before thy feet, and to know that I loved thee. ¹⁰ Because thou didst keep my word of patient endurance, I also will keep thee from the hour of temptation, which is about to come upon the whole world, to try those who dwell upon the earth.

¹¹ I come quickly; hold fast that which thou hast, that no one may take thy crown. ¹² He that overcomes, I will make him a pillar in the temple of my God, and he shall go out no more; and I will write upon him the name of my God, and the name of the city of my God, the new Jerusalem, which comes down out of heaven from my God, and my new name.

¹³ He that has an ear, let him hear what the Spirit says to the churches.

¹⁴ And to the angel of the church in Laodicea write: These things says the Amen, the faithful and true witness, the beginning of the creation of God. ¹⁵ I know thy works, that thou art neither cold nor hot. I would thou wert cold or hot. ¹⁶ So, because thou art lukewarm, and neither hot nor cold, I am about to vomit thee out of my mouth. ¹⁷ Because thou sayest: I am rich, and have gotten wealth, and have need of nothing, and knowest not that thou art the wretched and the pitiable one, and poor, and blind, and naked; ¹⁸ I counsel thee to buy of me gold refined by fire, that thou mayest be rich, and white garments, that thou mayest be clothed, and the shame of thy nakedness not be made manifest, and to anoint thine eyes with eye-salve, that thou mayest see. ¹⁹ As many as I love, I rebuke and chasten. Be zealous therefore, and repent.

²⁰ Behold, I stand at the door, and knock; if any one hear my voice, and open the door, I will come in to him, and I will sup with him and he with me. ²¹ He that overcomes, I will give to him to sit with me in my throne, as I also overcame, and sat down with my Father in his throne.

²² He that has an ear, let him hear what the Spirit says to the churches.

IV. After these things I saw, and, behold, a door set open in heaven, and that first voice (which I heard as of a

CHAPTER V.

trumpet speaking with me) saying: Come up hither, and I will show thee what things must take place after these. ² Immediately I was in the Spirit; and, behold, a throne was set in heaven, and one sat on the throne. ³ And he who sat was like in appearance to a jasper and sardine stone; and there was a rainbow round the throne, like in appearance to an emerald; ⁴ and around the throne were twenty-four thrones; and upon the thrones twenty-four elders sitting, clothed in white garments, and on their heads crowns of gold. ⁵ And out of the throne proceed lightnings, and voices, and thunders; and there were seven lamps of fire burning before the throne, which are the seven spirits of God; ⁶ and before the throne as it were a sea of glass like to crystal; and in the midst of the throne, and around the throne, four animals full of eyes before and behind. ⁷ And the first animal was like to a lion, and the second animal like to a calf, and the third animal having its face as of a man, and the fourth animal like to an eagle flying. ⁸ And the four animals had each of them six wings apiece; around and within they are full of eyes; and they have no rest by day and by night, saying: Holy, holy, holy, Lord God the Almighty, who was, and who is, and who is to come.

⁹ And when the animals shall give glory, and honor, and thanksgiving, to him who sits upon the throne, to him who lives forever and ever, ¹⁰ the twenty-four elders will fall down before him who sits upon the throne, and will worship him who lives forever and ever, and will cast their crowns before the throne, saying: Worthy art thou, our Lord and our God, to receive the glory, and the honor, and the power; because thou didst create all things, and because of thy will they were, and were created.

V. And I saw, on the right hand of him who sat on the throne, a book written within and on the back side, sealed up with seven seals. ² And I saw a strong angel proclaiming with a loud voice: Who is worthy to open the book, and to loose its seals?

³ And no one was able, in heaven, nor on the earth, nor

under the earth, to open the book, nor to look thereon. ⁴ And I wept much, because no one was found worthy to open the book, nor to look thereon.

⁵ And one of the elders says to me: Weep not; behold, the Lion that is of the tribe of Judah, the Root of David, prevailed to open the book, and its seven seals.

⁶ And I saw, in the midst of the throne and of the four animals, and in the midst of the elders, a Lamb standing, as if having been slain, having seven horns and seven eyes, which are the seven spirits of God sent forth into all the earth. ⁷ And he came, and has taken the book out of the right hand of him who sits upon the throne.

⁸ And when he took the book, the four animals, and the twenty-four elders, fell down before the Lamb, having each one a harp, and golden cups full of odors, which are the prayers of saints. ⁹ And they sing a new song, saying: Thou art worthy to take the book, and to open its seals; because thou wast slain, and didst redeem to God by thy blood out of every tribe, and tongue, and people, and nation; ¹⁰ and didst make them unto our God a kingdom and priests, and they will reign on the earth.

¹¹ And I saw, and I heard a voice of many angels, around the throne and the animals and the elders, and the number of them was ten thousand times ten thousand, and thousands of thousands, ¹² saying with a loud voice: Worthy is the Lamb that has been slain, to receive the power, and riches, and wisdom, and strength, and honor, and glory, and blessing. ¹³ And every creature which is in heaven, and on the earth, and under the earth, and on the sea, and all that are in them, I heard saying: To him who sits upon the throne, and to the Lamb, be the blessing, and the honor, and the glory, and the dominion, forever and ever. ¹⁴ And the four animals said: Amen. And the elders fell down and worshiped.

V. 10. *Some ancient copies omit :* **unto our God**

CHAPTER VI.

VI. ¹ And I saw, when the Lamb opened one of the seven seals, and I heard one of the four animals saying, as a voice of thunder: Come! ² And I saw, and behold a white horse, and he who sat on him having a bow; and a crown was given to him; and he went forth conquering, and to conquer.

³ And when he opened the second seal, I heard the second animal saying: Come! ⁴ And there went forth another horse that was red. And to him who sat thereon it was given to take away peace from the earth, and that they should slay one another; and there was given to him a great sword.

⁵ And when he opened the third seal, I heard the third animal saying: Come! And I saw, and behold a black horse, and he who sat on him having a balance in his hand. ⁶ And I heard a voice in the midst of the four animals, saying: A quart of wheat for a denáry, and three quarts of barley for a denáry; and: Hurt not the oil and the wine.

⁷ And when he opened the fourth seal, I heard the voice of the fourth animal saying: Come! ⁸ And I saw, and behold a pale horse; and he who sat on him, his name was Death, and the underworld followed with him. And authority was given to them over the fourth part of the earth, to kill with sword, and with famine, and with death, and by the beasts of the earth.

⁹ And when he opened the fifth seal, I saw under the altar the souls of those slain on account of the word of God, and on account of the testimony which they had. ¹⁰ And they cried with a loud voice, saying: How long, O Master, the holy and true, dost thou not judge and avenge our blood on those who dwell upon the earth? ¹¹ And a white robe was given to each one of them; and it was said to them, that they should rest yet a little time, until also their fellow-servants and their brethren, who are about to be killed as they were, should be fully numbered.

¹² And I saw when he opened the sixth seal, and there was a

V. 6. *A quart of wheat was commonly sold for one-eighth of a denáry. The denáry (about fifteen cents) was a third more than the daily pay of a Roman soldier.*

THE REVELATION.

great earthquake; and the sun became black as sackcloth of hair, and the moon became all as blood; ¹³ and the stars of heaven fell to the earth, as a fig-tree casts its untimely figs, when shaken by a great wind; ¹⁴ and the heaven parted asunder as a scroll rolled together; and every mountain and island were moved out of their places. ¹⁵ And the kings of the earth, and the great men, and the chief captains, and the rich men, and the strong men, and every bondman and freeman, hid themselves in the caves and in the rocks of the mountains; ¹⁶ and they say to the mountains and to the rocks: Fall upon us, and hide us from the face of him who sits on the throne, and from the wrath of the Lamb; ¹⁷ because the great day of his wrath is come, and who is able to stand?

VII. And after this, I saw four angels standing on the four corners of the earth, holding the four winds of the earth, that no wind should blow on the earth, nor on the sea, nor on any tree.

² And I saw another angel coming up from the rising of the sun, having the seal of the living God; and he cried with a loud voice to the four angels, to whom it was given to hurt the earth and the sea, ³ saying: Hurt not the earth, nor the sea, nor the trees, till we have sealed the servants of our God upon their foreheads.

⁴ And I heard the number of the sealed. A hundred and forty-four thousand were sealed, out of every tribe of the sons of Israel. ⁵ Out of the tribe of Judah were sealed twelve thousand; out of the tribe of Reuben, twelve thousand; out of the tribe of Gad, twelve thousand; ⁶ out of the tribe of Asher, twelve thousand; out of the tribe of Naphtali, twelve thousand; out of the tribe of Manasseh, twelve thousand; ⁷ out of the tribe of Simeon, twelve thousand; out of the tribe of Levi, twelve thousand; out of the tribe of Issachar, twelve thousand; ⁸ out of the tribe of Zebulun, twelve thousand; out of the tribe of Joseph, twelve thousand; out of the tribe of Benjamin, twelve thousand, were sealed.

⁹ After these things I saw, and behold a great multitude,

CHAPTER VIII.

which no one could number, out of every nation and all tribes and peoples and tongues, standing before the throne, and before the Lamb, clothed in white robes, and palms in their hands. ¹⁰ And they cry with a loud voice, saying: Salvation to our God, who sits upon the throne, and to the Lamb. ¹¹ And all the angels were standing round the throne and the elders and the four animals, and fell before the throne on their faces, and worshiped God, ¹² saying: Amen; the blessing, and the glory, and the wisdom, and the thanksgiving, and the honor, and the power, and the might, be to our God forever and ever. Amen.

¹³ And one of the elders answered, saying to me: These who are clothed in the white robes, who are they, and whence came they? ¹⁴ And I said to him: Sir, thou knowest. And he said to me: These are they who come out of the great affliction, and they washed their robes, and made them white in the blood of the Lamb. ¹⁵ Therefore are they before the throne of God, and they serve him day and night in his temple; and he who sits on the throne will spread his tabernacle over them. ¹⁶ They shall hunger no more, neither thirst any more; neither shall the sun fall upon them, nor any heat; ¹⁷ because the Lamb which is in the midst of the throne will be their shepherd, and will lead them to the fountains of the waters of life; and God will wipe away every tear from their eyes.

VIII. And when he opened the seventh seal, there was silence in heaven about half an hour.

² And I saw the seven angels who stand before God, and there were given to them seven trumpets. ³ And another angel came and stood over the altar, having a golden censer; and there was given to him much incense, that he should give it to the prayers of all the saints, upon the golden altar which is before the throne. ⁴ And there went up the smoke of the incense to the prayers of the saints, out of the hand of the angel, before God.

V. 15. See *Isaiah* iv., 6; *compare Leviticus* xxvi., 11; *Ezekiel* xxxvii., 27.

THE REVELATION.

⁵And the angel has taken the censer; and he filled it out of the fire of the altar, and cast it into the earth. And there followed thunders, and lightnings, and voices, and an earthquake.

⁶And the seven angels who had the seven trumpets prepared themselves, that they might sound.

⁷The first sounded; and there followed hail and fire mingled with blood, and they were cast into the earth, and the third part of the earth was burnt up, and the third part of the trees was burnt up, and all green grass was burnt up.

⁸And the second angel sounded; and as it were a great mountain burning with fire was cast into the sea, and the third part of the sea became blood; ⁹and the third part of the creatures that are in the sea, that have life, died; and the third part of the ships were destroyed.

¹⁰And the third angel sounded; and there fell out of heaven a great star, burning as a lamp, and it fell upon the third part of the rivers, and upon the fountains of the waters. ¹¹And the name of the star is called Wormwood. And the third part of the waters became wormwood; and many men died of the waters, because they were made bitter.

¹²And the fourth angel sounded; and the third part of the sun was smitten, and the third part of the moon, and the third part of the stars, that the third part of them might be darkened, and the day not shine for a third part of it, and the night in like manner.

¹³And I saw, and heard an eagle flying in mid-heaven, saying with a loud voice: Woe, woe, woe, to those who dwell upon the earth, by reason of the remaining voices of the trumpet, of the three angels who are about to sound!

IX. And the fifth angel sounded; and I saw a star fallen out of heaven to the earth, and there was given to him the key of the pit of the abyss. ²And he opened the pit of the abyss, and there went up a smoke out of the pit, as the smoke of a great furnace; and the sun and the air were darkened by reason of the smoke of the pit. ³And out of the

CHAPTER IX.

smoke went forth locusts into the earth; and there was given to them power, as the scorpions of the earth have power. ⁴ And it was said to them, that they should not hurt the grass of the earth, nor any green thing, nor any tree, but only the men who have not the seal of God upon their foreheads. ⁵ And it was given to them, that they should not kill them, but that they shall be tormented five months. And their torment is as the torment of a scorpion, when it has smitten a man.

⁶ And in those days men will seek death, and shall not find it; and they will desire to die, and death flees from them.

⁷ And the shapes of the locusts were like to horses prepared for battle; and on their heads were as it were crowns like gold, and their faces were as the faces of men. ⁸ And they had hair as the hair of women, and their teeth were as the teeth of lions. ⁹ And they had breastplates, as breastplates of iron; and the sound of their wings was as the sound of chariots of many horses running into battle. ¹⁰ And they have tails like to scorpions, and stings; and in their tails is their power to hurt men, five months. ¹¹ They have over them a king, the angel of the abyss. His name in the Hebrew tongue is Abaddon; but in the Greek tongue he has for a name, Apollyon.

¹² The first woe is past; behold, there come yet two woes, after these things.

¹³ And the sixth angel sounded; and I heard a voice out of the four horns of the golden altar which is before God, ¹⁴ saying to the sixth angel who had the trumpet: Loose the four angels who are bound, by the great river Euphrates. ¹⁵ And the four angels were loosed, who had been prepared for the hour, and day, and month, and year, that they may slay the third part of men. ¹⁶ And the number of the armies of the horsemen was two hundred thousand thousand. I heard the number of them.

¹⁷ And thus I saw the horses in the vision, and those who sat on them, having breastplates of fire, and of hyacinth, and like brimstone; and the heads of the horses were as the heads of lions, and out of their mouths issue fire, and smoke, and brimstone. ¹⁸ By these three plagues was the third part of men killed, by the fire, and the smoke, and the brimstone, which

issued out of their mouths. ¹⁹ For the power of the horses is in their mouth, and in their tails; for their tails are like to serpents, having heads, and with them they do hurt. ²⁰ And the rest of men, who were not killed in these plagues, repented not of the works of their hands, that they should not worship demons, and idols of gold, and of silver, and of brass, and of stone, and of wood, which can neither see, nor hear, nor walk; ²¹ and they repented not of their murders, nor of their sorceries, nor of their fornication, nor of their thefts.

X. And I saw another strong angel coming down out of heaven, clothed with a cloud, and the rainbow was upon his head, and his face was as the sun, and his feet as pillars of fire. ² And he had in his hand a little book opened. And he set his right foot upon the sea, and the left upon the land; ³ and he cried with a loud voice, as a lion roars; and when he cried, the seven thunders uttered their voices. ⁴ And when the seven thunders spoke, I was about to write; and I heard a voice out of heaven saying to me: Seal up the things which the seven thunders spoke, and write them not. ⁵ And the angel, whom I saw standing upon the sea and upon the land, lifted up his right hand to heaven, ⁶ and swore by him who lives forever and ever, who created heaven and the things therein, and the earth and the things therein, and the sea and the things therein, that there shall be time no longer; ⁷ but in the days of the voice of the seventh angel, when he is about to sound, then is the mystery of God finished, as he gave the joyful message to his servants the prophets.

⁸ And the voice which I heard out of heaven [I heard] again speaking to me, and saying: Go, take the little book which lies opened in the hand of the angel, who stands upon the sea and upon the land. ⁹ And I went to the angel, telling him to give me the little book. And he said to me: Take, and eat it up; and it will make thy belly bitter, but in thy mouth it will be sweet as honey.

V. 6. *The time here meant, is that spoken of in ch.* vi., 11.

CHAPTER XI.

¹⁰And I took the little book out of the hand of the angel, and ate it up; and it was in my mouth as honey, sweet; and when I had eaten it, my belly became bitter. ¹¹And they say to me: Thou must again prophesy of many peoples, and nations, and tongues, and kings.

XI. AND there was given me a reed, like to a staff, saying: Rise, and measure the temple of God, and the altar, and those who worship therein. ²And the court which is without the temple leave out, and measure it not; because it was given to the Gentiles, and they will tread down the holy city forty-two months. ³And I will give [power] to my two witnesses, and they shall prophesy a thousand two hundred and sixty days, clothed in sackcloth.

⁴These are the two olive-trees; and the two lamp-stands, which stand before the Lord of the earth. ⁵And if any one desires to hurt them, fire goes forth out of their mouth, and devours their enemies; and if any one desires to hurt them, he must in this manner be killed.

⁶These have power to shut heaven, that it rain not in the days of their prophecy; and have power over the waters to turn them to blood, and to smite the earth with every plague, as often as they will.

⁷And when they shall have finished their testimony, the beast that comes up out of the abyss will make war with them, and will overcome them, and will kill them. ⁸And their remains are on the street of the great city, which spiritually is called Sodom and Egypt, where their Lord also was crucified. ⁹And some out of the peoples, and tribes, and tongues, and nations, look on their remains three days and a half, and suffer not their dead bodies to be put into a tomb. ¹⁰And they who dwell on the earth rejoice over them, and are glad; and they will send gifts to one another, because these two prophets tormented those who dwell on the earth.

¹¹And after three days and a half, the spirit of life from God entered into them, and they stood upon their feet; and great fear fell upon those who beheld them. ¹²And they heard a

loud voice out of heaven, saying to them: Come up hither. And they went up into heaven in the cloud, and their enemies beheld them.

¹³ And in that hour there was a great earthquake, and the tenth part of the city fell; and in the earthquake were slain of men seven thousand names; and the rest became afraid, and gave glory to the God of heaven.

¹⁴ The second woe is past; behold, the third woe comes quickly.

¹⁵ And the seventh angel sounded; and there followed loud voices in heaven, saying: The kingdom of the world is become our Lord's, and his Christ's; and he will reign forever and ever. ¹⁶ And the twenty-four elders, who sit before God on their thrones, fell upon their faces, and worshiped God, ¹⁷ saying: We give thanks to thee, O Lord God the Almighty, who art, and who wast; because thou hast taken thy great power, and didst reign. ¹⁸ And the nations were enraged, and thy wrath came, and the time of the dead to be judged, and to give the reward to thy servants the prophets, and to the saints, and to those who fear thy name, the small and the great; and to destroy those who destroy the earth.

¹⁹ And the temple of God was opened in heaven, and the ark of his covenant was seen in his temple; and there were lightnings, and voices, and thunders, and an earthquake, and a great hail.

XII. And a great sign was seen in heaven; a woman clothed with the sun, and the moon under her feet, and upon her head a crown of twelve stars. ² And being with child she cries out, travailing in birth, and pained to be delivered.

³ And another sign was seen in heaven; and behold a great red dragon, having seven heads and ten horns, and on his heads seven crowns. ⁴ And his tail drags the third part of the stars of heaven; and it cast them to the earth.

And the dragon stands before the woman who was about to bring forth, that when she has brought forth, he may devour her child. ⁵ And she brought forth a man-child, who will rule

CHAPTER XII.

all nations with a rod of iron; and her child was caught up to God, and to his throne. ⁶ And the woman fled into the wilderness, where she has a place prepared by God, that they may nourish her there a thousand two hundred and sixty days.

⁷ And there was war in heaven, Michael and his angels fighting with the dragon. And the dragon fought, and his angels, ⁸ and prevailed not; neither was their place found any more in heaven.

⁹ And the great dragon was cast down, the old serpent, called the Devil and Satan, who leads astray the whole world; he was cast down to the earth, and his angels were cast down with him. ¹⁰ And I heard a loud voice in heaven, saying: Now is come the salvation, and the strength, and the kingdom of our God, and the authority of his Christ; because the accuser of our brethren is cast down, who accused them before our God day and night. ¹¹ And they overcame him, because of the blood of the Lamb, and because of the word of their testimony; and they loved not their life, unto the death. ¹² For this cause rejoice, ye heavens, and they who dwell in them. Woe to the earth and the sea! For the Devil is come down to you, having great wrath, knowing that he has little time.

¹³ And when the dragon saw that he was cast down to the earth, he persecuted the woman who brought forth the man-child. ¹⁴ And there were given to the woman the two wings of the great eagle, that she might fly into the wilderness, into her place, where she is nourished for a time, and times, and half a time, from the face of the serpent.

¹⁵ And the serpent cast out of his mouth water as a flood after the woman, that he might cause her to be carried away by the flood. ¹⁶ And the earth helped the woman; and the earth opened her mouth, and swallowed up the flood which the dragon cast out of his mouth.

¹⁷ And the dragon was enraged at the woman; and he departed to make war with the rest of her seed, who keep the commandments of God, and have the testimony of Jesus.

THE REVELATION.

XIII. And I stood upon the sand of the sea. And I saw a beast coming up out of the sea, having ten horns and seven heads, and upon his horns ten crowns, and upon his heads names of blasphemy; (²and the beast which I saw was like to a leopard, and his feet as of a bear, and his mouth as the mouth of a lion, and the dragon gave to him his power, and his throne, and great authority;) ³and one of his heads as it were wounded unto death. And his deadly wound was healed; and all the world wondered after the beast. ⁴And they worshiped the dragon, because he gave the authority to the beast; and they worshiped the beast, saying: Who is like to the beast, and who is able to make war with him?

⁵And there was given to him a mouth speaking great and blasphemous things; and power was given him to work forty-two months. ⁶And he opened his mouth in blasphemies against God, to blaspheme his name, and his tabernacle, those who tabernacle in heaven. ⁷And it was given him to make war with the saints, and to overcome them; and power was given him over every tribe, and tongue, and nation. ⁸And all who dwell upon the earth will worship him, whose names are not written in the book of life of the Lamb, which is slain from the foundation of the world.

⁹If any one has an ear, let him hear.

¹⁰If any one is for captivity, he goes into captivity; if any to be killed with the sword, he must be killed with the sword. Here is the patience and the faith of the saints.

¹¹And I saw another beast coming up out of the earth; and he had two horns like a lamb, and he spoke as a dragon. ¹²And he exercises all the authority of the first beast in his presence, and causes the earth and those who dwell therein to worship the first beast, whose deadly wound was healed. ¹³And he does great signs, so that also he causes fire to come down

---

V. 1. *In some ancient copies:* And he stood
V. 1. *In some copies:* a name of blasphemy

CHAPTER XIV.

out of heaven on the earth, in the sight of men; ¹⁴and he leads astray those who dwell on the earth, because of the signs which it was given him to do in the presence of the beast; saying to those who dwell on the earth, that they should make an image to the beast, which has the wound of the sword, and lived. ¹⁵And it was given him to give breath to the image of the beast, that the image of the beast should also speak, and should cause that as many as worship not the image of the beast should be killed. ¹⁶And he causes all, the small and the great, and the rich and the poor, and the free and the bond, to receive a mark on their right hand, or on their forehead; ¹⁷and that no one should be able to buy or sell, save he that has the mark, the name of the beast, or the number of his name.

¹⁸ Here is wisdom. Let him that has understanding count up the number of the beast, for it is the number of a man; and his number is Six hundred and sixty-six.

XIV. AND I saw, and behold, the Lamb stood on the mount Zion, and with him a hundred and forty-four thousand, having his name, and the name of his Father written on their foreheads.

² And I heard a voice out of heaven, as the voice of many waters, and as the voice of loud thunder; the voice which I heard was as that of harpers, harping with their harps. ³ And they sing as it were a new song before the throne, and before the four animals and the elders; and no one was able to learn the song, except the hundred and forty-four thousand, who are redeemed from the earth. ⁴ These are they who were not defiled with women; for they are virgins. These are they who follow the Lamb, whithersoever he goes. These were redeemed from men, a first-fruits to God and to the Lamb. ⁵ And in their mouth was found no falsehood; for they are blameless.

⁶ And I saw another angel flying in mid-heaven, having the

V. 15. *Or*, to give spirit
V. 16. *Or*, that they should give them a mark
V. 6. *Or*, having an eternal message of joy

everlasting gospel to preach to those who dwell on the earth, and to every nation, and tribe, and tongue, and people; ⁷ saying with a loud voice: Fear God, and give glory to him, because the hour of his judgment is come; and worship him who made heaven and earth, and sea, and fountains of waters.

⁸ And another, a second angel followed, saying: Babylon the great is fallen, is fallen, because she has made all the nations drink of the wine of the wrath of her fornication.

⁹ And another, a third angel followed them, saying with a loud voice: If any one worships the beast and his image, and receives a mark on his forehead, or on his hand, ¹⁰ he also shall drink of the wine of the wrath of God, which is poured out without mixture into the cup of his wrath, and shall be tormented with fire and brimstone in the presence of holy angels, and in the presence of the Lamb. ¹¹ And the smoke of their torment goes up forever and ever; and they have no rest day and night, who worship the beast and his image, and whoever receives the mark of his name.

¹² Here is the patience of the saints, who keep the commandments of God, and the faith of Jesus.

¹³ And I heard a voice out of heaven saying: Write, Happy are the dead who die in the Lord, henceforth; yea, says the Spirit, that they shall rest from their labors, for their works follow with them.

¹⁴ And I saw, and behold a white cloud, and upon the cloud one sitting like to the Son of man, having on his head a golden crown, and in his hand a sharp sickle. ¹⁵ And another angel came forth out of the temple, crying with a loud voice to him who sat on the cloud: Put forth thy sickle, and reap; because the time to reap is come; because the harvest of the earth is ripe. ¹⁶ And he who sat on the cloud thrust in his sickle upon the earth; and the earth was reaped.

¹⁷ And another angel came forth out of the temple which is in heaven, he also having a sharp sickle. ¹⁸ And another angel came out from the altar, who had power over fire; and he cried with a loud cry to him who had the sharp sickle, saying: Put forth thy sharp sickle, and gather the clusters of the vine

CHAPTER XV.

of the earth; for her grapes are fully ripe. ¹⁹ And the angel thrust in his sickle into the earth, and gathered the vine of the earth, and cast it into the great wine-press of the wrath of God. ²⁰ And the wine-press was trodden without the city, and blood came forth out of the wine-press, even to the bits of the horses, as far as a thousand and six hundred furlongs.

XV. And I saw another sign in heaven, great and marvelous, seven angels having seven plagues; which are the last, because in them is completed the wrath of God.

² And I saw as it were a sea of glass, mingled with fire; and those who had gained the victory over the beast, and over his image, and over the number of his name, standing by the sea of glass, having harps of God. ³ And they sing the song of Moses the servant of God, and the song of the Lamb, saying: Great and marvelous are thy works, Lord God the Almighty; just and true are thy ways, thou King of the nations. ⁴ Who shall not fear, O Lord, and glorify thy name? Because thou alone art holy; because all the nations shall come and worship before thee; because thy judgments are made manifest.

⁵ And after these things I saw, and the temple of the tabernacle of the testimony in heaven was opened; ⁶ and there came forth the seven angels having the seven plagues, clothed in pure, shining linen, and girded about the breasts with golden girdles. ⁷ And one of the four animals gave to the seven angels seven golden cups, full of the wrath of God, who lives forever and ever. ⁸ And the temple was filled with smoke from the glory of God, and from his power; and no one was able to enter into the temple, till the seven plagues of the seven angels should be completed.

XVI. And I heard a loud voice out of the temple, saying to the seven angels: Go, and pour out the seven cups of the wrath of God into the earth.

² And the first departed, and poured out his cup into the

V. 2. *Or*, on the sea

earth; and there fell a noisome and grievous sore upon the men who have the mark of the beast, and who worship his image.

³ And the second poured out his cup into the sea; and it became blood, as of a dead man; and every living thing died that was in the sea.

⁴ And the third poured out his cup into the rivers, and the fountains of water; and they became blood. ⁵ And I heard the angel of the waters saying: Righteous art thou, who art and who wast holy, because thou didst thus judge; ⁶ because they shed the blood of saints and prophets, and thou hast given them blood to drink. They are worthy. ⁷ And I heard, out of the altar, one saying: Even so, Lord God the Almighty, true and righteous are thy judgments.

⁸ And the fourth poured out his cup upon the sun; and it was given to it to scorch men with fire. ⁹ And men were scorched with great heat, and blasphemed the name of God, who has the power over these plagues, and repented not, to give him glory.

¹⁰ And the fifth poured out his cup upon the throne of the beast; and his kingdom became darkened; and they gnawed their tongues for pain, ¹¹ and blasphemed the God of heaven, because of their pains and their sores, and repented not of their works.

¹² And the sixth poured out his cup upon the great river, the Euphrates; and its water was dried up, that the way of the kings, who are from the rising of the sun, might be prepared. ¹³ And I saw come out of the mouth of the dragon, and out of the mouth of the beast, and out of the mouth of the false prophet,. three unclean spirits as frogs; ¹⁴ for they are spirits of demons, working signs, which go forth over the kings of the whole habitable world, to gather them to the battle of that great day of God the Almighty.

¹⁵ Behold, I come as a thief. Happy is he that watches, and keeps his garments, that he may not walk naked and they see his shame.

V. 7. *In ancient copies:* I heard the altar saying

CHAPTER XVII.

¹⁶ And they gathered them into the place called in the Hebrew tongue, Armageddon.
¹⁷ And the seventh poured out his cup upon the air; and there came forth a loud voice out of the temple of heaven, from the throne, saying: It is done. ¹⁸ And there were lightnings, and voices, and thunders; and there was a great earthquake, such as was not since there was a man upon the earth, so mighty an earthquake, so great. ¹⁹ And the great city was divided into three parts, and the cities of the nations fell; and Babylon the great was remembered before God, to give to her the cup of the wine of the fierceness of his wrath. ²⁰ And every island fled away, and mountains were not found. ²¹ And great hail, as of a talent's weight, comes down out of heaven upon men; and men blasphemed God on account of the plague of the hail; because the plague thereof was exceeding great.

XVII. And there came one of the seven angels who have the seven cups, and talked with me, saying: Come hither; I will show thee the judgment of the great harlot, that sits upon many waters; ² with whom the kings of the earth committed fornication, and the inhabitants of the earth were made drunk with the wine of her fornication. ³ And he carried me away in the spirit into the wilderness. And I saw a woman sitting upon a scarlet beast, full of the names of blasphemy, having seven heads and ten horns. ⁴ And the woman was clothed in purple and scarlet, and gilded with gold, and precious stones and pearls, having a golden cup in her hand, full of abominations and the impurities of her fornication. ⁵ And upon her forehead was a name written: MYSTERY, BABYLON THE GREAT, THE MOTHER OF THE HARLOTS AND OF THE ABOMINATIONS OF THE EARTH.
⁶ And I saw the woman drunken with the blood of the saints, and with the blood of the witnesses of Jesus; and I wondered when I saw her, with great wonder. ⁷ And the angel said to me: Wherefore didst thou wonder? I will tell thee the mystery of the woman, and of the beast that carries her, which has

the seven heads and the ten horns. ⁸ The beast that thou sawest was, and is not, and is to come up out of the abyss, and to go into perdition; and they will wonder who dwell on the earth, whose names are not written in the book of life from the foundation of the world, seeing the beast, that he was, and is not, and shall come.

⁹ Here is the mind that has wisdom. The seven heads are seven mountains, on which the woman sits. ¹⁰ And they are seven kings; the five are fallen, and the one is; the other is not yet come; and when he comes, he must remain a little time. ¹¹ And the beast that was, and is not, he also is an eighth, and is of the seven, and goes into perdition.

¹² And the ten horns which thou sawest are ten kings, who received no kingdom as yet; but receive authority as kings one hour, along with the beast. ¹³ These have one mind, and give their power and authority to the beast. ¹⁴ These will make war with the Lamb, and the Lamb will overcome them; because he is Lord of lords, and King of kings; and they who are with him are called, and chosen, and faithful.

¹⁵ And he says to me: The waters which thou sawest, where the harlot sits, are peoples and multitudes, and nations and tongues. ¹⁶ And the ten horns, and the beast, these will hate the harlot, and will make her desolate and naked, and will eat her flesh, and will burn her up with fire. ¹⁷ For God put it into their hearts to do his will, and to form one purpose, and to give their kingdom to the beast, until the words of God shall be fulfilled.

¹⁸ And the woman which thou sawest is the great city, which has a kingdom over the kings of the earth.

XVIII. After these things I saw another angel coming down out of heaven, having great authority; and the earth was lightened with his glory. ² And he cried with a strong voice, saying: Babylon the great is fallen, is fallen, and is become a habitation of demons, and a hold of every foul spirit, and a cage of every unclean and hateful bird. ³ Because all the nations have drunk of the wine of the wrath

CHAPTER XVIII.

of her fornication, and the kings of the earth committed fornication with her, and the merchants of the earth became rich out of the abundance of her luxury.

⁴ And I heard another voice out of heaven, saying: Come out of her, my people, that ye partake not in her sins, and that ye receive not of her plagues. ⁵ For her sins reached unto heaven, and God remembered her iniquities. ⁶ Reward her as she also rewarded, and render twofold according to her works; in the cup which she mixed, mix for her twofold. ⁷ By as much as she glorified herself, and lived luxuriously, so much torment and mourning give her; because in her heart she says: I sit a queen, and not a widow, and shall not see mourning. ⁸ Therefore shall her plagues come in one day, death, and mourning, and famine; and she shall be burned up with fire; because strong is the Lord God who judged her.

⁹ And the kings of the earth, who committed fornication and lived luxuriously with her, shall weep, and shall lament for her, when they see the smoke of her burning; ¹⁰ standing afar off for the fear of her torment, saying: Alas, alas, the great city Babylon, the mighty city! Because in one hour thy judgment is come.

¹¹ And the merchants of the earth shall weep and mourn over her, because no one buys their lading any more; ¹² the lading of gold, and of silver, and of precious stones, and of pearls, and of fine linen, and of purple, and of silk, and of scarlet; and all citron wood, and every vessel of ivory, and every vessel of most precious wood, and of brass, and of iron, and of marble, ¹³ and cinnamon, and amomum, and odors, and ointment, and frankincense, and wine, and oil, and fine flour, and wheat, and cattle, and sheep; and [lading] of horses, and of chariots, and of slaves; and souls of men. ¹⁴ And the fruit that thy soul desired departed from thee, and all the dainty and goodly things perished from thee, and thou shalt no more find them.

¹⁵ The merchants of these things, who became rich by her, shall stand afar off for the fear of her torment, weeping and mourning, ¹⁶ saying: Alas, alas, the great city, that was clothed in fine linen, and purple, and scarlet, and gilded with gold, and

precious stone, and pearls ; ¹⁷ because in one hour so great riches are made desolate.

And every pilot, and every one that sails to any place, and seamen, and as many as do business at sea, stood afar off, ¹⁸ and cried out when they saw the smoke of her burning, saying: Who is like to the great city! ¹⁹ And they cast dust upon their heads, and cried out, weeping and mourning, saying: Alas, alas, the great city, whereby all that have the ships in the sea became rich by reason of her costliness; because in one hour she is made desolate.

²⁰ Rejoice over her, thou heaven, and ye saints, ye apostles, and ye prophets; because God judged your cause upon her.

²¹ And a strong angel took up a stone like a great millstone, and cast it into the sea, saying: Thus with violence shall Babylon the great city be cast down, and shall be found no more. ²² And the voice of harpers, and of musicians, and of pipers, and of trumpeters, shall be heard in thee no more; and no craftsman, of whatever craft, shall be found any more in thee, and the sound of a millstone shall be heard in thee no more; ²³ and the light of a lamp shall shine in thee no more; and the voice of bridegroom and of bride shall be heard in thee no more; because thy merchants were the great men of the earth; because by thy sorcery all the nations were led astray.

²⁴ And in her was found the blood of prophets, and of saints and of all that have been slain upon the earth.

XIX. After these things, I heard as it were a loud voice of a great multitude in heaven, of those saying: Alleluia; the salvation, and the glory, and the power, are our God's; ² because true and righteous are his judgments; because he judged the great harlot, who corrupted the earth with her fornication, and avenged the blood of his servants at her hand. ³ And a second time they said: Alleluia. And her smoke goes up forever and ever.

⁴ And the twenty-four elders, and the four animals, fell down and worshiped God, who sits on the throne, saying: Amen; Alleluia.

CHAPTER XIX.

⁵ And a voice came out from the throne, saying: Praise our God, all ye his servants, and ye who fear him, the small and the great. ⁶ And I heard as it were the voice of a great multitude, and as the sound of many waters, and as the sound of mighty thunders, saying: Alleluia; because the Lord God the Almighty reigns. ⁷ Let us rejoice and exult, and we will give to him the glory; because the marriage of the Lamb is come, and his wife made herself ready. ⁸ And it was given her that she should be clothed in fine linen, pure and shining; for the fine linen is the righteousness of the saints.

⁹ And he says to me: Write, Happy are they who are called to the marriage-supper of the Lamb. And he says to me: These are the true sayings of God. ¹⁰ And I fell before his feet to worship him. And he said to me: See thou do it not. I am a fellow-servant of thee and of thy brethren who have the testimony of Jesus; worship God. For the testimony of Jesus is the spirit of prophecy.

¹¹ And I saw heaven opened, and behold a white horse, and he who sat upon him, called Faithful and True; and in righteousness he judges, and makes war. ¹² His eyes were as a flame of fire, and on his head were many crowns; and he had a name written, which no one knows but he himself. ¹³ And he was clothed with a garment dipped in blood; and his name is called, The Word of God. ¹⁴ And the armies which are in heaven followed him upon white horses, clothed in fine linen, white, pure. ¹⁵ And out of his mouth goes a sharp sword, that with it he may smite the nations; and he will rule them with a rod of iron; and he treads the wine-press of the fierceness of the wrath of God the Almighty. ¹⁶ And he has on his garment, and on his thigh, a name written: KING OF KINGS, AND LORD OF LORDS.

¹⁷ And I saw an angel standing in the sun. And he cried with a loud voice, saying to all the birds that fly in midheaven: Come, and gather yourselves together to the great supper of God; ¹⁸ that ye may eat the flesh of kings, and the flesh of captains of thousands, and the flesh of mighty men, and

the flesh of horses and of those who sit on them, and the flesh of all, both free and bond, both small and great.

¹⁹ And I saw the beast, and the kings of the earth, and their armies, gathered together to make war with him who sat on the horse, and with his army. ²⁰ And the beast was seized, and with him the false prophet that wrought the signs in his presence, with which he led astray those who received the mark of the beast, and who worship his image. The two were cast alive into the lake of fire, that burns with brimstone. ²¹ And the rest were slain with the sword of him who sat upon the horse, which went forth out of his mouth; and all the birds were filled with their flesh.

XX. And I saw an angel coming down out of heaven, having the key of the abyss, and a great chain in his hand. ² And he laid hold of the dragon, the old serpent, which is the Devil and Satan, and bound him a thousand years, ³ and cast him into the abyss, and shut it, and set a seal over him, that he mislead the nations no more, until the thousand years are finished; after these he must be loosed a little time.

⁴ And I saw thrones, and they sat upon them, and judgment was given to them; and the souls of those beheaded on account of the testimony of Jesus, and on account of the word of God, and whoever did not worship the beast, neither his image, and did not receive the mark upon the forehead, or upon their hand; and they lived and reigned with Christ a thousand years. ⁵ The rest of the dead lived not until the thousand years were finished. This is the first resurrection. ⁶ Happy and holy is he that has part in the first resurrection; on these the second death has no power, but they shall be priests of God and of Christ, and shall reign with him a thousand years.

⁷ And when the thousand years are finished, Satan will be loosed out of his prison, ⁸ and will go out to mislead the nations that are in the four corners of the earth, Gog and Magog, to gather them together to the war, the number of whom is as the sand of the sea. ⁹ And they went up upon the breadth of the earth, and encompassed the camp of the saints, and the

CHAPTER XXI.

beloved city; and fire came down from God out of heaven, and devoured them. ¹⁰ And the Devil who misleads them was cast into the lake of fire and brimstone, where are also the beast and the false prophet; and they will be tormented day and night forever and ever.

¹¹ And I saw a great white throne, and him who sat upon it, from whose face the earth and the heaven fled away, and no place was found for them.

¹² And I saw the dead, the great and the small, standing before the throne. And books were opened; and another book was opened, which is [the book] of life; and the dead were judged out of the things written in the books, according to their works. ¹³ And the sea gave up the dead which were in it; and death and the underworld gave up the dead which were in them; and they were judged each one according to their works.

¹⁴ And death and the underworld were cast into the lake of fire. This is the second death, the lake of fire. ¹⁵ And if any one was not found written in the book of life, he was cast into the lake of fire.

XXI. AND I saw a new heaven and a new earth; for the first heaven and the first earth passed away, and the sea is no more.

² And I saw the holy city, new Jerusalem, coming down out of heaven from God, prepared as a bride adorned for her husband. ³ And I heard a loud voice out of the throne, saying: Behold, the tabernacle of God is with men, and he will dwell with them, and they shall be his people, and GOD-WITH-THEM himself will be their God. ⁴ And he will wipe away every tear from their eyes; and death shall be no more, nor shall mourning, nor crying, nor pain be any more; because the former things are passed away.

⁵ And he who sat upon the throne said: Behold, I make all

V. 9. *Some ancient copies omit:* from God
V. 3. *Compare* Immanuel, *Matthew* i., 23.

things new. And he says: Write; because these words are faithful and true.

⁶ And he said to me: It is done. I am the Alpha and the Omega, the beginning and the end. I will give to him that thirsts, of the fountain of the water of life freely. ⁷ He that overcomes shall inherit these things; and I will be to him a God, and he shall be to me a son. ⁸ But the fearful, and unbelieving, and defiled with abominations, and murderers, and fornicators, and sorcerers, and idolaters, and all the liars, shall have their part in the lake which burns with fire and brimstone, which is the second death.

⁹ And there came one from among the seven angels, who have the seven cups full of the seven last plagues, and talked with me, saying: Come hither; I will show thee the bride, the wife of the Lamb. ¹⁰ And he carried me away in the spirit to a great and high mountain, and showed me the holy city Jerusalem, coming down out of heaven from God, ¹¹ having the glory of God; her luminary like to a most precious stone, as it were to a jasper stone, clear as crystal; ¹² having a wall great and high; having twelve gates, and at the gates twelve angels, and names written thereon, which are the names of the twelve tribes of the sons of Israel; ¹³ on the east three gates, and on the north three gates, and on the south three gates, and on the west three gates. ¹⁴ And the wall of the city had twelve foundation-stones, and on them twelve names of the twelve apostles of the Lamb.

¹⁵ And he who talked with me had a golden reed for a measure, that he might measure the city, and the gates thereof, and the wall thereof. ¹⁶ And the city lies foursquare, and its length is as great as the breadth. And he measured the city with the reed, twelve thousand furlongs. The length, and the breadth, and the height of it are equal.

¹⁷ And he measured the wall thereof, a hundred and forty-four cubits, the measure of a man, which is that of an angel. ¹⁸ And the structure of its wall was jasper; and the city was pure gold, like to pure glass. ¹⁹ The foundation-stones of the wall of the city were adorned with every precious stone. The first foun-

CHAPTER XXII.

dation-stone was jasper; the second, sapphire; the third, chalcedony; the fourth, emerald; ²⁰the fifth, sardonyx; the sixth, sardius; the seventh, chrysolite; the eighth, beryl; the ninth, topaz; the tenth, chrysoprasus; the eleventh, hyacinth; the twelfth, amethyst. ²¹And the twelve gates were twelve pearls; each several gate was of one pearl; and the street of the city was pure gold, as transparent glass.

²²And I saw in it no temple; for the Lord God the Almighty is its temple, and the Lamb.

²³And the city has no need of the sun, neither of the moon, to shine on it; for the glory of God lightened it, and the Lamb is the light thereof. ²⁴And the nations will walk by its light; and the kings of the earth bring their glory into it. ²⁵And its gates will not be shut by day; for there will be no night there; ²⁶and they will bring the glory and the honor of the nations into it. ²⁷And there shall not enter into it any thing unclean, or that works abomination or falsehood; but they who are written in the Lamb's book of life.

XXII. And he showed me a river of water of life, clear as crystal, proceeding out of the throne of God and of the Lamb. ²In the midst of its street, and on either side of the river, was a tree of life, bearing twelve fruits, yielding its fruit every month; and the leaves of the tree are for the healing of the nations. ³And there will be no more curse. And the throne of God and of the Lamb will be in it; and his servants will serve him, ⁴and will see his face, and his name will be upon their foreheads. ⁵And there will be no night there; and they will have no need of a lamp, nor of the light of the sun, because the Lord God will give them light; and they will reign forever and ever.

⁶And he said to me: These sayings are faithful and true; and the Lord, the God of the spirits of the prophets, sent his angel to show to his servants what things must shortly come to pass. ⁷Behold, I come quickly. Happy is he that keeps the sayings of the prophecy of this book.

⁸And I, John, am he who heard and saw these things. And

when I heard and saw, I fell down to worship before the feet of the angel, who showed me these things. ⁹And he says to me: See thou do it not. I am a fellow-servant of thee and of thy brethren the prophets, and of those who keep the sayings of this book; worship God.

¹⁰ And he says to me: Seal not the sayings of the prophecy of this book; for the time is at hand. ¹¹ He that is unjust, let him be unjust still; and he that is filthy, let him be filthy still; and he that is righteous, let him be righteous still; and he that is holy, let him be holy still.

¹² Behold, I come quickly; and my reward is with me, to give to each one according as his work is. ¹³ I am the Alpha and the Omega, the first and the last, the beginning and the end. ¹⁴ Happy are they who wash their robes, that they may have right to the tree of life, and may enter by the gates into the city. ¹⁵ Without are the dogs, and the sorcerers, and the fornicators, and the murderers, and the idolaters, and every one that loves and makes a lie.

¹⁶ I, Jesus, sent my angel, to testify to you these things in the churches. I am the root and the offspring of David, the bright, the morning star.

¹⁷ And the Spirit and the bride say: Come. And let him that hears say: Come. And let him that thirsts, come; let him that will, take the water of life freely.

¹⁸ I testify to every one that hears the words of the prophecy of this book, if any one shall add to them, God will add to him the plagues that are written in this book; ¹⁹ and if any one shall take away from the words of the book of this prophecy, God will take away his part from the tree of life, and out of the holy city, which are written of in this book.

²⁰ He who testifies these things, says: Yea, I come quickly. Amen; come, Lord Jesus.

²¹ The grace of the Lord Jesus be with the saints.

www.ingramcontent.com/pod-product-compliance
Lightning Source LLC
Chambersburg PA
CBHW051236300426
44114CB00011B/756